T0178552

Lecture Notes in Computer Science 14712

Founding Editors

Gerhard Goos
Juris Hartmanis

Editorial Board Members

The series Lecture Notes in Computer Science (LNCS), including its subseries Lecture Notes in Artificial Intelligence (LNAI) and Lecture Notes in Bioinformatics (LNBI), has established itself as a medium for the publication of new developments in computer science and information technology research, teaching, and education.

LNCS enjoys close cooperation with the computer science R & D community, the series counts many renowned academics among its volume editors and paper authors, and collaborates with prestigious societies. Its mission is to serve this international community by providing an invaluable service, mainly focused on the publication of conference and workshop proceedings and postproceedings. LNCS commenced publication in 1973.

Aaron Marcus · Elizabeth Rosenzweig ·
Marcelo M. Soares

Editors

Design, User Experience, and Usability

13th International Conference, DUXU 2024
Held as Part of the 26th HCI International Conference, HCII 2024
Washington, DC, USA, June 29 – July 4, 2024
Proceedings, Part I

 Springer

Editors
Aaron Marcus
Principal
Aaron Marcus and Associates
Berkeley, CA, USA

Elizabeth Rosenzweig
World Usability Day and Bubble Mountain
Newton Center, MA, USA

Marcelo M. Soares
Federal University of Pernambuco
Recife, Pernambuco, Brazil

ISSN 0302-9743   ISSN 1611-3349 (electronic)
Lecture Notes in Computer Science
ISBN 978-3-031-61350-0   ISBN 978-3-031-61351-7 (eBook)
https://doi.org/10.1007/978-3-031-61351-7

This Springer imprint is published by the registered company Springer Nature Switzerland AG
The registered company address is: Gewerbestrasse 11, 6330 Cham, Switzerland

If disposing of this product, please recycle the paper.

Foreword

This year we celebrate 40 years since the establishment of the HCI International (HCII) Conference, which has been a hub for presenting groundbreaking research and novel ideas and collaboration for people from all over the world.

The HCII conference was founded in 1984 by Prof. Gavriel Salvendy (Purdue University, USA, Tsinghua University, P.R. China, and University of Central Florida, USA) and the first event of the series, "1st USA-Japan Conference on Human-Computer Interaction", was held in Honolulu, Hawaii, USA, 18–20 August. Since then, HCI International is held jointly with several Thematic Areas and Affiliated Conferences, with each one under the auspices of a distinguished international Program Board and under one management and one registration. Twenty-six HCI International Conferences have been organized so far (every two years until 2013, and annually thereafter).

Over the years, this conference has served as a platform for scholars, researchers, industry experts and students to exchange ideas, connect, and address challenges in the ever-evolving HCI field. Throughout these 40 years, the conference has evolved itself, adapting to new technologies and emerging trends, while staying committed to its core mission of advancing knowledge and driving change.

As we celebrate this milestone anniversary, we reflect on the contributions of its founding members and appreciate the commitment of its current and past Affiliated Conference Program Board Chairs and members. We are also thankful to all past conference attendees who have shaped this community into what it is today.

The 26th International Conference on Human-Computer Interaction, HCI International 2024 (HCII 2024), was held as a 'hybrid' event at the Washington Hilton Hotel, Washington, DC, USA, during 29 June – 4 July 2024. It incorporated the 21 thematic areas and affiliated conferences listed below.

A total of 5108 individuals from academia, research institutes, industry, and government agencies from 85 countries submitted contributions, and 1271 papers and 309 posters were included in the volumes of the proceedings that were published just before the start of the conference, these are listed below. The contributions thoroughly cover the entire field of human-computer interaction, addressing major advances in knowledge and effective use of computers in a variety of application areas. These papers provide academics, researchers, engineers, scientists, practitioners and students with state-of-the-art information on the most recent advances in HCI.

The HCI International (HCII) conference also offers the option of presenting 'Late Breaking Work', and this applies both for papers and posters, with corresponding volumes of proceedings that will be published after the conference. Full papers will be included in the 'HCII 2024 - Late Breaking Papers' volumes of the proceedings to be published in the Springer LNCS series, while 'Poster Extended Abstracts' will be included as short research papers in the 'HCII 2024 - Late Breaking Posters' volumes to be published in the Springer CCIS series.

I would like to thank the Program Board Chairs and the members of the Program Boards of all thematic areas and affiliated conferences for their contribution towards the high scientific quality and overall success of the HCI International 2024 conference. Their manifold support in terms of paper reviewing (single-blind review process, with a minimum of two reviews per submission), session organization and their willingness to act as goodwill ambassadors for the conference is most highly appreciated.

This conference would not have been possible without the continuous and unwavering support and advice of Gavriel Salvendy, founder, General Chair Emeritus, and Scientific Advisor. For his outstanding efforts, I would like to express my sincere appreciation to Abbas Moallem, Communications Chair and Editor of HCI International News.

July 2024   Constantine Stephanidis

HCI International 2024 Thematic Areas and Affiliated Conferences

- HCI: Human-Computer Interaction Thematic Area
- HIMI: Human Interface and the Management of Information Thematic Area
- EPCE: 21st International Conference on Engineering Psychology and Cognitive Ergonomics
- AC: 18th International Conference on Augmented Cognition
- UAHCI: 18th International Conference on Universal Access in Human-Computer Interaction
- CCD: 16th International Conference on Cross-Cultural Design
- SCSM: 16th International Conference on Social Computing and Social Media
- VAMR: 16th International Conference on Virtual, Augmented and Mixed Reality
- DHM: 15th International Conference on Digital Human Modeling & Applications in Health, Safety, Ergonomics & Risk Management
- DUXU: 13th International Conference on Design, User Experience and Usability
- C&C: 12th International Conference on Culture and Computing
- DAPI: 12th International Conference on Distributed, Ambient and Pervasive Interactions
- HCIBGO: 11th International Conference on HCI in Business, Government and Organizations
- LCT: 11th International Conference on Learning and Collaboration Technologies
- ITAP: 10th International Conference on Human Aspects of IT for the Aged Population
- AIS: 6th International Conference on Adaptive Instructional Systems
- HCI-CPT: 6th International Conference on HCI for Cybersecurity, Privacy and Trust
- HCI-Games: 6th International Conference on HCI in Games
- MobiTAS: 6th International Conference on HCI in Mobility, Transport and Automotive Systems
- AI-HCI: 5th International Conference on Artificial Intelligence in HCI
- MOBILE: 5th International Conference on Human-Centered Design, Operation and Evaluation of Mobile Communications

List of Conference Proceedings Volumes Appearing Before the Conference

1. LNCS 14684, Human-Computer Interaction: Part I, edited by Masaaki Kurosu and Ayako Hashizume
2. LNCS 14685, Human-Computer Interaction: Part II, edited by Masaaki Kurosu and Ayako Hashizume
3. LNCS 14686, Human-Computer Interaction: Part III, edited by Masaaki Kurosu and Ayako Hashizume
4. LNCS 14687, Human-Computer Interaction: Part IV, edited by Masaaki Kurosu and Ayako Hashizume
5. LNCS 14688, Human-Computer Interaction: Part V, edited by Masaaki Kurosu and Ayako Hashizume
6. LNCS 14689, Human Interface and the Management of Information: Part I, edited by Hirohiko Mori and Yumi Asahi
7. LNCS 14690, Human Interface and the Management of Information: Part II, edited by Hirohiko Mori and Yumi Asahi
8. LNCS 14691, Human Interface and the Management of Information: Part III, edited by Hirohiko Mori and Yumi Asahi
9. LNAI 14692, Engineering Psychology and Cognitive Ergonomics: Part I, edited by Don Harris and Wen-Chin Li
10. LNAI 14693, Engineering Psychology and Cognitive Ergonomics: Part II, edited by Don Harris and Wen-Chin Li
11. LNAI 14694, Augmented Cognition, Part I, edited by Dylan D. Schmorrow and Cali M. Fidopiastis
12. LNAI 14695, Augmented Cognition, Part II, edited by Dylan D. Schmorrow and Cali M. Fidopiastis
13. LNCS 14696, Universal Access in Human-Computer Interaction: Part I, edited by Margherita Antona and Constantine Stephanidis
14. LNCS 14697, Universal Access in Human-Computer Interaction: Part II, edited by Margherita Antona and Constantine Stephanidis
15. LNCS 14698, Universal Access in Human-Computer Interaction: Part III, edited by Margherita Antona and Constantine Stephanidis
16. LNCS 14699, Cross-Cultural Design: Part I, edited by Pei-Luen Patrick Rau
17. LNCS 14700, Cross-Cultural Design: Part II, edited by Pei-Luen Patrick Rau
18. LNCS 14701, Cross-Cultural Design: Part III, edited by Pei-Luen Patrick Rau
19. LNCS 14702, Cross-Cultural Design: Part IV, edited by Pei-Luen Patrick Rau
20. LNCS 14703, Social Computing and Social Media: Part I, edited by Adela Coman and Simona Vasilache
21. LNCS 14704, Social Computing and Social Media: Part II, edited by Adela Coman and Simona Vasilache
22. LNCS 14705, Social Computing and Social Media: Part III, edited by Adela Coman and Simona Vasilache

23. LNCS 14706, Virtual, Augmented and Mixed Reality: Part I, edited by Jessie Y. C. Chen and Gino Fragomeni

24. LNCS 14707, Virtual, Augmented and Mixed Reality: Part II, edited by Jessie Y. C. Chen and Gino Fragomeni

25. LNCS 14708, Virtual, Augmented and Mixed Reality: Part III, edited by Jessie Y. C. Chen and Gino Fragomeni

26. LNCS 14709, Digital Human Modeling and Applications in Health, Safety, Ergonomics and Risk Management: Part I, edited by Vincent G. Duffy

27. LNCS 14710, Digital Human Modeling and Applications in Health, Safety, Ergonomics and Risk Management: Part II, edited by Vincent G. Duffy

28. LNCS 14711, Digital Human Modeling and Applications in Health, Safety, Ergonomics and Risk Management: Part III, edited by Vincent G. Duffy

29. LNCS 14712, Design, User Experience, and Usability: Part I, edited by Aaron Marcus, Elizabeth Rosenzweig and Marcelo M. Soares

30. LNCS 14713, Design, User Experience, and Usability: Part II, edited by Aaron Marcus, Elizabeth Rosenzweig and Marcelo M. Soares

31. LNCS 14714, Design, User Experience, and Usability: Part III, edited by Aaron Marcus, Elizabeth Rosenzweig and Marcelo M. Soares

32. LNCS 14715, Design, User Experience, and Usability: Part IV, edited by Aaron Marcus, Elizabeth Rosenzweig and Marcelo M. Soares

33. LNCS 14716, Design, User Experience, and Usability: Part V, edited by Aaron Marcus, Elizabeth Rosenzweig and Marcelo M. Soares

34. LNCS 14717, Culture and Computing, edited by Matthias Rauterberg

35. LNCS 14718, Distributed, Ambient and Pervasive Interactions: Part I, edited by Norbert A. Streitz and Shin'ichi Konomi

36. LNCS 14719, Distributed, Ambient and Pervasive Interactions: Part II, edited by Norbert A. Streitz and Shin'ichi Konomi

37. LNCS 14720, HCI in Business, Government and Organizations: Part I, edited by Fiona Fui-Hoon Nah and Keng Leng Siau

38. LNCS 14721, HCI in Business, Government and Organizations: Part II, edited by Fiona Fui-Hoon Nah and Keng Leng Siau

39. LNCS 14722, Learning and Collaboration Technologies: Part I, edited by Panayiotis Zaphiris and Andri Ioannou

40. LNCS 14723, Learning and Collaboration Technologies: Part II, edited by Panayiotis Zaphiris and Andri Ioannou

41. LNCS 14724, Learning and Collaboration Technologies: Part III, edited by Panayiotis Zaphiris and Andri Ioannou

42. LNCS 14725, Human Aspects of IT for the Aged Population: Part I, edited by Qin Gao and Jia Zhou

43. LNCS 14726, Human Aspects of IT for the Aged Population: Part II, edited by Qin Gao and Jia Zhou

44. LNCS 14727, Adaptive Instructional System, edited by Robert A. Sottilare and Jessica Schwarz

45. LNCS 14728, HCI for Cybersecurity, Privacy and Trust: Part I, edited by Abbas Moallem

46. LNCS 14729, HCI for Cybersecurity, Privacy and Trust: Part II, edited by Abbas Moallem

47. LNCS 14730, HCI in Games: Part I, edited by Xiaowen Fang
48. LNCS 14731, HCI in Games: Part II, edited by Xiaowen Fang
49. LNCS 14732, HCI in Mobility, Transport and Automotive Systems: Part I, edited by Heidi Krömker
50. LNCS 14733, HCI in Mobility, Transport and Automotive Systems: Part II, edited by Heidi Krömker
51. LNAI 14734, Artificial Intelligence in HCI: Part I, edited by Helmut Degen and Stavroula Ntoa
52. LNAI 14735, Artificial Intelligence in HCI: Part II, edited by Helmut Degen and Stavroula Ntoa
53. LNAI 14736, Artificial Intelligence in HCI: Part III, edited by Helmut Degen and Stavroula Ntoa
54. LNCS 14737, Design, Operation and Evaluation of Mobile Communications: Part I, edited by June Wei and George Margetis
55. LNCS 14738, Design, Operation and Evaluation of Mobile Communications: Part II, edited by June Wei and George Margetis
56. CCIS 2114, HCI International 2024 Posters - Part I, edited by Constantine Stephanidis, Margherita Antona, Stavroula Ntoa and Gavriel Salvendy
57. CCIS 2115, HCI International 2024 Posters - Part II, edited by Constantine Stephanidis, Margherita Antona, Stavroula Ntoa and Gavriel Salvendy
58. CCIS 2116, HCI International 2024 Posters - Part III, edited by Constantine Stephanidis, Margherita Antona, Stavroula Ntoa and Gavriel Salvendy
59. CCIS 2117, HCI International 2024 Posters - Part IV, edited by Constantine Stephanidis, Margherita Antona, Stavroula Ntoa and Gavriel Salvendy
60. CCIS 2118, HCI International 2024 Posters - Part V, edited by Constantine Stephanidis, Margherita Antona, Stavroula Ntoa and Gavriel Salvendy
61. CCIS 2119, HCI International 2024 Posters - Part VI, edited by Constantine Stephanidis, Margherita Antona, Stavroula Ntoa and Gavriel Salvendy
62. CCIS 2120, HCI International 2024 Posters - Part VII, edited by Constantine Stephanidis, Margherita Antona, Stavroula Ntoa and Gavriel Salvendy

https://2024.hci.international/proceedings

Preface

User experience (UX) refers to a person's thoughts, feelings, and behavior when using interactive systems. UX design becomes fundamentally important for new and emerging mobile, ubiquitous, and omnipresent computer-based contexts. The scope of design, user experience, and usability (DUXU) extends to all aspects of the user's interaction with a product or service, how it is perceived, learned, and used. DUXU also addresses design knowledge, methods, and practices, with a focus on deeply human-centered processes. Usability, usefulness, and appeal are fundamental requirements for effective user-experience design.

The 13th Design, User Experience, and Usability Conference (DUXU 2024), an affiliated conference of the HCI International conference, encouraged papers from professionals, academics, and researchers that report results and cover a broad range of research and development activities on a variety of related topics. Professionals include designers, software engineers, scientists, marketers, business leaders, and practitioners in fields such as AI, architecture, financial and wealth management, game design, graphic design, finance, healthcare, industrial design, mobile, psychology, travel, and vehicles.

This year's submissions covered a wide range of content across the spectrum of design, user-experience, and usability. The latest trends and technologies are represented, as well as contributions from professionals, academics, and researchers across the globe. The breadth of their work is indicated in the following topics covered in the proceedings, encompassing theoretical work, applied research across diverse application domains, UX studies, as well as discussions on contemporary technologies that reshape our interactions with computational products and services.

Five volumes of the HCII 2024 proceedings are dedicated to this year's edition of the DUXU Conference, covering topics related to:

- Information Visualization and Interaction Design, as well as Usability Testing and User Experience Evaluation;
- Designing Interactions for Intelligent Environments; Automotive Interactions and Smart Mobility Solutions; Speculative Design and Creativity;
- User Experience Design for Inclusion and Diversity; Human-Centered Design for Social Impact.
- Designing Immersive Experiences Across Contexts; Technology, Design, and Learner Engagement; User Experience in Tangible and Intangible Cultural Heritage;
- Innovative Design for Enhanced User Experience; Innovations in Product and Service Design.

The papers in these volumes were accepted for publication after a minimum of two single-blind reviews from the members of the DUXU Program Board or, in some cases, from Preface members of the Program Boards of other affiliated conferences. We would like to thank all of them for their invaluable contribution, support, and efforts.

July 2024   Aaron Marcus
                                                              Elizabeth Rosenzweig
                                                               Marcelo M. Soares

13th International Conference on Design, User Experience and Usability (DUXU 2024)

The full list with the Program Board Chairs and the members of the Program Boards of all thematic areas and affiliated conferences of HCII 2024 is available online at:

http://www.hci.international/board-members-2024.php

HCI International 2025 Conference

The 27th International Conference on Human-Computer Interaction, HCI International 2025, will be held jointly with the affiliated conferences at the Swedish Exhibition & Congress Centre and Gothia Towers Hotel, Gothenburg, Sweden, June 22–27, 2025. It will cover a broad spectrum of themes related to Human-Computer Interaction, including theoretical issues, methods, tools, processes, and case studies in HCI design, as well as novel interaction techniques, interfaces, and applications. The proceedings will be published by Springer. More information will become available on the conference website: https://2025.hci.international/.

General Chair
Prof. Constantine Stephanidis
University of Crete and ICS-FORTH
Heraklion, Crete, Greece
Email: general_chair@2025.hci.international

https://2025.hci.international/

Contents – Part I

Information Visualization and Interaction Design

Interaction Design for Territories: Fostering Community-Centered Design
Experiences in Peri-Urban Contexts 3
  Filipe Cruz and Marco Neves

Data Sins: Speculative Design Unveiling Data Colonialism Through AI
Imagery 22
  Fábio de Almeida and Sónia Rafael

Navigating Government Websites: Optimizing Information Architecture
on the US Department of Labor Site 38
  Fiorella Falconi, Arturo Moquillaza, Adrian Lecaros, Joel Aguirre,
  Carlos Ramos, and Freddy Paz

Conversations in the Cloud: Crafting Harmony in AliCloud Computing
Interaction Design 53
  Xintong Huang, Yiqi Chen, Dan Qiu, Xuan Zhou, Yuzhe Fang,
  Yiyang Liu, Zeyu Wu, Zhongbo Zhang, Qu Rong, Tianyu Wang,
  Xiaofan Wu, Mengke Liu, Yuwei Yang, Xiang Wang, Chenyu Li,
  Jiazhi Wen, Shihua Sun, and Wei Liu

The Impact of Correlated Colour Temperature on Physiological Responses,
Task Precision and Subjective Satisfaction in a Simulated Node3 Aft
Cabin of the Space Station 68
  Zhangchenlong Huang, Ao Jiang, Yan Zhao, Hao Fan, and Kun Yu

Positive Lab: Intentional Visualization of Positive Emotions in Everyday
Face-to-Face Communication 88
  Yukina Kato and Tatsuo Nakajima

European Luxury Fashion Brand Websites for the Chinese Market.
An Explorative Study on Localization 107
  Joanna Liu and Lorenzo Cantoni

Influence of Color on Information Perception Under AR Simulated Lunar
Surface Environment 121
  Yukun Lou, Ao Jiang, Kun Yu, and Haihai Zhou

From Modeling to Fractals: Research on Prototyping of Augmented
Fractal Tangram Blocks Set 132
   Qi Tan

Designing a Collaborative Storytelling Platform to Enrich Digital Cultural
Heritage Archives and Collective Memory 142
   Ana Velhinho, Mariana Alves, Pedro Almeida, and Luís Pedro

Designing Interactive Infographics for Traditional Culture: An Exploration
of Interaction Patterns 160
   Ying Zhang, DanDan Yu, and LiMin Wang

The Effect of Color on Responsiveness in the Interactive Interface
of the Space Station Alerting Task (SSAT) 175
   Liangliang Zhao, Ao Jiang, Yan Zhao, Hao Fan, and Kun Yu

Usability Testing and User Experience Evaluation

Workshop DUXAIT: Conducting Efficient Heuristic Evaluations
with the Duxait-Ng Tool. A Case Study 189
   Joel Aguirre, Adrian Lecaros, Carlos Ramos, Fiorella Falconi,
   Arturo Moquillaza, and Freddy Paz

A Study of the Usability and Experience of Public Space in Rural
Watershed Environments 201
   Yali Chen and Xin Tu

Optimization of Display Content Switching Under Multiple Large-Screen
Displays: A Multi-channel Interaction Usability Evaluation 217
   Jialing Chen, Xiaoxi Du, Xinhao Guo, Xiaozhou Zhou,
   and Chengqi Xue

Optimizing Information Seeking for Multi-person Collaboration:
Evaluating the Influence of Various Zoom Centers and Interaction Modals 232
   Xinhao Guo, Xiaoxi Du, Jialing Chen, Xiaozhou Zhou,
   and Chengqi Xue

Building the User Experience Evaluation Model of Bank Outlets
by Service Design 248
   Manhai Li and Yixuan Liu

Usability Testing for Electronic Remote Control Interaction Interface
for Smart Home Products 259
   Fanhao Li, Yonghong Liu, and Xiangtian Bai

Public Transparency in Brazil: Evaluation of Transparency Websites
and Portals of Local Governments with More Than 200 Thousand
Inhabitants 268
    João Marcelo Alves Macêdo, Valdecir Becker,
    Felipe Melo Feliciano de Sá, Edvaldo Vasconcelos da Rocha Filho,
    and Daniel de Queiroz Cavalcanti

DUXAIT-NG in Practice: Evaluating Usability on the Municipality
of Lima Website 285
    Arturo Moquillaza, Fiorella Falconi, Joel Aguirre, Adrian Lecaros,
    Carlos Ramos, and Freddy Paz

Proposal for Packaging Evaluation Methodology Based on Eye-Tracking
and Affective Evaluation 300
    Shuma Ohtsuka, Naoya Kumagai, and Midori Sugaya

Qualitative and Quantitative Approaches to Conduct Heuristic Evaluations:
A Comparison Study 310
    Freddy Paz, Freddy-Asrael Paz-Sifuentes, Arturo Moquillaza,
    Fiorella Falconi, Joel Aguirre, Adrian Lecaros, and Carlos Ramos

A Checklist for the Usability Evaluation of Artificial Intelligence (AI)
mHealth Applications Graphical User Interface 324
    Chanjuan Tu, Alessia Russo, and Ying Zhang

Research on User Experience Evaluation System of Popular Science
Games Based on Analytic Hierarchy Process 338
    Yu Wan and Yide Zhou

A Qualitative Study for Parametric Designed Custom-Fit Eyewear Frames:
Fit Test Evaluation and User Insights 354
    Yuanqing Tian, Lingyu Li, and Roger Ball

Quality Assessment of Interdisciplinary Virtual Simulation Comprehensive
Practical Training Program for Economics and Management Based
on Students' Experience 371
    Jixu Zhu and Xiaoshi Chen

Author Index 387

Information Visualization
and Interaction Design

Interaction Design for Territories: Fostering Community-Centered Design Experiences in Peri-Urban Contexts

Filipe Cruz[(✉)] [ID] and Marco Neves[ID]

CIAUD, Research Centre for Architecture, Urbanism and Design,
Lisbon School of Architecture, Universidade de Lisboa, Lisbon, Portugal
filipedacruz@gmail.com, mneves@fa.ulisboa.pt

Abstract. Territories serve as a cognitive system for local societies, consolidating languages, shared experiences, and identities. As cities expand and peri-urban areas emerge, territories evolve, prompting the development of new design models. These models adopt a multisectoral, collaborative, and localized approach to address issues such as local economic development, quality of life, and active population participation. Promoting social interaction through activities and/or services fosters lasting relationships, strengthening communities. These interactions celebrate diversity and unity, creating spaces for sharing, collaboration, dialogue, and empathy. Interaction design for territories aims to advance sustainable development by considering not only the physical aspects of the territory but also human relationships, heritage preservation, responsible resource use, and cultural identity. We aim to present opportunities for interaction design to intervene in peri-urban contexts by fostering more personalized and engaging community-centered experiences. This paper, structured as a literature review, explores interaction design for territories as a mindset, process, tools, and interdisciplinary language. It introduces key concepts for designing experiences for visitors and local communities, including authenticity, co-creation, storytelling, and emotional atmospheres. Examining the cultural mapping of Lousa in the Lisbon Metropolitan Area, Portugal, the paper proposes an augmented reality (AR) application to mediate social interactions and enhance cultural and natural heritage. It questions the synergy between interaction design for territories and service design, emphasizing their potential to foster trust and efficiency in the digital era. The analysis under-scores the profound impact of interaction design as a catalyst for behavioral change, creating cohesive and community-oriented social interactions within territories.

Keywords: interaction design for territories · community-centered experiences · cultural mapping · service design

1 Introduction

Territories represent a cognitive system through which local societies utilize their territorial context to consolidate languages, shared experiences, and identities. It not only establishes connections between different forms of thought and relationships but also

A. Marcus et al. (Eds.): HCII 2024, LNCS 14712, pp. 3–21, 2024.
https://doi.org/10.1007/978-3-031-61351-7_1

generates a wide diversity of variants distributed throughout the geography of a given region [1]. It is crucial in constructing local identity, serving as an intellectual mediator that continuously reinterprets this identity for distinctive use in global relations [2].

The concept of "territories" theoretically encompasses several dimensions, each with distinct implications, thus amplifying the complexity of this multifaceted construct. According to the authors [3–7], there are four fundamental dimensions that deserve attention in understanding territories: political, cultural, economic, and naturalistic.

In the political dimension, related to power relations in space, the most widespread interpretation of territories highlights that they are a delimited and controlled space, often linked to the political dominion of the State. The cultural dimension, associated with culturalism, emphasizes the importance of the symbolic and subjective dimension of territory. It is a product of the symbolic appropriation of a group in relation to its living space, constructing cultural identity within its territorial context. The economic dimension, less disseminated, directs attention to the spatialization of economic relations. Territories are conceived as a source of resources, influencing the struggle between social classes and the dynamics of capital and labor, highlighting the territorial division of labor. Finally, the naturalistic dimension, less common in contemporary social sciences, explores the interactions between society and nature. Territories are shaped by human interactions with nature and the geographical characteristics of space.

From this perspective, the intrinsic importance of territories is emphasized as an expression of the historical dynamics of power correlations, whether they be political or symbolic. The relevance of geographical location is an unavoidable factor in understanding contemporary scenarios, permeating all areas considered essential. Knowledge of territories, understood as the spatial mediation of forces over time, proves indispensable in unraveling the complexities of the political and symbolic relations that shape. Present reality [8]. Territories are not only a stage for human actions and passions but also a reflection of the deepest expressions of human existence. When considering power, weaknesses, intangible dimensions, and their inherent connection to the human condition, we realize that territories play a central role in shaping cultural, historical, and social identity [8, 9].

As societies evolve, their territories also transform and fragment, especially as cities expand beyond their usual limits and peri-urban areas emerge as transitional spaces between rural and urban environments.

Traditionally, peri-urban areas are understood as urban outskirts around the urban core, serving as a transition zone between the urban and the rural [10], creating a complex and hybrid landscape. Considered fragile territories, susceptible to constant intervention, the peri-urban area is in a state of continuous consolidation. Over the years, various taxonomies have been adopted. Fanfani [11] argues that peri-urban space is a "third space," situated between the urban and the rural. It is an area of interaction between urban clusters and surrounding rural areas, often the stage for conflicts of interest [12]. Gottero [13] expands the concept to "agro-urban," recognizing multifunctional agriculture in this context. This includes professional agriculture focused on the city as well as practices such as leisure farming and urban gardening. These activities contribute to the connection between people and nature [14].

The growing interest in peri-urban areas in recent years reflects the recognition of the importance of territorial capital in these complex and ambiguous spaces [15]. This multifaceted resource is vital to the development and prosperity of a region, exerting significant influence on various factors. The social aspect highlights the contribution of the local population through skills, knowledge, and relationship networks, emphasizing the importance of social capital for regional cohesion [16, 17]. The cultural perspective underscores the value of historical-architectural heritage, traditions, and artistic practices, which not only enrich the territory's identity but also have economic potential through cultural tourism and local cultural activities [16, 18, 19]. The economic perspective focuses on natural resources, infrastructure, and the concentration of economic activities as drivers of growth, highlighting the need to identify specific characteristics for sustainable exploitation [16, 19, 20].

Professionals from various fields such as design, geography, agronomy, urban and rural planning, as well as policymakers, are increasingly adopting a multisectoral, collaborative, and localized approach to address issues related to local economic development, quality of life, and citizen participation [21]. Understanding and valuing the potential of these areas is essential for balanced development.

2 Interaction Design for Territories: A Holistic Approach

Design, as an ever-evolving artistic practice, aims to enhance objects, processes, services, and systems throughout its lifecycle. Playing a crucial role in technological innovation, design is recognized as a creative discipline situated at the intersection of everyday culture, technology, and the economy. Beyond its aesthetic and functional dimensions, design is considered a strategic tool for valuing local resources, promoting the preservation of regional identities and cultures. This valorization goes beyond products, involving knowledge, people, and traditional techniques that define the essence of a specific region [22–27].

Design enables connection between a region and the outside world, allowing local products and services to reach global audiences without compromising their cultural identity. By effectively communicating local authenticity, design creates an opportunity to celebrate cultural diversity. This approach not only preserves regional identity but also facilitates global sharing, encouraging tourism, investment, and valorization of local resources. When properly applied, design contributes to a positive image of the region, driving economic development, sustainable innovation, and social inclusion [26, 28, 29].

The perspective of interaction design for territories views the territories as a complex system that includes not only physical infrastructure but also the social, cultural, and economic dynamics that compose it [30]. The goal is to promote sustainable development and improve well-being in local communities. Design aims to create solutions that benefit territories as a whole and the communities within them [31, 32].

In this approach, not only the physical aspects of the territories are considered, but also human relationships, heritage preservation, responsible resource use, and the promotion of cultural identity. It is a holistic view that recognizes the interconnection between physical and social elements of a region [33].

The principles of interaction design for territories include integrated sustainability, community participation from the outset, heritage preservation, resilience and adaptation to future challenges, connectivity and accessibility, functional diversity, and the promotion of a sustainable local economy [18, 34].

In the process of interaction design, the importance of contextual analysis is highlighted, understanding the history, culture, and specific challenges of territories. Community engagement is crucial, with meetings and workshops held to actively incorporate local perspectives [30]. Interdisciplinary collaboration among professionals from different fields is essential, as well as prototyping and concept testing before gradual implementation [35].

This approach seeks to create multifunctional, connected, and inclusive spaces or networks that respect local diversity. By adopting interaction design for territories, the aim is to promote activities or services that, when focused on promoting social interaction, can foster meaningful and lasting relationships among people, contributing to the formation of strong and resilient community bonds [25]. These interactions are designed with the intention of serving as meeting points for the celebration of diversity and unity, providing fertile ground for sharing, collaboration, and empathy [36].

Collaborative networks are a fundamental catalyst for establishing a balance between the local and the global. Collaboration is a process in which different parties constructively explore their differences to achieve common goals. These collaborative networks function as structures that bring together resources, actions, visions, and learnings cooperatively, enabling the achievement of goals that would otherwise be unattainable in isolation [37].

In this scenario, creative communities emerge as protagonists. These innovative groups, when facing everyday challenges, often combine local and global elements. They challenge traditional ways of approaching tasks and, in doing so, introduce new behaviors that align individual interests with social and environmental concerns. These communities not only solve local problems but also generate new ideas about society, production, and well-being. They become practical examples of how local and global can not only coexist but also enrich each other [38].

Global networks of communication and information, driven by the internet and digital technologies, reduce geographic distances, allowing for instant connections and information sharing among people anywhere in the world. This global connectivity not only facilitates the dissemination of local cultures and knowledge but also promotes global collaboration among individuals and communities [39–41].

Creative communities, in particular, take advantage of this interconnected environment, using networks to spread ideas and innovations, enriching creativity, and enabling the creation of unique products and services valued globally. The successful implementation of collaborative networks requires common goals, effective interaction, and management adapted to the specificities of each network [42].

Despite the benefits, technological globalization also presents challenges, especially in the quality of relationships and communications in a diverse global environment. Trust, mutual respect, and cultural sensitivity are crucial to avoid misunderstandings and conflicts. Additionally, the quality of access and the interface of technologies must be designed taking into consideration the different cultural backgrounds of people [25].

Digital platforms and social networks represent valuable tools that allow communities to share common interests and objectives, fostering collaboration and the valorization of unique products and services. Through these networks, local communities can establish connections globally, sharing knowledge and innovations, and achieving higher levels of competitiveness while preserving their unique identities and values [34]. This interconnection is crucial for the sustainable development of communities, offering opportunities for growth, learning, and innovation, such as the creation of experiences between local communities and visitors.

3 Beyond Aesthetics: The Impact of Experience Design in Tourism

The Tourism industry has been enhancing visitor experiences by increasingly adopting design as a central tool. This paradigm shift reflects the understanding that the quality of the tourist experience plays a crucial role in customer satisfaction and loyalty [43]. By focusing on experience design, companies in the tourism sector can establish a deeper connection with their customers, nurturing an emotional bond that goes beyond mere transactional satisfaction [44].

This approach is driven by two streams of thought: experience economy [45] and entertainment economy [46]. These streams emphasize the importance of generating value and meaning in consumer experiences through the creation of products or services that exceed expectations, providing tourists with exciting and transformative experiences [47, 48].

Thus, experience design in tourism is an iterative and creative process aimed at establishing an emotional connection between the visitor and the destination [49]. It goes beyond visual aspects and encompasses the entire visitor experience, including sensory, emotional, and interactive elements that contribute to the creation of lasting memories [50, 51].

Moreover, it is a human-centered and co-creative practice that enables a better understanding of visitor needs and behaviors. This facilitates the creation of more personalized and engaging tourist experiences [52, 53]. The integration of technologies such as mobile devices, augmented reality, and artificial intelligence has contributed to improving accessibility, convenience, and interactivity in tourist experiences [54]. Active participation of tourists in the design of tourism services and products promotes a stronger connection and commitment to the destination [55].

The use of storytelling in the design of tourism experiences is a common practice. It involves telling stories to transform initially uninteresting places into attractive tourist destinations [56]. This goes beyond mere narratives, however, incorporating emotional and cultural elements, thus establishing a deeper connection between visitors and destinations. These narratives celebrate individual qualities in overcoming real challenges, highlighting the historical and cultural richness of the place [57, 58].

Communication through storytelling is a participatory experience that seeks to explore individuals and territories, transcending conventional locations and leaving a lasting mark on collective memory. When expressed by attentive listeners, narratives prove to be a powerful tool for dismantling deeply ingrained negative beliefs, touching the most intimate fibers of the human experience and activating the senses [59, 60].

Authenticity is another essential aspect of the tourism experience. Authenticity emerges as a crucial criterion in the evaluation of experiences by modern tourists [61]. The pursuit of authenticity is closely associated with the preservation of traditional culture and its genuineness [62, 63], and it is one of the main underlying motivations of current tourism trends [64]. Destinations that offer authentic experiences have a significant competitive advantage [65–67].

The creation of emotional and atmospheric environments plays a fundamental role in influencing consumer responses and forming emotional bonds with tourism and hospitality brands [68]. Visual, auditory, olfactory, and tactile elements converge to shape the atmosphere of a place, providing visitors with memorable and unique sensations. Careful interaction with color palettes, choice of ambient music, introduction of distinctive scents, and attention to spatial textures all contribute to the construction of an engaging sensory narrative. This meticulous attention not only directs consumer affection but also triggers specific associations that positively impact customer behavior, such as purchase intention and brand loyalty [69].

With the advent of the digital era, the importance of atmospheric elements transcends physical space and extends to the virtual environment. The online experience has become a crucial extension of the tourist journey, where virtual suggestions of atmosphere influence attitudes, engagement, satisfaction, and purchase intentions [70]. In this scenario, the strategic use of background colors, visual schemes, digital soundtracks, and even the incorporation of olfactory elements into virtual platforms are innovative practices adopted by tourism and hospitality companies. The careful design of these online elements not only reflects the brand identity but also amplifies the user experience, creating an emotionally captivating environment [71, 72]. Thus, conscious management of the atmosphere, whether in the physical or digital world, emerges as an essential tool for success in the tourism industry, serving as a competitive advantage in experience design and fostering a lasting emotional connection between consumers and brands.

4 Service Design and Interaction Design: A Strategic Alliance

One approach that has been widely applied in various sectors of tourism, triggering significant transformations in the way services are perceived and experienced, is service design [44].

By integrating tangible and intangible aspects, service design enables smoother user journeys and more harmonious interactions with the offered service [73]. The application of innovation principles, collaboration, and design thinking allows tourism service providers to redefine the relationship between visitors and industry objectives, addressing not only functional but also emotional and psychological needs of tourists [74]. A human-centered approach is essential for developing services that are not only efficient but also attractive and memorable, fostering lasting and enriching relationships between visitors and hosts [75].

Service design can be analyzed from various perspectives, each providing a unique and complementary view. These approaches range from a specific mindset to a comprehensive management view, highlighting the inherent versatility of this dynamic discipline. According to several authors [76–79], service design incorporates a series of interconnected perspectives, characterizing it as a mindset, a process, a set of tools, an interdisciplinary language, and a management approach.

As a guiding mindset, service design promotes a pragmatic and co-creative approach, placing user needs at the forefront while also balancing technology and business objectives. As a process, it operates through iterative cycles of research and development, allowing rapid prototyping and continuous adaptation to innovative and market-aligned solutions. As a set of tools, the importance of visual representations, such as customer journey maps, stands out for facilitating collaborative dialogue and mutual understanding between disciplines.

As an interdisciplinary language, it promotes collaboration among experts from different areas, using shared visual representations and boundary objects to facilitate cooperation across silos. As a management approach, it guides both incremental and radical innovation, focusing on human-centered performance indicators, qualitative research methods, and rapid prototyping. Its implementation often results in adjustments to organisational structures and systems, while keeping a close eye on the organisation's business objectives.

Regarding the foundational principles of service design, new contexts emerge [73, 79, 80] to enhance and update the understanding of this discipline:

- The importance of a human-centered approach is highlighted, emphasizing the need to consider the experience of all people affected by the service, including employees, customers, and other stakeholders;
- The collaboration of all participants is vital to ensure a comprehensive and representative vision throughout the design process;
- The iterative approach emphasizes the exploratory and adaptive nature of service design, encouraging experimentation and learning through trial and error;
- The emphasis on research and prototyping in reality underscores the importance of grounding concepts and ideas in concrete and tangible data, ensuring the effectiveness and practical relevance of proposed solutions;
- The focus on sustainability and a holistic approach highlights the need to ensure that services meet the needs of all stakeholders, promoting a balance between business objectives and user experiences;
- The harmony of interactions takes on added importance. In an increasingly demanding world, this understanding and interaction becomes essential throughout the user's journey.

Thus, service design has found an essential ally in interaction design. The collaboration between these disciplines not only favors desirable human, digital, and physical interactions but also strengthens trust and efficiency of services in the digital era [81]. Utility (the service's ability to provide functionalities that meet user needs), usability (ease of service use), pleasantness (the emotional experience provided by the interaction), and desirability (acceptance and popularity of the service) emerge as crucial factors, driving tourism companies in the search for differentiation and market leadership [74, 82].

5 Cultural Mapping of Lousa

The negligent evolution of the local context and culture undermines the inherent unique-ness of the territory, resulting in the alienation of residents from their heritage and the erosion of their cultural identity. The spread of culture and tradition across genera-tions cultivates a sense of pride and belonging. To fully understand local development, adopting a holistic approach that takes into account the interconnection between cul-ture, community, and environment is crucial [19, 29]. Cultural mapping, by analyz-ing the territories, has become an essential tool in identifying and understanding these interconnections [83].

Cultural mapping is a process that involves the identification, documentation, and analysis of culturally distinctive elements and resources of a locality, as well as local needs, aspirations, and perceptions. This place-based approach requires a deep under-standing of the cultural character and ecology of the region, thus promoting a more profound understanding of the place, its people, and its culture. It can be used to publi-cize conservation and preservation efforts, as well as uncover stories from the past and gain knowledge about the present [84].

The concrete (existing as tangible objects) and the abstract (existing as intangible ideas and beliefs) are interdependent and together form a system. In this context, Pillai [85], suggests that the location and distribution of these elements should be framed within resource mapping, involving the identification of tangible and intangible resources for cultural production, and in identity and community mapping, which highlights intangible components such as principles and values that shape the practices and identity of a community.

By employing specific tools and techniques to identify and document the cultural ele-ments and resources of an area and assess their significance, cultural mapping contributes to informing decisions regarding the appropriate use of resources, future planning, and the promotion of a sense of community. Additionally, it stimulates appreciation and respect for diversity, contributing to the creation of a more sustainable environment [86, 87].

Cultural mapping techniques such as direct observation and fieldwork were employed to qualitatively approach physical environments. The selection of Lousa village (see Fig. 1), among 10 other peri-urban communities in the Lisbon region, was selected based on the following criteria: community engagement, available tourism offerings, and accessibility to local authorities. This choice was driven by the need to establish a representative case study, which will serve as a foundation for the future development of an augmented reality (AR) application to mediate social interactions that shape and impact the dynamics of the territories and promote the cultural and natural heritage of a region.

Lousa (see Fig. 2) is a parish belonging to the municipality of Loures, with an area of 16.54 km^2 [88]. It borders the municipality of Mafra to the North and West, the parish of Loures to the South, and the parish of Fanhões to the East. Situated in a valley, between the Atalaia, Carregueira, and Serves mountain ranges, and along the banks of the Sacavém stream, the parish has a population density of 194.7 inhabitants/km^2, totaling 3216 residents. The population is distributed across different age groups: 430 inhabitants between 0–14 years old, 305 inhabitants between 15–24 years old, 1678

Fig. 1. Lousa, a peri-urban village in the Lisbon Metropolitan Area (authors, 2024).

inhabitants between 25–64 years old, and 803 inhabitants over 65 years old [89]. There are 1544 buildings, 386 of which were built before 1945 [90]. The parish encompasses several localities, including Ponte de Lousa, Carrasqueira, Carcavelos, Carrascal, Lousa, Freixeira, Montachique, Cabeço de Montachique, Tocadelos e Salemas, Casal do Barril, Casais do Forno, Torneiro, Torre Pequena, Casais de Montegordo, and Fontelas.

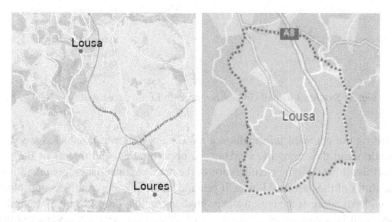

Fig. 2. Municipality of Loures and the neighboring area of the Lousa parish (Google Maps, 2024).

According to some toponym researchers, the name "Lousa" derives from the Latin lausia (flat stone, slate fragment), suggesting the existence of a prehistoric population in the region, corroborated by the caves of Salemas and the dolmens of Carcavelos. Others claim that the name comes from a royal slate workshop that existed in this location.

Fruit growing is the main economic activity in the area, although there is also a presence of metal production industries and commerce.

To organize the mapping process, cultural resources were segmented into six sub-categories: cultural organizations, spaces and facilities, cultural heritage, cultural and creative industries, festivals and events, and natural heritage (see Fig. 3). The figure reflects the categories presented in the report from the Agency for the Development of

Creative Industries [91] and in the Intangible Heritage Collection Kit from the Institute of Museums and Conservation [92].

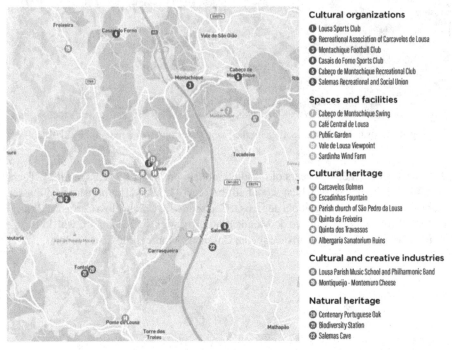

Cultural organizations

1. Lousa Sports Club
2. Recreational Association of Carcavelos de Lousa
3. Montachique Football Club
4. Casais do Forno Sports Club
5. Cabeço de Montachique Recreational Club
6. Salemas Recreational and Social Union

Spaces and facilities

7. Cabeço de Montachique Swing
8. Café Central de Lousa
9. Public Garden
10. Vale de Lousa Viewpoint
11. Sardinha Wind Farm

Cultural heritage

12. Carcavelos Dolmen
13. Escadinhas Fountain
14. Parish church of São Pedro da Lousa
15. Quinta da Freixeira
16. Quinta dos Travassos
17. Albergaria Sanatorium Ruins

Cultural and creative industries

18. Lousa Parish Music School and Philharmonic Band
19. Montiquejo - Montemuro Cheese

Natural heritage

20. Centenary Portuguese Oak
21. Biodiversity Station
22. Salemas Cave

Fig. 3. Synthesis map of cultural resources in Lousa parish (authors, 2024).

Based on the gathered information, a SWOT analysis was conducted (see Fig. 4) better understand the strengths, weaknesses, opportunities, and threats of the region. This analysis allowed for the identification of the main characteristics, potentialities, and vulnerabilities of the parish of Lousa. It provided a broader perspective, contributing to a better understanding of the region and its challenges. In order to evaluate strengths and weaknesses, it is necessary to evaluate tourist attractions, accessibility, infrastructure, tourism services, human resources, and other factors related to the internal environment. As for opportunities and threats, external factors such as tourism trends, regulations, technology, and the like need to be assessed.

Lousa parish presents a privileged location with a variety of historical, cultural, and natural attractions. To fully exploit the potential of this destination and achieve a competitive advantage, it is necessary to develop effective promotional strategies and offer differentiated experiences and a suitable tourism infrastructure. In this sense, the utilization of underused historical and cultural attractions, the adoption of new technologies for promotion, the creation of new types of tourism (such as regenerative and/or creative tourism), the development of "instagrammable" environments/spaces to increase visibility, and the creation of interactive routes to make the experience more playful and

STRENGTHS

INTERNAL FACTORS

• Strategic Location for Tourism: Lousa is close to Lisbon and Sintra, making it an ideal base for exploring the attractions of these cities;
• Historical and Cultural Attractions: Abundant monuments and historic sites await visitors to explore;
• Nature Encounter: Amidst the Atalaia, Carregueira, and Serves mountain ranges, it offers a lush natural setting with numerous trails to explore;
• Public Transport Access: Good connectivity with neighboring cities via public transport, facilitating easy arrival and departure for tourists;
• Accessibility: Just 4.8 km from the A8 highway, accessible via the N374-2.

WEAKNESSES

• Limited tourist infrastructure: scant offerings impacting the tourist experience;
• Low destination visibility: Less recognizable than others, making it challenging to attract tourists;
• Restricted range of tourist activities: Limited options for tourist activities, reducing visitor interest in the area;
• Insufficient investment: Less financial resources compared to more popular destinations, hindering improvements in infrastructure and tourist services.

OPPORTUNITIES

EXTERNAL FACTORS

• Local tourism growth: Capitalize on historical and natural attractions to attract more visitors;
• New technologies to promote the destination: Utilize new technologies to increase visibility and attract tourists;
• New forms of tourism: Regenerative and creative tourism offers experiences based on historical and cultural attractions, craft workshops, culinary demonstrations, and guided tours;
• Instagrammable environments: Create appealing spaces for social media sharing, enhancing visibility;
• Interactive routes: Provide entertaining and educational routes for tourists to explore the region.

THREATS

• Competition from other tourist destinations: Need to compete with more popular tourist destinations in the region, which may hinder attracting tourists;
• Changes in tourist consumption habits: Must be attentive to tourism trends and adapt to meet the needs of tourists.

Fig. 4. SWOT analysis of the Lousa parish (authors, 2024).

educational should be explored (see Fig. 5). However, it is important to consider existing threats, such as competition from other tourist destinations and changes in visi-tor consumption habits.

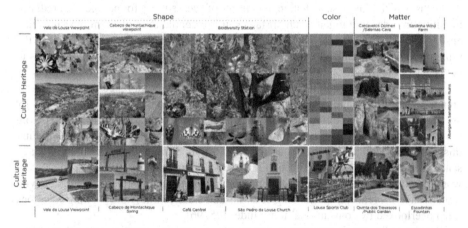

Fig. 5. Visual map of the cultural and natural heritage of Lousa parish (authors, 2024).

5.1 Further Research

The conception of a tourist itinerary encompassing the key historical, cultural, and natural attractions, both tangible and intangible, of the region is proposed with the aim of attracting new visitors and promoting the local culture of the region.

To achieve this objective, it is imperative to implement an interactive component of a playful nature, allowing visitors to interact with both the local residents and the itinerary itself. This component includes the development of a digital application that showcases the route and provides information about the main attractions through a historical narrative during the exploration of the parish. Through the use of augmented reality (AR) and GPS, visitors will have access to self-guided, personalized, and engaging routes, with video testimonials from local residents about the culture and history of the locality. The sensory and visual experiences provided by augmented reality add layers of information and context to tourist spots, making the visit more captivating and educational. This versatile tool raises awareness among users about a significant part of the locality's cultural heritage, possessing the ability to add value to visitors' experiences and the potential to redefine the interaction between tourists and the cultural heritage of a locality, establishing itself as a fundamental piece in the promotion and preservation of tourism in urban destinations.

Simultaneously, in order to optimize the visibility of the route, considering the ease with which images are shared through social media platforms, particularly Instagram, low-cost structures should be implemented in the main natural spaces. Given the absence of accommodation facilities for visitors in Lousa, the most suitable option is to create routes for Same-day visitors[1].

To improve the organization of the program, it is crucial to consider various elements, such as the time required for round trips, the duration of local activities, the opening hours of facilities, and the flexibility for spontaneous activities. It should be emphasized that, given the predominantly pedestrian nature of the route, some parts of the itinerary cover dirt paths, which may pose a challenge in terms of accessibility for people with reduced mobility. In order to mitigate such obstacles, it is essential to implement measures that ensure accessibility for all visitors, such as providing detailed information about the route through the mobile app, as well as the possibility of adapting certain activities to the needs of the traveler.

Additionally, it is recommended to consider the Hidden Florence project as a reference source during the design process of future application. Developed in 2014 by art history and visual culture professors Fabrizio Nevola and David Rosenthal from the University of Exeter, in collaboration with the digital innovation agency Calvium, this free-access application invites users to explore six distinct itineraries in the Renaissance city of Florence, Italy. Through the eyes of contemporary guides, such as wool workers, police officers, bankers, and matriarchs, users can imaginatively engage with Renaissance Florence, experiencing it as an authentic journey and visiting locations often overlooked by conventional tour guides [95, 96].

Before its launch, in order to generate interest among potential users, three communication channels were established in 2013: a dedicated website, a WordPress blog, and a YouTube channel. The WordPress site included teasers of the tours, presented in web page format, along with additional resources about the project, the team, and the city. Initially, three videos were added to the YouTube channel: a documentary about the project and promotional film for Hidden Florence, and a shorter 30-s edit. Although it was not part of the communication strategy itself, the application received an unexpected

---

[1] Same-day visitors, or excursionists, are a unique category of tourists exploring a destination for the day or as part of a tour. These visitors invest time and financial resources in the services and facilities offered by the destination [93, 94].

boost when it was featured on prime-time TV in the United Kingdom on December 26, 2016, and subsequently syndicated to several countries [95].

Currently, the application has been subject to updates, incorporating new narratives and protagonists, as well as establishing new collaborations that have allowed the integration of 3D tools into the route, thus enhancing immersion in the experience. The success of this project is reflected in its replication into other initiatives, such as the five new applications entitled, Hidden City, coordinated by the University of Exeter in partnership with Calvium.

6 Conclusion

This article emphasizes the importance of understanding and valuing the diverse dimensions of territories in order to promote equitable development. By highlighting the impact of interaction design for territories, and considering them as cognitive systems that consolidate languages, rituals, and shared experiences, the territories are recognized as more than just a delimited physical space. It plays the role of an intellectual mediator, continuously reinterpreting local identity to achieve global utility.

Exploring the political, cultural, economic, and naturalistic dimensions of the complexity of territories in shaping cultural, historical, and social identities is underscored. The growing recognition of the importance of peri-urban areas highlights the value of territorial capital, encompassing social, cultural, and economic contributions toward balanced and sustainable development in the region.

We conducted a preliminary study on interaction design for territories, considering it a complex system that integrates not only physical infrastructure but also social, cultural, and economic dynamics. This holistic approach seeks to create solutions that benefit the territories as a whole, incorporating principles such as integrated sustainability, community participation, heritage preservation, and fostering a sustainable local economy.

The importance of contextual analysis, community engagement, and interdisciplinary collaboration in the process of interaction design for territories is highlighted, aiming to create multifunctional, inclusive, and connected spaces or networks. These interactions not only preserve local identity but also promote long-lasting and meaningful relationships among people, contributing to the formation of strong and resilient community bonds.

Creative communities emerge as key players in this context, combining local and global elements to address challenges and generate new ideas about society, production, and well-being. Global connectivity, driven by communication and information networks, facilitates the dissemination of local cultures and knowledge, promoting global collaboration among individuals and communities.

Despite the benefits, technological globalization presents challenges, underscoring the need for trust, mutual respect, and cultural sensitivity to avoid misunderstandings. Digital platforms and social networks are essential for local communities to establish global connections, sharing knowledge and innovation, while preserving their unique identities. This interconnection is vital for sustainable development, offering opportunities for growth, learning, and innovation.

We analyzed the evolution of the tourism industry, highlighting the increasing importance of design in improving the visitor experience. This shift reflects the recognition that the quality of the tourism experience plays a crucial role in customer satisfaction and loyalty. The experience-centered design approach aims to establish deep emotional connections with customers, going beyond mere transactional satisfaction. Driven by the experience and entertainment economy, this practice aims to generate value and meaning, providing transformative experiences.

Experience design in tourism is an iterative and creative process that encompasses sensory, emotional, and interactive aspects, allowing for the creation of personalized experiences. The integration of technologies contributes to improved accessibility and interactivity. Storytelling stands out in creating emotional connections, while authenticity and the creation of atmospheric environments are crucial in influencing consumer responses. Both in physical and virtual spaces, conscious management of atmosphere emerges as a crucial tool for success in the tourism industry, driving emotional connections between consumers and brands.

We questioned the effectiveness of the alliance between interaction design for territories and service design as a strategy in the tourism context, given the service design's ability to trigger significant transformations in the perception and experience of tourism services. We conclude that by integrating tangible and intangible aspects, service design revolutionizes the appreciation and experience of tourism services. Adopting a human-centered approach, it fosters smoother interactions, taking into account functional, emotional, and psychological needs. This approach, under scrutiny as a mindset, process, set of tools, interdisciplinary language, and management approach, stands out for its remarkable versatility.

Simultaneously, factors such as utility, usability, enjoyability, and desirability act as drivers of differentiation and leadership in the tourism market by strengthening desirable and efficient interactions in the digital era.

Finally, we mapped Lousa, a peri-urban locality in the Lisbon Metropolitan Area, Portugal, with the purpose of proposing the creation of a comprehensive tourist itinerary. This itinerary aims to highlight the main historical, cultural, and natural attractions of the region, whether tangible or intangible, with the goal of attracting new visitors and promoting the local. To achieve this intent, we emphasize the importance of implementing an interactive component of a playful nature. This approach would allow visitors to interact not only with the environment but also with local residents, exploring the itinerary through a digital app.

The results of this research and its present reflections should not be interpreted as conclusive. However, the analyzed methods and raised questions constitute a valuable tool for interaction designers, and also offer a starting point for future investigations in this specific area of design. We aim to provide a solid foundation for professionals and researchers in the field of design, empowering them to create more attractive and dynamic interactive solutions within the scope of design for territories. Additionally, we aim to provide a solid theoretical basis on which to enrich the work of these professionals and researchers.

Acknowledgements. This work is financed by national funds through FCT - Fundação para a Ciência e a Tecnologia, I.P., under the Strategic Project with the references UIDB/04008/2020.

References

1. Rullani, E.: La Fabbrica dell'Immateriale. Produrre Valore con la Conoscenza. Carocci (2004)
2. Beccatini, G., Rullani, E.: Sistema Locale e Mercato Globale. In: Economia e Politica Industriale. Journal of Industrial and Business Economics. Franco Angeli (1993)
3. Bonomi, A.: Territorio e Politica. Einaudi, Torino, Italia (2013)
4. Godelier, M.: L'Idéel et le Matériel: Pensée, Économies, Sociétés. Librairie Arthème Fayard (1984)
5. Haesbaert, R.: O Mito da Desterritorialização: do "Fim dos Territórios" à Multiterritorialidade. Bertrand Brasil, Rio de Janeiro, Brasil (2004)
6. Levy, J.: Intercultural Training Design. In: Fowler, S.M., Mumford, M.G. (eds.) Intercultural Sourcebook: Cross-Cultural Training Methods, pp. 1–15. Intercultural Press, Yarmouth, Me. (1995)
7. Parente, M., Sedini, C.: Design for territories as practice and theoretical field of study. Des. J. **20**, S3047–S3058 (2017). https://doi.org/10.1080/14606925.2017.1352812
8. Santos, M.: O Dinheiro e o Território. Revista GEOgraphia **1**, 7–13 (1999). https://doi.org/10.22409/GEOgraphia1999.v1i1.a13360
9. Hogg, M.A., Terry, D.J., White, K.M.: A tale of two theories: a critical comparison of identity theory with social identity theory. Soc. Psychol. Q. **58**, 255–269 (1995). https://doi.org/10.2307/2787127
10. Pryor, R.J.: Defining the rural-urban fringe. Soc. Forces **47**, 202–215 (1968). https://doi.org/10.2307/2575150
11. Fanfani, D.: Il Governo del Territorio e del Paesaggio Rurale Nello Spazio "Terzo" Periurbano. Il Parco Agricolo come Strumento di Politiche e di Progetto. ri-vista. **6**, 54–69 (2006). https://doi.org/10.13128/RV-17443
12. Busck, A.G., Kristensen, S.P., Præstholm, S., Reenberg, A., Primdahl, J.: Land system changes in the context of urbanisation: examples from the peri-urban area of greater Copenhagen. Geografisk Tidsskrift-Danish J. Geogr. **106**, 21–34 (2006). https://doi.org/10.1080/00167223.2006.10649554
13. Gottero, E. (ed.): Agrourbanism. GL, vol. 124. Springer, Cham (2019). https://doi.org/10.1007/978-3-319-95576-6
14. Vejre, H., et al.: Can agriculture be urban? In: Urban Agriculture Europe, pp. 18–21. Jovis (2016)
15. Amirinejad, G., Donehue, P., Baker, D.: Ambiguity at the Peri-urban interface in Australia. Land Use Policy **78**, 472–480 (2018). https://doi.org/10.1016/j.landusepol.2018.07.022
16. Farrell, G., Thirion, S., Soto, P., Champetier, Y., Janot, J.-L.: La Competitività Territoriale. Costruire una strategia di sviluppo territoriale alla luce dell'esperienza LEADER. In: Innovazionne in Ambiente Rurale. p. 43. Osservatorio Europeo LEADER (1999)
17. Putnam, R.D.: Bowling Alone: The Collapse and Revival of American Community. Simon & Schuster, New York (2000)
18. Magnaghi, A.: Il Progetto Locale. Verso la Coscienza di Luogo. Bollati Boringhieri (2010)
19. Magnaghi, A.: Il Principio Territoriale. Bollati Boringhieri (2020)
20. Parente, M., Sedini, C.: Valorizzare il Capitale Territoriale con un Approccio Design Oriented: il Caso di Biella, Fabbrica Culturale Creativa. In: Scienze del Territorio: Rivista di Studi Territorialisti, pp. 212–222. Firenze University Press (2018)
21. Wandl, A., Magoni, M.: Sustainable planning of Peri-Urban areas: introduction to the special issue. Null **32**, 1–3 (2017). https://doi.org/10.1080/02697459.2017.1264191
22. Bonfim, G.A.: Idéias e Formas na História do Design: uma Investigação Estética. Editora Universitária, João Pessoa (1998)
23. Bonsiepe, G.: Design, Cultura e Sociedade. Edgard Blücher (2019)

24. Cross, N.: Designerly Ways of Knowing. Springer, London, England (2006)
25. Krucken, L.: Design e Território: Valorização de Identidades e Produtos Locais. Studio Nobel, São Paulo (2009)
26. Manzini, E., Meroni, A.: Design em Transformação. In: Krucken, L. (ed.) Design e Território: Valorização de Identidades e Produtos Locais, pp. 13–16. Studio Nobel, São Paulo, Brasil (2009)
27. WDO: Definition of Industrial Design. https://wdo.org/about/definition/. Accessed 01 Oct 2023
28. Manzini, E.: Design, When Everybody Designs: An Introduction to Design for Social Innovation. The MIT Press, Cambridge, Massachusetts (2015)
29. Paiva, F., Moura, C.: Territory. In: Paiva, F. (ed.) DESIGNA 2018 - Territory Proceedings, pp. 15–16. LABCOM.IFP, Covilhã, Portugal (2018)
30. Cruz, F., Neves, M.: Local Communities and Their Visitors: An Interaction Design Approach. In: Marcus, A., Rosenzweig, E., Soares, M.M. (eds.) Design, User Experience, and Usability. HCII 2023. LNCS, vol. 14030. Springer, Cham (2023). https://doi.org/10.1007/978-3-031-35699-5_8
31. Parente, M.: Design for Territories as Reflective Practice (2016). http://www.d4t.polimi.it/dissemination-and-networking/
32. Sharp, H., Rogers, Y., Preece, J.J.: Interaction Design: Beyond Human-Computer Interaction. John Wiley & Sons Inc, New York, USA (2019)
33. Saffer, D.: Designing for Interaction: Creating Innovative Applications and Devices. New Riders, California, USA (2010)
34. Manzini, E., M'Rithaa, M.K.: Distributed systems and cosmopolitan localism: an emerging design scenario for resilient societies. Sustain. Dev. 24, 275–280 (2016). https://doi.org/10.1002/sd.1628
35. De Luca, V.: Reality-based interaction design. a review of tools and products for people's participation in the challenges of sustainability. In: Paiva, F. (ed.) DESIGNA 2018 - Territory Proceedings, pp. 317–326. LABCOM.IFP, Covilhã, Portugal (2018)
36. Saffer, D.: A Definition of Interaction Design. http://www.odannyboy.com/blog/archives/001000.html. Accessed 21 Apr 2022
37. Gray, B., Wood, D.J.: Collaborative alliances: moving from practice to theory. J. Appl. Behav. Sci. 27, 3–22 (1991). https://doi.org/10.1177/0021886391271001
38. Meroni, A.: Creative Communities. People Inventing Sustainable Ways of Living. POLI.design, Milano, Italy (2007)
39. Kossoff, G.: Cosmopolitan Localism: The Planetary Networking of Everyday Life in Place. Cuadernos (2019). https://doi.org/10.18682/cdc.vi73.1037
40. Ramos, J., Bauwens, M., Ede, S.: Cosmo-Local Reader. Journal of Futures Studies (2023)
41. Sachs, W.: The Development Dictionary: A Guide to Knowledge as Power. Zed Books, New York, USA (2010)
42. Balestrin, A., Verschoore, J.: Redes de Cooperação Empresarial: Estratégias de Gestão na Nova Economia. Bookman (2008)
43. Karayilan, E., Cetin, G.: Tourism Destination: Design of Experiences. In: Sotiriadis, M. and Gursoy, D. (eds.) The Handbook of Managing and Marketing Tourism Experiences. pp. 65–83. Emerald Group Publishing Limited (2016). https://doi.org/10.1108/978-1-78635-290-320161004
44. Stickdorn, M., Zehrer, A.: Service design in tourism: customer experience driven destination management. In: Proceedings of the 1st Nordic Service Design Conference., Oslo, Norway (2009)
45. Pine II, B.J., Gilmore, J.H.: Welcome to the Experience Economy, https://hbr.org/1998/07/welcome-to-the-experience-economy. Accessed 21 Oct 2023

46. Wolf, M.J.: The Entertainment Economy: How Mega-Media Forces Are Transforming Our Lives. Crown (2003)
47. Rodríguez, B., Molina, J., Pérez, F., Caballero, R.: Interactive design of personalised tourism routes. Tour. Manage. **33**, 926–940 (2012). https://doi.org/10.1016/j.tourman.2011.09.014
48. Tussyadiah, I.P.: Toward a theoretical foundation for experience design in tourism. J. Travel Res. **53**, 543–564 (2014). https://doi.org/10.1177/0047287513513172
49. Trischler, J., Zehrer, A.: Service design: suggesting a qualitative multistep approach for analyzing and examining theme park experiences. J. Vacat. Mark. **18**, 57–71 (2012). https://doi.org/10.1177/1356766711430944
50. Csikszentmihalyi, M.: Flow: The Psychology of Optimal Experience. Harper Perennial, New York (1990)
51. Turkle, S.: Evocative Objects: Things We Think With. The MIT Press, Cambridge, MA (2011)
52. Gnoth, J.: Destinations and Value Co-creation: Designing Experiences as Processes. In: Fesenmaier, D.R., Xiang, Z. (eds.) Design Science in Tourism. TV, pp. 125–138. Springer, Cham (2017). https://doi.org/10.1007/978-3-319-42773-7_8
53. Tussyadiah, I.P.: Technology and Behavioral Design in Tourism. In: Fesenmaier, D.R., Xiang, Z. (eds.) Design Science in Tourism. TV, pp. 173–191. Springer, Cham (2017). https://doi.org/10.1007/978-3-319-42773-7_12
54. Magnini, V.: Designing Tourism Services in an Era of Information Overload. In: Fesenmaier, D.R., Xiang, Z. (eds.) Design Science in Tourism. TV, pp. 161–172. Springer, Cham (2017). https://doi.org/10.1007/978-3-319-42773-7_11
55. Richards, G.: Designing creative places: the role of creative tourism. Ann. Tour. Res. **85**, 102922 (2020). https://doi.org/10.1016/j.annals.2020.102922
56. Chronis, A.: Coconstructing Heritage at the Gettysburg Storyscape. Ann. Tour. Res. **32**, 386–406 (2005). https://doi.org/10.1016/j.annals.2004.07.009
57. Moscardo, G.: Stories as a Tourist Experience Design Tool. In: Fesenmaier, D.R., Xiang, Z. (eds.) Design Science in Tourism. TV, pp. 97–124. Springer, Cham (2017). https://doi.org/10.1007/978-3-319-42773-7_7
58. Sova, R., Sova, D.H.: Storyboards: A Dynamic Storytelling Tool. Usability Professionals' Association Conference (2006)
59. Liçaj, B., Matja, L.: Storytelling and cultural tourism. valorisation of past identities. In: Santoro, S. (ed.) Skills and Tools to the Cultural Heritage and Cultural Tourism Management, pp. 279–290. D'Errico (2015)
60. Stoica, I.S., Kavaratzis, M., Schwabenland, C., Haag, M.: Place brand co-creation through storytelling: benefits Risks Preconditions. Tourism Hospitality **3**, 15–30 (2022). https://doi.org/10.3390/tourhosp3010002
61. Cohen, E.: Contemporary Tourism: Diversity and Change. Elsevier Science (2004)
62. Meethan, K.: Mobile cultures? Hybridity, tourism and cultural change. J. Tour. Cult. Chang. **1**, 11–28 (2003). https://doi.org/10.1080/14766820308668157
63. Sharpley, R.: Tourism. Tourists and Society. Routledge, London, England (2018)
64. Kolar, T., Zabkar, V.: A consumer-based model of authenticity: an oxymoron or the foundation of cultural heritage marketing? Tour. Manage. **31**, 652–664 (2010). https://doi.org/10.1016/j.tourman.2009.07.010
65. Rickly, J.M., McCabe, S.: Authenticity for Tourism Design and Experience. In: Fesenmaier, D.R., Xiang, Z. (eds.) Design Science in Tourism. TV, pp. 55–68. Springer, Cham (2017). https://doi.org/10.1007/978-3-319-42773-7_5
66. Steiner, C.J., Reisinger, Y.: Understanding existential authenticity. Ann. Tour. Res. **33**, 299–318 (2006). https://doi.org/10.1016/j.annals.2005.08.002
67. Wang, N.: Rethinking authenticity in tourism experience. Ann. Tour. Res. **26**, 349–370 (1999). https://doi.org/10.1016/S0160-7383(98)00103-0

68. Spence, C., Puccinelli, N.M., Grewal, D., Roggeveen, A.L.: Store atmospherics: a multisensory perspective. Psychol. Mark. **31**, 472–488 (2014). https://doi.org/10.1002/mar.20709
69. Mattila, A.S., Gao, L.: Atmospherics and the Touristic Experience. In: Fesenmaier, D.R., Xiang, Z. (eds.) Design Science in Tourism. TV, pp. 151–160. Springer, Cham (2017). https://doi.org/10.1007/978-3-319-42773-7_10
70. McKinney, L.N.: Creating a satisfying internet shopping experience via atmospheric variables. Int. J. Consum. Stud. **28**, 268–283 (2004). https://doi.org/10.1111/j.1470-6431.2004.00368.x
71. Richard, M.-O.: Modeling the impact of internet atmospherics on surfer behavior. J. Bus. Res. **58**, 1632–1642 (2005). https://doi.org/10.1016/j.jbusres.2004.07.009
72. Wu, C.-S., Cheng, F.-F., Yen, D.C.: The atmospheric factors of online storefront environment design: an empirical experiment in Taiwan. Inf. Mana. **45**, 493–498 (2008). https://doi.org/10.1016/j.im.2008.07.004
73. Stickdorn, M., Hormess, M., Lawrence, A., Schneider, J.: This Is Service Design Doing: Applying Service Design Thinking in the Real World. A Practitioners' Handbook. O'Reilly, Sebastopol, California (2018)
74. Moritz, S.: Service Design: Practical Access to an Evolving Field. KISD, London, England (2005)
75. Tassi, R.: #Service Designer. Il Progettista Alle Prese con Sistemi Complessi. Franco Angeli, Milano, Italy (2019)
76. Azizpour, A.: Outside-in Service Design: A Practical Guide. YouCaxton (2015)
77. IxDF: What is Service Design?. https://www.interaction-design.org/literature/topics/service-design. Accessed 22 Oct 2023
78. Kimbell, L.: Designing for service as one way of designing services. IJDesign. **5**, 41–52 (2011)
79. Stickdorn, M., Schneider, J.: This is Service Design Thinking: Basics, Tools. Cases. BIS Publishers, Amsterdam, Netherlands (2011)
80. IxDF: The Principles of Service Design Thinking - Building Better Services., https://www.interaction-design.org/literature/article/the-principles-of-service-design-thinking-building-better-services. Accessed 22 Oct 2023
81. IDEOU: Human-Centered Service Design: Design the Moments That Matter. https://www.ideou.com/products/human-centered-service-design. Accessed 20 Oct 2023
82. Clatworthy, S.: Interaction Design: Services as a Series of Interactions. In: Stickdorn, M., Schneider, J. (eds.) This is Service Design Thinking: Basics, Tools, Cases, pp. 74–81. BIS Publishers, Amsterdam, Netherlands (2011)
83. Duxbury, N., Garrett-Petts, W., MacLennan, D.: Cultural Mapping as Cultural Inquiry. Introduction to an Emerging Field of Practice. Routledge, London, England (2015)
84. Lee, D., Gilmore, A.: Mapping cultural assets and evaluating significance: theory. Methodol. Pract. Cult. Trends **21**, 3–28 (2012). https://doi.org/10.1080/09548963.2012.641757
85. Pillai, J.: Cultural Mapping: A Guide to Understanding Place, Community and Continuity. Gerak Budaya, Selangor/Kuala Lumpur (2020)
86. Gibson, C.R.: Mapping Culture, Creative Places: Collisions of Science and Art. Presented at the Local-Global: Identity, Security, Community, Wollongong, Australia (2010)
87. Stewart, S.: The Creative City Network of Canada's Cultural Mapping Toolkit. Creative City Network of Canada, Vancouver (2007)
88. DGT: Carta Administrativa Oficial de Portugal - CAOP2021 (2021). https://www.dgterritorio.gov.pt/Carta-Administrativa-Oficial-de-Portugal-CAOP-2021
89. INE: Censos 2021. XVI Recenseamento Geral da População. VI Recenseamento Geral da Habitação: Resultados definitivos. Instituto Nacional de Estatística, Lisboa (2022)
90. INE: Censos 2011. Resultados Definitivos - Portugal. Instituto Nacional de Estatística, Lisboa (2012)

91. Mateus, A.A.: A Economia Criativa em Portugal. Relevância para a Competitividade e Internacionalização da Economia Portuguesa. ADDICT - Agência para o Desenvolvimento das Indústrias Criativas (2016)
92. IMC: Kit de Recolha de Património Imaterial. MatrizPCI (2011)
93. United Nations: International Recommendations for Tourism Statistics 2008. United Nations Publication, New York (2010)
94. Urry, J.: O Olhar do Turista: Lazer e Viagens nas Sociedades Contemporâneas. Nobel, São Paulo (1996)
95. Nevola, F., Coles, T., Mosconi, C.: Hidden florence revealed? Critical insights from the operation of an augmented reality app in a world Heritage City. J. Herit. Tour. **17**, 371–390 (2022). https://doi.org/10.1080/1743873X.2022.2036165
96. Rosenthal, D., Nevola, F.: Locating Experience in the Renaissance City Using Mobile App Technologies. The Hidden Florence Project. In: Terpstra, N. and Rose, C. (eds.) Mapping Space, Sense, and Movement in Florence, pp. 187–209. Routledge, London (2016)

Data Sins: Speculative Design Unveiling Data Colonialism Through AI Imagery

Fábio de Almeida[1] 🆔 and Sónia Rafael[2(✉)] 🆔

[1] Faculdade de Belas-Artes, Universidade de Lisboa, Largo da Academia Nacional de Belas Artes, 1249-058 Lisbon, Portugal
[2] ITI/LARSyS, Faculdade de Belas-Artes, Universidade de Lisboa, Largo da Academia Nacional de Belas Artes, 1249-058 Lisbon, Portugal
srafael@campus.ul.pt

Abstract. The Data Sins project aims to provoke reflection on the concept of data colonialism by exploring its key underpinnings as an emerging phenomenon in the early 21st century. Through the discipline of speculative design, the project seeks to emphasize how many of the rationales surrounding the ideals of connectivity and progress within the realm of big data, in fact, conceal a new form of neocolonial appropriation.

The storytelling is based on conjectures that reveal contemporary aspects of the interconnected relationships between political, economic, and religious power. In this context, the rise of conservative right-wing movements observed in Brazil over the last decade solidifies the marriage between religious moralism, authoritarianism, and economic liberalism. The materialization of the project adopted a discursive approach, with the methodology relying on the use of artificial intelligence to construct the visual universe of speculative scenario. Furthermore, it was crucial for recognizing and highlighting biases and prejudices related to gender, race, and culture within the training models of the platform.

Keywords: Critical and Speculative Design · Storytelling · Data Colonialism · Artificial Intelligence Art Generator · Digital Bias

1 Introduction

The objective of this article is to research possible futures for capitalist practices in Brazil. The research seeks to relate aspects of data colonialism to contemporary social concerns in Brazil, such as the rise of religious and conservative nationalism in politics, along with the numerous data collection events observed in recent decades.

In this context, the document is structured in two parts, with the first dedicated to a theoretical framework that serves as the basis for the project. This includes the characteristics of data colonialism, power relations and their agents, as well as an analysis of issues related to social quantification processes, surveillance, and behavioral change through life gamification. These conditions position the self as the last frontier of colonization.

The second part focuses on understanding speculative design as a critical and discursive discipline that not only considers the plurality of existing realities in the world but also addresses the structural problems of technologies at the economic, political, and social levels. This part is centered on the creation of a speculative scenario, where the visual construction of the narrative and scenarios is carried out using artificial intelligence (AI).

Through an AI image generation software, the discursive practice seeks to investigate how natural language processing combined with the ability to generate images via textual descriptions enables a creative process in which the analysis and appropriation of visual speculations generated by algorithms offer the opportunity to not only highlight gender, race, and cultural biases present in the "machine's" decisions but also challenge historical images that depict the beginning of the colonization of Brazil.

The goal is to demonstrate how the rationalizations surrounding the "civilizing missions" of the world conceal a variety of social violence and injustices. Thus, it is through humor and exaggeration that the project, called Data Sins, introduces fictional entities, artifacts, and sacred rituals that reflect possible developments for capitalism in Brazil, considering its colonial legacy reflected in past struggles, current warnings, and potential challenges for the future.

2   Theoretical Background

2.1   Colonialism and Colonization Strategies

One of the first objects with which the natives communicated with the newly arrived colonizers in the region known as the Island of the True Cross, in the year 1500, was a white rosary. This event was recorded in a letter written by Pêro Vaz de Caminha, addressed to the King of Portugal, King Manuel. This record is considered the first historical document that describes the initial contacts between the Portuguese and the local peoples, marking the beginning of Portuguese colonization in Brazil [1].

Therefore, the natives' interest in the rosary, a Christian religious symbol, and their appreciation, "as if they were willing to offer gold in exchange," had a symbolic function of supporting a discourse intentionally aimed at legitimizing a colonization project. The coercion of peoples and the forced appropriation of lands for economic purposes were often justified by a divine and universal mission of "civilizing" the world. This mission had the power to transcend linguistic barriers and become true even to the most reluctant natives, who, in one way or another, would ultimately succumb to the faith and dominion of the colonizers.

In this context, reflecting on the strategies of Spanish colonization in the late 15th century, Zuboff (2018) highlights that the "pattern of conquest" of peoples and territories unfolded in three fundamental phases: a) the creation of legal measures that provided a justification for the invasion; b) the declaration of territorial claims; and c) the establishment of a city to legitimize and institutionalize the conquest [2]. Similarly, to the Portuguese colonizers, the Spanish monarchy and conquerors also conducted a kind of performance, a ritual, to legitimize the taking of possession of newly discovered lands and the inevitable confrontation with native peoples.

The reading of the *Requerimiento* [3] before invasions was a practice whose purpose was to announce to the native peoples that the Spanish colonizers embodied, at that time, the authority of God, the Pope, and the King, and that all would be subject to their power and punishments if any orders were not obeyed.

Just as the natives did not understand the language of the invaders, the latter did not try to make themselves understood, as the intention was solely to justify the use of extreme violence to subdue indigenous peoples and establish dominion over the invaded territory [2]. Consequently, as the author continues, it would not be surprising that the sailors involved in the colonial ventures of the 16th century, with their acts of "conquest by declaration" established a pattern of exercising power that transcends time and space, reaching the digital world of the 21st century.

2.2　From Historical Colonialism to Data Colonialism

For a deeper understanding of the concept of data colonialism, it is initially helpful to highlight the role of European colonialism of the 16th century as a structuring condition that enabled the evolution of global capitalism and its power relations over more than 500 years [4]. In this context, we can observe how the continuation of these logics reveals a phenomenon involving the reconfiguration of colonialism itself into a new order, where social relations and all aspects of human life are transformed into data. If we consider "data" as the flow of information from all aspects of human life (and its various forms) to data collection and processing infrastructures, we can assert that the exponential growth of the Internet over the last three decades has enabled the emergence of data colonialism due to the profound interconnection of human life with digital technology, driven by capitalism [4]. Thus, the rapid development of technological infrastructures capable of extensively connecting humans, objects, and systems, along with the continuous extraction of data, forms the basis for this new phase of colonialism.

It becomes evident how data accumulation and management activities for commercial exploitation view data, especially personal data, as a raw material freely available *in natura* for appropriation and use for profitable purposes. It is important to emphasize that data colonialism is not merely a metaphor describing contemporary capitalist phenomena, as it evolves within the same structures that were present in historical colonialism – the exercise of power and the large-scale acquisition of resources from which economic value can be extracted.

On the other hand, considering colonialism and its contemporary manifestations solely as an evolution of capitalism as the dominant world system entails adopting a Eurocentric narrative that, in part, overlooks social relations in favor of economic relations [5].

In this context, the colonial experience, whether it involves exploitation or colonization, laid the foundations for the formation of global centers of power. The core zones of the capitalist world-economy are predominantly composed of societies of European and Euro-American origin, such as Western Europe, Canada, Australia, and the United States, while the peripheral zones are occupied by non-European colonized peoples, often seen as in a process of "development" toward an ideal of "civilization" that is still under construction [6].

This "colonial power matrix" serves as an organizing principle that encompasses the exercise of exploitation and domination across various dimensions of social life, from the economic and sexual aspects to gender relations, political organizations, structures of knowledge, state institutions, and family units [7].

Therefore, it is relevant to investigate how certain decolonial concepts, originating from a Global South perspective, demonstrate that both historical colonialism and data colonialism are grounded in the same power structures that underpin the patriarchal, capitalist, and modern world system. From this perspective, it is possible to explore how advanced technological structures, such as big data and artificial intelligence, replicate, through their networks and algorithms, the same power relations present in colonialism [4].

2.3 Cloud Metaphor and Self Datafication

A fitting symbol to illustrate the functioning of contemporary new colonialism is the concept of the "cloud." The National Institute of Standards and Technology defines cloud computing as a model that enables ubiquitous, convenient, on-demand network access to a shared pool of configurable computing resources (e.g., networks, servers, storage, applications, and services) that can be rapidly accessed with minimal management effort [8].

The cloud serves as the central metaphor of the internet in contemporary times, it is ethereal and benign, an icon found on screens and smartphones, so ingrained in our daily lives that we can look through it [9]. In this sense, the empire of clouds can act as an episteme, a knowledge model that organizes social realities into structures that facilitate their "datafication." Datafication is a contemporary phenomenon that refers to the quantification of human life through digital information, often with economic implications [4].

One way to explain the political power of the cloud is through sovereignty [10]. By asserting that the cloud is a subtle tool tied to sovereign power, Hu (2015) seeks to emphasize that the illusion of security and participation promoted by these technologies aims primarily to establish the belief that the cloud, where data and content from personal hardware and smartphones are deposited, is truly "yours" [10].

Furthermore, the apparent "marketing feedback" supporting many user interaction initiatives, as well as the supposed freedom offered by the gig economy system, for instance, subtly embed the individual in the logic of liberal capitalism. However, this integration occurs within economic and data policy structures that leave individuals at the mercy of the sovereign power of corporations that control the cloud's operation [10]. On the other hand, Zuboff (2018) reveals that the emerging power relations in surveillance capitalism cannot be equated with a return to totalitarian power. References from the past are insufficient to comprehend the internal dynamics of this new form of power in the 21st century [2]. According to the author, in the contemporary world-system, the means of production serve the means of behavioral change, and human processes are gradually being replaced by machine learning processes, with the goal of replacing "trust" with "certainty."

In this context, a relationship is established where the greater the control of knowledge accumulation structures, the better the production of "predictions" that become valuable as they approach "certainty" [2]. Hence, the consecration of "certainty" produced by machines as the definitive solution to social uncertainty is linked to the intertwining of state institutions and market institutions, reflecting a shared commitment to the relentless pursuit of guaranteed outcomes.

2.4   The Quantified Self as the Ultimate Frontier of Colonization

Just as early industrial capitalism initially relied on the exploitation of nature, regardless of the consequences for the planet, surveillance capitalism relies exclusively on the exploitation of human nature. However, in this context, the impacts are directly felt by individuals [2].

The central issue lies in the informal and invasive way data is collected [4]. The application of extensive surveillance jeopardizes what the authors define as the "minimal integrity of the self." This minimal integrity can be understood as the boundaries that determine what the "self" is.

These boundaries constitute what Hegel would refer to as the "space of the self," which is the domain of fundamental material possibilities that provide the self with a horizon of action and imagination [4].

While personal tracking technologies gained momentum from the 1970s through practices like "lifelogging" and the use of wearable technologies, it was in 2007 that the term "Quantified Self" was coined to promote a movement in which people engage in the creation, use, and sharing of activities related to digital self-tracking technologies [11, 12].

With the evolution in recent decades of internet-connected mobile devices, digital sensors, and cloud technologies, the monitoring of bodies, activities, and behaviors has become more agile and detailed. Consequently, the concept of the "quantified self" has gained relevance and entered the cultural lexicon not only due to the development of digital self-tracking means but also because of the normalization of "datafication" processes [13]. In this context, as datafication of life expands and encroaches on the minimal space of self-integrity, notions of autonomy are being reconfigured. This raises questions about how the practices of collecting and processing personal data are shaping privacy.

A study by Pedersen (1997) defines privacy as a boundary control process in which the right to restrict or seek interaction is of primary importance. The study identifies six categories of privacy behaviors, including solitude, isolation, anonymity, discretion, intimacy with friends, and intimacy with family. These privacy behaviors serve important functions for psychological health and the development of behaviors such as contemplation, autonomy, rejuvenation, openness to others, freedom, creativity, recovery, catharsis, and dissimulation [14]. However, capitalist practices forged in the constant surveillance seem to authorize an invasion, a kind of authorized destruction, of the space of minimal self-integrity.

Therefore, we recognize that we are in the early stages of these transformations, and any proposed solution should prioritize the preservation of autonomy. What is at risk is the inner experience of a self being able to formulate its own desires and creatively experience them in spaces that grant it this right [2, 4].

3 Framing the Context Through Speculative Design

As a starting point for the design development, principles guiding speculative design and critical design practices were considered, particularly in reclaiming the discursive nature of design and its understanding within the postmodernist context.

The term postmodern refers to a movement characterized by "distrust of metanarratives" [15], the significance of discourse in postmodernism lies in deconstructing dominant metanarratives and challenging their meanings [16]. Examples of such metanarratives include Patriarchy, Christian ideals, and even the deterministic nature of genetics in human development.

Hence, the postmodern ideal rejects the notion of an absolute truth in religion, science, or philosophy. In this way, skepticism toward established theories, anti-foundationalism, self-reflective attitudes are among its fundamental characteristics, which, along with the use of irony and satire, are absorbed by the practice of speculative critical design, and thus guide the development of this proposal.

Prado & Oliveira (2016) emphasize the importance of a plural approach to understanding and practicing design, where the questioning attitude extends beyond established narratives that differentiate those with knowledge from those with beliefs and opinions [17], as well as what belongs to civilization, barbarism, science, or magic.

By recognizing design's complicity with systems that reinforce racism, classism, sexism, and xenophobia, the authors teach us that it is possible to envision this "leap," which changes not only the content but also the very terms of the conversation [17].

By rethinking how design formulates its questions, it is possible to act not only in denouncing but also directly in how to articulate the questions.

Furthermore, considering design production articulated through a decolonial attitude becomes relevant, as the proposed debate is carried out from what Ansari (2016) defines as "from the border," [18] where breaking with the dominant hegemonies present in the discipline of speculative design itself allows the "what if...?" approach to come closer to other global and systemic realities.

3.1 Defining the Speculative Scenario

The creation of the dystopian scenario will consider the issues of technological advancements at the level of infrastructures beyond the Global North, that is, at the political level of other realities [19]. In this sense, the choice of Brazil as the scenario takes into consideration the care needed in producing dystopian realities that are already a reality in many parts of the world [20].

The established dystopian future will be based on conjectures that reveal contemporary aspects of the interchangeable relationships between political power, economic power, and religion. These aspects are particularly evident in the rise of conservative far-right movements observed in Brazil over the last decade, which consolidates the marriage between religious moralism, authoritarianism, and economic liberalism. This marriage is most evident in the expansion of the political agenda of segments of neo-Pentecostal churches in Brazil [21].

The neo-Pentecostal movement originated in the United States in the mid-20th century and soon arrived in Brazil, with the Universal Church of the Kingdom of God as its primary institution. With a greater emphasis on "spiritual healing" and the "theology of prosperity" [22], the meritocratic logic and the pursuit of material success here and now are explicitly preached through exuberant, emotional, and interactive rituals, within a simple and easily accessible language [21]. Unlike classical Protestant ethics, in which economic success is achieved through methodical work conduct, for neo-Pentecostals, financial reward and material success can be attained through immediate conversion, coupled with a more entrepreneurial attitude toward life's adversities [23]. This ultimately favors the convergence of religious moralism with the agendas of economic neoliberalism.

In this sense, the growing number of evangelical Christians in the country, within a plurality of denominations, combined with an increasingly prominent role of churches in politics, can be considered signs of what some authors call a silent transformation. This transformation suggests a realignment of power dynamics and Brazilian democracy in the coming decades.

The project's objective is to speculate on how a possible technological crusade can legitimize the ongoing exploitation of data for capital generation while relating the colonization of the self [4] to the concept of salvation of the soul.

According to the conjectures presented, the "what if...?" approach develops the following proposal: What if, in the future, Brazilian citizens had complete control over their data and could delegate their control to evangelical religious institutions, in such a way that the Church becomes a new kind of data broker in a political, economic, and social rearrangement with the Government and technological corporations (Big Techs). In this context, the Church becomes a data worship platform within the awakening of a new religious nationalism, where the governance of citizens occurs through the creation of a Christian Social Credit System, integrated into a variety of sacred services and rituals. These not only ensure the predictability of social relations but also reconfigure capitalist practices that obliterate the dualities between the public and the private, the real and the virtual, faith and certainty.

The narrative as a satire of a technological Christian crusade reinforces the idea that individuals, having legal control over their own data, have the freedom to offer it to the Christian cause (the Church) in exchange for material gains (prosperity) and the certainty of salvation for the soul (self). Consequently, the narrative marks the beginning of the official extinction of the secular government and the reorganization of the Church's role as a mask for maintaining the power of Big Techs. Therefore, the words "Order and Progress" on the Brazilian national flag begin to take on new and extreme contours.

In the speculative scenario, various denominations of evangelical neo-Pentecostal churches unite in a kind of para-government entity called the *Christian Data Union* (CDU). This entity manages the personal data of the faithful within a range of public and private services organized within a *Christian Social Credit System* (CSCS). Physical spaces become a true fusion of church, lan house, cyber cafe, notary, school, financial institution, and electronics store. Consequently, the sacred temple is transformed into safe socialization spaces where individuals have access to a range of sophisticated devices and technologies that connect them to digital realms in which they can find guidance, prosperity, and peace. The creation of this fictitious entity refers to the formation of Big Tech monopolies in which the Cloud represents all private data technology infrastructure.

The CSCS satirizes the Chinese Social Credit System. In the scenario, the CSCS represents the score that the faithful receive for accumulating virtues within a logic that uses recurring data from individuals' daily activities, with metrics calculated in accordance with biblical precepts and other Christian codes of conduct. The metrics apply to captured, organized, and grouped data in five categories: biometrics (body); civil (official public obligations); labor (formal and informal work, professional development); social (social networks and communication); and Christian (participation in religious services and daily evangelization). The accumulation or loss of credits is calculated in real time based on the user's activities, and daily life thus becomes a grand game.

Under the name PAX-BR, the digital currency officially managed by the CSCS criticizes the maximum capitalization of human social experience and the future of money within technologies that are supposedly decentralizing the financial system, such as cryptocurrencies.

The narrative transforms the temple into a platform of products and services converted into sacred data worship rituals. Therefore, the narrative presents the individual's integration into the sanctuary under five aspects, where each stage represents a critical component of data colonialism metaphorically illustrated in the user's journey (Fig. 1). These aspects are:

1. Baptism – login as an act of conquest: baptism directly critiques the "terms of acceptance of products and services," drawing a direct analogy to the patterns of "conquest by declaration" that date back to the Spanish colonial expansion. Baptism is the ritual symbolizing an individual's adherence to the Christian Social Credit System (PAX-BR) and their registration in the CDU of Brazil. By accepting the terms of the "Declarations of Rights and Responsibilities", the citizen acknowledges the Church as the sole entity responsible for analyzing their life, and, consequently, the unrestricted provision of personal data takes on the form of a new type of tithe. Thus, the "First Access Login" marks the beginning of the fusion between the pursuit of salvation for the soul and the user's journey, transforming it into a myriad of products, tools, and systems that legitimize the "act of conquest" of the human experience, while profitable surveillance becomes omnipresent in the bodies and spaces it occupies.
2. Worship – gamification of life: in a moment of complete fusion between physical and virtual realities, and with cities saturated with mediatic spaces, the concept of "attending worship" expands across time and space through augmented reality, virtual reality, wearable devices, and the Internet of Things. These technologies serve as instruments for both evangelization and immediate financial rewards. Mobile devices and augmented reality technologies allow users to "collect" rewards at sacred locations scattered throughout urban centers. These virtual sanctuaries are found in places such as bus stations, parks, churches, clubs, and shopping centers, enabling users to interact with sacred words through rituals such as prayer, singing, and dance, performed individually or collectively. Thus, Worship highlights the control strategies of technological addictions, where techniques of compulsion, reward, recognition, acceptance, belonging, and inclusion aim to create a subjective experience similar to that of casino slot machines, where there is a reverse dynamic with the player being "played" by the machine.

3. Confession – life analytics, the truth through data: how can the user have more direct contact with the data analysis underlying the CSCS? How to understand the fluctuations between positive and negative balances converted into the PAX-BR currency? In this scenario, the act of Confession aims to put the user in direct contact with their sins and virtues so that they can understand when, how, and why their experiences are converted into credits or debits. Confession redefines privacy and the fetishization of data. It becomes a sacred and useful time for contemplating the "truth" contained in data. It is the time to review one's life – should I get married? Should I change jobs? Should I spend more time with my family? Should I be more patient? Thus, the account statement becomes the material instrument connecting the individual with their inner self. The processes of quantifying the soul become the manifestation of the sacred, where algorithmic certainty replaces faith. In the Confession ritual, the criticism is directly related to the phenomenon of the "quantified self" in the evolution of self-tracking technologies.

4. Exorcism – efficient herding of humans: in the Exorcism, highly unusual user behavior triggers alerts that result not only in the account and user credits being blocked but also in a summons to acts of "purification." In this case, to reinstate their account and recover points and financial balance, the faithful must undergo rituals at specific centers. In these spaces, known as "Labs," smart devices apply digital visual and auditory drugs, along with other techniques, with the aim of rehabilitating the individual.

5. Death – logout and restart: digital death signifies earthly demise. The annihilation of PAX-BR credits symbolizes the inability to navigate and prosper in secure seas protected by the Church, the Government, and technologies designed for the common good. There are various exit conditions, ranging from voluntary user departure to CDU's decision, as punishment for serious transgressions. In both cases, the citizen's account is canceled and directed to the so-called "digital limbo," where the possibility of rebirth is guaranteed in most cases through the purification of cloud files and a game reset. In this limbo, individuals become phantoms identified by surveillance system alerts and roam the Earth as "wandering souls." Thus, the impossibility of escaping surveillance and the connection of earthly prosperity to these processes ultimately elevate "digital life" to the status of life itself.

3.2 Materializing the Fiction and Defining the Visual Language

After the structuring of the speculative scenario, the next step is to determine the most suitable means and languages to bring the fiction to life. We have chosen a linear fictional narrative[1] that explores techniques of visual production in animation, storyboard creation, and scriptwriting. This choice aims to introduce emerging practices within the tradition of storytelling, creating room for a multiplicity of personal interpretations that foster relevant discussions on the theme and the practice [24, 25].

With the goal of exploring an emerging and experimental practice that utilizes metadata to generate images through artificial intelligence techniques, all the visual language used in materializing the narrative was developed using an AI image generation platform

---

[1] The video can be seen at: https://vimeo.com/763602632.

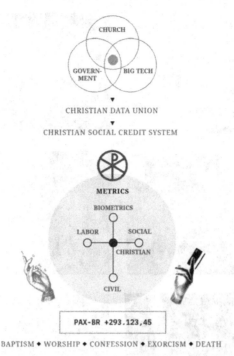

Fig. 1. Conceptual framework to illustrate the organization of a new social order, where we have the relationship between the institutions of power, the CDU, and the personal data metrics that make up the CSCS converted into digital currency (PAX-BR).

called Midjourney. This independent research laboratory employs proprietary artificial intelligence software to create images based on textual descriptions.

Interaction with this tool takes place through a chatbot, in which the textual description, known as a "prompt," serves as how the program recognizes what type of image is intended to be generated. The activation of the prompt begins with the command "/imagine," initiating the conversation with the software to construct the image. Images generated in response can be refined with specific commands or guided by other images.

As stated by Holz (2022), this platform is an "engine for imagination" [26]. The objective is not to create art or produce deepfakes but to provide a tool for research and experimentation that expands the human capacity to imagine.

In this speculative design context, the images are essentially speculative. The visual result arises from choices made during the experimentation with input data (text) and the inclusion of the unexpected as part of the creative process (Fig. 2). Like a game, interaction with the algorithm is the sole means of communication.

Fig. 2. Some images generated by Midjourney included in the video, representing an individual's integration into the sanctuary, based on the aspects of the storytelling

4   Findings and Discussion of Results

During the research, it was observed that the input of data in the construction of images ultimately provided an opportunity to challenge the biases related to gender, race, and religion present in the program. All these biases are reflections of the political condition within the structures where such emerging technologies are developed.

Thus, the materialization of satire takes place within this framework, offering a means of interrelating the social injustices perpetrated by algorithmic decision systems with the intertwined narratives at the outset of the colonization of Brazil, which also concealed the injustices inherent in the progress of those expeditions.

Therefore, all the images created were generated from prompts that embody ideas and terms related to critical components.

Here's an example of the image construction process for the concept of a "speculative church" within what Zuboff (2018) teaches about the relationships of instrumental power with the design of vices, in which casino slot machines illustrate the space and moment where a human being can enter a subjective experience of total symbiosis with the machine [2].

- Prompt: /imagine religious slot machine, church casino hallway, futuristic, dramatic atmosphere, divine, octane render, 4k, wallpaper
- Composition:

  - Description of the scene: religious slot machine and church casino hallway
  - Scene mood: futuristic, dramatic atmosphere, divine
  - Technical guidelines: octane render, 4k
  - Image size: wallpaper

The result comprises four images generated based on the prompt. Was requested the generation of additional compositions based on image number 2, resulting in four more images (Fig. 3). Then, we choose to enhance the resolution of image number 4 by a factor of 2X.

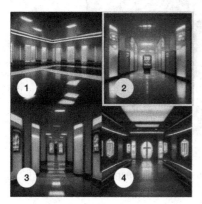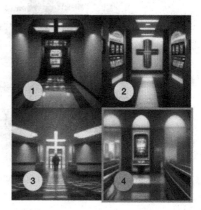

Fig. 3. Images generated by Midjourney based on the introduced prompt related to religious slot machine and church casino hallway

After obtaining the higher resolution image, the following prompt was added: /imagine religious game screen showing points, sins and virtues, slot machine, coins, sci-fi UX, divine, octane render, 4k. The resulting image is presented in Fig. 4.

The final composition, shown in Fig. 5, results from the combination of the two generated images, providing a visualization of *Worship – gamification of life* technologies. These technologies enable users to "collect" rewards at sacred locations, thereby emphasizing the control mechanisms of technological addictions designed to create a subjective experience akin to that of casino slot machines.

In further image developments, it was observed that certain algorithmic decisions reinforce stereotypes when inputs like "Jesus," "woman," and "evangelical" automatically default to an image of a light-skinned Jesus and a white woman, in addition to adding formal attire – a suit and tie – as something related to evangelical religion (Fig. 6).

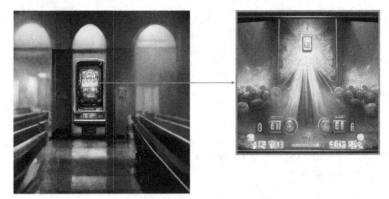

Fig. 4. Image generated by Midjourney upon adding a new prompt related to a religious game

Fig. 5. Final composition based on previously images generated by Midjourney

The inserted prompt was */imagine public confessionary with evangelical woman on the street, photo booth cabin with Jesus' picture. 16:9,* uplight, v3, q2.

Fig. 6. Result of the images generated by Midjourney based on the introduced prompt related to Jesus and evangelic religion

5 Conclusion

The project aimed to propose a dystopian scenario to expose the often overlooked, invisible violence and to reveal the fragile illusions associated with connectivity utopias. The project's proposal is to recognize the importance of discussing the immediate discriminations and injustices arising from data collection dynamics in everyday life. This includes, for example, black individuals who fall victim to errors in facial recognition systems, women whose professional resumes are overlooked by sexist algorithms on job search platforms, employees of large corporations whose performance is assessed by systems that monitor their real-time movements, and especially communities whose basic internet access is controlled by private organizations, often disguised as humanitarian actions. In this sense, the project seeks to highlight how the democratic state and its public policies are gradually being influenced by a new order of power.

Within this context, the materialization of the project relied on a discursive approach, with the methodology of active research incorporating the use of artificial intelligence to construct the visual universe of speculative scenarios. The use of the AI image generation platform, Midjourney, allowed for the creation of visual elements from textual inputs, establishing a creative method for appropriating unexpected results. Furthermore, it was crucial in recognizing and highlighting biases and prejudices related to gender, race, and culture present in the platform's algorithm training models.

By addressing the contradictions and opportunities offered by Midjourney, the project's execution not only acknowledged the potential for new practices in speculative design but also enabled a design investigation that confronts both the evident and subtle forms of violence and discrimination that pervade the discipline. Thus, the outcome of the video encompasses the visualization of the conceptual universe of data colonialism within a speculative scenario generated through dialogue with algorithms.

Acknowledgements. Research funded by ITI/LARSyS (LA/P/0083/2020).

References

1. Cortesão, J.: A Carta de Pero Vaz de Caminha. Imprensa Nacional Casa da Moeda, Lisboa (2010)
2. Zuboff, S.: The Age of Surveillance Capitalism: The Fight for a Human Future at the New Frontier of Power. Public Affairs, New York (2018)
3. De Viveros, J.L.: Notificación y requerimiento que se ha dado de hacer a los moradores de las islas en tierra firme del Mar Océano que aún no están sujetos a Nuestro Señor. Memoria histórica de México, 1500 Requerimiento de la Monarquía Española (1512). http://www.mem oriapoliticademexico.org/Textos/1Independencia/1500RME.html. Accessed 03 Nov 2023
4. Couldry, N., Mejias, U.A.: The Costs of Connection: How Data is Colonizing Human Life and Appropriating it for Capitalism. Stanford University Press, California (2019)
5. Grosfoguel, R.: Transmodernity, border thinking, and global coloniality: decolonizing political economy and postcolonial studies. Transmodernity: J. Peripheral Cult. Prod. Luso-Hispanic World 1(1), 1–36 (2011). https://doi.org/10.5070/T411000004

6. Lander, E.: Marxismo, eurocentrismo y colonialismo. In: Boron, A., Amadeo, J., González, S. (eds.). La teoría marxista hoy: problemas y perspectivas. CLACSO, Consejo Latinoamericano de Ciencias Sociales, pp. 209–243 (2006). http://biblioteca.clacso.edu.ar/clacso/formacion-virtual/20100720062844/boron.pdf. Accessed 16 Oct 2023

7. Quijano, A., Ennis, M.: Coloniality of Power, Eurocentrism, and Latin America. Nepantla: Views South **1**(3), 533–580 (2000). https://www.muse.jhu.edu/article/23906, last accessed 2023/10/05

8. Mell, P., Grance, T.: The NIST Definition of Cloud Computing. National Institute of Standards and Technology, Special Publication 800–145. U.S. Department of Commerce (2011). https://csrc.nist.gov/pubs/sp/800/145/final. Accessed 02 Oct 2023

9. Bridle, J.: Under the cloud. BBC Radio 4 (2020). https://www.bbc.co.uk/programmes/m000 0nc1n. Accessed 22 Sep 2023

10. Hu, T.-H.: A prehistory of the Cloud. MIT Press, Massachusetts (2015)

11. Wolf, G.: What is The Quantified Self? Quantified Self, Self-Knowledge through Numbers (2011). https://quantifiedself.com/blog/what-is-the-quantified-self. Accessed 23 Sep 2023

12. Lupton, D.: The diverse domains of quantified selves: self-tracking modes and dataveillance. Econ. Soc. **45**(1), 101–122 (2016)

13. Van Dijck, J.: Datafication, dataism and dataveillance: big data between scientific paradigm and ideology. Surveill. Soc. **12**(2), 197–208 (2014). https://doi.org/10.24908/ss.v12i2.4776, last accessed 2023/09/15

14. Pedersen, D.M.: Psychological functions of privacy. J. Environ. Psychol. **17**(2), 147–156 (1997). https://doi.org/10.1006/jevp.1997.0049

15. Johannessen, L.K.: The young designer's guide to speculative and critical design. Norwegian University of Science and Technology (2017)

16. Lyotard, J.-F.: The Postmodern Condition: A Report on Knowledge. University of Minnesota Press, Minnesota (1984)

17. Prado, L., Oliveira, P.: Shapeshifting: towards decolonizing design. Design, Identidade e Complexidade. III Encontros do Design de Lisboa. Faculty of Fine-Arts, University of Lisbon. CIEBA, Lisboa, pp. 88–101 (2016)

18. Ansari, A.: Towards a Design of, from and with the Global South. Carnegie Mellon University, Pennsylvania (2016)

19. Laranjo, F.: Design should be decolonised. Speculative. Post-Design Practice or New Utopia? The XXI International Exhibition of the Triennale di Milano, The 21st Century. Design After Design (2016). https://speculative.hr/en/francisco-laranjo. Accessed 1 Nov 2023

20. Tonkinoise, C.: Speculative practice needs diverse cultures. Speculative. Post-Design Practice or New Utopia? The XXI International Exhibition of the Triennale di Milano, The 21st Century. Design After Design (2016). https://speculative.hr/en/cameron-tonkinwise/. Accessed 1 Nov 2023

21. Spyer, J.: Povo de Deus: Quem são os evangélicos e porque eles importam. Geração Editorial, São Paulo (2020)

22. Alves, J.E.D., Cavenaghi, S.M., Barros, L.F.W., Carvalho, A.A.: Distribuição espacial da transição religiosa no Brasil. Tempo Social **29**(2), 215–242 (2017). https://doi.org/10.11606/0103-2070.ts.2017.112180

23. Mariano, R.: Os neopentecostais e a teologia da prosperidade. Novos Estudos **1**(44), 24–44 (1996)

24. Dunne, A., Raby, F.: Speculative Everything: Design, Fiction, and Social Dreaming. The MIT Press, Massachusetts (2013)

25. Mitrović, I.: Speculative – Post-Design Practice or New Utopia? Ministry of Culture of the Republic of Croatia & Croatian Designers Association, Zagreb (2016)
26. Vincent, J.: An engine for the imagination: the rise of AI image generators. An interview with Midjourney founder David Holz. The Verge (Aug 2022). https://www.theverge.com/2022/8/2/23287173/ai-image-generation-art-midjourney-multiverse-interview-david-holz. Accessed 30 Oct 2023

Navigating Government Websites: Optimizing Information Architecture on the US Department of Labor Site

Fiorella Falconi[✉] [ID], Arturo Moquillaza[ID], Adrian Lecaros[ID], Joel Aguirre[ID], Carlos Ramos[ID], and Freddy Paz[ID]

Pontificia Universidad Católica del Perú, Av. Universitaria 1801, San Miguel, Lima 32, Lima, Perú

{ffalconit,adrian.lecaros,aguirre.joel,
carlos.ramosp}@pucp.edu.pe, {amoquillaza,fpaz}@pucp.pe

Abstract. Government websites serve as sources of information and services related to public affairs, playing an essential role in connecting citizens with government institutions. The responsibility of government websites extends beyond just providing information; they must ensure that the information is easily accessible and understandable. This paper analyzes and redesigns the United States Department of Labor's website. The research began by examining user-generated content on social media and online forums, shedding light on user grievances and challenges. The analysis revealed a significant issue with the website's information architecture, causing users to need help finding the information they needed. A heuristic evaluation was conducted, and issues related to problems with usability heuristics, including "Help and documentation," "Visibility of system status," and "Aesthetic and minimalist design," were also identified. To initiate the redesign, a virtual card sorting activity engaged potential users to reorganize content and categories. User interface (UI) components were developed, presenting a fresh color palette aligned with the Department of Labor's branding. Remote Usability Testing (RUT) with seven diverse users, leading to further refinements for responsiveness and consistency. Usability tests on the prototypes demonstrated the value of a user-centric approach. If implemented on the United States government website, this redesign could alleviate user pain points, particularly information accessibility. In conclusion, optimizing government website information architecture is vital for improving user experience. This research and redesign process serves as a valuable case study for enhancing the usability of government online platforms, ultimately benefiting citizens and their interactions with government services.

Keywords: E-Government · User-centered design · Architecture information · Prototyping · Human-Computer Interaction · User Experience

A. Marcus et al. (Eds.): HCII 2024, LNCS 14712, pp. 38–52, 2024.
https://doi.org/10.1007/978-3-031-61351-7_3

1 Introduction

Government websites play a pivotal role in providing information related to public affairs in countries. Users seeking information or some procedure on these websites often have limited alternatives, as governmental institutions are the primary sources of such information and services [24, 25].

Government websites are often the only source of information, procedures, or services on a wide range of topics, from taxation and employment to healthcare and social services.

Users of these websites bring diverse needs and expectations, ranging from information acquisition to seeking assistance and access to essential services. In the digital age, where users have unrestricted access to global information, citizens are aware of the disparities in government-provided services [1].

Consequently, it is imperative that government websites are meticulously designed with a focus on usability, credibility, and accessibility. These factors are significant as they impact how citizens utilize and embrace e-government services and shape their daily interactions with e-government websites.

Historically, the origins of government websites can be traced back to the pioneering efforts of internet entrepreneur Eric Brewer, who set the stage for the inception of the first government website known as Firstgov.gov in 1999 [2]. Over time, these initial portals have evolved from rudimentary search engine counterparts into sophisticated platforms, bolstering their capabilities with advanced search functionalities, enriched content offerings, and enhanced user control [3].

Due to particular dynamics that emerged after the pandemic in the workplace that showed a tight and competitive labor market with rates of vacant positions and resignations [26], the importance of verifying the usability that users had to deal with when navigating the United States Department of Labor's website. The Department of Labor's website, as it exists today, emerged in 2009, stemming from the efforts of the Wirtz Labor Library, which began collecting and providing access to select agency websites associated with the department [4]. Presently, this portal assumes a pivotal role as a comprehensive resource for information and services pertinent to employment, labor laws, and workforce development. The department's overarching mission revolves around "fostering, promoting, and developing the welfare of wage earners, job seekers, and retirees in the United States." It is dedicated to improving working conditions, advancing employment opportunities, and ensuring work-related benefits and rights [5]. To accomplish this formidable mission, it is indispensable that the website's design and functionality align with the diverse needs of its user groups. This paper is structured as follows: An introduction and the theoretical framework to understand the essential concepts of this paper; the third chapter starts to explain the process and the user research executed to understand the website's pain points. This research includes Heuristic evaluation, card sorting, and usability testing. The fourth chapter explains the prototyping process performed for mobile and desktop versions. The fifth chapter explains how the test of the interactive prototype was designed and the tasks the seven users had to execute. In the last two chapters, we explain the test made on the final prototypes and the results. Also, we explain the importance of the user-centered design on government websites.

2   Theoretical Framework

This chapter delves into the theoretical framework and concisely explores foundational elements, offering insights into the key theoretical dimensions that shape modern digital governance experiences.

2.1   User-Centered Design

User-centered design process (UCD) is also known as a human-centered design process [6], where development proceeds with the user as the center of focus [7]. The central goal of this framework is to develop an optimal product that aligns with user needs, steering away from imposing a product's features on users and tailoring the design to enhance user satisfaction and functionality [8].

2.2   E-government

E-Government is the reference for electronic government because governments at the local, regional, and national levels worldwide are responsible for harnessing this capability to establish an electronic presence [9]. E-government entails leveraging information and communication technologies, especially web-based applications, to facilitate quicker, simpler, and more efficient access to and delivery of information and services to the public [10].

Given the importance of e-government, the United Nations published an E-Government Survey, the sole worldwide report evaluating the e-government progress of the 193 UN Member States. Its purpose is to function as a resource for countries to exchange insights, recognize strengths and challenges in e-government, and influence their policies and strategies [11].

2.3   Information Architecture

The usability.gov website explains Information Architecture (IA) as focusing on organizing, structuring, and labeling content effectively and sustainably [12]. The key objective in constructing a website's IA is establishing a coherent and user-friendly knowledge system, ensuring that content is easily locatable and accessible for users [13]). To achieve this objective, there are some specific tools related to IA: Content inventory, Taxonomy development, card sorting, tree testing, and usability testing, among others.

The author L. Rosenfeld, mentions the difficulty of mapping the boundaries of the IA and specifies that we can't confuse Information architecture with Graphic design, software development, or usability engineering [14].

2.4   Heuristic Evaluation

The heuristic evaluation is an evaluation that helps us to identify problems in how a system's interface works. We can do this by following clear guidelines. The main goal of the evaluators is based on the use of rules called heuristics, which look at the design to spot these problems [15]. The author Lecaros explains, based on Nilsen, that for the execution, it's best to have 3 to 5 evaluators for the most value. Each person checks independently, and when they're done, they compare results to get an overall view of usability [16].

2.5 Card-Sorting

Card sorting is a tool to help understand the users for whom we are designing something [17]. The proper definition is that this tool is a UX research technique where participants group labels written on notecards based on criteria that make sense to them. Figure 1 shows the basic steps to perform card sorting. This method reveals how the target audience organizes their knowledge and helps create an information architecture aligned with users' expectations [18].

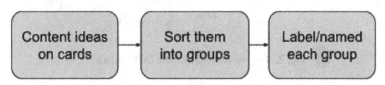

Fig. 1. Card-sorting process (extract from [17])

2.6 Responsive Design

The growing population of internet users and the prevalence of mobile devices, such as smartphones and tablets, have generated a necessity to customize the content presented on each device. Responsive design is identified by its ability to dynamically adjust content to fit the screen size, ensuring a favorable viewing experience on any web access device [19]. To achieve maximum usability and impact, a website's content should intelligently re-shaped itself [20].

3 Process and User Research

Göransson et al. (2003) presented a detailed usability design process encompassing three phases. However, for this redesign, only the first two significant phases were taken into account, as the development aspect of the redesign was beyond the scope. Figure 2 illustrates the adapted process implemented in this redesign effort.

To commence the user-centered design process, the information gathering and research phase was initiated to identify pain points and improvement opportunities on the DOL's website. As a first step, a review of the current website was conducted to understand the number of pages and the material covered. The examined website is hosted at https://www.dol.gov/ [21].

Given the extensive user base of this website, input was gathered from forums and social media, where users shared real difficulties encountered while interacting with the

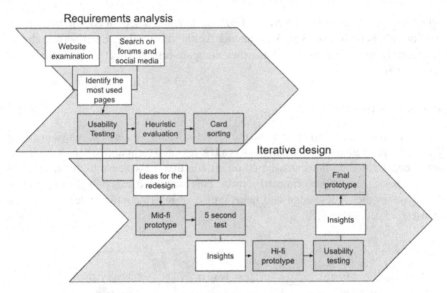

Fig. 2. Process redesign for the DOL website

website in search of specific information. Since this information is public and freely accessible, an analysis of these comments was performed, helped by word cloud generators and search engines associated with the web, revealing a common theme of users searching for information on the web, not finding it, and subsequently attempting to contact other points of contact within the Department of Labor. Additionally, the topics most frequently referenced by social media users in their searches were identified. The results indicated that users recurrently sought information on pages such as the Contact DOL page, Unemployment Insurance, Continuation of Health Coverage, and Frequently Asked Questions.

Based on these results, two evaluations were conducted: a remote usability test with potential users and a heuristic evaluation. The usability test, conducted with 7 participants using the Useberry tool, revealed that only 4 participants could complete all assigned tasks, and the average time to complete the tasks was 5 min. Figure 3 displays the results obtained in the Useberry tool format.

Furthermore, pain points identified from the usability test included the following:

- The website information is hard to recognize and understand for first-time users.
- The navigation menu and labels are not descriptive enough to quickly find what users are searching for.
- Too many links listed make it overwhelming to use the website.
- Users are uncomfortable using the website due to the technical language.

Table 1 presents the issues identified in the pages analyzed in the heuristic evaluation.

With these research findings, a clearer panorama emerged regarding why users face difficulties and the specific usability issues that need resolution.

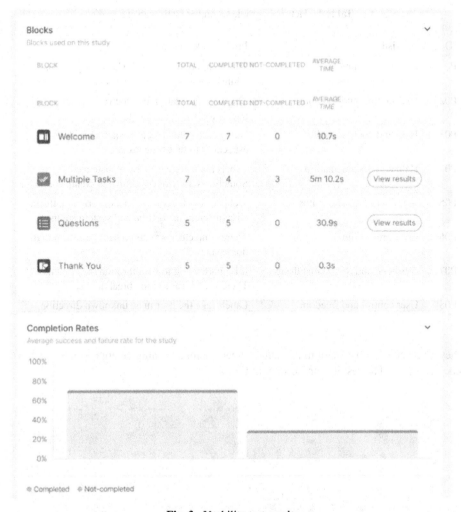

Fig. 3. Usability test results

The research findings revealed the need for a significant overhaul of the website's information architecture, navigation, and language. Key improvements included are the following:

- Streamlined Information Architecture: Reorganizing website content into a clear and intuitive hierarchy, making it easier for users to locate the information they need.
- Enhanced Navigation: Redesigning the navigation menu with descriptive labels and drop-down menus to facilitate quick and efficient access to specific sections.
- Simplified Language: Replacing complex jargon with plain language to improve comprehension and accessibility for all users.

A remote card-sorting session was conducted using the FigJam tool to reorganize the website's information architecture. Participants were tasked with grouping content

Table 1. Heuristic problems on the DOL website

ID	Heuristic	Problem Description
P01	Help and documentation	The search option doesn't show suggestions while typing
P02	User control and freedom	The main navigation bar doesn't remain on the page's top while scrolling
P03	Help and documentation	Navigation menu labels are not very clear, especially to first-time users
P04	Help and documentation	Labels are not clear in every instance. Sometimes, they overwhelm and create confusion
P05	Visibility of system status	Webpages redirect users to a different platform with different navigation and system status
P06	Error prevention	There is no clear way to go back or return to the homepage
P07	Aesthetic and minimalist design	It is challenging to scan through the content. There is no clear section breakdown
P08	User control and freedom	Labels take the user in an unknown direction

they believed should remain in the same category and assigning an appropriate name to each category. The results can be seen in Fig. 4.

Fig. 4. Remote card sorting

4 Prototyping

Prototypes are widely recognized as a foundational method for exploring and expressing designs for interactive computer artifacts [22]. They serve as a visual tool to illustrate the evolution of a design and experiment with different concepts.

Using the Figma tool, we developed prototypes for this redesign ranging from low to high fidelity. This choice was informed by the team's pre-existing knowledge and the ease of creating interactive prototypes for future usability testing. Key highlights implemented in the medium-fidelity prototypes included:

- Utilizing the hero space to showcase important news with brief descriptions, aiming to provide users with quick and easy access to the latest information.
- Introducing new categories in headers and labels.
- Designing drop-down menus to display options within each category, enhancing navigation and information retrieval.
- Standardize the internal pages' design with the homepage and incorporate breadcrumbs to aid navigation.

A glimpse of some design proposals is depicted in Figs. 5 and 6.

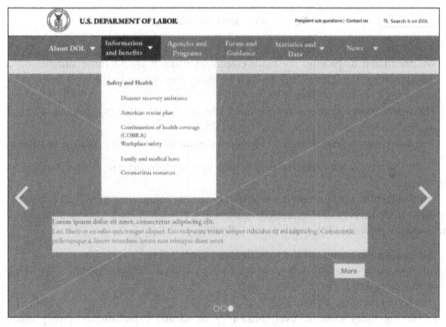

Fig. 5. Mid-fidelity Main Page

Medium-fidelity prototypes were also created for the mobile version. To ensure a responsive design, we implemented the following changes:

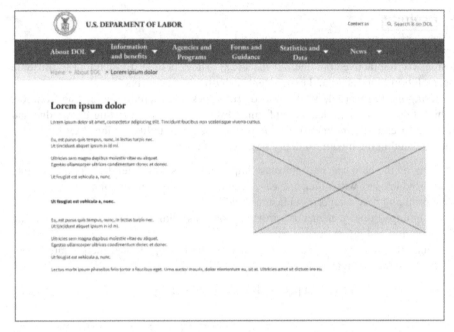

Fig. 6. Mid-fidelity Internal Page

- We prioritized displaying the main categories using a layout more suitable for a mobile screen. We retained the desktop version's dropdowns and utilized typography to highlight internal options.
- The search component was repositioned after the menu, allowing users to search if the desired information is not found manually.
- The footer was redesigned to incorporate social media links and language assistance.

Table 2 presents the proposed design decisions to solve the pain points founded on the research.

To validate the user comprehension of the content within the redesigned pages and the ease of identifying new components, a 5-s test was conducted. This method, based on Gronier's protocol [23], involves the following:

1. Introducing the context of the page that users will assess.
2. Informing users that they will see a page for 5 s and should try to remember everything in that short time.
3. Displaying the page for precisely 5 s.
4. Prompting users to share everything they recall and explaining how they could accomplish a specific task.

The feedback obtained from this test guided improvements to be implemented in the high-fidelity interactive prototype, as shown in Fig. 7. Some established enhancements include:

Table 2. Design decisions related to pain points.

Problem Description	Design Proposal
Information is hard to recognize and difficult to navigate menú	Architecture information restructuration
There are too many links listed	Links are grouped by categories and with the help of images
Difficulty in language translation	Highlight the bilingual options by placing them at the beginning
Redirection to different pages with different navigation	Use the same layout of components and breadcrumbs for all pages
There is no clear way to go back to the homepage	The home option is always available
The search option doesn't show suggestions while typing	Help display content while writing
The main navigation bar disappears with scrolling	Stick the bar always to have the options available

- Dividing the hero image into three sections to display more news simultaneously; hovering over the image reveals additional information.
- Placing language assistance within the header facilitates access for those seeking the Spanish version.
- Adjusting font sizes for better visualization.
- Add a blog section, Twitter, Contact Us, and federal government websites to the homepage.

5   User Testing

After the high-fidelity prototypes are prepared and interactive, the next step involves planning the usability test and defining the tasks that users will perform during the test.

For this usability test, three tasks were formulated based on information gathered from forums and social media, where the most sought-after information by real users was analyzed. The defined tasks were as follows:

- Find the phone number to call for information.
- Locate information about the Continuation of Health Coverage (COBRA) on the website.
- Review the main page and identify the different sections.
- The test was strategically planned to be conducted remotely to engage a larger pool of participants. In total, the test was administered to 7 users.

6   Results and Findings

After we finished the seven tests, the data was processed, and the insights were clustered. The outcomes were as follows:

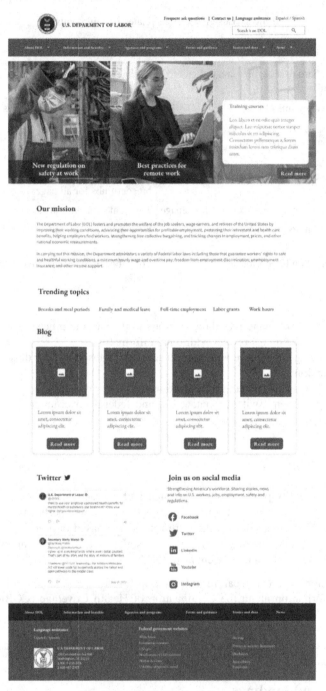

Fig. 7. Hi-fidelity Main DoL page

- All seven users successfully located information in the dropdown menus, finding the experience intuitive.
- All seven users noted consistency across the two website versions.
- Four users faced challenges in reading certain texts.
- Two users expected to find the site map under the "About Us" category.

Fig. 8. Hi-fidelity iterations

Responding to these findings, a subsequent iteration was deemed necessary to address the identified pain points from the usability test. The following improvements were implemented:

- We increased the font size for menu options to 18px.
- We altered the position and layout of trending topics.
- We included the site map option within the "About Us" category without removing it from the footer.

- We incorporated the language assistance option in the header of the mobile version.

The final prototype, showcasing these four modifications post-usability test, is illustrated in Fig. 8.

7 Conclusions and Future Works

In conclusion, optimizing the information architecture of government websites is crucial to ensure users can access the information and services they need. This research and redesign process on the US Department of Labor's website serves as a valuable case study for improving the usability of governmental online platforms, ultimately benefiting citizens and enhancing their interactions with government services. The user-centric approach, encompassing analyses of user-generated content, heuristic evaluations, and usability testing, unveils a strategic roadmap for addressing challenges in government website design. By prioritizing usability, this research contributes to the broader understanding of the evolving significance of government websites and underscores their pivotal role in fostering effective citizen-government interactions.

Government websites are indispensable hubs for citizens seeking information and services related to public affairs, and their design significantly influences user experiences. In acknowledging the limitations of current government websites, this research advocates for a proactive and user-centered redesign approach. The Department of Labor's website, a critical resource, becomes a testing ground for implementing vital improvements. The iterative analysis, redesign, and usability testing process offers valuable insights into the multifaceted nature of user interactions with government platforms. This case study is relevant to the Department of Labor and provides a broader framework for enhancing the usability of government websites, aligning them more closely with citizens' evolving expectations.

In future works, the insights gleaned from this research and redesign process open avenues for future exploration in enhancing various government websites. Analyzing and improving the usability of governmental online platforms is an ongoing endeavor, and the success of the Department of Labor's website redesign provides a blueprint for similar initiatives.

Acknowledgments. The authors thank all the participants involved in this experience, which has allowed the development of the present work. This study is highly supported by the HCI, Design, User Experience, Accessibility & Innovation Technologies Research Group (HCI-DUXAIT). HCI-DUXAIT is a research group of the Pontificia Universidad Católica del Perú (PUCP).

References

1. Prins, J.E.J.: Electronic government. variations on a concept. In: Prins, J.E.J. (ed.) Designing E-Government: On the Crossroads of Technological Innovation and Institutional Change 1–5. Kluwer Law International (2001). ISBN 978–9041116215
2. Department of Labor. USAGov's mission and History. Department of Labor (2023). https://www.usa.gov/mission-history

3. Gant, J., Gant, D.B.: Web portal functionality and state government e-service. In: Proceedings of the 35th Hawaii International Conference on System Sciences (2003). https://doi.org/10.1109/hicss.2002.994073

4. Department of Labor. Website archive. DOL (2023). https://www.dol.gov/general/aboutdol/history/digital-archive

5. Department of Labor. About us. DOL (2023). https://www.dol.gov/general/aboutdol

6. Shawn Lawton Henry and Justin Thorp. Notes on User-Centered Design Process (UCD). W3.org (2004). https://www.w3.org/WAI/redesign/ucd

7. Rubin, J.: Handbook of Usability Testing: How to Plan, Design, and Conduct Effective Tests. John Wiley and Sons, Inc (2008)

8. Argumanis, D., Moquillaza, A., Paz, F.: Challenges in integrating SCRUM and the user-centered design framework: a systematic review. En Commun. Comput. Inf. Sci. 6(6), 52–62 (2020) https://doi.org/10.1007/978-3-030-66919-5_6

9. Huang, Z.H., Benyoucef, M.: Usability and credibility of e-government websites. Gov. Inf. Q. 31(4), 584–595 (2014). https://doi.org/10.1016/j.giq.2014.07.002

10. Lee, J.: 10year retrospect on stage models of e-Government: a qualitative meta-synthesis. Gov. Inf. Q. 27(3), 220–230 (2010). https://doi.org/10.1016/j.giq.2009.12.009

11. United Nations. New global survey shows e-government emerging as a powerful tool (2023). https://www.un.org/en/desa/new-global-survey-shows-e-government-emerging-powerful-tool

12. Department of Health and Human Services. Information Architecture Basics (2023). https://www.usability.gov/what-and-why/information-architecture.html

13. Tankala, S.: Information architecture vs. sitemaps: What's the difference? Nielsen Norman Group (2023). https://www.nngroup.com/articles/information-architecture-sitemaps/

14. Rosenfeld, L., Morville, P.: Information Architecture for the World Wide Web. Inc, O'Reilly Media (2002)

15. Nielsen, J.: Usability Engineering. Morgan Kaufmann Publishers Inc., San Francisco (1993)

16. Lecaros, A., Paz, F., Moquillaza, A.: Challenges and Opportunities on the Application of Heuristic Evaluations: A Systematic Literature review. In: Soares, M.M., Rosenzweig, E., Marcus, A. (eds.) HCII 2021. LNCS, vol. 12779, pp. 242–261. Springer, Cham (2021). https://doi.org/10.1007/978-3-030-78221-4_17

17. Spencer, D., Garrett, J.J.: Card sorting: Designing Usable Categories. Rosenfeld Media (2009). ISBN 978–1933820026

18. Sherwin, K.: Card Sorting: Uncover users' mental models for better information architecture. Nielsen Norman Group (2018). https://www.nngroup.com/articles/card-sorting-definition/

19. Almeida, F., Monteiro, J.: The role of responsive design in web development. Webology 14(2), 157 (2017). http://www.webology.org/2017/v14n2/a157.pdf

20. Subic, N., Krunic, T., Gemovic, B.: Responsive web design – Are we ready for the new age?. Online J. Appl. Knowl. Manag. 2(1), 93–103 (2014). https://www.iiakm.org/ojakm/articles/2014/volume2_1/OJAKM_Volume2_1pp93-103.pdf

21. Department of Labor. DOL (2023). https://www.dol.gov/

22. Houde, S., Hill, C.: What Do Prototypes Prototype? In: Handbook of Human-Computer Interaction (2nd Ed.), Helander, M., Landauer, T., Prabhu, P. (eds.): Elsevier Science (1997). https://doi.org/10.1016/B978-044481862-1.50082-0

23. Gronier, G.: Measuring the first impression: testing the validity of the 5 second test. J. Usability Stud. 12, 8–25 (2016). https://doi.org/10.5555/3040226.3040228

24. Cabinakova, J., Kroenung, J., Eckhardt, A., Bernius, S.: The Importance of Culture, Trust, And Habitual Patterns - Determinants of Cross-Cultural Egovernment Adoption (2013). ECIS 2013 Completed Research. 182. http://aisel.aisnet.org/ecis2013_cr/182

25. The World Bank. Digital Government for Development. The World Bank. IBRD. IDA. https://www.worldbank.org/en/topic/digitaldevelopment/brief/digital-government-for-development
26. Domash, A., Summers, L.H.: How Tight are U.S. Labor Markets? (2022). https://doi.org/10.3386/w29739

Conversations in the Cloud: Crafting Harmony in AliCloud Computing Interaction Design

Xintong Huang[1], Yiqi Chen[1], Dan Qiu[1], Xuan Zhou[1], Yuzhe Fang[1], Yiyang Liu[1], Zeyu Wu[1], Zhongbo Zhang[1], Qu Rong[1], Tianyu Wang[1], Xiaofan Wu[1], Mengke Liu[1], Yuwei Yang[2], Xiang Wang[2], Chenyu Li[2], Jiazhi Wen[2], Shihua Sun[2(✉)], and Wei Liu[1(✉)]

[1] Beijing Key Laboratory of Applied Experimental Psychology, National Demonstration Center for Experimental Psychology Education (Beijing Normal University), Faculty of Psychology, Beijing Normal University, Beijing 100875, China
202328061013@mail.bnu.edu.cn

[2] AliCloud Design Center Beijing, Alibaba Cloud Computing Co., Ltd., Beijing 100020, China

Abstract. With the rapid development of cloud services, it has become the core driving force for innovation and business development in the digital era. The emerging technology of cloud computing has transformed cloud services from simple resource providers into comprehensive ecosystems, offering users unprecedented convenience, flexibility, and efficiency. In this context, this project focuses on the application of conversational interaction design in the field of cloud services, aiming to enhance the user interface and provide a more convenient and comfortable user experience (UX). Conversational interaction design, based on human-computer interaction (HCI), aims to deliver a more natural, intuitive, and personalized UX. By integrating artificial intelligence technology with cloud services, an intelligent conversational interface is created, allowing users to interact, manage, and optimize cloud services effortlessly. Through in-depth research and practical implementation, this project explores the diversity of user needs to ensure that conversational interaction design can meet the requirements of different user groups.

Keywords: User eXperience · Human-Centered Design · Cloud Service · Elastic Compute Service · Generation Z · Interaction Design

1 Introduction

In recent years, the vigorous development of cloud services has profoundly altered the landscape of the digital era, becoming a key driving force for innovation and business growth [1, 2]. The rise of cloud computing technology has transformed cloud services from mere storage and computing resource providers into comprehensive ecosystems, offering unprecedented convenience, flexibility, and efficiency for both enterprises and individuals. From data analytics to artificial intelligence applications, cloud services play a crucial role, providing a solid foundation for progress. In this context, this project

A. Marcus et al. (Eds.): HCII 2024, LNCS 14712, pp. 53–67, 2024.
https://doi.org/10.1007/978-3-031-61351-7_4

aims to explore the application of conversational interaction design in the field of cloud services to enhance UX. Conversational interaction design, integrating artificial intelligence technology with cloud services, creates intelligent conversational interfaces, allowing users to effortlessly interact, manage, and optimize cloud services [3, 4]. This project strives to improve the user interface of cloud services through in-depth research and practical implementation of conversational interaction design, aiming to meet user needs, enhance user satisfaction, and drive innovation in the field of cloud services. By studying the diversity of user needs, the project aims to ensure that conversational interaction design can meet the requirements of different user groups, providing valuable insights and solutions for the future development of cloud services and advancing the digital era.

This collaborative project with AliCloud focuses on exploring conversational interaction design in the era of cloud computing. The project concentrates on two common cloud computing scenarios, employing mental models to identify different user profiles, map UX operation chains, and contemplate the entry points and forms of conversational interface. It proposes conversational interaction design solutions tailored to typical user groups for two selected topics: (1) Building a Cloud-based Blog using Cloud Servers and (2) Quickly Getting onto the Cloud in Five Minutes. The former aims to optimize the Elastic Compute Service (ECS) setup experience through conversational interaction for users with different technical backgrounds, while the latter seeks to help students or developers better understand cloud services, uncover the potential uses of the cloud, and experience its convenience.

Despite the numerous conveniences provided by cloud services, challenges such as high technical barriers and user bottlenecks persist. Novices may struggle to grasp cloud computing concepts due to a lack of computer expertise, making it challenging to get started. Additionally, users often encounter various problems while using cloud services, and existing tutorials and documentation may fail to provide personalized solutions, leading to confusion and uncertainty. Enhancing the accessibility and UX of cloud services is crucial. Considering these challenges, this project aims to explore the following questions:

- What are the typical scenarios and journeys of users using AliCloud services?
- What pain points and needs do users have in the process of using AliCloud services?
- What kind of conversational interaction design can help users better use AliCloud services?

Through reasonable division of labor and transdisciplinary collaboration, this project has produced some forward-looking results. It enables students to apply theoretical knowledge from the perspective of enterprise requirements, assess their capabilities, and continuously reinforce and strengthen theoretical knowledge to better adapt to the practical environment of frontline production. Furthermore, the project provides students with a comprehensive understanding of the latest technological developments and market trends. While the application of cloud services by individual users is still evolving, this project has preliminarily explored the scenarios of personal users using cloud services on the AliCloud platform. It envisions the lifestyle of individuals in the future deep big data era, designing interactive methods suitable for corresponding cloud service scenarios, and provides references for the integration of cloud services with individual users in the future.

2 Related Works

2.1 Analysis of the Cloud Services Market

In the past three years, the Chinese cloud services market has experienced rapid growth due to the significant increase in online activities and cloud adoption. Cloud services are widely utilized in various sectors, including finance, manufacturing, energy, urban planning, healthcare, and media, providing substantial support for enterprises' digital transformation. The market exhibits a pattern of "one superpower and several major powers," with market share highly concentrated among a few leading providers. AliCloud holds the top position in market share, followed by Tencent Cloud, Huawei Cloud, ECloud, and Amazon Web Services. In specific industry verticals, cloud service providers have also achieved success. For instance, Tencent Cloud leads in market share for public cloud in gaming and video clouds, while Baidu AI Cloud tops the charts in intelligent media and industrial quality inspection solutions. Overall, China's cloud services market shows robust growth, intense market competition, and continuous expansion of market share by leading cloud service providers [5, 6]. They also offer differentiated solutions in various industries and verticals. As China's digital transformation progresses, cloud computing would continue to play a crucial role in meeting the growing needs of enterprises and governments.

2.2 Overview of Conversational Interaction Design for Cloud Services

With the advancement of technology, HCI has taken on various forms, and technological progress allows users to engage in natural and comfortable conversational interactions. Conversational interaction involves a two-way exchange of information between humans and machines through natural language, whether in textual or voice form, simulating natural communication between individuals. In the past, interactions, such as phone-based customer service, faced challenges like lengthy processing times and overly complex menu interfaces. Users often had to go through multiple rounds of dialogue to meet their actual needs. However, with the improvement of cloud computing capabilities and enhanced data processing power, precise text recognition and direct voice interaction have become possible, greatly enhancing UX [7, 8]. Conversational interaction has addressed issues like complex menus, allowing users to communicate directly with machines through text and voice, getting immediate guidance, and significantly improving UX. This approach eliminates the need for users to navigate through layers of menu options, enabling quick jumps and searches, saving time, and increasing work efficiency.

Conversational interaction is a key technology in artificial intelligence, determining the quality and UX. It not only assists in handling relevant tasks but also autonomously analyzes massive datasets. The goal of natural language processing technology is to help computers better understand and process human language. Its evolutionary stages include small-scale expert knowledge, shallow machine learning, deep learning, pre-trained language models, with each stage having a roughly half-cycle of the previous one, demonstrating increasingly rapid iteration. ChatGPT is a significant advancement in the field of natural language processing, improving the quality of conversational interaction and enabling roles such as intelligent customer service, chatbots, and voice assistants [9, 10]. Firstly, humans can communicate with ChatGPT using a more informal and conversational style, like everyday conversations with friends, enabling ChatGPT to understand the user's actual intent. During conversational interaction, there is a significant reduction in non-contextual responses to questions. Secondly, users can ask follow-up questions during the conversation, allowing ChatGPT to continuously improve based on previous responses, establishing meaningful connections between questions, creating a tightly knit context, rather than the traditional one-question-one-answer format. Thirdly, Chat-GPT possesses logical reasoning capabilities like humans in problem-solving. It not only provides answers but also explains the process and reasons behind the answers, allowing for detailed follow-up questions about the entire process. In the interaction, humans feel as if they are engaging with someone with logical thinking and extensive knowledge, resembling real-life conversations with friends or teachers.

2.3 Competitor Analysis

In recent years, conversational interaction design has made significant progress, yielding numerous cutting-edge developments and outstanding design cases. These advancements play a crucial role in enhancing UX within cloud services. Notably, the rapid development of natural language processing (NLP) technology and the application of pre-trained models like GPT-3 and BERT have contributed to more natural and fluent conversational interactions. The rise of personalized dialogues, multi-channel conversation design, as well as the emergence of intelligent assistants and virtual agent technologies, enables users to have more personalized and diversified experiences. Simultaneously, the integration of augmented reality (AR) and virtual reality (VR) provides users with immersive experiences, emotion recognition technology better understands user emotional needs, interpretable AI enhances transparency and user trust, while automation and machine learning technologies reduce design and maintenance costs, improving efficiency [11, 12]. These advancements and cutting-edge technological achievements collectively drive the development of conversational interaction design, offering more possibilities for applications in the field of cloud services.

The forefront progress of NLP technology is prominently evident in virtual assistants and chatbots within the financial services sector. For instance, e-commerce giants such as Amazon and Alibaba's Taobao have successfully provided consumers with intelligent customer service and product recommendations through conversational interaction. These chatbots assist users in browsing products, obtaining detailed information, and receiving personalized shopping suggestions, thereby enhancing the overall shopping experience. Products like Amazon Echo and Google Home have successfully integrated voice assistants, allowing users to control various smart home devices through voice commands and providing real-time information and entertainment. Siri, Apple's virtual assistant, utilizes NLP technology to enable users to engage in natural language conversations. Google Assistant possesses advanced natural language processing capabilities, allowing users to interact with it through voice or text, performing tasks such as checking account information and paying bills. IBM Watson Assistant, a cloud-based virtual assistant, utilizes NLP technology and machine learning algorithms to provide intelligent dialogue solutions for businesses. It can be used to build custom virtual assistants to support customer service, transaction queries, and other functions. These cases demonstrate the diverse applications of conversational interaction in different domains, providing richer, more natural, and personalized UX, while also offering extensive inspiration and insights for future improvements in cloud service conversation design.

3 Methodology

In the project, students employed a series of methods and theoretical frameworks such as user journey maps, affinity diagrams, flower mind maps, and the MoSCOW method to dive into the key principles and concepts of UX design. Two methods were emphasized in this project: researcher introspection and one-on-one qualitative interviews.

3.1 Researcher Introspection

Researcher introspection is a valid approach to investigating subjective experiences in human-centered design (HCD) research [13–15]. It challenges the pursuit of objectivity and the designer-user dualism, proposing introspection as a method to understand subjective phenomena. Introspection is an ongoing process of tracking, experiencing, and reflecting on one's thoughts, feelings, and behaviors. Although criticized for lacking objectivity, it is recognized as valuable in investigating experiential aspects. There are two scopes of introspection: narrow conception, involving a researcher's self-introspection, and broader conception, including guided introspection. Guided introspection, often used in HCD, elicits sensory feelings and meaning perceptions. The designer-user dualism, arising during usability research, encourages design researchers to use themselves as a measuring instrument for human understanding.

Researcher introspection contributes to more empathetic designs by incorporating subjective experiences. AliCloud researchers engage with cloud services, documenting encounters, reflections, and emotions. This enables a profound understanding of cognitive processes, informing design. Using a first-person perspective, researchers seek answers to improve experiences, empowering innovative solutions. Guided introspection prompts participants to express sensory feelings and emotional reactions, providing insights. It is employed in methods like in-depth interviews, guiding participants to introspect for valuable insights. Guided introspection is crucial in mapping user journeys, uncovering visible and subconscious feelings. By empathizing with users, it identifies service improvements and opportunities. In interviews, researchers engage in open-ended conversations to explore subjective experiences.

3.2 One-On-One Qualitative Interviews

One-on-One qualitative interviews refer to a research method where researchers engage in face-to-face communication with individual participants to gain in-depth insights into their personal experiences, feelings, and perspectives. This method is commonly used in qualitative research [16–18]. One-on-One interviews help researchers establish a trusting relationship with participants, uncover deeper feelings, motivations, and the reasons behind their behaviors and decisions. Typically conducted in a semi-structured format, open-ended questions are employed to encourage participants to express their viewpoints and emotions. In terms of sampling methods, qualitative research often uses non-probability sampling. Common specific sampling methods in interviews include purposive sampling, heterogeneity sampling, quota sampling, and snowball sampling. The steps of One-on-One qualitative interviews mainly include the following: (1) Define research purpose and questions: Before starting the interview, it is essential to clarify the research objectives and questions. (2) Develop the interview outline: Based on the research goals and questions, create an interview outline with open-ended questions to gather more information from participants. (3) Conduct the interview: During the interview, researchers need to build a trusting relationship with participants to encourage them to express their viewpoints and feelings. Additionally, researchers must employ interview techniques such as listening, guiding, and probing to help participants fully articulate their thoughts. The interview is generally conducted in a semi-structured manner. (4) Record and analyze interview content: Researchers need to maintain accurate records during the interview, including participants' viewpoints, feelings, and behaviors. After the interview, analyze the recorded content to extract useful information and conclusions, contributing to the research report. (5) Summarize and apply: Based on the analysis results, summarize valuable information and conclusions, applying them to practical research and implementation.

In this project, focusing on the topics, we formed four teams. Each conducted relevant literature and report research based on different topics and user groups. Through the research results, each team gained a deeper understanding of their target audience. We combined demographic data such as gender, age, and education with existing internet technologies, cloud service business, and conversational interaction forms for analysis. Additionally, we employed offline situational observations, observing users' real-life situations to identify product opportunities and development directions, providing practical data support for enhancing UX. Subsequently, each team outlined typical user profiles based on the analysis mentioned above, depicting the items, environments, information accessed, and potential services users might use while using the product. Each team formulated an interview outline based on their goals and questions. Utilizing methods like online surveys and offline poster placements, we contacted over a hundred participants, and after screening, conducted interviews with 24 participants. The interviews were mainly conducted in a semi-structured format, with deeper probing based on users' personal characteristics during the process to uncover genuine pain points and needs. After the interviews, the transcripts were analyzed, and each point raised by the users was written on sticky notes. Through affinity clustering, several dimensions were identified, providing direction and guidance for future product design.

4 Results

4.1 CloudSpace

In the era of personal media, platforms with low entry barriers such as Xiaohongshu and Douyin provide avenues for self-employed individuals, including artisans, to promote themselves and monetize their skills. However, the restrictions and constraints imposed by these platforms on individual bloggers create new challenges, prompting them to seek a transition from social media platforms to personal websites. Yet, cloud servers like ECS, designed for professional programmers, struggle to adapt well to the website-building attempts of non-professional beginners with zero foundations. The use of professional terminology and a complex console presents significant limitations and difficulties for them.

Yun, a 28-year-old inheritor of paper-cutting craftsmanship, operates two self-media accounts on different platforms, earning income by selling paper-cut artworks. The throttling mechanism on social media platforms has driven her to make a personal website, but she faces challenges due to a lack of relevant skills and experience. She expressed, "I want to combine my craftsmanship with the internet and create my own small website to keep up with the times."

In the following jobs-to-be-done (JTBD), "Quickly grasping the various components of the ECS console every time I open the interface" is highly emphasized. (1) Understandable: Quickly grasping the various components of the cloud server console every time I open the interface. (2) Easy to build: From now on, the cloud server can always realize my ideas. (3) Powerful features: Using the cloud server for website construction should save me money and time. (4) Cost reduction: The website construction process is smooth and efficient, without any hitches. (5) After successful website construction, I should gain more traffic and sales.

This design centers around 3D-style construction as the core, with intelligent conversational assistant as a supplement, creating the CloudSpace personal website building assistant tool. It provides users with more intuitive operations, flexible interactions, and user-friendly guidance. Twelve target users underwent rapid usability testing, revealing that the product lacked clarity and was somewhat dull. Therefore, the design was iterated to further simplify the interaction process, enrich the operation interface, and enhance its appeal. The design results are shown in Figs. 1 and 2.

4.2 Agricultural Assistance

Young individuals and small farmers play crucial roles in the digital transformation of agriculture. They attempt to quickly and cost-effectively establish websites to promote agricultural products. However, during the website building process, issues such as complex consoles, numerous technical terms, and cumbersome procedures make their journey filled with anxiety and confusion. To address this problem, the team designed an assistance system to help users build websites quickly and easily.

Ling, a 23-year-old university student majoring in a non-computer-related field, loves his hometown. He is trying to establish an agricultural assistance website to support the local economy and promote the culture of his hometown. Due to his lack of relevant

Fig. 1. The user scenario.

Fig. 2. The user interface design.

knowledge and experience, he hopes to build a website with low economic and learning costs. He often says, "I hope to use a more convenient website to serve more fellow villagers."

In the JTBDs, efficiency, speed, and low cost are the key focus. (1) Let me always make a website in 10 min with 10 China Yuan (CNY). (2) Let me always experience joy and a sense of accomplishment in the process of building a website. (3) Let me always have a tutorial butler who is as intimate as a nanny during website construction. (4) Let the websites I create always showcase the characteristics of my hometown, full of love and warmth. (5) Network construction is always secure, modular, with rich interfaces, feedback, and smooth operation.

Fourteen target users underwent rapid usability testing of low-fidelity interfaces and core functions. The results showed that practicality > enjoyment. They generally believed that the design was simple, efficient, and helpful, but the user experience lacked fun. In the product iteration, the team made improvements in three dimensions: (1) More eye-catching voice image. (2) More direct operational assistance. (3) More interesting material collection. The results are presented in the storyboards and high-fidelity interfaces shown in Figs. 3 and 4.

Fig. 3. The user scenario.

Fig. 4. The user interface design.

4.3 Photography

Since the birth of cloud services, it has provided people with convenient storage and computing functions. With the integration of breakthrough technologies such as artificial intelligence, its capabilities have been further strengthened. Maslow's hierarchy of needs theory points out that aesthetic needs make people willing to discover and appreciate beautiful things [19]. With the improvement of living standards and the development of convenient technology, people's need to record beautiful moments through photography continues to increase. However, throughout the entire process from preparation, shooting, storage to photo editing and sharing, people often encounter various problems that hinder them from smoothly capturing and expressing themselves through photography.

Xiao, a 25-year-old office worker, loves traveling. She often plans trips with friends during holidays or travels alone to another city. She recently started exploring photography and fell in love with the feeling of capturing the colorful world through the lens. However, due to limited technical skills and capabilities, she is often dissatisfied with the results. She says, "I aspire to capture the wonderful moments I encounter during my travels through the lens, but many times, I cannot shoot or edit the photos to evoke the feelings I want."

In the JTBDs, "Editing satisfying photos anytime, anywhere" is highly emphasized. (1) Travel light: Carry fewer equipment during shooting. (2) More and faster: Quickly upload many photos anytime, anywhere. (3) Say goodbye to choose difficulties: Filtering functions that understand me better. (4) Reduce editing troubles: Edit satisfying photos anytime, anywhere. (5) Diversified sharing: Share photos in various forms anytime, anywhere.

Twelve target users underwent rapid usability testing of low-fidelity interfaces and core functions. The results showed that users generally felt that the functions could effectively help them, but the design was conventional and lacked excitement. In the product iteration, the team optimized the interface design of the product homepage image display, added community functions, enriched the specific functions of the product, resulting in the final storyboards and high-fidelity interfaces shown in Figs. 5 and 6.

Fig. 5. The user scenario.

Fig. 6. The user interface design.

4.4 Investment

In the era of big data, information is crucial for investors. Every day, investors use multiple software and devices simultaneously to obtain the most up-to-date information possible, helping them make better decisions through data analysis. This multitasking operation is exhausting, and the powerful computing power and features of AliCloud can help investors reduce procedural work, enabling them to conduct investment analysis more rationally. However, the powerful features of AliCloud and the high entry requirements deter users. The abundance of professional terms, complex interfaces, and difficulties in finding functions create a strong sense of difficulty for users. The high learning and cognitive costs make it challenging for users. Rather than emphasizing powerful features, users expect AliCloud to be user-friendly for quick adoption. They desire a more user-friendly AliCloud.

Yilong, a 24-year-old financial graduate student, is an entrepreneur in the investment industry. He aims to achieve financial freedom through rational investment relying on concise and accurate information obtained through data analysis in the web3 era. He wants to create software that integrates automated streaming, analysis, and presentation, relying on cloud computing power and storage for personal use. In the future, he plans to offer paid services to people with similar needs. He often says, "Strive for a life of freedom."

In the JTBDs, "Lower my usage threshold and alleviate my reluctance before use" is highly emphasized by the researchers. (1) Have a more complete and comfortable experience during use. (2) Match AliCloud features directly to my needs during use to reduce time. (3) Make it easier and simpler to reduce my cognitive load during use. (4) Make it less boring during use, making me more willing to use it again. (5) Lower my usage threshold and alleviate my reluctance before use.

Twelve target users underwent rapid usability testing of low-fidelity interfaces and core functions. The results showed that the current prototype has a low enjoyment quality, although it can complete the work content completely, the process is somewhat uninteresting. The team made improvements and iterations to enhance the enjoyment, optimize the product, resulting in the storyboards and high-fidelity interfaces shown in Figs. 7 and 8.

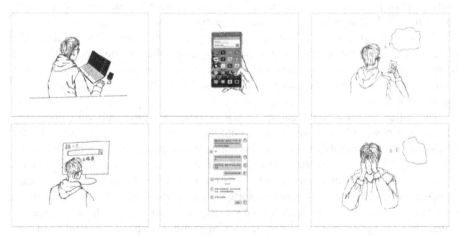

Fig. 7. The user scenario.

Fig. 8. The user interface design.

5 Discussion and Reflection

This project has made the following discoveries in response to the initial three questions. For the first question, it was found that users typically engage with AliCloud in the context of "Internet," and their journey often involves "Opening the webpage—Feeling overwhelmed—Learning—Completing operations." Regarding the second question, users' pain points and needs while using AliCloud generally revolve around "not understanding professional terms," "finding the interface too complex to operate," "customizing the interface automatically based on user needs," and "diverse sharing." Concerning the third question, it was discovered that an intelligent, automatically customized, and interactive interface with interesting and eye-catching materials can significantly enhance the user's experience when interacting with web interfaces.

5.1 Collaboration with the AliCloud Design Center

The enterprise presented two topics for selection in the interaction design of the product, providing detailed information about the current product and the issues to be addressed. Throughout the project, the enterprise team offered valuable suggestions to assist the project team in adjusting. In less than two months of collaboration, not only did the project team experience rapid improvement in practical knowledge, but communication with the AliCloud team also nurtured a basic understanding of executing enterprise requirements.

The collaboration with the enterprise posed some challenges and difficulties. AliCloud, as a powerful and diverse cloud computing platform, presented a significant challenge for team members who were encountering cloud computing products for the first time. Understanding its basic functions and identifying modules for optimization on the platform was a challenging task. To better comprehend user experiences, team members personally engaged with the platform, facing difficulties that mirrored those of potential users. By studying AliCloud's existing learning materials, they acquired foundational usage knowledge. After the learning phase, a deeper understanding of current user pain points was gained, leading to the creation of user personas before the design phase. This process involved studying user behavior, needs, and preferences to better understand the target audience and make design adjustments accordingly. However, ensuring the authenticity and comprehensiveness of data during persona creation was crucial to avoid biased or misleading results. This process also guided the team in formulating interview outlines for future reference.

During the design process, the team used petal diagrams to propose and select solutions. Balancing and prioritizing among various features and design elements based on factors such as user needs and technical feasibility were crucial. The team had to make trade-offs to ensure the final design maximally met user requirements and provided a user-friendly experience in interface design. This realization was a new understanding given to the team during this phase. In the creation of low-fidelity interfaces, the team faced the challenge of translating conceptual designs into preliminary interface representations, considering layout, interaction details, and other optimizations. The production of high-fidelity interfaces involved refining and optimizing low-fidelity interfaces to better align with user experience and visual requirements. This stage presented challenges related to the design of product flows and the presentation of interfaces, requiring multiple adjustments to the logical sequence of product use. The initial creation of pages had to address various technical details and interaction issues, demanding continuous learning and iterative improvement. This stage involved a high level of technical expertise, and the team navigated challenges related to product flow design and interface presentation.

The four teams in the project produced conceptual designs for AliCloud products and interaction methods, providing innovative solutions to address difficulties in user experience. The teams delivered conceptual designs that assisted the enterprise in overcoming existing challenges in user experience and offered inspirational design concepts for future development. This process not only facilitated the rapid improvement of the team's practical knowledge but also developed a fundamental understanding and execution capability to meet enterprise requirements, enhancing the overall capabilities of the team.

5.2 Reflection on Professional Knowledge

Throughout the collaboration with AliCloud, we not only applied the knowledge we gained to practice for the first time but also deepened our understanding of the concepts learned in our courses. For instance, the introduction of the user journey concept initially seemed abstract and unfamiliar. However, as we repeatedly crafted user journey maps during the project, we gained a clearer understanding of how to visually represent the goals, actions, emotions, and pain points of users using this method. We also better grasped the significance of user journey in the entire process from conceptualizing a product to its final implementation. Beyond theoretical insights, this project provided an excellent opportunity for honing our skills. Throughout the project, we needed to transform our ideas into professional prototypes, prompting us to self-learn and utilize various software tools, such as the widely used Axure for prototype design. The hands-on experience with these tools significantly elevated our skill set.

5.3 Innovations in Conversational Interaction Design

During the project, the four teams explored different aspects of improvements and innovations in conversational interaction design, focusing primarily on two areas. Firstly, traditional conversational interfaces continuously integrated artificial intelligence services. This technological integration made conversations more natural, aligning with users' habits and expectations, thereby enhancing user efficiency and providing a smoother and more convenient experience when using AliCloud products. Secondly, the introduction of emotion recognition and response features expanded the scope of communication beyond verbal language, allowing interactions to include non-verbal emotional expressions. This comprehensive approach enriched the user experience, deepening the interaction between humans and technology and increasing user emotional engagement. These innovations are not only technological breakthroughs but also demonstrate a profound understanding of user experience and needs [20]. By integrating artificial intelligence and emotion recognition technologies into conversational interactions, the improvements enhanced the product's functionality and strengthened the emotional connection between users and the product. These enhancements not only endowed AliCloud products with greater competitiveness but also conveyed a sense of HCD care and thoughtfulness to users during their usage, further boosting user satisfaction and loyalty to AliCloud products, services, and systems.

References

1. Marston, S., Li, Z., Bandyopadhyay, S., Zhang, J., Ghalsasi, A.: Cloud computing—the business perspective. Decis. Support. Syst. **51**(1), 176–189 (2011)
2. Bello, S.A., et al.: Cloud computing in construction industry: use cases, benefits and challenges. Autom. Constr. **122**, 103441 (2021)
3. Dubberly, H., Pangaro, P.: What is conversation? How can we design for effective conversation. Interactions **16**(4), 22–28 (2009)
4. Ouerhani, N., Maalel, A., Ben Ghézela, H.: SPeCECA: a smart pervasive chatbot for emergency case assistance based on cloud computing. Clust. Comput. **23**, 2471–2482 (2020)
5. Deuerlein, C., Langer, M., Sessner, J., Heß, P., Franke, J.: Human-robot-interaction using cloud-based speech recognition systems. Procedia Cirp **97**, 130–135 (2021)
6. Grassi, L., Recchiuto, C.T., Sgorbissa, A.: Knowledge-grounded dialogue flow management for social robots and conversational agents. Int. J. Soc. Robot. **14**(5), 1273–1293 (2022)
7. Moore, R.J., Arar, R.: Conversational UX design: A practitioner's guide to the natural conversation framework. Morgan & Claypool (2019)
8. Shevat, A.: Designing bots: Creating conversational experiences. O'Reilly Media, Inc. (2017)
9. Borangiu, T., Trentesaux, D., Thomas, A., Leitão, P., Barata, J.: Digital transformation of manufacturing through cloud services and resource virtualization. Comput. Ind. **108**, 150–162 (2019)
10. Luitse, D., Denkena, W.: The great transformer: Examining the role of large language models in the political economy of AI. Big Data Soc. **8**(2), 20539517211047736 (2021)
11. Al Mahmud, A., Mubin, O., Shahid, S., Martens, J.B.: Designing social games for children and older adults: two related case studies. Entertainment Comput. **1**(3–4), 147–156 (2010)
12. Zhu, Y., Tang, G., Liu, W., Qi, R.: How post 90's gesture interact with automobile skylight. Int. J. Hum.-Comput. Interact. **38**(5), 395–405 (2022)

13. Visser, F.S., Stappers, P.J., Van der Lugt, R., Sanders, E.B.: Contextmapping: experiences from practice. CoDesign **1**(2), 119–149 (2005)
14. Liu, W., Lee, K.P., Gray, C.M., Toombs, A.L., Chen, K.H., Leifer, L.: Transdisciplinary teaching and learning in UX design: a program review and AR case studies. Appl. Sci. **11**(22), 10648 (2021)
15. Desmet, P.M., Xue, H., Xin, X., Liu, W.: Demystifying emotion for designers: a five-day course based on seven fundamental principles. Adv. Des. Res. **1**(1), 50–62 (2023)
16. Schrepp, M., Hinderks, A., Thomaschewski, J.: Design and evaluation of a short version of the user experience questionnaire (UEQ-S). Int. J. Interact. Multimedia Artif. Intell. **4**(6), 103–108 (2017)
17. Ohashi, T., Watanabe, M., Takenaka, Y., Saijo, M.: Real-time assessment of causal attribution shift and stay between two successive tests of movement aids. Integr. Psychol. Behav. Sci. **55**(3), 541–565 (2021)
18. Gray, C.M., Hasib, A., Li, Z., Chivukula, S.S.: Using decisive constraints to create design methods that guide ethical impact. Des. Stud. **79**, 101097 (2022)
19. Desmet, P., Fokkinga, S.: Beyond Maslow's pyramid: Introducing a typology of thirteen fundamental needs for human-centered design. Multimodal Technol. Interact. **4**(3), 38 (2020)
20. Verganti, R.: Design, meanings, and radical innovation: a metamodel and a research agenda. J. Prod. Innov. Manag. **25**(5), 436–456 (2008)

The Impact of Correlated Colour Temperature on Physiological Responses, Task Precision and Subjective Satisfaction in a Simulated Node3 Aft Cabin of the Space Station

Zhangchenlong Huang[1], Ao Jiang[1($\boxtimes$)], Yan Zhao[2], Hao Fan[3], and Kun Yu[4]

[1] Nanjing University of Aeronautics and Astronautics, Nanjing, China
aojiang@nuaa.edu.cn
[2] Key Laboratory of Biomimetic Robots and Systems of the Chinese Ministry of Education, Beijing Institute of Technology, Beijing, China
[3] Southeast University, Nanjing, China
[4] China Ship Development and Design Center, Wuxi, China

Abstract. This study investigated the impact of different Correlated Color Temperatures (CCT) on task accuracy, Galvanic Skin Response (GSR), emotional responses, and task load in a simulated Node3 aft port cabin environment. Findings indicated that higher CCT levels (6500K) significantly enhanced task accuracy, physiological arousal (as indicated by GSR), positive emotional states, and reduced task load, suggesting a pivotal role of CCT in optimizing environmental conditions for improved performance and well-being in space habitats. The use of high-fidelity simulations, though not entirely replicating the microgravity conditions of space, provided valuable insights into the potential benefits of CCT adjustments in space station lighting design. Future research is recommended to explore the long-term effects of CCT on crew health and performance in microgravity, employing a longitudinal study design to further validate these findings and contribute to the design of habitable space environments.

Keywords: correlated colour temperature · fine work · space station compartment · physiological response · emotion

1 Introduction

In long-duration manned space missions, astronauts may face unstable physiological and psychological states in an enclosed, cramped, and isolated environment. This situation poses unprecedented challenges to space mission support and manned space engineering [1, 2]. To ensure the success of manned space missions, habitability research has become a key area. This involves not only the coordination of astronauts' biomechanics but also their psychological and physical health [3] NASA's previous studies have emphasized that habitability is closely related to human factors, behavioral health, environmental interaction, and human-machine interaction [4]. The core goal of habitability is to provide comprehensive physical, psychological, social, and spiritual support for astronauts.

As early as 1985, NASA recognized that the habitability of long-duration spacecraft needs to meet operational requirements and consider the needs for long-term sustainable living [5]. Design elements of spacecraft, such as spatial layout, lighting, color, air circulation, and odor, are considered to have significant impacts on the level of habitability. [6] Especially environmental factors like lighting and color, which directly affect human visual functions and become a focus of habitability research [7]. In this regard, the color temperature (CCT) of lighting plays an important role in emotional regulation and can affect the habitability level of the space station. Studies have shown significant differences in the impact of different CCT lighting conditions on human psychological and physiological responses within the space station. These findings highlight the importance of considering lighting conditions in the design of space station environments to maintain astronauts' psychological and physical health. Therefore, the importance of integrating considerations of astronauts' physiological and psychological states with environmental interactions in the design and evaluation of long-duration manned space environments cannot be overlooked [8].

Lighting has a broad range of non-visual effects on human biological functions, particularly in terms of emotional regulation and the maintenance of the circadian rhythm. [8] In this context, the significance of Correlated Color Temperature (CCT) has become increasingly prominent due to its substantial impact on human physiological and psychological states [9, 10]. Thus, the selection and application of lighting technology in manned spacecraft environments are especially critical. The International Space Station (ISS) currently utilizes Solid State Lighting Assemblies (SSLAs) [11] equipped with Light Emitting Diodes (LEDs) to illuminate the astronauts' working and living environments [12]. This lighting system, capable of adjusting CCT, not only aids in protecting astronauts' vision but also serves as an effective means to counteract emotional stress and performance decline caused by isolation, confinement, and lack of social support on the ISS. In terms of repetitive task efficiency, properly adjusted CCT can reduce visual fatigue, enhancing work efficiency and precision [13]. Moreover, the impact of CCT on emotions cannot be overlooked. Adjusting lighting CCT can effectively alleviate emotional fluctuations and stress caused by isolated environments, thereby enhancing astronauts' psychological stability and work performance [14].

Research conducted in terrestrial environments has already revealed significant effects of CCT on human cognitive abilities and emotions. Higher CCTs, [15] typically exceeding 4000 K and approaching blue-white light, are considered cool tones, while lower CCTs, not exceeding 3000 K and closer to red light, are regarded as warm tones [16]. These studies indicate that, compared to cool-toned fluorescent lighting (4000 K), warm tones (3000 K) tend to induce negative emotions during cognitive tasks. Meanwhile, compared to fluorescent lights, LED sources at higher CCTs can significantly reduce fatigue and enhance cognitive abilities, an effect particularly crucial in simulated environments like the aft port cabin of the space station's Node3 [17].

Further research has shown that a comfortable Correlated Color Temperature (CCT) can significantly improve satisfaction and well-being, especially in environments with high-quality lighting where people perceive their workspace as more attractive and experience enhanced mood and well-being. This research has also linked CCT to a range of physiological responses, including core body temperature and heart rate, underscoring its critical role in confined spaces such as the International Space Station (ISS) [18]. Proper adjustment of CCT in such environments is crucial for astronauts' physical and mental health, alleviating the stress of prolonged spaceflights and ensuring overall well-being and mission efficiency [19]. The balance between visual comfort and physiological impact highlights the importance of CCT in designing lighting systems for space habitats, aimed at maintaining astronauts' health and performance [20].

According to ISS anecdotes, the aft port cabin of Node3 provides a challenging work environment for astronauts, primarily due to its cramped and enclosed space characteristics, along with multiple environmental stressors present [21]. This unique setting demands high standards for visual comfort, operational precision, and emotional stability from astronauts, especially during long-duration, high-precision, and monotonous tasks. Furthermore, the physical constraints under microgravity conditions and the complexity of the environmental control systems add to the operational difficulty, posing additional challenges to astronauts' psychological and physiological states. On May 28, 2016, NASA recorded a meticulous control expansion process in the ISS's Bigelow Expandable Activity Module (BEAM), involving 25 air injections totaling 2 min and 27 s over 7 h [22]. Operator Jeff Williams emphasized the importance of maintaining attention and ensuring visual and manual coordination during such high-precision [23, 24], long-duration, monotonous tasks. This places higher demands on the cabin's lighting CCT, especially during pressurization operations, significantly affecting astronauts' visual comfort, operational precision, and emotional state. This study, targeting the simulated aft port cabin environment of the space station, explored the effects of six different CCTs [25] (2700 K to 6500 K) on astronauts' Galvanic Skin Response (GSR), task accuracy, mood, and task load [26].

2 Materials and Methods

2.1 Participants

A total of 48 healthy participants were included in the study, comprising 24 males and 24 females, with an age distribution of 28.3 ± 6.2 years. This age group was selected as it reflects the typical age range of most astronaut candidates. The selection process for participants followed the screening procedures used for astronaut candidates [24]. All participants had passed a standard physical examination. They were assessed through interviews and two screening questionnaires, including the Pittsburgh Sleep Quality Index and the Stanford Sleepiness Scale, ensuring that all were non-smokers without any medical, psychiatric, or sleep disorders. Participants had normal or corrected-to-normal visual acuity better than 0.6 (in minutes of visual angle and normal color vision), assessed before and after the study using the Ishihara Test (International 36-plate edition). Prior to the experiment, participants received specialized operational training involving a Dataq Instruments human factors data acquisition system (DI4180-E, USA) [27] and a custom-developed aft port cabin chamber simulator. To ensure the accuracy of the simulated experimental tasks, participants were required to avoid consuming caffeine and alcohol for 24 h before the experiment and to maintain a regular daily routine, including normal eating habits and fluid intake [28]. Specifically, participants were instructed to go to bed at approximately 10 p.m. and wake up at 7 a.m. the following morning [9]. Before the start of the experiment, all participants signed an informed consent form, confirming their comprehensive understanding of the experiment's objectives, procedures, and potential risks involved [29].

2.2 Virtual Reality Equipment

The virtual reality system (Vive, HTC Corporation, Taiwan) was employed to present a model of the Node3 aft port cabin of the virtual space station. Participants were able to: (a) explore the interior of the habitat using the Vive controllers, denoted as Intra-Vehicular Activity (IVA) for activities inside the cabin [30]; (b) open the outer hatch and secure themselves with a safety tether for extravehicular activities (EVA) to explore the external space; (c) simulate the operation of manually pressurizing the BEAM module by adjusting the Manual Pressure Equalization Valve (MPEV) according to the procedure (ECSS-E-ST-35) [31]. The MPEV, designed as a safety measure, facilitates pressure regulation between the aft port cabin of Node3 and the BEAM module [32]. Before undertaking the MPEV pressurization task in Earth's gravity using VR, participants underwent a 20-min familiarization session with the VR equipment and system to acquaint themselves with its functional properties for this experiment [33].

Participants were required to wear a virtual reality headset and microphone. This setup allowed researchers to effectively communicate instructions and guide participants through hatch operations within the Node3 aft port cabin, as well as to complete experimental tasks inside the space station (IVA), such as moving within the virtual Node3 aft port cabin and simulating manual adjustments of air pressure on either side of the hatch using controllers [34]. Furthermore, these tasks were designed to assess participants' reaction capabilities within the aft port cabin under different color temperature lighting conditions, building on their familiarity with the task procedures to evaluate their adaptability and accuracy in specific environments [35].

2.3 Experimental Apparatus and Scenario

A virtual model of the Node3 aft port cabin was designed and constructed (Fig. 1), with detailed optimization of the interior functional modules according to the "Human Factors Requirements" outlined in NASA-STD-3001 [36], Volume 2. This optimization aimed to provide a comprehensive virtual experimental platform for the aft port cabin area. The virtual platform encompasses four primary sub-modules: a pressure monitoring module, a lighting system module, a physiological parameters monitoring module, and a simulated Manual Pressure Equalization Valve (MPEV) module. These sub-modules collectively form a multifunctional virtual environment to support complex experimental operations and data collection, ensuring high fidelity and practicality of the experiment.

In this experiment, virtual reality (VR) technology was utilized to recreate the lighting system of the Node3 aft port cabin area. To ensure the precision of the experiment, the virtual environment's air pressure displays employed non-reflective, monochrome, and backlight-free high-definition electronic ink technology, eliminating potential interference from the display's light source on the experimental participants' task performance under different Correlated Color Temperature (CCT) conditions. Figure 2 and Table 1 detail the vestibule cabin environment LED lighting parameters input into the virtual

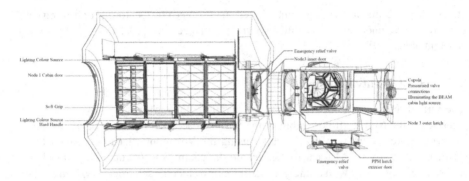

Fig. 1. Simulated Environment of Node3 Aft Port Cabin

reality system, including the spectral distribution of six different CCTs, their corresponding Duv values, and illuminance levels, aiming to accurately simulate the aft port cabin's
lighting environment and provide a realistic background for the virtual experiment. In
the experimental scenario, the colors of the walls and ceiling were set to gray-white,
with reflectance values set at 66% and 72%, respectively, while the light gray floor had
a reflectance value of 25%, and the off-white operation panels had a reflectance value of
67%. The brightness distribution on the floor and walls was set between 200-250 cd/m^2,
and the wall brightness was set at 120-140cd/m^2. The lighting fixtures were installed
on the ceiling of the virtual aft port cabin, ensuring that the experimental participants
could clearly observe them, even though their primary focus was on the operation panels
ahead.

2.4 Experimental Procedure

1. To ensure the effectiveness and reliability of the experiment, the preparation phase
   before the official start of the experiment included proper rest guidance for participants. It was mandated that participants rest for a period of 5 min before the commencement of the experiment to stabilize their mood, acclimate to the experimental
   environment, and master the simulated manual operation of the Pressure Equalization
   Valve (MPEV) [37]. This measure aimed to mitigate unfamiliarity with the experimental setup and prevent psychological fluctuations due to dealing with unknown
   scenarios.
2. To guarantee the validity of the experiment, participants conducted virtual operation
   experiments under six different Correlated Color Temperature (CCT) conditions in
   a randomized order. The study was designed with six independent experimental sessions, each separated by at least 24 h to eliminate potential residual effects (as shown
   in Fig. 3). To control experimental conditions, participants were required to perform
   the experiments within 3 to 5 h after waking, a period considered to have relatively
   stable cognitive performance [38]. The laboratory environment was set up to simulate
   the Node3 aft port cabin, aimed at providing participants with an immersive experience for adaptation before entering the virtual vestibule chamber. During the experiment, participants were equipped with Shimmer GSR (Galvanic Skin Response)

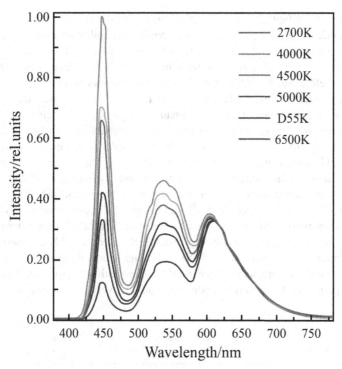

Fig. 2. Spectral Distribution of Indoor Lighting for Nominal CCTs of 2700 K, 4000 K, 4500 K, 5000 K, 6500 K, and Sunlight D55

Table 1. Duv and illuminance of each nominal CCT at the operator panel volume after setting up the illumination

	Nominal Color Temperature (K)	Duv	Illumination (Lux)
1	2700 K	−0.0021	529.6
2	4000 K	0.00230	528.9
3	4500 K	0.00240	529.1
4	5000 K	0.00251	529.4
5	6500 K	0.00230	530.1
6	D55Light	0.00270	529.4

sensors to monitor their physiological reactions. Once the virtual reality equipment was donned, participants were exposed to dim multicolor white light (≤ 5 lx) for 5 min to ease emotional tension and minimize the impact of external environments on the experimental outcomes. Through this methodology, the study aimed to evaluate participants' virtual operational performance under different lighting conditions in a controlled environment [38].

Following the adaptation period, continuous monitoring of the Galvanic Skin Response (GSR) of the 48 participants was conducted under six different Correlated Color Temperature (CCT) lighting conditions for thirty minutes. This duration was chosen based on the average time required for standard astronaut tasks within the Node3 aft port cabin, as referenced by NASA (2015). The duration was set to effectively simulate astronauts' real experiences in this environment, avoiding data bias due to inappropriate length of time. While certain studies have identified significant impacts of CCT lighting on physiological indicators within shorter time frames, this experiment maintained a one-hour observation window to comprehensively assess effects and maintain equivalence with real-world tasks. During the experiment, all participants' operational procedures followed the space station safety pressurization standards document (ECSS-E-ST-35) established by the European Space Agency Technical Center (ESA-ESTEC) (European Space Agency, 2016). The specific design and steps of the experiment are detailed in Fig. 4. Upon completion, to assess psychological states and task load, participants were required to complete the Positive and Negative Affect Schedule (PANAS) and the NASA Task Load Index (Hart & Staveland, 1988) [39]. After data collection, the experimental personnel assisted participants in removing the virtual reality equipment, followed by a 10-min rest period in D55 lighting conditions to aid recovery before participants left the laboratory.

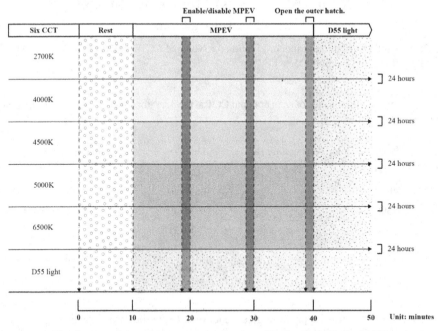

Fig. 3. Experimental Operational Procedures Under Six Different CCTs

The experimental task involved using virtual reality controllers to operate a Manual Pressure Equalization Valve (MPEV) within a simulated environment, repeatedly and safely pressurizing the BEAM module until it expanded to its predetermined volume.

This operation ensured pressure balance between the Node3 aft port cabin and the BEAM module, allowing for safe extravehicular activities (EVA) [40]. The MPEV operation process strictly adhered to the NASA standard V2 8024 [41], requiring operators to precisely control the opening and closing times of the pressure balance valve under a standard atmospheric pressure condition of 101.3 kPa, with each operation's duration controlled within six seconds. This procedural regulation was referenced from the pressurization operation standards during the BEAM module expansion in 2016[42]. The intent of this simulation was to validate the operators' ability to perform prolonged precise operations under specified pressure conditions, ensuring efficient control of hatch operations while maintaining safe pressure levels, thereby ensuring the safety and success rate of the entire task [43].

In this experiment, the process was divided into three key stages, with specific steps as shown in Fig. 4: The first stage was the preparation phase, where participants initially tapped the "menu button" on the virtual reality controller to activate the pressure monitoring task, followed by carefully reading the manual and observing the pressure gauge under different Correlated Color Temperatures (CCT). The next stage involved manually opening the Pressure Equalization Valve (MPEV), requiring participants to tap the "trigger" button on the controller to switch it to the "open" state, and tapping again to switch to the "close" state, closing the valve within the specified time. The final stage was the hatch opening phase, where participants needed to continuously press the "grip button" to ensure communication with the ground control center, aiming to confirm if the Tranquility Node's aft port cabin and the BEAM module had reached equilibrium pressure. This step simulated the standard operational protocols of the International Space Station (NASA-STD-3001) and the operations for ensuring pressure consistency between chambers [44]. If the pressure had not reached the preset equilibrium value, participants would continue the pressurization task; if it had, they would proceed with the established extravehicular procedure, requiring a series of precise gestures in the virtual environment, including continuous tapping of the "trackpad" button and performing a circular motion in a 30 cm radius clockwise while extending the arm horizontally forward (Johnson & Williams, 2019). This series of actions was designed based on historical mission data to ensure the accuracy of task execution and astronaut safety (Brown et al., 2018).

2.5 Materials and Data Collection

To ensure the validity and accuracy of the data, this experiment utilized a human factors data acquisition system provided by Dataq Instruments, complemented by Shimmer sensors as wireless data collection tools for recording participants' Galvanic Skin Response (GSR). To enhance signal quality during data collection, GSR sensor electrodes were attached to the index and ring fingers of the participant's left hand, after the skin surface was cleaned with medical alcohol and conductive gel was applied. This arrangement was chosen considering that the right hand would be operating the virtual reality controller, while the left hand remained relatively stationary, thereby minimizing the potential for hand movements to interfere with the GSR signal [45].

For assessing the emotional states of the experimental participants, this study employed the Positive and Negative Affect Schedule (PANAS), a scale with well-established validity and reliability. The scale is divided into two dimensions, Positive

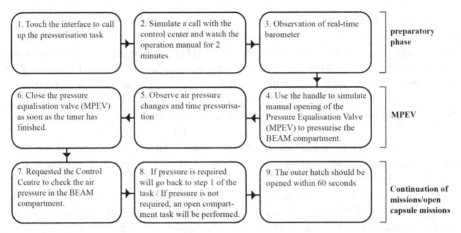

Fig. 4. Operational Procedure for Pressurizing the BEAM Module Using the MPEV

Affect (PA) and Negative Affect (NA), each consisting of nine adjectives to quantify emotional experiences (Watson, Clark & Tellegen, 1988). In this experiment, the Cronbach's α coefficients for the PANAS scale were 0.90 (PA) and 0.92 (NA), indicating high internal consistency (Thompson, 2007). Following each experimental phase, participants were invited to complete the PANAS scale using a five-point Likert scale, where 1 represented "not at all" and 5 represented "extremely strong" emotional experiences (Crawford & Henry, 2004).

In terms of cognitive load assessment, the NASA Task Load Index (NASA-TLX) is widely regarded as a reliable tool for measuring cognitive load across various task environments, including space missions. This scale integrates six dimensions: mental demand, physical demand, temporal pressure, personal performance, effort, and frustration level, to comprehensively reflect the task burden (Hart & Staveland, 1988). Each dimension is scored on a scale from 0 to 100, with gradations indicating the level of load, where higher scores imply a greater workload (Hart, 2006). According to psychometric standards, Cronbach's alpha coefficient is used to evaluate the internal consistency of the scale, with values closer to 1 indicating higher consistency. Typically, an alpha coefficient of 0.70 or above is considered suitable for research purposes (Nunnally, 1978). In this study, after each experimental session, participants were asked to provide feedback on these six dimensions using a 100-point scale, where 0 represented no load and 100 indicated extreme load. This quantitative assessment method enables researchers to precisely measure and analyze the correlation between cognitive load and task performance in specific space mission simulation environments [46].

The Visual Comfort Probability (VCP) scale is an assessment tool designed to quantify the likelihood of observers experiencing discomfort under specific lighting conditions. Scores on this scale range from 0 to 100, with higher scores indicating greater visual comfort, i.e., less likelihood of discomfort due to lighting quality (IESNA, 2000). The VCP scale demonstrates high internal consistency, with a Cronbach's alpha value set at 0.9, indicating the tool's high reliability (Boyce et al., 2003). Especially in lighting research, such as assessing the impact of different Correlated Color Temperatures (CCT) on observer satisfaction, the VCP scale is extensively applied [47].

2.6　Statistical Analysis

Before conducting the main statistical analysis, this study first assessed the normality and homogeneity of variances of the dataset using the Shapiro-Wilk test and Levene's test, respectively, to ensure that the data met the prerequisite conditions for one-way Analysis of Variance (ANOVA) [48]. One-way ANOVA was utilized to evaluate whether there were statistically significant differences in accuracy, Galvanic Skin Response (GSR), and NASA Task Load Index (TLX) scores under different Correlated Color Temperature (CCT) conditions. The significance level was set at $\alpha < 0.05$ to determine the statistical significance of differences (Field, 2013). Upon finding significant ANOVA results, further pairwise comparisons were conducted using Tukey's Honestly Significant Difference (HSD) post-hoc test, with Bonferroni correction applied to control the risk of Type I errors (Hochberg & Tamhane, 1987). All data analyses were performed using SPSS software (version 24; IBM Corporation; Armonk, NY, USA), ensuring the accuracy and scientific integrity of the analysis.

3　Results

3.1　Accuracy

The results demonstrated a statistically significant impact of color temperature on participants' accuracy in completing the MPEV task ($F = 9.323$, $p = 0.045 < 0.05$), indicating differences in accuracy across the six CCT conditions. As depicted in Fig. 5, post hoc analysis further revealed that under the 6500 K lighting condition, participants' task accuracy was significantly higher than under the other three lighting conditions ($p = 0.037 < 0.05$), while no statistically significant differences in accuracy were observed among the other five CCT conditions ($p > 0.05$). The analysis indicated that task accuracy improved with increasing CCT, with the highest accuracy observed at 6500 K (Standard Deviation SD $= 0.0112$, Mean M $= 0.004$), and the lowest accuracy at 2700 K (Standard Deviation SD $= 0.0122$, Mean M $= 0.002$).

3.2　Galvanic Skin Response Variations

A one-way Analysis of Variance (ANOVA) was conducted to assess the Galvanic Skin Response (GSR) under different color temperature conditions, revealing a significant main effect of CCT on GSR ($F = 7.541$, $p = 0.041 < 0.05$). This indicates that changes in CCT significantly affected participants' physiological responses. As shown in Fig. 6, GSR increased with rising CCT, particularly under the 6500 K condition, where the GSR value was the highest and the difference was statistically significant ($p = 0.039 < 0.05$). In contrast, differences in GSR values among the 2700 K, 4000 K, and D55 lighting conditions did not reach statistical significance ($p = 0.051 > 0.05$). Specifically, the average GSR value under the 6500 K condition was 0.1327 with a standard deviation of 0.2326, while the lowest average GSR value was observed under the 2700 K condition, at 0.1143 with a standard deviation of 0.1569.

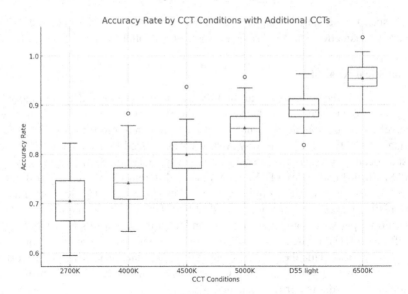

Fig. 5. Differences in Task Accuracy Under Different CCTs

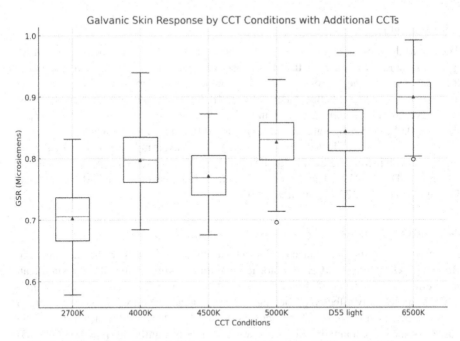

Fig. 6. Differences in Galvanic Skin Response (GSR) Under Different CCT Conditions

3.3 PANAS Emotional Scale

In the univariate analysis of variance for positive emotion indicators, the six different Correlated Color Temperature (CCT) conditions demonstrated a significant main effect ($F = 14.752$, $p = 0.038 < 0.05$), as shown in Fig. 7, revealing significant differences in participants' levels of positive emotions under different CCTs. Post hoc multiple comparisons indicated that under the 6500 K lighting condition, participants' scores for positive emotions were significantly higher than those under other CCT conditions ($p = 0.041 < 0.05$), suggesting that an increase in CCT is associated with elevated levels of positive emotions. Specifically, under the 6500 K condition, the mean score for positive emotions was 4.8333 with a standard deviation of 1.26, while the lowest mean score was observed under the 2700 K condition, at 3.0313 with a standard deviation of 1.35.

In the analysis of negative emotions, although the impact of CCT variations on levels of negative emotions was not significant ($F = 27.986$, $p = 0.064 > 0.05$), data trends indicated a tendency for negative emotions to decrease with increasing CCT. This suggests that under the six CCT conditions, despite the lack of statistically significant differences, participants' scores for negative emotions tended to be lower under higher CCT conditions, albeit the difference was not significant.

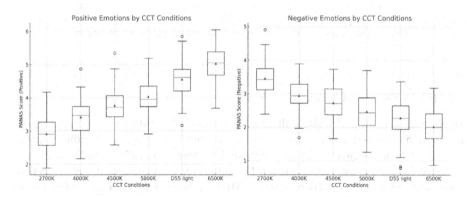

Fig. 7. Emotional Differences Under Different CCT Conditions

3.4 Visual Comfort Probability (VCP)

Further assessment was conducted on the differences in visual comfort under varying color temperature environments. Statistical results revealed a significant main effect in the Visual Comfort Probability index across the six CCT conditions studied ($F = 14.093$, $p = 0.045 < 0.05$), as depicted in Fig. 8, indicating significant variations in comfort levels experienced by participants in different CCT environments. Further post hoc analysis revealed that under the 6500K lighting condition, participants reported significantly higher levels of light comfort compared to other CCT conditions ($p = 0.042 < 0.05$), while differences in comfort indices between the 2700 K, 4000 K, 4500 K, 5000 K, and D55 lighting conditions did not reach statistical significance ($p > 0.05$).

In further analysis regarding visual fatigue, a significant main effect was also observed ($F = 14.928$, $p = 0.046 < 0.05$), indicating significant differences in levels of visual fatigue across different CCT environments. Notably, under the 6500 K CCT condition, participants experienced significantly lower levels of visual fatigue compared to other CCT conditions, suggesting that higher CCTs may help reduce visual fatigue ($p < 0.05$). These findings emphasize the crucial role of CCT in influencing visual comfort and fatigue perception, providing important scientific evidence for the optimization of lighting design.

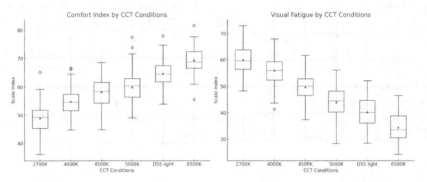

Fig. 8. Differences in Visual Comfort Under Different CCT Conditions

3.5 NASA Task Load Index (TLX) Scale

Upon examining the standardized data of the NASA Task Load Index (TLX) Scale, we analyzed the effects of color temperature across multiple dimensions, including Mental Demand, Physical Demand, Temporal Demand, Performance, Effort, and Frustration.

Specifically, the analysis of Mental Demand revealed a significant main effect of color temperature ($F = 11.210$, $p = 0.043 < 0.05$), indicating that the impact of different CCTs on mental demand is statistically significant. Further post-hoc comparison analysis pointed out significant differences in mental demand between 6500 K and 2700 K CCT conditions ($p = 0.038 < 0.05$). However, comparisons between the D55 light source and 4000 K, 2700 K, as well as 5000 K did not show statistically significant differences ($p = 0.065$, although lower than 0.1 but higher than 0.05), suggesting that changes in mental demand under these specific conditions are not significant. Moreover, while there was a slight increase in mental demand under 6500 K compared to the D55 light source, the difference was minimal, possibly indicating no significant change in mental demand within the CCT range from D55 to 6500 K.

In analyzing the data for the NASA TLX Scale, we noted that color temperature significantly impacted multiple task performance indicators. Specifically, Physical Demand showed a significant decrease under the 6500 K CCT condition ($F = 21.056$, $p < 0.05$), with participants experiencing the lowest physical demand at this CCT compared to others ($p = 0.044$), while no significant differences in physical demand were observed among other CCTs ($p > 0.05$).

Analysis of the impact on Temporal Demand also revealed a significant main effect of CCT ($F = 19.850$, $p < 0.05$), with participants experiencing the lowest temporal demand under the 6500 K condition ($p = 0.033$), indicating that less time was needed to complete tasks at this CCT.

In terms of Performance, the 6500 K CCT also showed a positive main effect, with participants performing best under this condition ($F = 21.588$, $p < 0.05$; $p = 0.033$), suggesting that higher CCTs may facilitate better work performance.

Analysis of Effort indicated that participants exerted less effort under the 6500 K CCT condition ($F = 19.915$, $p < 0.05$; $p = 0.033$), suggesting that participants may feel that less effort is required under high CCT lighting.

Analysis of Frustration pointed out that under the 6500 K CCT, participants' levels of frustration were significantly lower than under other CCT conditions ($F = 19.459$, $p < 0.05$; $p = 0.044$), potentially reflecting a more positive and relaxed working environment (Fig. 9).

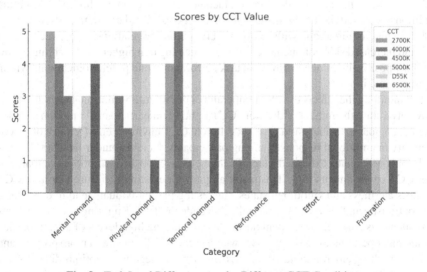

Fig. 9. Task Load Differences under Different CCT Conditions

4 Discussion

This study aimed to investigate the impact of different Correlated Color Temperature (CCT) lighting conditions on participant task performance through a simulated MPEV task in the Node3 aft port cabin environment [49]. The experiment analyzed multiple dimensions, including accuracy, Galvanic Skin Response (GSR), emotional response, satisfaction, visual comfort, and task load. The results indicated observable differences in work performance, GSR, emotional states, and lighting satisfaction across different CCT settings. Specifically, with increasing CCT values, participants showed higher levels of GSR [50], more positive emotional responses, and enhanced satisfaction with the lighting settings, with a notable improvement in task accuracy. These changes suggest that higher CCT values may promote physiological arousal, thereby improving emotional states and the accuracy of task execution [51].

Results showed that under the 6500 K CCT condition, task accuracy was the highest, while it was relatively lower under the 2700 K CCT condition. Notably, apart from 6500 K, there were no significant differences in accuracy between other CCTs [52]. Further analysis indicated that maintaining a 6500 K light source condition not only significantly improved task accuracy but also associated GSR indicators showed active variations, reflecting higher levels of physiological arousal. Although no significant differences in task performance were observed under CCT conditions other than 6500K [53], an increase in participant work efficiency was observed with rising CCT, peaking at 6500 K. This suggests that a higher CCT lighting environment facilitates quick and effective responses from participants in critical situations, crucial for the smooth conduct of the MPEV task [54].

The significant changes in GSR within the brief thirty-minute experimental period further validated the activity of skin conductance responses under high CCT lighting conditions, with activity being most pronounced at 6500K and comparatively weaker at 2700 K. This finding aligns with existing literature on the relationship between higher CCT and increased skin conductance activity, indicating that higher CCT lighting conditions may positively influence astronaut task performance and psychological state within the aft port cabin [49].

In examining the effects of color temperature conditions on emotional responses, our study delved into the impact of different CCT lighting on participants' emotional states. Through comparative analysis across six different CCT environments [55], we observed variability in emotional responses among participants. Notably, under the 6500 K CCT condition, participants exhibited a significant increase in positive emotions compared to other CCT environments [56]. This result aligns with existing literature that high CCT enhances alertness and emotional states, suggesting that individuals tend to experience more optimistic and energetic emotional states under high CCT lighting conditions. This phenomenon is particularly evident during tasks requiring high levels of attention, such as manually operating the MPEV valve, where higher CCT provides a more positive and effective working environment. However, the impact on negative emotions did not show significant changes, indicating that while CCT may influence emotions, this effect seems limited under short-term experimental conditions. These findings reinforce the consideration of lighting CCT in environmental design, suggesting that the potential impact of CCT on occupants' emotions should be fully considered when designing spaces for long-term living and work. Nonetheless, further research is needed to validate the long-term effects and mechanisms of emotional responses under different CCT conditions.

Considering the impact of CCT on human visual comfort, CCT also significantly influences visual comfort and experience. In the experiment, the 6500 K CCT lighting environment was found to significantly enhance participants' visual comfort and reduce visual fatigue, while at 2700 K CCT, comfort was at its lowest, and visual fatigue relatively increased [57]. This phenomenon may be related to the brightness and clarity of light under high CCT conditions, which can induce positive visual and psychological responses. These results have particular implications for practical lighting design, such as the International Space Station's lighting system, which uses adjustable CCT LED lighting to improve astronauts' working and living conditions. In this context, the 2700 K CCT facilitates relaxation and quicker sleep onset in sleeping areas, while 6500 K CCT optimizes visual clarity and alertness in working areas [58].

Analysis of the NASA Task Load Index (TLX) Scale revealed that CCT significantly affects the six dimensions of mental demand, physical demand, temporal demand, performance, effort, and frustration. At 6500K CCT, participants showed significant reductions in physical demand, lower temporal demand, optimal performance, reduced effort, and the lowest levels of frustration, indicating that under high CCT conditions, participants could complete tasks more efficiently with lower psychological and physiological loads. In contrast, at 2700 K CCT, participants exhibited higher mental demand and did not show advantages in other indicators, suggesting that low CCT may increase the difficulty and load of task execution [59]. Choosing an appropriate CCT in the simulated Node3 aft port cabin environment is crucial for optimizing astronauts' work performance and reducing their task load. Specifically, the high CCT of 6500K not only aids in enhancing work performance but also creates a more positive and relaxed work atmosphere, reducing psychological and physical stress [60]. Future research should further explore the impact of lighting CCT on crew members' spatial orientation, information processing capabilities, and psychological states, providing comprehensive needs fulfillment and optimization solutions for lighting design. This will offer important references for environmental design in long-duration space missions, ensuring the effectiveness and adaptability of lighting strategies.

5 Limitations and Future Research

This study systematically analyzed the impact of color temperature on operational tasks in a simulated aft port cabin environment; however, several limitations within the research design point towards directions for future research [61]. Firstly, although high-fidelity simulation technology was used to recreate the aft port cabin environment, differences still exist between the simulated conditions and the real space environment. Under actual microgravity conditions, the interaction between astronauts and equipment, as well as lighting conditions, may differ, potentially affecting the complexity and outcomes of operational tasks. Secondly, the study participants were not individuals with professional astronaut training. Considering the psychological and physiological differences between professional astronauts and the general population, future research should focus on individuals with specialized training, such as astronauts, pilots, or military personnel, to obtain data closer to actual conditions. Additionally, the current study did not fully explore the effects of color temperature changes under different lighting intensities and exposure durations. Human physiological and psychological responses are closely linked to daily circadian rhythms, and future research should consider how the effects of color temperature might vary under long-term exposure and different lighting conditions [62]. Therefore, while this study provides preliminary insights into the impact of color temperature, further verification is needed in a broader range of environments and conditions closer to reality. Future research should delve deeper into these aspects to ensure the broad applicability and accuracy of the research findings.

6 Conclusion

This study delved into the effects of lighting color temperature (CCT) on accuracy, GSR, emotions, task load, and subjective satisfaction within a simulated Node3 aft port cabin environment. The findings reveal that conducting the MPEV operation task under 6500 K lighting conditions led to higher accuracy, improved Galvanic Skin Response (GSR), positive emotional responses, and reduced task load, thereby providing scientific backing for lighting design in the Node3 aft port cabin. These results underscore the importance of CCT adjustment in enhancing the physiological and psychological responses of crew members within simulated space habitats. Given this, to deepen the understanding of CCT's comprehensive impact on habitat habitability in microgravity environments, future research is encouraged to adopt longitudinal study designs. Such studies should further explore the role of CCT adjustments in long-duration space missions on crew health, performance, and psychological well-being.

References

1. Wang, Y., Jing, X., Lv, K., et al.: During the long way to Mars: effects of 520 days of confinement (Mars500) on the assessment of affective stimuli and stage alteration in mood and plasma hormone levels. PLoS ONE **9**(4), e87087 (2014)
2. Gushin, V., Shved, D., Vinokhodova, A., et al.: Some psychophysiological and behavioral aspects of adaptation to simulated autonomous Mission to Mars. Acta Astronaut. **70**, 52–57 (2012)
3. Tafforin, C.: Ethological indicators of isolated and confined teams in the perspective of missions to Mars. Aviat. Space Environ. Med. **76**(11), 1083–1087 (2005)
4. Schlacht, I.L.: Integrating human factors into the design. Process Enhance Habitability Long Duration Missions **52**, 3892–3897 (2012)
5. Clark, T.A.: Addressing challenges to the design and test of operational lighting environments for the international space station. In: Strategies in Light 2016 Conference (JSC-CN-35069) (2016)
6. Horneck, G., Facius, R., Reichert, M., et al.: HUMEX, a study on the survivability and adaptation of humans to long-duration exploratory missions, part II: missions to Mars. Adv. Space Res. **38**(4), 752–759 (2006)
7. Lin, J., Westland, S., Cheung, V.: Effect of intensity of short-wavelength light on electroencephalogram and subjective alertness. Light. Res. Technol. **52**, 413–422 (2020)
8. Peldszus, R., Dalke, H., Pretlove, S., et al.: The perfect boring situation—addressing the experience of monotony during crewed deep space missions through habitability design. Acta Astronaut. **94**(1), 262–276 (2014)
9. Jiang, A., et al.: The effect of correlated colour temperature on physiological, emotional and subjective satisfaction in the hygiene area of a space station. Int. J. Environ. Res. Public Health **19**(15), 9090 (2022)
10. Maciejewski, W.F., Using virtual reality in quantifying the relation between colour temperature of public lighting and perceived personal safety. Jan Matejko. Acad. Fine Arts Krakow, Fac. Ind. Des. Krakow, Poland, 181–186 (2018).
11. Brainard, G.C., Barger, L.K., Soler, R.R., Hanifin, J.P.: The development of lighting countermeasures for sleep disruption and circadian misalignment during spaceflight. Curr. Opin. Pulm. Med. **22**, 535–544 (2016)

12. Van Bommel, W.J.M., van den Beld, G.J.: Lighting for work: a review of visual and biological effects. Light. Res. Technol. **36**, 255–266 (2004)

13. Kar, A. and Kar, A., New generation illumination engineering-an overview of recent trends in science and technology. In: 2014 First International Conference on Automation, Control, Energy and Systems (ACES). IEEE, pp. 1–6 (2014)

14. Bishop, S., Haeuplik-Meusburger, S. and Wise, J.A., habitability and the golden rule of space architecture. In: 51st International Conference on Environmental Systems (2022)

15. Simon, M., Whitmire, A., Otto, C., et al.: Factors impacting habitable volume requirements: results from the 2011 Habitable Volume Workshop, pp S–1114 (2011)

16. Mathew, V. and Kurian, C.P., 2020. A framework for the selection of tunable LED luminaire for human centric lighting design. In: 2020 Internationl Conference on Smart Technologies

17. Häuplik-Meusburger, S., Bishop, S.: Habitability as SPACE. In: Space Habitats and Habitability: Designing for Isolated and Confined Environments on Earth and in Space, pp. 25–49. Springer International Publishing, Cham (2021)

18. Sleegers, P.J.C., Moolenaar, N.M., Galetzka, M., et al.: Lighting affects students' concentration positively: Findings from three Dutch studies. Light. Res. Technol. **45**(2), 159–175 (2013)

19. Brainard, G.C., Barger, L.K., Soler, R.R., et al.: The development of lighting countermeasures for sleep disruption and circadian misalignment during spaceflight. Curr. Opin. Pulm. Med. **22**(6), 535–544 (2016)

20. Rahman, S.A., Kent, B.A., Grant, L.K., et al.: Effects of dynamic lighting on circadian phase, self-reported sleep and performance during a 45-day space analog mission with chronic variable sleep deficiency. J. Pineal Res. **73**(4), e12826 (2022)

21. Kakitsuba, N.: Comfortable indoor lighting conditions evaluated from psychological and physiological responses. LEUKOS **12**, 163–172 (2016)

22. Cajochen, C., Kräuchi, K., Wirz-Justice, A.: Role of melatonin in the regulation of human circadian rhythms and sleep. J. Neuroendocrinol. **15**(4), 432–437 (2003)

23. Räuchi, K., Cajochen, C., Wirz-Justice, A.: Circadian and homeostatic regulation of core body temperature and alertness in humans: What is the role of melatonin. Circadian Clock Entrainment **7**, 131–146 (1998)

24. Yang, W., Jeon, J.Y.: Effects of correlated colour temperature of LED light on visual sensation, perception, and cognitive performance in a classroom lighting environment. Sustain. **12**(10), 4051 (2020)

25. Knez, I.: Effects of indoor lighting on mood and cognition. J. Environ. Psychol. **15**(1), 39–51 (1995)

26. Denk, E., Jimenez, P., Schulz, B.: The impact of light source technology and colour temperature on the well-being, mental state and concentration of shop assistants. Light. Res. Technol. **47**(4), 419–433 (2015)

27. Suzer, O.K., Olgunturk, N., Guvenc, D.: The effects of correlated colour temperature on wayfinding: a study in a virtual airport environment. Displays **51**, 9–19 (2018)

28. Boyce, P.R., Cuttle, C.: Effect of correlated colour temperature on the perception of interiors and colour discrimination performance. Light. Res. Technol. **22**(1), 19–36 (1990)

29. Connolly, J.H. and Arch, M., 2005. NASA Standard 3000, Human Systems Integration Standards (HSIS) Update. In: Proc. Hum. Factors Ergon. Soc. Annu. Meet., 49, pp. 2018–2022

30. Fleri, E.L., Jr., Galliano, P.A., Harrison, M.E., Johnson, W.B. and Meyer, G.J., 1989. Proposal for a Zero-Gravity Toilet Facility for the Space Station. NASA: Washington, DC, USA

31. NASA.https://www.nasa.gov/centers/johnson/pdf/123838main_iss_shuttle_joint_ops_book.pdf. Accessed 03 Sep 2023

32. Chlacht, I.L.: Space habitability integrating human factors into the design process to enhance habitability in long duration missions (2012)

33. Ja'Mar, A.W.: Statistically architected human spaceflight missions to Mars. Acta Astronautica **160**, 155–162 (2019)

34. Russo, D., Foley, T., Stroud, K., et al., 2007. NASA space flight human system standards. In: Proceedings of the Human Factors and Ergonomics Society Annual Meeting. Sage CA: Los Angeles, CA: SAGE Publications, 51(21), pp. 1468–1470 (2007)

35. Childress, S.D., Williams, T.C. and Francisco, D.R., 2023. NASA Space Flight Human-System Standard: enabling human spaceflight missions by supporting astronaut health, safety, and performance. NPI Microgravity, 9(1), p. 31

36. Wohlwill, J.F.: Human adaptation to levels of environmental stimulation. Hum. Ecol. **2**, 127–147 (1974)

37. Hoffer, A.: A theoretical examination of double-blind design. Can. Med. Assoc. J. **97**(3), 123 (1967)

38. Moore, M.P., Martin, R.A.: On the evolution of carry-over effects. J. Anim. Ecol. **88**(12), 1832–1844 (2019)

39. Chen, R., Tsai, M.C., Tsay, Y.S.: Effect of color temperature and illuminance on psychology, physiology, and productivity: An experimental study. Energies **15**(12), 4477 (2022)

40. Holt, A. and Underwood, S.D., 1999. Leak Rate Testing of the International Space Station Hatch in a Thermal Vacuum Environment. In: NASA Conference Publication. NASA, pp. 131–140

41. Wang, L., Sun, L., Zhang, H., et al.: Spacecraft hatch leak testing. Vacuum **189**, 110233 (2021)

42. Liu, C., Sun, L., Jing, X., et al.: How correlated color temperature (CCT) affects undergraduates: A psychological and physiological evaluation. Journal of Building Engineering **45**, 103573 (2022)

43. Shalamanov, V. and Yaneva, N., 2018. Color space distribution of luminaire for dynamic „tunable white" lighting at different color temperatures. In: 2018 Seventh Balkan Conference on Lighting (BalkanLight). IEEE, pp. 1–4

44. Ru, T., de Kort, Y.A.W., Smolders, K.C.H.J., et al.: Non-image forming effects of illuminance and correlated color temperature of office light on alertness, mood, and performance across cognitive domains. Build. Environ. **149**, 253–263 (2019)

45. Kürkçü, E., 2017. The Effects of Color Temperature on Performance and Mood of Users: A Color Task Implementation Model. Bilkent Universitesi (Turkey)

46. Chou, C., Lin, J.F., Chen, T.Y., et al., 2013. An Evaluation of LED Ceiling Lighting Design with Bi-CCT Layouts. In: Proceedings of the Institute of Industrial Engineers Asian Conference 2013. Springer Singapore, pp. 1279–1287

47. Bakker, J., Pechenizkiy, M. and Sidorova, N., 2011. What's your current stress level? Detection of stress patterns from GSR sensor data. In: 2011 IEEE 11th international conference on data mining workshops. IEEE, pp. 573–580

48. Smolders, K.C.H.J., de Kort, Y.A.W.: Investigating daytime effects of correlated colour temperature on experiences, performance, and arousal. J. Environ. Psychol. **50**, 80–93 (2017)

49. Mills, P.R., Tomkins, S.C., Schlangen, L.J.M.: The effect of high correlated colour temperature office lighting on employee wellbeing and work performance. J. Circadian Rhythms **5**(1), 1–9 (2007)

50. Gou, Z., Gou, B., Liao, W., et al.: Integrated lighting ergonomics: a review on the association between non-visual effects of light and ergonomics in the enclosed cabins. Building and Environment, p. 110616 (2023)

51. Shin, Y.B., Woo, S.H., Kim, D.H., et al.: The effect on emotions and brain activity by the direct/indirect lighting in the residential environment. Neurosci. Lett. **584**, 28–32 (2015)

52. Mostafavi, A., Tong Bill, X., Kalantari, S.: Effects of illuminance and correlated color temperature on emotional responses and lighting adjustment behaviors. J. Build. Eng. **86**, 108833 (2024). https://doi.org/10.1016/j.jobe.2024.108833

53. Zhu, Y., Yang, M., Yao, Y., et al.: Effects of illuminance and correlated color temperature on daytime cognitive performance, subjective mood, and alertness in healthy adults. Environ. Behav. **51**(2), 199–230 (2019)
54. Wu, T.Y., Wang, S.G.: Effects of LED color temperature and illuminance on customers' emotional states and spatial impressions in a restaurant. Int. J. Affect. Eng. **14**(1), 19–29 (2015)
55. Wang, Q., Xu, H., Zhang, F., et al.: Influence of color temperature on comfort and preference for LED indoor lighting. Optik **129**, 21–29 (2017)
56. Román, M.O., Wang, Z., Sun, Q., et al.: NASA's Black Marble nighttime lights product suite. Remote Sens. Environ. **210**, 113–143 (2018)
57. Chellappa, S.L., Steiner, R., Blattner, P., et al.: Non-visual effects of light on melatonin, alertness and cognitive performance: can blue-enriched light keep us alert? PLoS ONE **6**(1), e16429 (2011)
58. Elvidge, C.D., Keith, D.M., Tuttle, B.T., et al.: Spectral identification of lighting type and character. Sensors **10**(4), 3961–3988 (2010)
59. Liu, Y., Peng, L., Lin, L., et al.: The impact of LED spectrum and correlated color temperature on driving safety in long tunnel lighting. Tunn. Undergr. Space Technol. **112**, 103867 (2021)
60. Zhang, Q., Ding, L., Sun, C., et al.: Effects of human thermophysiology and psychology in exposure to simulated microgravity. Acta Astronaut. **201**, 445–453 (2022)
61. Bogner, A.: The paradox of participation experiments. Sci. Technol. Human Values **37**(5), 506–527 (2012)
62. Wieczorek, J., Blazejczyk, K., Morita, T.: Changes in melatonin secretion in tourists after rapid movement to another lighting zone without transition of time zone. Chronobiol. Int.. Int. **33**(2), 220–233 (2016)

Positive Lab: Intentional Visualization of Positive Emotions in Everyday Face-to-Face Communication

Yukina Kato[✉] and Tatsuo Nakajima

Department of Computer Science and Engineering, Waseda University, Tokyo, Japan
{yukna1011001xw,tatsuo}@dcl.cs.waseda.ac.jp

Abstract. Recent developments in biometric data acquisition, artificial intelligence, and the widespread adoption of extended reality (XR) devices have facilitated the emergence of various technologies for emotion visualization. However, research focused specifically on daily face-to-face communication is scarce. The visualization of emotions carries the risk of privacy infringement, and displaying all emotions does not necessarily facilitate communication. In particular, individuals may wish to avoid displaying negative emotions. Additionally, users feel discomfort if they cannot control the visualization of their emotions. Therefore, this study introduces an everyday face-to-face communication support service called "Positive Lab," which focuses on positive emotions. This service constructs a system that displays "emotion objects" in augmented reality (AR) space by using the user's gesture as a trigger, which allows users to express their emotions whenever they want. Experimental results suggest that the system facilitates emotional transmission, enhances the communication experience, and amplifies positive emotions, revealing the usefulness of the service. Moreover, the potential applications of the service were demonstrated.

Keywords: Positive Emotion · Visualization · AR · Communication

1 Introduction

Recent advancements in devices that acquire biometric information such as brainwaves, augmented reality (AR), and virtual reality (VR) technologies have led to their proliferation. Concurrently, artificial intelligence (AI) technology has evolved at a swift pace. Utilizing these innovations, a variety of studies and services that visualize emotions have emerged. It includes the Emotion Analyzer[1], which utilizes brainwaves for emotion visualization, and Empath[2], a technology that visualizes emotions from voice data. Such services have improved customer service satisfaction in various business sectors.

Nonetheless, there is still a shortage of studies and related services focused on emotion visualization within the context of everyday face-to-face communication, which is

---

[1] Emotion Analyzer: https://www.dentsusciencejam.com/kansei-analyzer/en/index.html.

[2] Empath: https://webempath.net/lp-eng/.

A. Marcus et al. (Eds.): HCII 2024, LNCS 14712, pp. 88–106, 2024.
https://doi.org/10.1007/978-3-031-61351-7_6

the most familiar emotional interaction in our lives. The PERMA model [7] underscores the importance of positive interpersonal relationships, suggesting that advancements in research on face-to-face communication could contribute to improved well-being.

Visualizing emotions in public leads to some concerns. Psychological study suggests the propagation of emotions [4]. Another study on emotion propagation reveals that when a leader displays negativity, these emotions spread to group members. Conversely, a positive demeanor in the leader results in the spread of positive emotions among members [10]. In essence, displaying visualized negative emotions may prove detrimental to the community engaged in face-to-face communication.

Existing studies on visualizing emotions with biometrics have indicated that the uncontrolled visualization of emotions makes users anxious [11]. The majority of studies on emotion visualization are reliant on biometric data, which fails to reflect whether users wish to exhibit their emotions. Nevertheless, there is a user demand for a feature that honors their emotional state and provides the option to control the disclosure of such information.

In this paper, we propose "Positive Lab," a service designed to visualize emotions with the goal of enhancing everyday face-to-face communication, with a particular emphasis on positive emotions. For this service, we developed a system that displays objects symbolizing positive emotions on AR glasses. This system enables users to visualize their emotions at will through their gestures.

This study aims to assess the usefulness of the service. To achieve this, we examine its effects on communication and the psychological impacts of users deliberately visualizing positive emotions during daily in-person interactions with the system.

A workshop was conducted as the initial phase of the research to collect insights on the importance of positive emotions in daily face-to-face communication and to gather opinions on the visualization of emotions. Based on the workshop's findings, the system was designed and subsequently evaluated through experiments. Finally, the paper presents a discussion on the effects and usefulness of the proposed service, as well as its future prospects.

2   Related Work

2.1   Visualizing Emotions in Everyday Face-to-Face Communication

Semertzidis et al. devised a system that infers emotions from ElectroEncephaloGraphy (EEG) data and displays them as objects in AR [9]. The study conducted a three-day experiment, and the findings indicated that the visualized emotions could augment emotional exchange between individuals. It became apparent that conveying emotional cues, which are inaccessible through conventional communicative means, has the potential to provide a preternatural communicative experience. Furthermore, the visualized personal emotions promoted users' conscious appreciation and reflection.

2.2   Social Action of Positive Emotions

Sels et al. synthesized existing research on the societal impacts of positive emotions [8]. They identified three primary functions of positive affect: (1) enhancing intimacy, (2) improving the impressions made on others, and (3) influencing others. For example, individuals adept at expressing positive emotions frequently sustain superior interpersonal relationships [2] and benefit from improved reputations [3]. Furthermore, the expression of positive emotions can boost motivation across communities [10]. The mimicry of positive emotions also facilitates social interaction [5].

3 Service Design

3.1 Service Overview

This service is AR communication support specifically designed for daily face-to-face interactions. The AR overlay effect visualizes positive emotions, allowing users to visually recognize their emotions. Figure 1 illustrates the flow of service usage in the current system. The representations of User A and User B in Fig. 1 correspond to the visual perspectives provided by the AR glasses for each respective user; in other words, they depict User B as seen from User A's viewpoint and conversely.

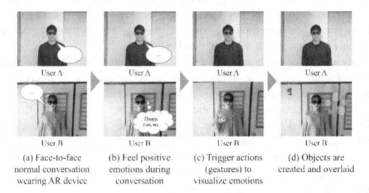

Fig. 1. Service flow

(a) Face-to-face normal conversation wearing AR device
   The user engages in face-to-face communication as usual wearing the AR glasses. Currently, AR glasses represent the preferred technology; however, future projections suggest an integration with more user-friendly apparatuses, like smart contact lenses.
(b) Feel positive emotions during conversation
   In communication, users may occasionally encounter positive emotions. Such instances arise when they are commended, experience joy, or convey gratitude to others.
(c) Trigger actions (gestures) to visualize emotions
   During communication, when users experience positive emotions and wish to express them, they perform an action as a trigger for the creation of objects representing their positive emotions. In this study's system, a specific gesture operated as the trigger, hereinafter denoted as a "trigger gesture."

The expression of emotions through the trigger gesture is at the user's discretion, free from any temporal restrictions during the communication. While "Feel positive emotions during conversation" is outlined in (b), users may execute the gesture irrespective of their current emotional state, an approach that accommodates user intentionality in the expression of emotions.

(d) Objects are created and overlaid

Performing the trigger gesture results in the generation of objects that represent positive emotions, hereafter termed "emotion objects". These emotion objects are overlaid in the AR glasses in proximity to the gesturing user. Although Fig. 1 illustrates the perspective of an observer, users can view their own generated emotion objects via the AR glasses in the actual service.

3.2 A Workshop for System Development

In the study, a prototype was developed, followed by a workshop to facilitate the initial phase of system development. Participants in the workshop assessed the prototype and offered feedback on the emotional visualization. Figure 2 depicts the trigger gesture, that is, putting hands on top of each other, and emotion objects of the prototype.

Participants. Ten participants (nine males and one female) aged between 20 and 24 attended the workshop. All participants were native Japanese speakers.

Workshop Overview. The workshop began with an introduction to its objectives and an overview, followed by discussion and evaluation of the following five topics:

1. Current emotion visualization services in real-life face-to-face environments and related concerns.
2. Experiences or situations where there is a need to visually express emotions in everyday face-to-face communication.
3. Psychological evaluation of the prototype
4. Design evaluation of the prototype
5. Overall service evaluation and suggested improvements based on prototype experience.

For the prototype evaluation during the workshop for points (3) to (5), we created a scenario that allowed even first-time users to easily use the service. Participants were asked to engage in communication using the following scenario:

Character Setting: Senior A and Junior B in the laboratory

Location: Laboratory

Conversation flow:

1. Junior B is having trouble understanding how to use a device.
2. Senior A, who is familiar with the device, decides to help Junior B.
3. With Senior A's assistance, Junior B grasps how to use the device, experiencing feelings of gratitude and joy from learning.
4. Junior B decides to use the service and visually expresses his positive emotions.

During the workshop, participants formed pairs to engage with the prototype. Five individuals played the role of Senior A, and the remaining five were Junior B for the evaluation. Each pair interacted utilizing the prototype.

Fig. 2. Trigger gesture (left) and emotion objects (right) in prototype

Extraction of Obtained Opinions. The workshop identified the following five key aspects. Each of the 10 participants is represented as P1 through P10.

Privacy Awareness of Display of Emotions. P3 noted, "Emotions are personal information. If I'm not enjoying something, I might pretend to enjoy it. Thus, I especially prefer not to display negative emotions to others." P8 conveyed comfort with emotional expression during conversations but opposed third-party observation outside the conversational context. Many participants were not uncomfortable with the visualization of positive emotions within their conversation partner's visual field.

Opportunity to Display Positive Emotions. P6 reported "I once had a situation where I thought I was enjoying the conversation, but the other person perceived that I was angry." P3 agreed with P6, highlighting the challenge of discerning enjoyment in individuals whose facial expressions do not readily convey emotions. Thus, despite privacy concerns associated with visualizing emotions, it is evident that the display of positive emotions is beneficial in certain conversational contexts. Furthermore, for some users, emotion visualization services may offer a communicative capacity that supplements facial expressions and body language, thereby enriching the communicative environment.

Gap Between the User's Intended Information and the Emotion Objects. P9 highlighted the complexity of visualizing emotions in face-to-face communication, where facial expressions and other factors can impact the user. P4 felt uneasy role-playing as Senior A because the facial expressions did not match the positive emotion indicated by the objects. These opinions suggest the potential for misreading emotions or discomfort when visual emotion cues, such as facial expressions, contradict the intended positive emotions. To resolve this, narrowing the gap between the intended emotion and its display is crucial. The current prototype uses heart-shaped objects, which means positive emotions directly, which could be misunderstood. It is important to find ways to convey positivity through neutral visuals not associated with specific emotions.

The Style of Trigger Gesture. P3 mentioned that a trigger gesture would likely be accepted by users within a service designed for the expression of positive emotions. However, P3 emphasized the necessity for the gesture to be easily learnable and executable with one hand. Conversely, P5 suggested that smaller gestures could be less obtrusive and more comfortable for users compared to the existing, larger and more conspicuous alternatives.

Count Function. Although not introduced in the prototype, P8 mentioned the possibility of enhancing psychological effects by adding a count function. Increased frequency of positive emotion presentations/receptions could contribute to an enhanced mood state.

3.3 System Design

As following the workshop discussions, enhancements and augmentations of functions were integrated into the prototype. Figure 3 exhibits the actual trigger gesture and system interface.

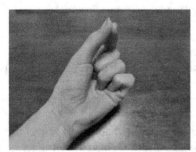 

Fig. 3. Trigger gesture (left) and system interface on AR glass (right) in actual system

Triger Gesture. The system uses a one-handed gesture, where the index finger and thumb overlap (Fig. 3, left). This gesture was chosen for its ease of use based on workshop feedback and its scalability for more emotion objects in the future.

Emotion Objects. The emotion objects had rounded designs, since study [1] showed such shapes evoke favorable feelings. Neutral shapes were also employed to avoid eliciting strong positive associations, as indicated by workshop findings. For colors, green was chosen to represent "trust," and yellow was selected to represent "joy," in accordance with Plutchik's Wheel of Emotions and the eight primary emotions [6].

Count Function. Following feedback from the workshop, we added a count function that tallies the number of times emotion objects are presented by the user and their conversational partner. this function is designed to maintain user enjoyment, regardless of their partner's presentation frequency.

3.4 Implementation

To utilize the system, each user wears AR glasses connected to an Android device. The left image of Fig. 4 illustrates the relationship between each device and user within the system. The system operates as depicted in the diagram, items (1) through (3).

The Positive Lab system app, created with Unity[3], is installed on each Android device and operates as shown in the right image of Fig. 4.

---

[3] Unity: https://unity.com/

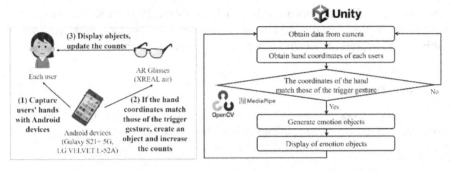

Fig. 4. System linkage diagram (left) and the program flow (right)

1. Capture users' hands with Android devices

   The Android device camera captures hand images of all conversation participants, including the user, during a conversation.
2. If the hand coordinates match those of the trigger gesture, create an object and increase the counts

   The program for the system uses OpenCV[4] and MediaPipe[5] to extract the hand coordinates of each user from the video images; if these match the trigger gesture, emotion objects are created and their count increases.
3. Display objects, update the counts

   The generated emotion objects are displayed on each user's AR glasses, and the incremental count is also displayed.

4   Experiment

4.1   Hypothesis for Usefulness Validation

In this paper, we have formulated the following three hypotheses to evaluate the usefulness of the service:

H1: The system for the service enhances emotional communication.

H2: The system for the service enhances the communication experience.

H3: The system for the service influences positive emotions.

H1, H2. The workshop revealed that some people struggle to express emotions and that visualizing emotions could improve expression beyond just facial cues and personal attitudes, leading to better emotional communication. This could set up H1 and H2.

H1 also considers the aspect of visual emotion transfer without encountering resistance. The workshop results revealed that, while some participants hesitated to visually express negative emotions, many displayed a positive inclination toward expressing positive emotions. In essence, this system, focused on positive emotional expression, may effectively convey emotions without inducing anxiety or resistance.

---

[4] OpenCV: https://opencv.org/

[5] MediaPipe: https://developers.google.com/mediapipe.

H3. Prior study has established the propagation of emotions [4]. Within the context of H1, which posits the superior communicability of positive emotions, it is possible that such emotions are transmitted more frequently than in typical conversations. Furthermore, extending the findings of Semertzidis et al., which suggest that visual representations of self-emotions facilitate introspection [9], it is anticipated that visual identification of personal positive emotion objects may induce positive affect in individuals. This concept forms H3.

4.2 Experiment Overview

The experiment examined H1-H3 with 18 participants (17 male and one female, aged 20–24), including 16 native Japanese individuals, one Chinese individual, and one English speaker. They were paired and followed the procedures outlined in Fig. 5.

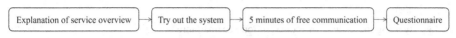

Fig. 5. Experiment flow

Experiment of Service Overview. An overview of the service and the experiment's objectives was presented to the participants.

Try Out the System. The participants had three minutes to learn the system's operation, and all mastered it within that time.

5 min of Free Communication. The participants engaged in normal conversations for five minutes using the system at least once. All pairs of participants communicated in Japanese. When a participant performed a trigger gesture, emotion objects and counts, as shown in Fig. 3 (right), were displayed on the AR glasses. Figure 6 depicts the actual experimental scene, including the display on the AR glasses.

Fig. 6. Experiment (left) and display on the participant's AR glass (right)

Questionnaire. Participants answered questions on H1-H3, system design, and overall system evaluation, as outlined in the Table 1: Q1 on H1, Q2 on H2, Q3 on H3, Q4 on design features, and Q5 on overall evaluation. Qualitative feedback was gathered in Q6.

Table 1. Questionnaire questions

No.	Question	Answer Style
Q1–1	By using the system, feel that you were able to express your positive emotions better than normal conversation	5-point Likert scale (1: Disagree - 5: Agree)
Q1–2	By using the system, it became easier to read others' emotions	
Q1–3	Feel that it is useful to be able to show your emotions whenever you want to	
Q1–4	Feel uncomfortable to show emotions using this system	
Q2–1	Seeing the emotional objects made you want to express your positive feelings to the other person more than usual	5-point Likert scale (1: Disagree - 5: Agree)
Q2–2	Feel that you will talk about positive topics and engage in active conversations in order to elicit positive feelings from others	
Q2–3	By using the system, the conversation became more enjoyable	
Q2–4	By using the system, communication with others has improved	
Q2–5	By using the system, you felt closer to your partner and improved relationships with him/her	
Q3–1	Seeing own visualized positive emotions amplified and enhanced own positive emotions	5-point Likert scale (1: Disagree - 5: Agree)
Q3–2	By seeing the positive emotions of others, you feel your own positive emotions amplified as well	
Q3–3	Seeing the emotion objects made you want to see more positive feelings from your partner	
Q4–1	Seeing the count of positive emotions of your partner and yourself made you want to show more positive emotions to the partner	5-point Likert scale (1: Disagree - 5: Agree)
Q4–2	Seeing the count of positive emotions of your partner and yourself made you want to see more positive emotions from the partner	
Q4–3	Gesture for emotion objects were easy to use	
Q4–4	Gesture for emotion objects were suitable for the system	
Q4–5	The shape of the emotion objects was appropriate to represent positive emotions	
Q4–6	Colors of the emotion objects were appropriate to represent positive emotions	

(*continued*)

Table 1. (*continued*)

No.	Question	Answer Style
Q5–1	The system was complex	5-point Likert scale (1: Disagree - 5: Agree)
Q5–2	Quickly understand how to use the system	
Q5–3	System can be used on a daily basis	
Q5–4	Want to use the system on a daily basis	
Q6–1	Advantages of the system	Descriptive expression
Q6–2	Improvements to this system	
Q6–3	Everyday situations where you want to use the system	
Q6–4	Other comments	

4.3 Results and Reviews

Below are the experiment results, displayed as pie charts for each item.

Emotional Communication. The responses of the Q1 group regarding the effect on emotional communication are as Fig. 7. This question group was evaluated using a 5-point Likert scale (1: Disagree - 5: Agree).

The average score for Q1–1 was 3.89, and upon considering the standard deviation, it becomes evident that the system aids participants in conveying positive emotions. Furthermore, the pie chart reveals that over 80% of participants responded with a score of 4 or 5. However, the results for Q1–2, as depicted in the pie chart, show that one-third of the participants hold negative opinions about the ease of emotion recognition using the system. Although approximately 60% of participants found it more straightforward to interpret emotions, it cannot be conclusively stated that emotion recognition has become universally more straightforward.

Regarding the resistance to emotion presentation, the average score and standard deviation for Q1–3 suggest that the ability to express emotions at will could potentially enhance convenience for users. Nevertheless, Q1–4 revealed that there is a subset of individuals who still feel resistance, even in an environment where they can present their emotions autonomously, as indicated by three participants' evaluations expressing resistance. The experiment showed that 77% of individuals were able to present emotions through the system without any resistance.

Effects on Conversation. The responses of the Q2 group regarding the effect on the conversation experience are as Fig. 8. This question group was evaluated using a 5-point Likert scale (1: Disagree - 5: Agree).

For Q2–1, the average score was 3.78 with a standard deviation of 1.00, suggesting the system potentially enhances users' active emotional expression via visual cues. However, Fig. 8 indicates that only approximately two-thirds of participants felt an increased inclination to express more positive emotions, precluding definitive conclusions about the system's impact. For Q2–2 to Q2–5, all evaluations yielded average scores above 4.00 with standard deviations below 1.00, indicating the system's probable role in fostering more positive and active communication, as well as augmenting conversational

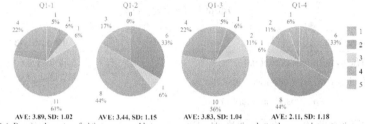

AVE: 3.89, SD: 1.02   AVE: 3.44, SD: 1.15   AVE: 3.83, SD: 1.04   AVE: 2.11, SD: 1.18

Q1-1: By using the system, feel that you were able to express your positive emotions better than normal conversation.
Q1-2: By using the system, it became easier to read others' emotions.
Q1-3: Feel that it is useful to be able to show your emotions whenever you want to.
Q1-4: Feel uncomfortable to show emotions using this system.

Fig. 7. Aggregate results of Q1 answers

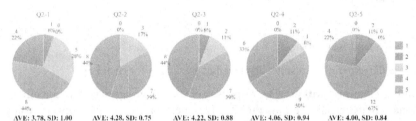

AVE: 3.78, SD: 1.00   AVE: 4.28, SD: 0.75   AVE: 4.22, SD: 0.88   AVE: 4.06, SD: 0.94   AVE: 4.00, SD: 0.84

Q2-1: Seeing the emotional objects made you want to express your positive feelings to the other person more than usual.
Q2-2: Feel that you will talk about positive topics and engage in active conversations in order to elicit positive feelings from others.
Q2-3: By using the system, the conversation became more enjoyable.
Q2-4: By using the system, communication with others has improved.
Q2-5: By using the system, you felt closer to your partner and improved relationships with him/her.

Fig. 8. Aggregate results of Q2 answers

enjoyment. The system may also influence users' relationships with their conversation partners.

Effects on Positive Emotion. The responses of the Q3 group regarding the effect on positive emotions are as Fig. 9. This group of questions was rated using a 5-point Likert scale (1: Disagree - 5: Agree).

Q3–1 data indicates that personal emotion objects positively influenced the affective states of 80% of participants. The Q3–2 data, with an average score of 4.22 (SD = 0.73), imply a notable impact of the partner's emotion objects on participants' positive emotions, corroborated by over 90% reporting enhanced positivity. Analysis of Q3–3, yielding an average of 3.89 (SD < 1), hints at the role of emotion objects recognition in seeking positive emotional experiences. Although, only 67% of participants scored 4 or 5 on the scale, which precludes a definitive conclusion and suggests a potential trend.

Evaluation of System Design. Responses to the Q4 group regarding the evaluation of the system design, including functions, are as Fig. 10. This group of questions was evaluated using a 5-point Likert scale (1: Disagree - 5: Agree).

Questions Q4–1 and Q4–2 both had an average score of 3.61, with a standard deviation close to 1. However, while 57% of respondents rated Q4–1 with a 4 or 5, 67%

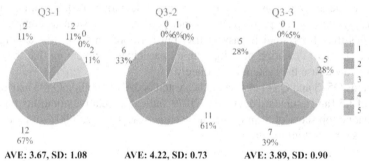

AVE: 3.67, SD: 1.08   AVE: 4.22, SD: 0.73   AVE: 3.89, SD: 0.90

Q3-1: Seeing own visualized positive emotions amplified and enhanced own positive emotions.
Q3-2: By seeing the positive emotions of others, you feel your own positive emotions amplified as well.
Q3-3: Seeing the emotion objects made you want to see more positive feelings from your partner.

Fig. 9. Aggregate results of Q3 answers

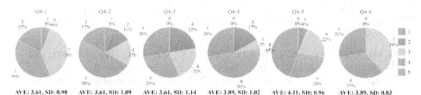

AVE: 3.61, SD: 0.98   AVE: 3.61, SD: 1.09   AVE: 3.61, SD: 1.14   AVE: 3.89, SD: 1.02   AVE: 4.11, SD: 0.96   AVE: 3.89, SD: 0.83

Q4-1: Seeing the count of positive emotions of your partner and yourself made you want to show more positive emotions to the partner

Q4-2: Seeing the count of positive emotions of your partner and yourself made you want to see more positive emotions from the partner.

Q4-3: Gesture for emotion objects were easy to use.

Q4-4: Gesture for emotion objects were suitable for the system.

Q4-5: The shape of the emotion objects was appropriate to represent positive emotions.

Q4-6: Colors of the emotion objects were appropriate to represent positive emotions.

Fig. 10. Aggregate results of Q4 answers

did so for Q4–2, suggesting that the count function does not always correlate with the conveyance of positive emotions, even though it has the potential to influence the pursuit of a partner's positive response.

Regarding the trigger gesture, about half of the participants in Q4–3 reported usability concerns. However, nearly 80% in Q4–4 recognized its compatibility with the system, evidenced by an average score of 3.89 and a standard deviation close to 1, indicating its overall suitability.

Assessment of the emotion objects' design via Q4–5 and Q4–6 revealed an average score of 4.11 (SD < 1) for Q4–5, suggesting the shape effectively conveyed positive emotions. The color received an average of 3.89 (SD = 0.83), with 60% rating it 4 or 5. While color assessments were not negative, a substantial proportion of participants expressed neutrality, indicating ambivalence towards the color scheme.

Evaluation of the Entire System. The Q5 responses for the overall system evaluation are as Fig. 11. This question group was evaluated using a 5-point Likert scale (1: Disagree - 5: Agree).

In Q5–1, the average was 1.56 with a standard deviation of 0.86, indicating that approximately 90% of the participants did not perceive the system as complex. This demonstrates that the system is easy to use. Furthermore, in Q5–2, the average was 4.78 with a standard deviation of 0.43, with all participants indicating that they could understand how to use the system immediately.

Questions Q5–3 and Q5–4 evaluated the system's daily usability. Q5–3 had an average score of 3.50 and a standard deviation of 0.79, indicating relative suitability for everyday use, but no top score of 5. In Q5–4, the average was 3.39, with 60% of participants willing to use the system regularly.

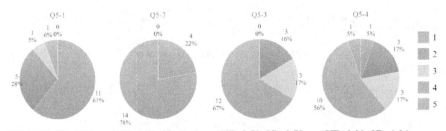

AVE: 1.56, SD: 0.86   AVE: 4.78, SD: 0.43   AVE: 3.50, SD: 0.79   AVE: 3.39, SD: 1.04

Q5-1: The system was complex. ; Q5-2: Quickly understand how to use the system.
Q5-3: System can be used on a daily basis. ; Q5-4: Want to use the system on a daily basis.

Fig. 11. Aggregate results of Q5 answers

Qualitative Evaluation Results. Participants provided qualitative opinions from Q6–1 to Q6–4, which are summarized below. Each participant is labeled as P1 to P18.

Advantages of the System. In Q6–1, users were asked about the advantages of the system. Furthermore, in Q6–4, additional benefits of the system were articulated. From the comments of the participants, three primary points of the system's advantages were extracted.

Visualized Emotions. According to the opinions of the participants, some participants found merit in the visualization of emotions itself. P14 described the potential application of visible emotions to communication with people who are unable to speak.

Empathic Mutual Communication Experience. Several participants perceived an advantage in the ability to convey their emotions. P10 noted the capability to confirm their partner's enjoyment of the interaction. P11 and P16 stated that the visual ascertainment of their partner's enjoyment facilitated non-verbal agreement, such as nodding, and the more effective selection of conversation topics. P6 described perceiving empathy from their partner's expression of emotions. Furthermore, P18 highlighted the benefit of communicating visualized emotions without disrupting the conversational flow.

System Functions. P8 and P17 cited the simplicity of the trigger gesture as an advantage, with P8 specifically mentioning the expandability of the gesture. P2 gave a positive assessment of the display of emotion objects. In addition, P16 and P17 discussed the characteristics of the AR glasses, noting that the glasses' resemblance to sunglasses is likely to elicit favorable impressions and allow visibility of facial expressions. The lightweight nature of the glasses and their ease of wear also received commendation. Furthermore, there were opinions regarding the count function, which suggested that it fostered motivation to increase the count.

Improvements to this System. In Q6–2, users were asked regarding potential improvements to the system. In Q6–4, additional points of improvement as well as problems with the system were highlighted. Five primary areas for system enhancement were identified based on these responses.

Accuracy of Hand Recognition System Multiple Participants Reported Enhancements in Hand Recognition Accuracy. Furthermore, P6 and P16 highlighted that the precision limitations of the current system necessitate bringing the hand closer to the camera, which leads to arm fatigue.

Types of Emotion Objects and Trigger Gesture. Several participants provided insights regarding the variety of gestures and emotion objects. P9 and P14 mentioned the potential for customization of emotion objects through variations in color and shape. In addition, P2 commented that the gesture was a bit embarrassing. P7 suggested that a greater variety of gestures would allow users to enjoy the system more.

Display Position of Emotion Objects and Counts. P11 and P12 noted difficulties in adjusting their gaze during the display of emotion objects. They reported that focusing on the partner's facial expressions led to a dispersion of attention towards the emotion objects and the count function. P11 suggested the implementation of auditory notifications during the generation of emotion objects. P18 expressed concerns about the possibility of emotion objects overlapping with the other's face position.

AR Device. While positive attitudes towards the AR glass have been noted, P1 and P12 articulated concerns regarding the visibility of facial expressions, as the eyewear can obscure the user's eyes. Furthermore, P3 has identified the limited field of vision as an inherent limitation associated with the use of the AR glass.

System Usage. P2 and P17 highlighted the risk of forgetting to present emotion objects while being engrossed in a conversation. However, P2 noted that as adaptation to the system progressed, the use of gestures would become more intuitive.

Everyday Situations Where the System Can Be Used. In Q6–3, participants were asked about their usage of the system in everyday life. Since descriptions related to usage scenarios are also present in Q6–2 and Q6–4, these were synthesized and summarized.

A majority of participants expressed a desire to use the system for conversations about hobbies, casual chats, and during initial encounters with new acquaintances. Furthermore, individuals such as P2 and P5 highlighted the potential for its application in online calls conducted on platforms like Zoom[6]. Scenarios including presentations, classes, and meetings were also cited as possible use cases. P8 stated that the use of emotion objects to share feelings between users could facilitate the initiation of communication and promote effective dialogue. P17 suggested that sharing emotions with distant individuals might enable effortless commencement of communication.

---

[6] Zoom: https://www.zoom.com/en/products/virtual-meetings/.

As for the communication partners, opinions among participants varied, ranging from strangers to close family and friends, and extending to superiors.

5 Discussion

The results obtained in Sect. 4.3 will be combined and discussed. In addition, the hypotheses from H1 to H3 will be verified.

5.1 Emotional Communication

In the study of systems used for facilitating emotional communication, it has become evident that there is a coexistence of ease in expressing positive emotions and difficulty in interpreting the emotions of others. Specifically, the challenge of facial recognition when utilizing AR glasses has become a barrier to interpretation. Furthermore, participants have noted ambiguity in where to focus their attention among emotion objects, facial expressions, and count function. Although emotion objects were intended to augment information, their effectiveness may be compromised if focus is dispersed. Therefore, to enhance users' perceptual abilities, optimization of the arrangement of AR space is necessary. Additionally, the consideration of auditory notifications during the creation of emotion objects should be explored.

Concerning the reluctance to exhibit emotions, numerous participants engage with the system unhesitatingly; however, a subset still experiences a degree of resistance. The embarrassment associated with the current gesture is posited as one contributing factor to this resistance. To mitigate this issue, the introduction of a variety of gestures or the provision of customization options is necessary. Given that the extant gesture has received positive assessments, the incorporation of additional features, while preserving the current gesture, is essential.

Based on these discussions, we address H1. The current system is effective in facilitating the expression of emotions; however, it presents challenges in the interpretation of others' emotions. Nevertheless, anticipated improvements in AR devices and user interfaces are expected to enhance the interpretation of emotions. At this stage, H1 is only partially supported, but with system enhancements, full support is anticipated to be achievable in the future.

5.2 Effects on Conversation

In communication, it was confirmed through experiment that our system promotes a communication improvement cycle in both scenarios where the partner is the focal point of the conversation and where the user themselves is at the center.

When the partner is the central topic of topic, emotion objects allow for a visual capture of the partner's enjoyment. This facilitates the selection of conversation topics that are likely to be received favorably by the partner, thereby creating a feedback loop that elicits positive responses.

Conversely, when the user is the center of the conversation, the visualization of the partner's emotions enables a more profound perception of empathy from the partner and simplifies the comprehension of their reactions. Receiving empathy from others enhances the user's enjoyment. Consequently, the user's selection of conversation topics tends to prioritize empathy and enjoyment, which, in turn, further amplifies the partner's positive emotional responses.

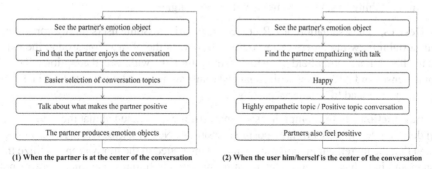

(1) When the partner is at the center of the conversation   (2) When the user him/herself is the center of the conversation

Fig. 12. Communication improvement cycle

The formation of the cycle during conversations is believed to have facilitated smooth and satisfying communication for both parties, which has been observed to enhance feelings of closeness and relationship quality.

Consequently, it can be stated that the use of this communication system improved the communication experience, thereby supporting H2 with the current system.

However, the responses to Q2–1 indicate that merely observing visualized emotions does not necessarily lead to more active emotional expression by the user. In other words, the natural enhancement of this cycle illustrated in Fig. 12 becomes crucial in communication facilitated by the system.

5.3 Effects on Positive Emotion

The experimental data from Group Q3 suggest a likelihood that both the user's and the partner's emotion objects significantly influence the user's positive emotions. Notably, the visualization of the partner's positive emotions was confirmed to have a marked effect on the user's emotional state.

Furthermore, as pointed out in the previous section, this system enhances the quality of the communication experience and facilitates more enjoyable interactions. This implies not only a direct promotion of positive emotions through the use of the system but also an indirect approach to emotions through communication.

In light of these findings, it can be concluded that H3 is supported in the context of the current system.

5.4 System Function and Devices

System Accuracy. The survey results revealed deficiencies in the accuracy of the hand recognition system. This system is confined to the camera recognition range of Android devices, and the limitations and lack of precision are suggested to be diminishing the operability of gesture. Furthermore, the fact that affirmative responses regarding daily use remained at 60% is conjectured to stem from issues with usability. To resolve these challenges, enhancements in recognition accuracy and a reassessment of camera selection are necessary. In pursuit of a more practical system, consideration should also be given to switching to smaller cameras with wider angles.

AR Devices. The evaluation of AR devices is polarized. Some users highly appreciate their portability, while others express discomfort with the obstruction around the eyes and the limitation of their field of vision. In the future, the widespread adoption of smart contact lenses and AR glasses with enhanced transparency is anticipated to alleviate user discomfort and lead to broader acceptance.

Count Function. In the comprehensive analysis, it was concluded that the count function does not definitively promote positive emotions. Nevertheless, one participant suggested that the increment in numerical values contributed to the motivation to utilize the system and introduced a gaming element to the service. Initially, gamification was not incorporated into the design of this system, but its potential value has been signified.

5.5   Potential Usage Opportunities.

Analysis of the comments revealed the diverse usage scenarios provided by the system, highlighting its advantages. Interestingly, users expressed a desire to utilize the system not only with intimate acquaintances but also in interactions with strangers and individuals in superior positions. It became evident that this service is applicable to conversations regardless of the degree of relationship. For this service, which targets everyday communication, it is a crucial element to offer opportunities for use without discriminating against the user's choice of partner. Furthermore, beyond casual conversation, the use of the system was proposed for specific contexts such as presentations and lectures, demonstrating its versatility.

Moreover, this service has the potential to support communications between individuals with different cultural backgrounds. In this experiment, two pairs of participants with different native languages took part. Specifically, P1 paired with P9, and P2 paired with P3. What follows are their responses to a set of questions regarding their communication experience (Q2). (Table 2)

Due to the limited dataset, it is not possible to make definitive conclusions; however, results indicating that the average exceeded 4 for items Q2-2, Q2-4, and Q2-5 suggest the potential of a system to foster active conversation, enhance communication, and strengthen relationships among participants with different cultural backgrounds and native languages. Furthermore, proposals have been made regarding the social contribution of services that could be applied to communication with individuals who have speech impairments or hearing disabilities.

Table 2. Aggregate results of Q2 answers for participants with different native languages

Participant No	Native language	Answers of each participant				
		Q2–1	Q2–2	Q2–3	Q2–4	Q2–5
P1	English	4	3	4	5	4
P2	Chinese	1	5	3	3	4
P3	Japanese	4	5	4	4	4
P9	Japanese	3	4	4	4	4
Average		3.00	4.25	3.75	4.00	4.00

6 Conclusion and Future Work

In this study, we proposed Positive Lab, an AR communication support service designed to visualize positive emotions in accordance with user intentions. For this service, we developed a system that includes a feature displaying emotion objects symbolizing positive emotions during a conversation by utilizing the trigger gesture, and its usefulness and areas for future challenges were identified through experimentation.

The system exhibited three key effects: facilitation of emotional conveyance, enhancement of the communication experience, and influence on positive emotions. In the experiment, participants were able to communicate their emotions more effectively, which led to reported improvements in the quality of conversation and interpersonal relationships. Furthermore, the system proved to be adaptable to various situations and user demographics. While there is room for refinement in the existing system, our service has been revealed to have usefulness as a communication support tool.

Future challenges include enhancing the accuracy of gesture recognition, diversifying the range of emotional expressions and gestures, simplifying daily use through device improvements, and refining the user interface. These advancements are expected to yield a service that enhances user satisfaction. Additionally, in this paper, we conducted an evaluation experiment solely with this system. In future research, by comparing and examining it against existing proposed methods for emotion visualization, it is likely that further insights can be gained.

References

1. Bar, M., Neta, M.: Humans prefer curved visual objects. Psychol. Sci. **17**(8), 645–648 (2016). https://doi.org/10.1111/j.1467-9280.2006.01759.x
2. Choi, I., Lim, S., Catapano, R., Choi, J.: Comparing two roads to success: self-control predicts achievement and positive affect predicts relationships. J. Res. Pers. **76**, 50–63 (2018). https://doi.org/10.1016/j.jrp.2018.07.001
3. Fischer, A.H., Manstead, A.S.R.: Social functions of emotion and emotion regulation. Handb. Emot. **4**, 424–439 (2016)
4. Hatfield, E.: Emotional contagion. Cambridge University Press, Cambridge, England (1993)

5. Mauersberger, H., Hess, U.: When smiling back helps and scowling back hurts: individual differences in emotional mimicry are associated with self-reported interaction quality during conflict interactions. Motiv. Emot. **43**, 471–482 (2019). https://doi.org/10.1007/s11031-018-9743-x

6. Plutchik, R., Kellerman, H.: Theories of emotion. Academic Press, New York (1980)

7. Seligman, M.E.P.: Flourish: a visionary new understanding of happiness and well-being. Atria, New York (2013)

8. Sels, L., Tran, A., Greenaway, K.H., Verhofstadt, L., Kalokerinos, E.K.: The social functions of positive emotions. Curr. Opin. Behav. Sci. **39**, 41–45 (2021). https://psycnet.apa.org/record/2021-77975-006

9. Semertzidis, N., et al.: Neo-noumena. In: Proceedings of the 2020 CHI Conference on Human Factors in Computing Systems, pp. 1–6 (2020). https://doi.org/10.1145/3313831.3376599

10. Sy, T., Côté, S., Saavedra, R.: The contagious leader: Impact of the leader's mood on the mood of group members, group affective tone, and group processes. J. Appl. Psychol. **90**, 2, 295–305 (2005). https://psycnet.apa.org/record/2005-02538-007

11. Valente, A. et al.: Empathic Aurea: exploring the effects of an augmented reality cue for emotional sharing across three face-to-face tasks. In: Proceedings of 2022 IEEE Conference on Virtual Reality and 3D User Interfaces (VR), pp. 158–166 (2022). https://ieeexplore.ieee.org/document/9756731

European Luxury Fashion Brand Websites for the Chinese Market. An Explorative Study on Localization

Joanna Liu^(✉) and Lorenzo Cantoni

USI – Università della Svizzera italiana, Lugano, Switzerland
joanna.bing.liu@usi.ch

Abstract. Globalization of digital communication, made available by the internet, has highlighted elements that are still very different in different markets, among them, those dimensions related to different languages and cultures. Digital communication has tackled such differences, and the need to address different target locales in different ways, through so-called "Localization", which can be considered as a cultural translation. Localization includes also changes related to different legal systems, or time/season zones, as well as currencies, payment systems, social media used in given areas.

However, while a company is requested to ensure high quality contents and functionalities for specific markets, it has also to ensure identity and consistency across different regions. Striking the right equilibrium between consistency and identity on one side, and localization on the other, is particularly relevant for luxury brands, which leverage their (cultural) identity as a major dimension of their (perceived) value.

This study analyzes how five European Luxury brands – Bulgari, Cartier, Gucci, La Prairie, and Rolex – adapt their websites for the Chinese market; such analysis is done through a comparison between their websites for the French, Italian, and Swiss markets and the Chinese one, how and how much they localize.

Keywords: Localization · European Luxury Fashion Brand · Chinese Market

1 Introduction

In an age of globalized digital communication, fueled by the internet, it becomes increasingly evident the importance of localization strategies of a company's website, e-commerce and social media. These strategies encompass a wide range of activities, taking into account linguistic and cultural diversity, time zones, currencies, payment systems, and even the choice of social media platforms in specific regions [17].

In this context, companies face a dual challenge. They must not only ensure the delivery of high-quality content and functionalities tailored to specific markets but also maintain a coherent brand identity and consistency across diverse regions [26]. Striking the right balance between preserving brand identity and embracing localization is particularly relevant for European luxury fashion brands. In fact, these brands, known for their

A. Marcus et al. (Eds.): HCII 2024, LNCS 14712, pp. 107–120, 2024.
https://doi.org/10.1007/978-3-031-61351-7_7

cultural identity, often hinge their perceived value on the preservation and celebration of their unique heritage [1].

This study embarks on an exploration of how five prominent European luxury brands – Bulgari, Cartier, Gucci, La Prairie, and Rolex – adapt their digital presence in order to communicate and operate in a specific context; more precisely, we explore how these luxury fashion brands navigate the complex landscape of digital communication and cultural value adaptation in the pursuit of global success, especially in the Chinese market. Hence, the addressed research questions are:

- RQ1: Do European luxury companies have different website versions for France, Italy, Switzerland and for China?
- RQ2: If yes, which are the differences?

Through a meticulous comparison of their websites designed for the Chinese, French, Italian, and Swiss market, we aim to analyze the strategies they employ for localization and the extent of their application. Our analysis is also informed by elements derived from the Hofstede model, which offers valuable insights into the cultural dimensions.

European luxury fashion brands need to understand and respect the cultural values, traditions, and lifestyles of different local markets. They adopt local elements, symbols, brand ambassadors, influencers [19] or other themes to communicate their products, to define the packaging, or to design marketing campaigns [10, 28]. This includes translating content into local languages, using culturally relevant imagery, employing local celebrities or influencers as brand ambassadors [19], and adopting appropriate marketing channels such as their website and local social media to engage with local consumers. This approach helps the brand establish a deeper connection with consumers and enhances the brand perception in the local market [7, 8].

Localization of a luxury brand refers to the adaptation and customization of the brand's products, services and marketing strategies in order to better accommodate to the language, culture and other specific local market conditions of the target region. Research shows that the localization involves tailoring the brands offering to the local target audience while maintaining the essence of the luxury brand image [17].

A successful luxury fashion brand localization requires a delicate balance between maintaining the brand's core identity and adapting to the specific needs and expectations of the local market in China [26]. An efficient website can help the European luxury fashion brand to build its online brand community and foster meaningful relationships with local customers in different regions, ultimately driving brand loyalty and achieving a healthy business growth.

To connect with local customers in the target market, it is important to stay up-to-date and publish information about new products. Engaging with local customers through storytelling is another effective strategy. One of the best platforms for luxury fashion companies to communicate with local customers is to use dedicated websites (versions) and their own social media. This research utilizes content analysis methodology to systematically analyze five selected luxury fashion brands from Europe, which encompass various product categories, including watches, skincare, clothing, shoes, bags, and jewelry.

The findings emphasize the importance of (some) localization strategies, encompassing adaptations of language, payment-related elements, as well as more subtle cultural adaptations. Such findings highlight the significance European luxury fashion companies place on catering to their Chinese customers.

The paper is organized as follows: a Literature review will present main relevant elements linked with Digital Fashion Communication and Localization, then the methodology will be presented, followed by results and discussion. A brief conclusion will outline main results, suggest further research and indicate some limitations.

2 Literature Review

In this section, the research context of Digital Fashion Communication will be outlined, together with the area of Localization, namely for the Chinese market.

2.1 Digital Fashion Communication

The global fashion industry has undergone a transformative shift with the widespread adoption of digital media [16], and this trend is particularly pronounced in dynamic markets like China [19]. Digital platforms enable fashion brands to connect with local customers, boost sales, and respond to evolving trends and consumer behaviors [18, 20].

One significant aspect of online multi-channels is their role in providing pre-purchase sales information [4]. The rapid growth of the online luxury market emphasizes the importance of maintaining and developing *ad-hoc* websites to reach local customers effectively [6]. However, despite the dynamic nature of the luxury landscape, only a few brands integrate local culture into their strategies, indicating a need for further development in this area [6]. Website content infused with local cultural context emerges as a key localization strategy.

The impact of websites extends beyond information provision up to promoting user engagement, directly influencing customers' brand loyalty [36]. Recognizing the importance of communication, luxury brand companies leverage their websites as efficient tools for interacting with audiences, addressing gaps and challenges, and seizing opportunities [38]. To effectively reach local consumers online, assessing the suitable level of website contents and functionalities is crucial, especially considering cultural differences [30].

Tong and Hawley note the diminishing allure of traditional mass media among the Chinese youth, emphasizing the significance of web advertising with its innovative content and interactive features [35]. Internet technology enhances customer experience, increasing brand familiarity and influencing perceptions of website performance [10]. Customers' e-loyalty, indicative of their intention to revisit or make future purchases, is intricately linked with their attitudes shaped by website content, particularly within cultural contexts [7].

Successful web design integrated with cultural content opens access to different marketplaces and facilitates engagement with clients through personalized, multicultural approaches [29]. Luxury fashion brands aiming for success in the Chinese market need to generate navigable and innovative information, building trust and loyalty among local customers [20]. The intangible value of a brand is conveyed through strategic web content, influencing customers' buying decisions and fostering trust in online vendors [15].

From a broader perspective, awareness and knowledge of a website's content and functionality impact brand benefits, customer trust, and product perception [9]. Website performance correlates strongly with brand understanding at the local audience level [6]. Brands must consider the local cultural background, as some customers may not favor personalized recommendations [1]. Online localization becomes a vital aspect of actual business conduct and operations [7], with measurement considerations rooted in the local cultural background as a fundamental standard [21].

Consumer engagement, facilitated through website content, emerges as a valuable predictor of business success, aiding sales growth and enhancing profitability [8]. The ability to position and market a brand as luxurious hinges on a comprehensive understanding of consumer perceptions and preferences [8, 12]. The online channel for luxury goods plays a pivotal role, especially considering the developed nature of digital strategies in the industry [27].

Luxury fashion brands face the challenge of navigating the "global-local dilemma," particularly in emerging markets with low brand awareness and loyalty [11]. Striking a balance between maintaining exclusivity and brand consistency across diverse markets is crucial for success, especially in challenging circumstances [13].

2.2 Localization

Localization, defined as the process of adapting products, services, and content to meet local cultural requirements [21], plays a pivotal role in the online strategy of consumer engagement [8].

Website design underscores the importance of consumer experiences perceived as trustworthy [5]. Localization strategies vary, particularly for luxury fashion brands aimed at local customers in different geographical regions. A localized website should incorporate cultural metaphors [2].

Website localization processes, initially focusing on language translation and basic elements like time and currency, have evolved up to include a comprehensive range of adjustments so to encompass cultural values, functionalities, human-computer interfaces, information architecture, optimization for specific search engines, symbols, videos etc. [31, 33].

The cultural shift brought about by the internet has significantly impacted business operations, customer behavior, and shopping habits, especially with the growing popularity of online shopping in emerging markets like China [24]. Culture differences emerge as crucial elements in localization strategies, particularly when focusing on higher sales. A well-designed website can effectively win customers' hearts and minds, contributing to marketing effectiveness [25].

The influence of Confucian collectivism philosophy on contemporary consumption behavior in the Chinese market emphasizes the importance of integrating local cultural content into luxury fashion brand websites as part of localization strategies [35]. Differences between individualistic societies in the West and the influence of collectivism on consumption in Southeast Asia, particularly China, underscore the importance of considering functional motives over emotional motives for luxury fashion brand purchases

[13]. Ensuring website content is culturally neutral or sensitive showcases the standardization and localization of luxury brands [28]. Websites and web tools emerge together with social media, engaging customers directly and influencing purchase intentions [5].

Localization of European Luxury Fashion Brands in the Chinese Market. Culturally relevant website content, as evidenced in the case of website localization for the Chinese market, engages local customers more effectively [22]. Incorporating localized features such as tailored product recommendations based on regional preferences, influenced by local cultural backgrounds, proves impactful [20, 27]. European luxury fashion brands entering multicultural markets, such as China, benefit from interesting website content with culturally relevant context, leading to purchase intentions and heightened research interests [25].

While the inclusion of translated local languages and currency, date, and time on websites are fundamental elements for localization strategies, research suggests that websites adopting culturally relevant content and features such as multilingual chatbots or dedicated local helplines might enhance customer satisfaction, resolve queries effectively, and contribute to positive brand perception, ultimately increasing revisit frequency and purchase intention [24, 30].

Comprehensive website adaptations that allow personalized and tailored shopping experiences based on the customer's location enable European luxury fashion brands to enhance customer satisfaction, brand loyalty, and higher retention rates [7]. Leveraging website communication to showcase culturally relevant content, including models, imagery, and styling, resonates better with local consumers, thereby improving brand perception in specific regions [8]. Furthermore, the integration of localized payment methods, shipping options, and customer service support reduces barriers during the purchase [10].

European luxury fashion brands utilizing their website (analytics) to collect and analyze customer data, gain valuable insights into market segments, enabling them to develop more effective localization strategies [25, 36, 37]. The strategic use of websites proves crucial in adapting to the local culture background, traditions, and aesthetics, leading to increased brand acceptance, higher sales, and market segmentation [23, 29]. Cultural sensitivity and respect, demonstrated by acknowledging and incorporating local cultural values and symbols, enhance authenticity, trust, preference, and higher levels of customer engagement [4, 25].

A model that has guided several localization practices is the one proposed by Hofstede, a framework designed to understand cultural variations. Hofstede's model, comprising various cultural dimensions, provides businesses with a valuable tool for navigating diverse cultural contexts. Companies can tailor their strategies, communication, and management practices to foster cross-cultural communication and collaboration [11]. Hofstede's model serves as a structured framework for cultural analysis, particularly in the context of online content localization, it might also assist luxury brands in identifying cultural differences impacting digital communication, marketing, and product adaptation. Recognizing that culture is multidimensional and complex, the model provides insights into various aspects of it, with the potential of creating cultural value for luxury brands in the Chinese market.

However, acknowledging its limitations is also crucial. The model might oversimplify cultural differences and lack precision in measuring individual variations within a culture. Furthermore, it may not capture rapid cultural changes and evolving trends. Despite its challenges in practical business contexts, considering the Hofstede model into localization strategies, while at the same time taking into account its limitations, can assist European luxury brands in navigating cultural diversity and achieving successful global expansion, especially in complex and very different markets such as the Chinese one.

3   Methodology

In order to answer the above introduced two research questions, the websites of five selected European luxury fashion companies (Bulgari, Cartier, Gucci, La Prairie, and Rolex) have been studied, adopting content analysis to systematically investigate their contents. The approach has also considered the cultural framework proposed by Hofstede, in particular tentatively identifying peculiar cultural dimensions such as power distance, individualism vs. collectivism, uncertainty avoidance and time orientation.

Different pages and services within the selected websites have been analyzed, the primary focus has been on each brand's homepage, on product pages, checkout processes, language options, payment methods, chatbot availability as well as on other culturally relevant content, such as storytelling webpages.

The research took place from October 2023 to January 2024. During this period, more than 100 web pages from the websites of the five selected European luxury fashion brands have been thoroughly examined, accessing them from Europe to China, using a laptop. The analysis encompassed web pages in multiple languages, namely French, German, Italian, and Chinese. Furthermore, also images have been scrutinized.

4   Results and Discussion

Hereafter, an analysis of each individual company's website communication is offered, highlighting the ways they have chosen in order to communicate and operate digitally in the European market as well as in the Chinese one. The presentation of results is done along the following dimensions: Domain, Design, Language, Rebranding, Social Media, Currency and Price, Ambassador, Online Chatbot.

4.1   Bulgari

Examining the Bulgari website reveals interesting distinctions between its European (France, Italy, Switzerland) and Chinese versions, catering to some cultural specificities of their respective audiences.

Domain. The choice of domains emphasizes regional considerations. The European website utilizes the.com domain with country-specific abbreviations, recognizing regional distinctions. On the other hand, the Chinese website employs the.cn domain, aligning with China's online identity.

Design. The website maintains a consistent design across the various European countries. Conversely, the Chinese website takes a culturally sensitive approach, featuring a special Chinese New Year edition. This bespoke design aligns with Chinese festivities, reflecting an understanding and adaptation to cultural events.

Language. Language is a notable distinction, with the European website, featuring different languages corresponding to respective countries. In contrast, the Chinese website exclusively employs Chinese, aligning with linguistic preferences in the Chinese market.

Rebranding. The approach to branding remains consistent on the European website, retaining the same brand name. On the Chinese website, there is a deliberate use of a translated Chinese brand name (宝格丽 – Bulgari), demonstrating a commitment to linguistic nuances and cultural preferences in China.

Social Media. Social media strategies diverge as well. The European website features Western platforms such as Instagram, YouTube, Facebook, Pinterest, and LinkedIn. In contrast, the Chinese website strategically includes Chinese social media – WeChat, Bulgari official WeChat, A Little Red Book, TikTok (Douyin), and Weibo – attuning to the preferences of the Chinese audience.

Currency and Price. Currency presentation on the European website reflects local currencies (Euro & CHF), while the Chinese website, in adherence to local preferences, displays prices in RMB.

Ambassador. In ambassadorial representation, the European website employs a common approach, utilizing the same ambassador and featuring a video with American superstars, Zendaya and Anne Hathaway. In contrast, the Chinese website opts for a more localized strategy, engaging a Chinese ambassador. This tailored approach demonstrates a recognition of the importance of cultural representation. Both the special Chinese New Year edition and the use of Chinese ambassadors reflect a high uncertainty avoidance and a focus on long-term orientation, aligning with Chinese cultural values.

Online Chatbot. The European does not offer an online chat robot; in contrast, the Chinese website incorporates an online chat robot, recognizing the importance of interactive communication in the Chinese market.

4.2 Cartier

The Cartier website exhibits distinct characteristics catering to the cultural nuances of the European (France, Italy, Switzerland) and Chinese markets, reflecting some adaptations aligned with Hofstede's cultural dimensions.

Domain. The European website utilizes the.com domain with country-specific subsections, while the Chinese one employs the.cn domain, aligning with regional distinctions in web domains.

Design. In the European website, a uniform design prevails across different European countries, presenting a cohesive visual identity. In contrast, the Chinese website features a special Chinese New Year edition, showcasing a cultural responsiveness by recognizing and celebrating Chinese festivities. Such presence is aligned with a long-term orientation.

Language. The European website employs different languages based on the respective countries, emphasizing a localized approach. Conversely, the Chinese Website is exclusively presented in Chinese, acknowledging, and aligning with linguistic preferences prevalent in the Chinese market.

Rebranding. Consistency in branding is maintained on the European website, retaining the same brand name. In contrast, the Chinese Website opts for a translated Chinese brand name (卡地亚– Cartier), demonstrating an adaptation to linguistic nuances and cultural preferences in China.

Social Media. Distinct social media strategies are employed. The European website displays Western social media platforms, including Instagram, YouTube, Facebook, Pinterest, Twitter, and LinkedIn. On the other hand, the Chinese website strategically features Chinese social media such as WeChat, Bilibili, A Little Red Book, TikTok (Douyin), and Weibo, aligning with the social media preferences prevalent in China.

Currency and Price. On the European website, prices are displayed in local currencies (Euro & CHF); in contrast, the Chinese website presents prices exclusively in the local currency (RMB), catering to the familiar currency in the Chinese market.

Ambassador. Neither the European website nor the Chinese one incorporate an ambassadorial representation. This absence suggests a consistent strategy across regions. The absence of ambassadors on both websites may reflect a certain level of uncertainty avoidance and a more reserved communication strategy.

Online Chatbot. The European website adopts a standardized approach without incorporating an online chatbot. Conversely, the Chinese website features an online chatbot, recognizing the importance of interactive communication in the Chinese market.

4.3 Gucci

Exploring the Gucci website unveils nuanced differentiations between the European and Chinese versions, showcasing tailored adaptations that resonate with Hofstede's cultural dimensions.

Domain. There is a divergence in the choice of domains, with the European website utilizing the.com domain with country-specific sub-sections, while the Chinese website adopting the.cn domain. This decision aligns with regional distinctions and reflects an understanding of China's unique online identity.

Design. A cohesive and consistent design is maintained across different European countries, presenting a unified visual identity. The Chinese website shares the same layout as its European counterpart but incorporates different images, indicating a localization to align with the visual preferences and cultural aesthetics of the Chinese audience.

Language. The European website employs different languages based on respective countries, emphasizing a localized approach. In contrast, the Chinese website exclusively presents content in Chinese, acknowledging and adhering to the linguistic preferences prevalent in the Chinese market.

Rebranding. Consistency is maintained in branding on the European website, retaining the same European brand name. Conversely, the Chinese website adopts a translated Chinese brand name (古驰– Gucci), exemplifying an awareness of linguistic nuances and cultural preferences in China.

Social Media. Distinct social media strategies are evident, with the European website integrating Gucci's own Western social media channels and an online exhibition. In contrast, the Chinese website exclusively features popular Chinese social media, including WeChat, A Little Red Book, and Weibo, reflecting a nuanced approach to the unique social media landscape in China.

Currency and Price. On the European website, prices are displayed in local currencies (Euro & CHF); also the Chinese website presents prices in the local currency (RMB).

Ambassador. The European website strategically features Western ambassadors and models, aligning with the cultural inclinations of the European market. On the Chinese website, a cross-cultural approach is adopted, utilizing both Chinese and Western ambassadors and models. This reflects a recognition of the diverse audience in China and an effort to connect with consumers from various cultural backgrounds. The utilization of both Chinese and Western ambassadors on the Chinese website might reflect an adaptation to a more collectivist cultural orientation, emphasizing the importance of diverse cultural representations.

Online Chatbot. The European website adopts an interactive approach by incorporating an online chatbot, enhancing customer engagement in the European market. Similarly, the Chinese website features an online chatbot, recognizing the importance of interactive communication in the Chinese market and ensuring a seamless user experience.

4.4 La Prairie

La Prairie online communication appears to have chosen only a few localization strategies, be it for a strategic long-term decision or for a temporary tactical one.

Domain. All websites utilize the same.com domain with country-specific sub-sections.

Design. In the European website, La Prairie maintains a consistent and uniform design across different countries, presenting a cohesive visual identity that resonates with Western aesthetics. No localization at this level has been applied, reducing the opportunity to cater for different publics, while ensuring a fully consistent brand image.

Language. The European website employs different languages corresponding to respective countries, adhering to a localized approach that caters to linguistic diversity in Europe. The Chinese website exclusively presents content in Chinese, aligning with linguistic preferences prevalent in the Chinese market.

Rebranding. On the European website, La Prairie maintains consistency by using the brand name across different countries, contributing to a cohesive and recognizable brand identity. Conversely, the Chinese section adopts a translated Chinese brand name (莱珀妮– La Prairie), showcasing an acknowledgment of linguistic nuances and cultural preferences in China.

Social Media. La Prairie's European sections integrate only Western social media platforms, including Instagram and YouTube, catering to the social media preferences in European countries. In contrast, the Chinese section exclusively features Chinese social media, such as WeChat, A Little Red Book, and Weibo, attuning to the distinct social media landscape in China. This social media adaptation reflects an awareness of cultural differences in online behavior and ensures effective engagement with the target audience in each region.

Currency and Price. On the European website, La Prairie displays prices in local currencies, the same happens in the Chinese website, which presents prices in the local currency (RMB).

Ambassador. On both the European and the Chinese sections, no ambassadorial representation is visible.

Online Chatbot. The European sections do not incorporate an online chatbot, opting for a hotline as the primary means of customer communication. The same choice has been done for the Chinese section.

4.5 Rolex

In examining the Rolex website, variations between the European (France, Italy, Switzerland) and Chinese versions become evident, reflecting cultural considerations in line with Hofstede's cultural dimensions.

Domain. The European website utilizes the.com domain with language-specific subsections. In contrast, the Chinese website uses the.cn domain, demonstrating a recognition of regional distinctions.

Website Design. The website design maintains consistency across European countries. Similarly, the Chinese website shares the same design elements as its European counterparts, indicating a unified visual approach irrespective of cultural differences.

Language. The European website tailors its language to specific countries, featuring French, Italian, and German languages. Conversely, the Chinese website exclusively employs Chinese.

Rebranding. While the European website maintains the same European brand name, the Chinese website employs a translated Chinese brand name (劳力士– Rolex). This adaptation reflects an acknowledgment of the importance of linguistic differences.

Social Media. Consistency extends to the presentation of social media platforms on both websites, where nine platforms are always linked, indicating a shared global social media strategy tailored to the preferences of both European and Chinese consumers.

Currency and Price. The European website displays prices in local currencies such as Euro and CHF, allowing for easy comparison. On the other hand, the Chinese website exclusively presents prices in the local currency (RMB), catering to the preferences and familiarity of the Chinese market.

Ambassador. Both the European and Chinese websites feature the same ambassador. This consistency implies a shared global brand image, where roles and representations remain uniform across diverse regions.

Online Chatbot. Both versions, European and Chinese, lack an online chatbot. This absence suggests a similarity in customer engagement approach across markets.

5 Conclusion and Limitation

Overall, the analyzed luxury fashion brands appear to strike a balance between maintaining a consistent global brand identity and adapting to local cultural nuances. Their approach reflects their understanding of the cultural, consumer, and regulatory differences between Europe and China [3], as well as their commitment to effectively penetrate and succeed in these diverse markets. These strategies help them resonate with local consumers while upholding their prestigious brand image.

Hereafter, we can answer the two research questions.

RQ1: Do European luxury companies have different website versions for France, Italy, Switzerland and for China? Yes, the analysis revealed that all five studied Brands have different website versions for the European and the Chinese markets.

RQ2: If yes, which are the differences? In terms of content localization, all selected brands localize somehow their content to cater to Chinese audiences. This localization always includes translation in Mandarin, provision of prices in RMB and inclusion of Chinese-specific social-media. Additionally, some brands incorporated Chinese cultural elements, such as ambassadors, symbols, colors, and motifs, to resonate with the local audience and create a sense of belonging.

In conclusion, the characteristics and functionality of websites of European luxury fashion brands for the Chinese market not only demonstrate their commitment to localizing content but also their understanding of the cultural values that influence consumer behavior in this dynamic and growing market. The localization of European luxury fashion brand's websites involves more than just language translation and other basic adaptations; it encompasses a wide range of adjustments including accessibility, cultural metaphors, information architecture, and navigation, etc. [2].

European luxury fashion brands need to be sensitive to the local cultural background to understand local customer behavior, cultural values, traditions, and lifestyle, which are crucial to resonate with the intended publics [14, 34]. Localization should align with the brand's global positioning while addressing local market demands. At the same time, reflecting local culture is essential for luxury fashion brands, such as incorporating strong design, visual communication, customer service with local experience, in order to connect with local customers [39]. By adapting to local cultural contexts, luxury fashion brands can build a strong connection with their targeted customers and promote a deeper understanding of their products, allowing to extend their presence beyond their home markets and seek recognition in different contexts [32].

Websites not only impact consumer engagement but also influence brand loyalty and purchase intentions [24]. Through effective website design and content, luxury fashion brands can provide valuable customer experiences, enhance brand familiarity, and generate positive electronic word-of-mouth [5]. Personalized recommendations and culturally relevant content further contribute to customer satisfaction and long-term engagement [8, 10] to approach the local customers in the Chinese market.

The understanding of consumer perceptions and preferences in different cultural backgrounds is essential for European luxury fashion brands to position themselves successfully as luxurious. By integrating culturally sensitive website content, European luxury fashion brands can create a strong connection with local consumers and build trust and loyalty [7]. The ability to balance between standardization and localization is crucial for European luxury fashion brands to maintain exclusivity while adapting the local market demands in China [19].

This study has contributed to online communication and localization research, unveiling how European luxury brands are adapting their communication to reach the Chinese market, showing different approaches and exploring the inner tension between localization and brand consistency. Furthermore, this research provides also a value to the industry, presenting and discussing different approaches that might be considered by further brands.

This research presents some limitations that need to be mentioned here. First, all navigation activities have been performed from Switzerland and Spain: while it seems to be quite unlikely, we cannot ensure that navigations from China might have yielded to (partially) different results. Second, results cannot be generalized beyond the specific studied cases, however – as we believe – they might be somehow "exemplar" ones within their respective categories. Third, as highlighted above, it is just an exploratory analysis, which has offered a first insight in this field. An insight that has been able to demonstrate the relevance of the studied process and suggests further explorations.

In particular, further studies might include a structured analysis of Hofstede's dimensions, following up on the observations that have been possible in this first analysis. Moreover, it would be very important to understand the reasons why the respective companies are operating the way we have seen, framing their actual practices within their strategic goals or (tactical) constraints. That would help positioning the synchronous picture taken through this research as a frame within medium and long term processes, encompassing communication, marketing and business activities.

References

1. Aaker, J.L., Maheswaran, D.: The effect of cultural orientation on persuasion. J. Consum. Res. **24**(3), 315–328 (1997). https://doi.org/10.1086/209513
2. Al-Badi, A., Naqvi, S.: A conceptual framework for designing localized business websites. J. Manage. Market. Res. **2**, 1 (2009)
3. Bain & Co. China Luxury Market Study (2011). http://www.bain.com/publications/articles/2011-china-luxury-market-study.aspx
4. Balabanis, G., Reynolds, N.L.: Consumer attitudes towards multi-channel retailers' web sites: the role of involvement, brand attitude, internet knowledge and visit duration. J. Bus. Strat. **18**(2), 105–132 (2001). https://doi.org/10.54155/jbs.18.2.105-132
5. Cheung, C.M., Lee, M.K., Rabjohn, N.: The impact of electronic word-of-mouth: the adoption of online opinions in online customer communities. Internet Res. **18**(3), 229–247 (2008). https://doi.org/10.1108/10662240810883290

6. Creevey, D., Coughlan, J., O'Connor, C.: Social media and luxury: a systematic literature review. Int. J. Manag. Rev. **24**(1), 99–129 (2021). https://doi.org/10.1111/ijmr.12271

7. Cyr, D.: Modeling web site design across cultures: relationships to trust, satisfaction, and e-loyalty. J. Manag. Inf. Syst. **24**, 47–72 (2008). https://doi.org/10.2753/MIS0742-122224040

8. Dessart, L., Veloutsou, C., Morgan-Thomas, A.: Consumer engagement in online brand communities: a social media perspective. J. Prod. Brand Manage. **24**(1), 28–42 (2015). https://doi.org/10.1108/JPBM-06-2014-0635

9. United Nations ESCAP. E-commerce in Asia and the Pacific (2018). https://www.unescap.org/resources/embracing-e-commerce-revolution-asia-and-pacific

10. Ha, H.Y., Perks, H.: Effects of consumer perceptions of brand experience on the web: brand familiarity, satisfaction and brand trust. J. Consum. Behav. **4**(6), 438–452 (2005). https://doi.org/10.1002/cb.29

11. Hofstede, G.: Dimensionalizing cultures: the Hofstede model in context. Online Read. Psychol. Culture **2**, 1 (2011). https://doi.org/10.9707/2307-0919.1014

12. Hudders, L., Pandelaere, M., Vyncke, P.: Consumer meaning making: the meaning of luxury brands in a democratised luxury world. Int. J. Mark. Res. **55**(3), 391–412 (2013). https://doi.org/10.2501/IJMR-2013-036

13. Hudders, L.: Why the devil wears Prada: Consumers' purchase motives for luxuries. J. Brand Manag. **19**, 609–622 (2012). https://doi.org/10.1057/bm.2012.9

14. Husic, M., Muris, C.: Luxury consumption factors. J. Fash. Mark. Manag. **13**(2), 231–245 (2009). https://doi.org/10.1108/13612020910957734

15. Jung, J., Shen, D.: Brand equity of luxury fashion brands among Chinese and U.S. young female consumers. J. East-West Bus. **17**, 1, 48–69 (2013). https://doi.org/10.1080/10669868.2011.598756

16. Kalbaska, N., Sádaba, T., Cantoni, L.: Fashion communication: between tradition and digital transformation. Stud. Commun. Sci. **18**(2), 269–285 (2019). https://doi.org/10.24434/j.scoms.2018.02.005

17. Kapferer, J., Valette-Florence, P.: Is luxury sufficient to create brand desirability? A cross-cultural analysis of the relationship between luxury and dreams. Luxury Res. J. **1**(2), 110–127 (2016). https://doi.org/10.1504/LRJ.2016.078129

18. Landa, R.: Storybuilding and content creation in the digital age. In: Advertising by design: generating and designing creative ideas across media, pp. 110–127. Wiley, New Jersey (2016)

19. Liu, J., Cantoni, L.: European fashion companies and chinese social media influencers. In: Sabatini, N., Sádaba, T., Tosi, A., Neri, V., Cantoni, L. (eds.) Fashion communication in the digital age. FACTUM 2023. Springer proceedings in business and economics. Springer, Cham (2023). https://doi.org/10.1007/978-3-031-38541-4_12

20. Liu, S., Perry, P., Moore, C., Warnaby, G.: The standardization-localization dilemma of brand communications for luxury fashion retailers' internationalization into China. J. Bus. Res. **69**(1), 357–364 (2016). https://doi.org/10.1016/j.jbusres.2015.08.008

21. Mele, E., De Ascaniis, S., Cantoni, L.: Localization of three european national tourism offices' websites. an exploratory analysis. In: Inversini, A., Schegg, R. (eds.) Information and communication technologies in tourism 2016. Springer, Cham (2016). https://doi.org/10.1007/978-3-319-28231-2_22

22. Mele, E., Cantoni, L.: Localising Websites of National Tourism organisations: The Case of ETC Members. European Travel Commission, Brussels (2017). https://etc-corporate.org/reports/localising-websites-of-national-tourism-organisations/

23. Mele, E., Kerkhof, P., Cantoni, L.: Analyzing cultural tourism promotion on Instagram: a cross-cultural perspective. J. Travel Tour. Mark. **38**(3), 326–340 (2021). https://doi.org/10.1080/10548408.2021.1906382

24. Netherlands Consulate-General Shanghai. Guidebook China Cross-Border E-Commerce; Netherlands Consulate-General Shanghai. Shanghai, China (2017). https://www.rvo.nl/sites/default/files/2017/03/Cross-Border%20E-Commere%20Guidebook%20FINAL%20FINAL.PDF

25. Nguyen, H.Q., Nguyen, T.K., Duong, T.H.N., Nguyen, T.K.N., Le, T.P.: The influence of website brand equity, e-brand experience on e-loyalty: The mediating role of e-satisfaction. Manage. Sci. Let. **10**(1), 63–76 (2019). https://doi.org/10.5267/j.msl.2019.8.015

26. Noris, A., SanMiguel, P., Cantoni, L.: Localization and cultural adaptation on the web: an explorative study in the fashion domain. In: Nah, F.H., Siau, K. (eds.) HCI in business, government and organizations. HCII 2020. LNCS, vol. 12204. Springer, Cham (2020). https://doi.org/10.1007/978-3-030-50341-3_36

27. Pauwels, K., Erguncu, S., Yildirim, G.: Winning hearts, minds and sales: How marketing communication enters the purchase process in emerging and mature markets. Int. J. Res. Mark. **30**(1), 57–68 (2013). https://doi.org/10.1016/j.ijresmar.2012.09.006

28. Phan, M., Thomas, R., Heine, K.: Social media and luxury brand management: the case of Burberry. J. Glob. Fash. Market. **2**(4), 213–222 (2011). https://doi.org/10.1080/20932685.2011.10593099

29. Liu, S., Perry, P., Gadzinski, G.: The implications of digital marketing on WeChat for luxury fashion brands in China. J. Brand Manag. **26**, 395–409 (2019). https://doi.org/10.1057/s41262-018-0140-2

30. Singh, N., Baack, D.: Web site adaptation: a cross-cultural comparison of U.S. and mexican web sites. J. Comput.-Mediated Commun. **9**, 4 (2004). https://doi.org/10.1111/j.1083-6101.2004.tb00298.x

31. Singh, N., Pereira, A.: The culturally customized web site: customizing web sites for the global marketplace. Routledge, London (2005)

32. Singh, N., Kumar, V., Baack, D.: Adaptation of cultural content: evidence from B2C e-commerce firms. Eur. J. Mark. **39**(1/2), 71–86 (2005). https://doi.org/10.1108/03090560510572025

33. Singh, N., Zhao, H., Hu, X.: Cultural adaptation on the web: a study of american companies' domestic and chinese websites. J. Glob. Inf. Manag. **11**(3), 63–80 (2003). https://doi.org/10.4018/jgim.2003070104

34. Tigre Moura, F., Gnoth, J., Deans, K.R.: Localizing cultural values on tourism destination websites: the effects on users' willingness to travel and destination image. J. Travel Res. **54**(4), 528–542 (2015). https://doi.org/10.1177/0047287514522873

35. Tong, X., Hawley, J.M.: Creating brand equity in the Chinese clothing market: the effect of selected marketing activities on brand equity dimensions. J. Fash. Mark. Manag. **13**(4), 566–581 (2009). https://doi.org/10.1108/13612020910991411

36. Wigand, R.T.: Commerce. In: Cantoni, L., Danowski, J. (eds.) Communication and technology. Berlin, München, Boston, De Gruyter Mouton, pp. 57–78 (2015). https://doi.org/10.1515/9783110271355-021

37. Wong, N.Y., Ahuvia, A.C.: Personal taste and family face: luxury consumption in Confucian and western societies. Psychol. Mark. **15**(5), 423–441 (1998). https://doi.org/10.1002/(SICI)1520-6793(199808)15:5%3C423::AID-MAR2%3E3.0.CO;2-9

38. Xiao, L., Guo, F., Yu, F.M., Liu, S.N.: The effects of online shopping context cues on consumers' purchase intention for cross-border e-commerce sustainability. Sustainability **11**, 2777 (2019). https://doi.org/10.3390/su11102777

39. Zheng, X., Cheung, C.M., Lee, M.K., Liang, L.: Building brand loyalty through user engagement in online brand communities in social networking sites. Inf. Technol. People **28**(1), 90–106 (2015). https://doi.org/10.1108/ITP-08-2013-0144

Influence of Color on Information Perception Under AR Simulated Lunar Surface Environment

Yukun Lou[1(✉)], Ao Jiang[2], Kun Yu[3], and Haihai Zhou[2]

[1] Sichuan University, Chengdu, Sichuan, People's Republic of China
levilyk@gmail.com
[2] Nanjing University of Aeronautics and Astronautics, Nanjing, People's Republic of China
{aojiang,zhouhai}@nuaa.edu.cn
[3] China Ship Development and Design Center, Wuhan, People's Republic of China

Abstract. At present, China, the United States, Russia and Europe are continuously exploring the moon, especially the development and development of spacecraft, in order to look forward to the establishment of a lunar base and human activities on the lunar surface in the future [1]. As an adjunct technology in this process, augmented reality (AR) is a display mechanism that combines real and virtual world content on a single screen [2]. However, current AR technology is not sufficient to function efficiently in practical operations. One of the key issues is the legibility of the text displayed via AR head-mounted displays [3]. Therefore, it can be concluded that the readability of text on AR head-mounted display can be improved by selecting colors that are suitable for the environment, so as to promote the in-depth application of AR in the aerospace field. This paper aims to explore the influence of AR symbols and text colors on astronaut information capture efficiency under simulated lunar surface environment, and put forward suggestions for improvement of color selectio, so as to guide the AR interface color design of spacesuit helmets for extravehicular operations. A total of 10 men and 10 women participated in the experiment to simulate the lunar surface environment by wearing AR glasses. In the experiment, two kinds of judgment pictures of symbol and text were set, the recognition speed and accuracy of participants were collected, and the experimental data were processed with the help of data analysis software to get the corresponding data map. The results show that the experimental data of yellow and blue-green are more prominent. Green visibility is strong but the judgment accuracy rate is low. The white indicators are more balanced but not prominent. Red, blue, magenta indicators are relatively poor. The preliminary conclusion of the experimental results is that the colors with better recognition effect on the lunar surface are cyan and yellow. All these colors can be well identified and understood, and can be used as the color to display key information. Other colors can be used for auxiliary information display as needed. Other colors can be used for auxiliary information displays as required. This paper provides the basis for the design and use of AR color of extravehicular space suit in the manned space flight project.

Keywords: Augmented Reality · Head-Mounted Display · Aerospace · Moon · Color Perception · Legibility

© The Author(s), under exclusive license to Springer Nature Switzerland AG 2024
A. Marcus et al. (Eds.): HCII 2024, LNCS 14712, pp. 121–131, 2024.
https://doi.org/10.1007/978-3-031-61351-7_8

1 Introduction

During the past 20 or so years, AR technologies have slowly made their way into several application domains. Concepts and applications of augmented reality have begun to gain new momentum in the public eye; through location-aware handheld augmented reality applications [4], increasing augmented reality demonstration YouTube, TV advertising and live sports events, continue to utilize augmented reality concepts, more sophisticated video augmented reality systems into the mainstream automotive industry (e. g., covering graphics to rear and side cameras), and Google announced the Glass Project (a head-mounted display with voice-enabled smartphones, GPS and Internet capabilities).

In the aerospace, AR has been used for decades to enhance navigation in civilian and military aviation for civilian and unmanned vehicles [5]. Engineers and technicians also use AR systems to improve the workflow and the environment in designing, maintaining, and assembling aerospace vehicles [6]. A literature survey conducted by Dini and Mura [7] found that 29% of articles related to Lifetime Engineering Services (TES) received aerospace training and operations. A TES is the engineering support provided for a high-value product or system throughout its lifetime.

The earliest use of AR in aviation history is the Oigee Reflector Sight developed by German optics manufacturer Optische Anstalt Oigee in 1918 for use in the Imperial German Army Air Service's Albatross D.III and Fokker DDS1 fighter aircraft [8]. In 1958, the first HUD capable of dynamic displays of flight data was introduced, then used in the early 1960s on the Royal Navy Blackburn Buccaneer, a British carrier-borne combat aircraft [5]. In 1969, Thomas A. Furness III designed the helmet-mounted display (HMD) as part of the US Air Force's Super Cockpit program [9, 10]. These inventions inspired the Boeing company to research and create an AR tool to enhance assembly operations by helping technicians and engineers in wiring harnesses in the fuselage [11]. Caudell and Mizell coined the term "augmented reality" and presented its potential in aerospace engineering for the first time at the Twenty-Fifth Hawaii International Conference in a proceeding titled "Augmented reality: An application of headsup display technology to manual manufacturing processes." [12].

Today, rapid advances in technology and tracking mechanisms make AR technology more versatile, able to support tasks in manufacturing, assembly, maintenance, training, simulation, payload missions, data analytics, flying entertainment and communications (IFEC), crew support, customer support, marketing and sales. As shown in Fig. 1, these fields can be divided into two main categories: engineering, navigation, training and simulation, and emerging services [13].

In the aerospace industry, the use of AR can effectively improve the efficiency and quality of operators' task completion, and the following cases can be used as effective evidence. In the early 2010s, Boeing conducted a study in collaboration with Iowa State University to compare the workload of workers performing assembly tasks using model-based instructions (MBI). The study found that AR MBI minimizes error compared to traditional devices [14]. In 2010, the Airbus military conducted a similar comparative study called the Moon Project (an intelligent author for augmented reality). This project found a 90% reduction in overall preparation and maintenance time for AR-based instructions compared to conventional approaches [15]. TAE Aerospace has developed

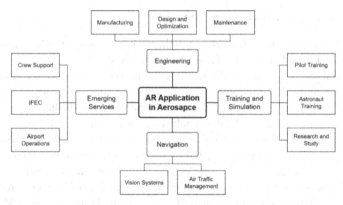

Fig. 1. Areas of AR application in aerospace organized by scope.

an auxiliary reality (AsR) technology called FountX AsR, which uses AR during conference calls to allow technicians to communicate with engineers when inspecting or repairing aircraft engines. Cameras mounted on FountX AsR provide live video for engineers, who provide guidance and feedback to technicians through interaction with their computer or tablet devices, eliminating the need for engineers to travel to the work site, thus reducing the time required for maintenance [16]. Within the space industry, many companies have designed and tested tools to support engineering and space operations using AR. In 2015 to 2016, the European Space Agency (ESA) completed a detailed study on augmented reality for product (or quality) assurance to evaluate AR usage in the assurance of space missions [17]. The study found that AR is a significant contributor for reducing error and interoperability, while increasing compliance and customization cost. The wearable augmented reality (WEAR) system was an early space project that used AR to assist astronauts in performing various tasks on the International Space Station [18, 19].

Based on the function of AR remote command and auxiliary operation, we can expect the further application of AR in the field of manned space flight. In this paper, we study and quantify the effect of AR color on information reception in a simulated lunar surface environment, given a representative set of lunar surface background images. This paper aims to provide the basis for the design and use of AR color of the extravehicular space suit in manned space flight program through the experiment of color visual effect test.

2 Method

2.1 Participants

A total of 20 participants, including 10 males and 10 females, were 18 to 23 years old college students who had never conducted similar experiments before. Their corrected visual acuity was above 1.0, and they had no color blindness.

2.2 Experimental Environment & Materials

Experiments were performed in quiet, low-light closed rooms where illumination values were guaranteed to be below 300 lx and volume below 40dB.

Experiments were written by the E-prime 2.0 program, experimental images were performed automatically, randomly, and experimental data recorded. The program obtained the raw data, summarized the experimental data with the Excel table, and finally analyzed the data using the data analysis software IBM SPSS. The experimental equipment included Lenovo Legion Y7000P 2020 laptops and Rokid Air AR glasses. The resolution ratio of the laptop is 1920 * 1080, so as to ensure that the color gamut of the LCD screen is suitable and color deviation of screen is under control. The visual effect of AR glasses is equivalent to the human eye viewing a 120-inch screen from a distance of 3–4 m, with a resolution of 1080P and an angular resolution of 55 PPD.

2.3 Experimental Variables

Based on the CIE1976 chromaticity space, the experiment selected seven objected colors that widely used in AR. CIEl976, stimulated by International Commission on illumination, is a well distributed chromaticity space that closer to the visual perception results of eyes, as shown in Fig. 2 and Table 1.

In addition, in view of the color deviation that is difficult to avoid, we believe that even if there is a difference between the rgb value of the display color and the standard value, it is difficult to detect for the human eye and will not change the identification result. So the error does not affect the experimental data, nor does it affect the experimental results [20–24].

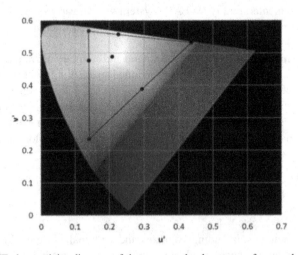

Fig. 2. 1976 CIE chromaticity diagram of the measured color space of a sample full-color LCD [4].

The triangle connects the three primaries (red, green, and blue). The middle points between the main colors are yellow, cyan, and magenta. Dots within the triangle represent white.

Table 1. Primary values for the selected colors.

	Red	Green	Blue	Yellow	Cyan	Magenta	White
R	255	0	0	255	0	255	255
G	0	255	0	255	255	0	255
B	0	0	255	0	255	255	255
L	54.29	87.82	29.57	97.61	90.67	60.17	100.00
a	80.81	−79.29	68.30	−15.75	−50.67	93.55	0.00
b	69.89	80.99	−112.03	93.39	−14.96	−60.50	0.00

We chose four representative images of the human eye perspective on the lunar surface as the background to place the test content on the background, as Fig. 3 has shown.

(a)   (b)

(a)   (b)

Fig. 3. Four representative images used as background.

2.4 Tasks Setting

In the experiment, there were 56 experimental samples, namely 4 scene pictures multiplied by 7 color symbol information as one group, and two groups of experiments [25–27].

First, the participants underwent a symbol-recognition test. Symbols of the seven colors are presented in turn on four background plots, with four images of each color grouped for a total of seven groups. Participants need to identify the meaning of the symbol and compare it with the text given below the symbol to determine whether the meaning of the symbol is consistent with the content of the text, as shown in Fig. 4:

Fig. 4. Symbol-recognition test image sample.

After the symbol-recognition test, participants continued with the text-recognition test. The background plots and testing steps used in the text-recognition test remained unchanged, as shown in Fig. 5. Participants needed to identify a string of letters given on the background and judge whether it was scrambled or a simple common English word. The purpose of this test is to prevent participants from having poor symbol recognition ability. The symbol is replaced with the text, and the key element for judgement is changed from the pattern language to the combination form of the text, which makes the whole experiment more robust.

After both tests were completed, participants completed a subjective evaluation questionnaire. The questionnaire includes two questions, namely, scoring the visibility of the seven colors and the understandability of the text respectively. The score range is from 0 to 10 points, 0 is the worst, 10 is the best, and only integer points. The details are as shown in Table 2.

2.5 Procedure

Before the start of the experiment, the participants wore the experimental equipment and adjusted the equipment parameters to ensure comfort. After the equipment debugging, participants need to take a 5-min closed eye rest to prevent eye fatigue from affecting the

Fig. 5. Text-recognition test image sample.

Table 2. Subjective evaluation table.

0 to 10	Red	Green	Blue	Yellow	Cyan	Magenta	White
Visibility							
Understandability							

Visibility: I was able to distinguish the symbols and texts from the background. (0: not at all, 10: very much so).

Understandability: I was able to quickly recognize and understand the symbols and texts. (0: not at all, 10: very much so).

test results. Then start the experiment with standing posture, touch the keyboard X key with the left hand and the keyboard O key with the right hand. First get familiar with the test rules through the tutorial part, and then officially make the judgment according to the task requirements. For example, if the symbol has the same meaning as the text, press the O key on the laptop, and press the X key instead. Similarly, in the text recognition test, the O key is pressed if it is a word, and the X key if it is scrambled. After each completion of one group test in the same color, participants took a short 3-min, closed-eye break. After both tests were completed, participants filled in the subjective evaluation form and the experiment ended [28–30].

3   Result

Through the collation and analysis of the experimental data, the subjective evaluation of different colors, reaction time and accuracy in four backgrounds were obtained (Figs. 6, 7, 8 and 9). As can be seen from the chart, red, blue and magenta do not perform well in the indicators. Therefore, it is not recommended to choose these three colors as the AR interface color. All aspects of the white indicators are moderate performance. Although green shows easily recognizable features, the recognition accuracy is low, so it is recommended as the minor choice instead of a primary one. In addition, each index of yellow and blue-green is excellent, so they are ideal color choices.

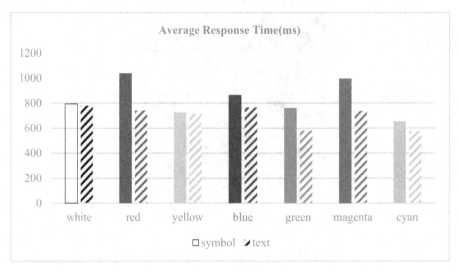

Fig. 6. Average response time(ms).

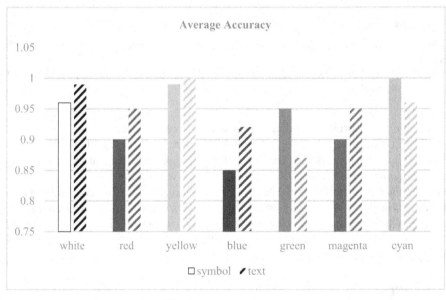

Fig. 7. Average accuracy.

This paper mainly studies the influence of color on information perception under the AR simulated lunar surface environment, which has certain guiding significance for the color design of AR interface of extravehicular space suit. The experiment was conducted in the laboratory and was difficult to restore accurately due to the complexity of the actual environment on the lunar surface. This experiment has some limitations, and further experiments are necessary to judge its reliability.

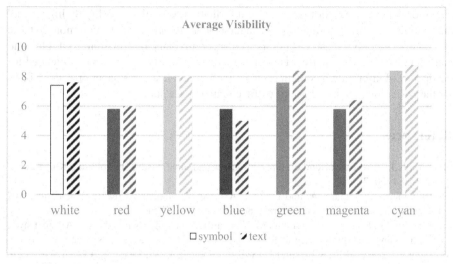

Fig. 8. Average visibility.

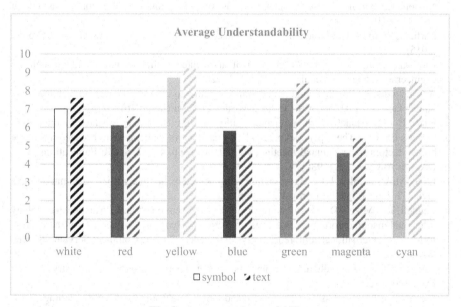

Fig. 9. Average understandability.

4   Conclusion

Under the condition of AR simulating the lunar surface environment, the choice of color will affect the efficiency of AR information reception. Choosing the appropriate color can improve the speed and accuracy of recognition. On the surface, yellow and blue green have excellent and stable visual effects, which can be used as colors to display key information. The error rate of green information recognition is slightly higher, and the visibility of white information and understandability are relatively common, so these two colors can only be used as colors to display auxiliary information. Red, blue and magenta visual reception effect is poor, not easy to identify, it is not recommended for the display of information content such as symbols and text. This paper provides a basis for the AR color design and use of extravehicular space suit.

References

1. Kim, K.J.: A research trend on lunar resources and lunar base. J. Petrol. Soc. Korea **26**(4), 373–384 (2017)
2. Billinghurst, M., Clark, A. and Lee, G.: A survey of augmented reality. Foundations and Trends® in Human. Comput. Interact. **8**(2–3), 73–272 (2015)
3. Gattullo, M., Uva, A.E., Fiorentino, M., Gabbard, J.L.: Legibility in industrial AR: text style, color coding, and illuminance. IEEE Comput. Graphics Appl. **35**(2), 52–61 (2015)
4. Jiang, A., Foing, B.H., Schlacht, I.L., Yao, X., Cheung, V., Rhodes, P.A.: Colour schemes to reduce stress response in the hygiene area of a space station: a Delphi study. Appl. Ergon. **98**, 103573 (2022)
5. Nicholl, R.: Airline head-up display systems: human factors considerations. Available at SSRN 2384101 (2014)
6. Barfield, W. (ed.): Fundamentals of wearable computers and augmented reality. CRC press (2015)
7. Dini, G., Dalle Mura, M.: Application of augmented reality techniques in through-life engineering services. Procedia Cirp **38**, 14–23 (2015)
8. Aukstakalnis, S.: Practical augmented reality: a guide to the technologies, applications, and human factors for AR and VR. Addison-Wesley Professional (2016)
9. Furht, B. (ed.): Handbook of augmented reality. Springer Science & Business Media (2011)
10. Furness III, T.A.: The super cockpit and its human factors challenges. In: Proceedings of the human factors society annual meeting, vol. 30, no. 1, pp. 48–52. SAGE Publications, Sage CA, Los Angeles, CA (1986)
11. Frigo, M.A., da Silva, E.C., Barbosa, G.F.: Augmented reality in aerospace manufacturing: a review. J. Indust. Intell. Inform. **4**(2) (2016)
12. Caudell, T.P., Mizell, D.W.: Augmented reality: an application of head-up display technology to manual manufacturing processes, research & technology. In: Proceedings of the twenty-fifth Hawaii international conference on system sciences. Boeing Computer Services. Seattle, WA, USA(1992)
13. Safi, M., Chung, J., Pradhan, P.: Review of augmented reality in aerospace industry. Aircraft Eng. Aerospace Technol. (2019)
14. Richardson, T., et al.: Fusing self-reported and sensor data from mixed-reality training (2014)
15. Serván, J., Mas, F., Menéndez, J.L., Ríos, J.: Using augmented reality in AIRBUS A400M shop floor assembly work instructions. In: Aip conference proceedings, vol. 1431, no. 1, pp. 633–640. American Institute of Physics (2012)
16. Jiang, A., et al.: The effect of colour environments on visual tracking and visual strain during short-term simulation of three gravity states. Appl. Ergon. **110**, 103994 (2023)
17. Youtube.com (2016). AREA Webinar: Augmented Reality in the Aerospace Industry. https://www.youtube.com/watch?v=u8rPFMGzOrw. Accessed 13 Oct 2022
18. Di Capua, M.: Augmented reality for space applications. University of Maryland, College Park (2008)

19. Di Capua, M., Akin, D., Brannan, J.: MX-3: design and technology development of an advanced all-soft high mobility planetary space suit. In: 40th international conference on environmental systems, p. 6176 (2010)

20. Thomas, B., Close, B., Donoghue, J., Squires, J., Bondi, P.D., Piekarski, W.: First person indoor/outdoor augmented reality application: ARQuake. Pers. Ubiquit. Comput. 6(1), 75–86 (2002)

21. Yu, K., Jiang, A., Wang, J., Zeng, X., Yao, X., Chen, Y.: Construction of crew visual behaviour mechanism in ship centralized control cabin. In: Stanton, N. (eds.) Advances in human aspects of transportation. AHFE 2021. LNNS, vol. 270. Springer, Cham (2021). https://doi.org/10.1007/978-3-030-80012-3_58

22. Jiang, A., et al.: Space habitat astronautics: multicolour lighting psychology in a 7-day simulated habitat. Space: Science & Technology (2022)

23. Jiang, A., et al.: Short-term virtual reality simulation of the effects of space station colour and microgravity and lunar gravity on cognitive task performance and emotion. Build. Environ. 227, 109789 (2023)

24. Gabbard, J.L., Swan, J.E., Zarger, A.: Color blending in outdoor optical see-through AR: the effect of real-world backgrounds on user interface color. In: 2013 IEEE virtual reality (VR), pp. 157–158. IEEE (2013)

25. Merenda, C., Smith, M., Gabbard, J., Burnett, G., Large, D.: March. Effects of real-world backgrounds on user interface color naming and matching in automotive AR HUDs. In: 2016 IEEE VR 2016 workshop on perceptual and cognitive issues in AR (PERCAR), pp. 1–6. IEEE (2016)

26. Jiang, A., Yao, X., Westland, S., Hemingray, C., Foing, B., Lin, J.: The effect of correlated colour temperature on physiological, emotional and subjective satisfaction in the hygiene area of a space station. Int. J. Environ. Res. Public Health 19(15), 9090 (2022)

27. Jiang, A.O.: Effects of colour environment on spaceflight cognitive abilities during short-term simulations of three gravity states (Doctoral dissertation, University of Leeds) (2022)

28. Jiang, A., Zhu, Y., Yao, X., Foing, B.H., Westland, S., Hemingray, C.: The effect of three body positions on colour preference: an exploration of microgravity and lunar gravity simulations. Acta Astronaut. 204, 1–10 (2023)

29. Huang, Z., Wang, S., Jiang, A., Hemingray, C., Westland, S.: Gender preference differences in color temperature associated with LED light sources in the autopilot cabin. In: Krömker, H. (eds.) HCI in mobility, transport, and automotive systems. HCII 2022. LNCS, vol. 13335. Springer, Cham (2022). https://doi.org/10.1007/978-3-031-04987-3_10

30. Jiang, A., Yao, X., Hemingray, C., Westland, S.: Young people's colour preference and the arousal level of small apartments. Color. Res. Appl. 47(3), 783–795 (2022)

From Modeling to Fractals: Research on Prototyping of Augmented Fractal Tangram Blocks Set

Qi Tan[✉]

Central Academy of Fine Arts, No. 8 Hua Jia Di Nan Jie, Beijing 100102, China
tanqi@cafa.edu.cn

Abstract. To further the previous research about Tangram and to discover the possibilities of Tangram Blocks, a new versatile model developed from Tangram, this paper will explore and develop Tangram Blocks into an augmented puzzle game based on the methodology of fractals. Fractals could be considered as a reversed process of modeling, which is another playable process combining of science and art. This paper starts from using fractal thinking to analysis Tangram shapes. Then we can composite Tangram patterns using fractal formulas, such as the Pythagoras tree. If 2D Tangram shapes can fit in the concept of fractals well, we will use Tangram Blocks to try to build a fractal Tangram Blocks set. After finishing the prototyping of material objects, we can get a set of extended Tangram Blocks with enough pieces in different scales that can form some typical fractal patterns in three dimensions. To examining the possible and novel variations and extensions of Tangram Blocks in fractals, then we will model it in the virtual world. There are different methods to generative fractal transitions into animation, we will compare the visual effect of each fractal animation and choose the most suitable one to link to the play of Tangram Blocks. Music will also be generated by the fractal method and add on to the animations. How to combine the physical fractal Tangram Blocks set with the virtual fractal audiovisuals is also will be discussed in this paper. From the technical and aesthetic aspects of argument reality, the scan of 3D object, attached sensors on the blocks and the use of Apple Vision Pro glasses or other AR glasses will be experimenting and evaluating. Modeling and fractals may be the two sides of the real world's operation; the augmented Tangram Blocks could open a window to witness this scene.

Keywords: Fractal · Mixed Reality · Augmented Tangram Blocks · Fractal Thinking

1 Introduction: Modeling and Fractals, The Complementary Representation of Real World

In my previous paper "Playable Modeling: Interactive Learning Process in Science and Art" for SCII 2023, I tried to analysis and explain modeling as a gamified learning process through Tangram, an ancient Chinese puzzle. Therefore, I have adapted and developed

Tangram to Tangram Blocks, a prototyped new versatile model can be play in 3D. To further the previous research and to discover the possibilities of Tangram Blocks, this paper will continue to explore and develop Tangram Blocks into an augmented puzzle game based on the methodology of fractals.

Fractal could be considered as a reversed process of modeling. If modeling is to simplify and idealize the complex real world, fractal is to geometrically repeat and vary simple shapes and elements to represent and reproduce the complexity of real world. From nature to geometry, and then in computer-based modeling, fractal shows the tremendous magic and potentiality in science research and art creation, it is also one of the core thinking and internal logic to form Artificial Intelligence. In this paper, Tangram is deemed to be a set of fractal patterns, and it can be differentiated following fractal process. Using fractal thinking, the physical puzzle game can be extended to the virtual computer world and be developed in various scales and infinite changes. Therefore, from 2D to 3D, from real to virtual, Tangram Blocks as the variant of Tangram will be augmented to learn about more complex world.

2   Fractal, Formatting the World from Simple to Complex

In 1975, the mathematician Benoît Mandelbrot coined the term "fractal" from the Latin word *frāctus*, to indicate the geometric patterns in the nature and their manners of formation as "broken" or "fractured" [1]. In the nature world, from cells to diamonds, from branches of trees to neurons in our body, many materials in the world evolve from monomer to complexes through the process of fractal. Fractal not only exhibits as similar patterns duplicate at increasingly smaller scales, which is called self-similarity; but also describes the growing logic and processes in time about how a complex thing be formed by a simpler or previous version of itself, which is called recursion.

2.1   What is a Fractal and How It Works?

Although fractal is easy to be understood by morphologic observation, but it was hard to be formally defined by mathematics. "A fractal is a rough or fragmented geometric shape that can be split into parts, each of which is (at least approximately) a reduced-size copy of the whole." [2] This was a simplified definition about fractal in mathematics by Mandelbrot in 1983. In general, a fractal has some common characteristics listed as below:

Self-Similarity. Most of fractals have some similarities in shapes or structures, each type of fractals exploits some parts of an original theme and copying it by isomorphism or by information-preserving transformation. In mathematics theory, regular fractals, such as the Mandelbrot set, the Sierpiński triangle and the Koch snowflake has strict self-similarity; but in the nature, irregular fractals, such as the coastlines, the fire flames, and the crystals, only have self-similarity within a certain scale-invariant region.

Fractal Dimension. A fractal pattern is used to be quantified by its roughness and complexity with an index, which is called fractal dimension. Normally, fractal dimension strictly exceeds the topological dimension, it characterizes details of complicated geometric forms. Topological dimension is an integer value to describe an ordinary geometric shape, 0 for a geometrical set describing a point; 1 for a set describing a line; 2 for a set describing a surface; 3 for a set describing a volume. But the fractal index can take non-integer values to indicate a more detailed geometric shape in between two ordinary geometric shapes. If a curve, its fractal dimension is 1.10 that is close to 1, it appears more like a line; but if its fractal dimension is 1.90 near to 2, it has more convolutedly small curves winding through space that looks more like to a surface.

Chaos Game. To create a fractal, there is a method to "pick a point at random inside a regular n-gon, then draw the next point a fraction r of the distance between it and a polygon vertex picked at random" [3], after iteratively creating a sequence of points for a large number of times, a fractal may be formed. Chaos game is the most common algorithm to compute IFS (Iterated function system) fractals that are often self-similar.

2.2 Fractal Art

The interesting of fractal research firstly comes from its complicated and changeable beauty in the nature. Then, people tried to use algorithm to simulate and visualize the fractal patterns discovered in the nature or by mathematics deduction. Nowadays, fractal art normally refers to a kind of algorithmic art by computer calculating, the results can be still images, animations, and media.

2.3 Fractal Thinking in Chinese Culture, Art, and Design

Fractal thinking is naturedly planted in Chinese culture, we would like to think everything with the whole and parts relation, for example, Eight Tri-grams from Yi Jing.

Chinese Characters in Fractal Structure. Because Chinese character is ideogram, the structures in-between some related characters are self-similar. It looks like a simple shape character copies itself 2 or 3 times in different positions to form a new character.

Manual of the Mustard Seed Garden. This is a guidebook for learning traditional Chinese ink painting dated back in the Qing Dynasty. In order to teach how to draw and compose trees, flowers, and stones, the book shows the iterated process from one element to many complexes (see Fig. 1).

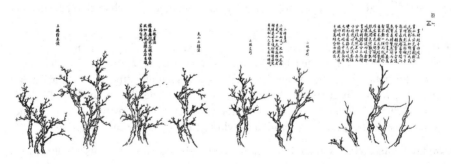

Fig. 1. The method of drawing trees in the book.

Chinese Papercut. Using a paper to fold several times, then cutting it to create continuous patterns, it is the main method of traditional Chinese papercut art.

3   Thinking Tangram in a Fractal Way

Tangram as a puzzle game, it can be split out and integrate together. All 7 tans inside the Tangram are regular geometric shapes, such isoscele right triangle, square and parallelogram; through diversely compositing and combining, it can form more than 1600 shapes, some are regular geometric shapes, some are not. Thus, Tangram may can be considered as a simple, pervious version to format a fractal, if displaying Tangrams in different scales and manners, it should be nowhere differentiable. In case Tangram cannot be strictly fitted in theorical mathematic fractals, it also can be seen as a form of fractal art. In this section, Tangram Blocks, hereafter this text will be abbreviated as TB, the developed model of Tangram, will be used to explore the fractal possibilities of Tangram, in order to continue deriving a new version of TB in a fractal way.

3.1   Tangram: The Simple Model of a Fractal

There are many fractals iterated from triangles and squares, for example, the famous Sierpiński triangle and T-square. Looking Tangram as an entirety, it is a square; looking Tangram as a set of 7 portions, it can be seen as 16 isoscele right triangles in 5 permutations and combinations. Thus, using Tangram to construct the fractals will depend on the transformations in between squares and triangles *ad infinitum*. In order to keep the derive fractals be more attributed to the original Tangram shapes, we only use isoscele right triangle to differentiate Tangram square. To find out how to develop the Tangram into fractals, we start from researching Tangram itself.

Self-Similarity Inside Tangram. If we regard a Tangram as a fractal, 7 tans are split out from a square into self-similar isoscele right triangles and their combinations. The 2 pieces of small size isoscele right triangles can form the 1 pieces of middle size triangle and 2 pieces of large size triangles can be seen as the double size of the middle one. They are duplications in the arithmetic scales, and then the square and the parallelogram can be seen as combinations of 2 small size triangles in different symmetric ways. Therefore, the smallest triangle in the Tangram also is the smallest scale of this fractal stage.

Fractal Tangram Series. Because the smallest triangle can piece together to form the rest of shapes in the Tangram, an isoscele right triangle can be used as the basic simple shape to be duplicated, and then repeating this process to form a fractal. There are 3 equidifferent scales of isoscele right triangle in one Tangram, if using one of the large size triangles to be the middle size triangle of the next Tangram, it will link these equidifferent size Tangrams together as a continuous fractal pattern. This fractal pattern can repeat itself in smaller or larger scales that could be infinite.

To Form Pythagoras Tree Fractal. Based on Pythagorean theorem, the Dutch mathematics teacher Albert E. Bosman invented a plane fractal iterated from squares in 1942. Each triple of touching squares encloses a right triangle; this configuration of Pythagorean theorem can be demonstrated by 2 sets of Tangram. The integral Tangram square displays in the bottom, upon this square are 2 squares composed separately by 2 large triangle tans and the other 5 tans. Regarding to the in-and-out complementary principle, if the area of the integral Tangram below is 1, the added area of 2 split squares upon is also 1. The area of the enclosed right triangle of these 3 squares equals to the area of the large triangle tan as $\frac{1}{4}$ of the Tangram area. Upon the 2 small squares will be constructed 4 scaled down integral Tangrams, each smaller Tangrams is $\frac{1}{4}$ area of the initial Tangram. Then the tans of the 4 small Tangrams will split out to form 8 smaller squares following previous procedure. The recursive process can be continued infinite, but some of the squares will begin to overlap after the order 5 iteration. Because the puzzle pieces can't be too small to handle, there are only order 1–4 iteration composed by tan pieces, the rest of iterations will be generated as computer graphics.

3.2 To Develop Fractal Version of TB

TB is a versatile model developed from Tangram to allow the 2D puzzle game building in 3D. If we would like to continue exploring the fractal possibilities of Tangram, TB can be used to form a new fractal version. Regarding to the features of a fractal, such self-similarity and recursion, the original 7 pieces of TB should be increased to ensure there are enough pieces to construct at the least first 3 orders of a fractal iteration. Then, the incremental pieces should be cohered with the original 7 pieces to become a new integral pattern.

The Design of Fractal TB Set. The original design of the TB is to cut grooves in the middle of sides or hypotenuse of 7 tans. The decision of position and size of the grooves are mainly to balance weight and to enlarge interlock area, but it doesn't accord with fractal regularity. In order to develop TB to a fractal set, we need to redesign the cutting of grooves. As discussed in pervious section, a Tangram as a fractal is a square to be split out to 5 isoscele right triangles, 1 square and 1 parallelogram, which is the 7 tans; then these 7 tans can be split out again to 16 pieces of the smallest isoscele right triangle in the set. So, the smallest isoscele right triangle is the basic self-similar shape in the Tangram, a groove cutting in the middle of the hypotenuse of the triangle will turn it into a basic shape of fractal TB set. The cut groove reaches the barycentre of the triangle, its length is $\frac{1}{4}$ of side length and its width is as the thickness of the piece.

Piecing together the grooved basic triangles, it can form the middle size triangle with 2 basic grooves on each right-angle side; the square with 1 groove in the middle of it, the length of the groove is double size of the basic groove; the parallelogram with 2 basic grooves on each long side. Then, the middle size triangle will continue to take shape of the large size triangle with 2 grooves on the hypotenuse and 1 same size groove of the square groove in the middle. Therefore, the smallest fractal TB square is formatted (see Fig. 2).

At this stage, using the reversed fractal process, we are going to structure the whole fractal TB set. The middle size triangle of the smallest TB square will be the small size triangle of the next larger TB square, then using it to set up the rest of shapes in the TB square. Actually, the large triangle in the small TB square is the middle triangle in the larger one, thus, it will be used as the chained block of the two TB squares. Repeating in the manner for another 2 times, there is a chain of 4 TB squares in arithmetic scales

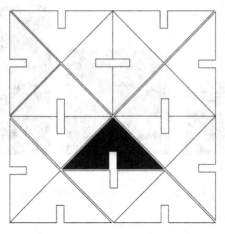

16 pieces of the small isoscele right triangle to from the Tangram

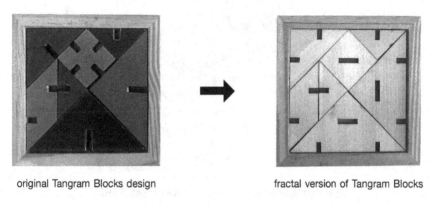

original Tangram Blocks design   fractal version of Tangram Blocks

Fig. 2. The changes of design in the Tangram Blocks.

composited. Considering the size and amount of TB blocks, the prototype of fractal TB set (hereinafter referred to as FTBS) is limited in 25 pieces and 3 steps of fractal iteration (see Fig. 3).

The outline of entirety FTBS as the 3rd generation of fractal iteration, is like a branch of tree. Drawing a straight line to link the center point of each TB squares, it will be a spiral after the 10th generation of fractal iteration. Using this new designed FTBS, we can further to explore the gameplay of it.

The Gameplay of FTBS. FTBS has 25 pieces in total, it has more pieces to construct patterns and solid figures than TB. Because TB is an evolutive Tangram, it has all the gameplays inherited from Tangram, and FTBS is the iteration of TB, so, it has both gameplays of Tangram and TB in 2D and 3D. FTBS has added fractal possibilities to TB, for example:

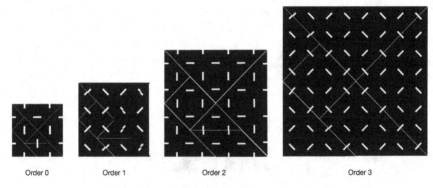

3 steps of fractal Tangram Blocks iteration

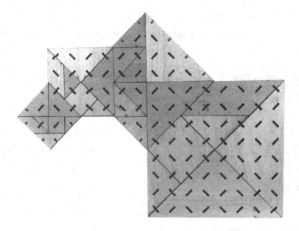

the puzzle of Fractal Tangram Blocks Set (FTBS)

Fig. 3. The prototype of fractal TB set.

2D Fractal Patterns. FTBS's whole pattern is similar with one branch of the Pythagoras Tree fractal. Thus, using 2 sets of FTBS can compose the whole Pythagoras Tree following the method demonstrated in Sect. 2.1. Because each TB inside FTBS also can be split out, some blocks can take out to piece together as other shapes and don't affect to recognize the square shape, variants of the tree fractal can be constructed. If every piece of 2 sets of FTBS will be placed, the whole pattern is like a flying bird with big beak (see Fig. 4). T-square is also a plane fractal can be composed and varied by multiple sets of FTBS. The whole set of TB can transfer from a square to an isoscele right triangle, thus, with the self-similar triangles inside TB, multiple sets of FTBS also can construct the Sierpiński triangle.

3D Fractal Solids. The 25 pieces of FTBS can piece and insert together to be some 3D fractal structures. The grooves on the side of shapes can interlock each other and the holes in the middle of shapes can strengthen the 3D structures. If constructing all pieces of FTBS upon each other vertically, it will form a semi-symmetry 3D fractal tree. The

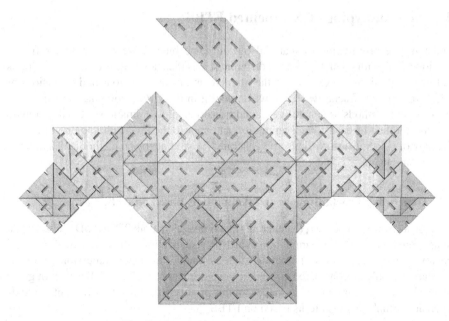

Fig. 4. The whole pattern of 2 sets of FTBS.

whole solid shape also looks like a dance woman with her arms opening (see Fig. 5). As 3D fractals are normally very complex, they need many iterations to become a significant fractal modeling. The FTBS only can show 3 generations of iteration, if we would like it to be more fractal, the best choice is to generate more iterations in CG.

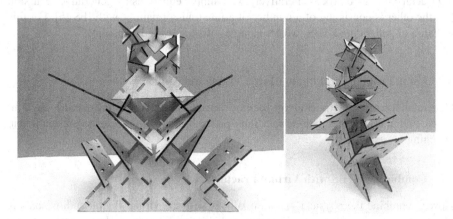

Fig. 5. The 3D fractal figure composed by FTBS.

4 The Prototyping of Augmented FTBS

Finishing the prototyping of material puzzle game blocks, we have gotten a fractal version of TB with enough pieces in different scales that can form some fractal patterns in three dimensions. To examining the possible and novel variations and extensions of FTBS in different fractal ways, we will model it in the virtual computer world. There are different methods to generative fractal transitions into animation, we will compare the visual effect of each fractal animation and choose the most suitable one to link to the play of FTBS. Music will also be generated by similar fractal method and add on to the animations.

4.1 Generating Fractal Images and Animations Based on FTBS

A lot of software can be used to generate fractal images in both 2D and 3D, these fractal images are for either model simulation or artistic visualization, which have mathematical beauty. The characteristics of fractals, such as fractal dimension, recursion, and self-similarity, should be considered during the generating process. As FTBS is a set of game blocks having regular geometric shapes, in this prototype, we will try different methods to create virtual fractal patterns based on FTBS.

Repeatedly Drawing FTBS in Different Scales. During the prototyping of FTBS, the feasibility of related fractal method is already proved. So, we can simply use vector graphics software, for example, Adobe Illustrator, to create patterns following the same method. Gradient ramp and transparency will be applied on the shapes to make the visual effect more distinct.

Using Fractal-generating Software. There are two major methods used in generating 2D fractals: one is to process iteratively with simple equations by generative recursion [4]; the other is consisting of a number of affine transformations with IFS [5]. For this research of generating FTBS, we are using a software, called "Chaotica".

4.2 Using Fractal Thinking to Match Visual and Audio

Generated fractals sometimes create for music visualization. According to music rhythm, speed, and tunes, the animations vary their patterns, colors and scales to present music changing.

4.3 Combining FTBS with Virtual Fractals

How to combine the physical Tangram Blocks with the virtual fractal audiovisuals is also the important issue will be discussed in this paper. From the technical and aesthetic aspects of argument reality, the scan of 3D object, attached sensors on the blocks and the use of Apple Vision Pro glasses will be experimenting and evaluating.

5   Conclusion: The Augmented FTBS, a Novelty Tryout in Collaboration with Modeling and Fractals

Mentioned by McLuhan in his famous book "The Medium is the Massage" that "When two seemingly disparate elements are imaginatively poised, put in apposition in new and unique ways, startling discoveries often result." [6] Modeling and fractals may be the two sides of the real world's operation; the augmented Tangram Blocks could open a window to witness this scene.

References

1. Mandelbrot, B.: Objects fractals, p. 4 (1975)
2. Mandelbrot, B.B.: The fractal geometry of nature. Macmillan (1983). ISBN 978-0-7167-1186-5
3. Eric, W.W.: Chaos Game. MathWorld
4. Shiffman, D.: Chapter 8. Fractals. The Nature of Code. Retrieved 22 Jan 2024
5. Chen, Y.Q., Guoan, B.: 3-D IFS fractals as real-time graphics model. Comput. Graph. **21**(3), 367–370 (1997). https://doi.org/10.1016/S0097-8493(97)00014-9
6. McLuhan, M., Fiore, Q.: The medium is the massage, p. 10. Penguin Classics, London, UK (2008)

Designing a Collaborative Storytelling Platform to Enrich Digital Cultural Heritage Archives and Collective Memory

Ana Velhinho(✉) , Mariana Alves , Pedro Almeida , and Luís Pedro

Digimedia, Department of Communication and Art, University of Aveiro, Aveiro, Portugal
{ana.velhinho,marianaalves20,almeida,lpedro}@ua.pt

Abstract. Polariscope is an R&D project resulting from a consortium between the academia and a municipal historical archive. The project is focused on developing a participatory digital experience of cultural archives and events from multiple perspectives using collaborative storytelling to share, visualize and co-create collective memories. Designed as an online community that gathers contributions from citizens and institutions, the platform intends to promote rich digital experiences through interactive and narrative visualizations around meaningful cultural events and heritage data, presenting multimedia visualizations built from archives and testimonies shared by people. The methodological approach of the project adopts a User-Centered Design (UCD) iterative process comprising four phases: 1) Literature review and related work; 2) User research and functional requirements specification; 3) Laboratory evaluation of a medium-fidelity prototype with users; 4) Pilot case studies in field trials related to cultural events. This paper is focused on presenting phases 1 and 2, which are dedicated to the definition and ideation of the digital experience proposed by the platform, validated by an empirical study using focus groups with experts. In overall, the results allowed the validation of the functional requirements, and the identification of the expected features and interaction patterns related to the processes of content contribution, validation, discovery, and curation to include in the next iteration of the prototype to be tested with users.

Keyword: Participatory platform · Digital experience · Collaborative storytelling · Artificial intelligence

1 Introduction

Polariscope is an R&D project in the field of Digital Humanities, resulting from a consortium between the academia – the University of Aveiro and Nova University Lisbon – and the Historical Archive of Aveiro, who joined efforts to develop and a participatory platform to share collective memories. To assess if such a mobile-first platform that eases multimedia content sharing and generates correlated visualizations may contribute to enhancing the digital experience of memories of places and events, the team is working with pilot use cases and adopting a User Centre Design (UCD) approach through an iterative cycle of data gathering, prototyping, and testing. For this, it is crucial to take into consideration the theoretical background of recent studies and projects, current trends, and available platforms, as well as new research lines, along with the expectations of potential users and stakeholders. This data will inform the research and development of a prototype envisioning an innovative product that aims to contribute both to the sector of cultural heritage and participatory media services, by bringing together specialists and non-specialists.

1.1 Aggregation Portals of Digital Collections

Regarding the provision of digital explorations using digital collections to be communicated to a less specialist audience, the focus of the large aggregating portals of cultural and artistic heritage, such as Google Arts & Culture[1] and Europeana[2], has been setting the trends of playful approaches, based on games and challenges, that put users in contact with heritage digital resources. In the case of Google Arts & Culture, it stands out for the dynamism of its interface and for putting the robustness of this technological giant's tools at the service of this platform. Examples include the possibility of geographic exploration (using Maps, Street View and 360° technology, to navigate virtual spaces and galleries with high-resolution images). It also uses semantic correlation with machine learning approaches, which allow content recommendation based on the user's activity. This permanent update (recommendations of stories, collections, experiences, artistic movements, historical figures, or locations by geographic proximity) and the use of gamification strategies (achievements, scores, and games) offer a tailored digital experience showcasing cutting-edge technological innovation, namely in the feature *Experiments*[3]. In the case of the Europeana portal, which makes available an extensive digital collection of resources from several European member-states cultural institutions, it offers virtual exhibitions and galleries that can also be created by users. As an editorial project, the content is organized by Themes, Collections or Stories, grouped into Topics and Features. It also highlights trending topics each day and month, according to what people are viewing, downloading, liking, and adding to their curations. Europeana is also betting on more disruptive initiatives to captivate younger audiences such as the annual competition *GIF IT UP – Remixing Cultural Heritage*[4], which values the emotional dimension of the experiences of digital collections, to give visibility to resources from open access collections, through creative appropriations produced by users and shared on social media.

These dynamics, inherent to an increasingly participatory culture, along with the transversal digital transformation of our lives, have led the institutions of memory, referred to as GLAM (galleries, libraries, archives, museums), to adapt their ways of working, namely by intensifying mediation and digital participation strategies. This change also brought the opportunity to direct people's participation to enrich collections

---

[1] https://artsandculture.google.com.

[2] https://www.europeana.eu/.

[3] https://experiments.withgoogle.com/collection/arts-culture.

[4] https://gifitup.net/en.

and integrate community archives with records of personal stories and everyday experiences to document and archive contemporary times, bringing together specialists and
non-specialists.

1.2 Relevant Studies on Storytelling and Visualization Strategies in Digital Cultural Heritage Platforms

To gain an overview of current and future trends in the use of visualization and storytelling approaches in projects and platforms linked to cultural heritage, two studies were
considered [1, 2]. These studies present a mapping of characteristics of user profiles,
tasks, types of content, forms of presentation, modalities of interactivity, and the gran-
ularity of forms of presentation, as well as narrative approaches, both at the language
level and at the structuring content level.

In the study about visualization of digital collections [1], the authors focus on interfaces and prototypes that explore information visualization techniques based on data and
metadata from collections and cultural heritage objects. This study aimed to systematize
these visualization practices linked to heritage from a sample of 70 cases (50 prototypes
referring to academic research and 20 implemented web-based products).

The results regarding the visualization methods and techniques used in the sample
indicate that "timelines", "slideshows", "maps", "networks", and "image mosaics" are
the most used methods in cultural heritage visualization interfaces. Based on a critical analysis of the gathered results, the authors propose seven interrelated concepts to
address perspectives on future trends and challenges within the scope of visualization
interfaces for cultural heritage: 1) *Serendipity* – focusing on curiosity through more
open experiences. To this end, multiple views and access to content, playful strategies
and challenges may be relevant; 2) *Generosity* – promoting a richest, most accessible
and contextualized presentation and navigation with quality information, from multiple perspectives and different levels of detail and favouring the participation of casual
users; 3) *Criticality* – supporting interpretative approaches to explore cultural objects,
through visualization interfaces that promote plurality and users' appropriation; 4) *User
guidance and narration* – using strategies to enrich visualizations open to exploration
by the user, namely through onboarding techniques, educational initiatives and narrative
guidance, as well as the possibility of sharing personal stories; 5) *Remote or in-person
access* – using various types of digital access interfaces to representations of collections,
including remote access, to make the collection's artifacts more accessible; 6) *Uncertainty* – recognizing the need for managing imprecision, ambiguity and interpretative
openness of data and metadata; 7) *Contextualization* – considering emerging linked-
data standards through the open access availability of structured and quality databases,
to enhance correlated visualizations.

Furthermore, another survey carried out to assess storytelling practices brings additional insights for the current research [2]. Considering a commitment to digital transformation, the European Commission, through Europeana, brought together in 2020 a
Task Force of experts to survey and analyse examples of digital storytelling approaches
that incorporate cultural heritage resources, to consolidate an internal strategy that aims
to make Europeana a "powerful platform for storytelling", a motto that gave the name to

the study report [2]. Between September, 2020 and March, 2021, the Task Force identified and analysed examples of storytelling implemented by entities linked to cultural heritage, and proposed guidelines and recommendations, including seven digital storytelling tips in the field of cultural heritage: 1) *Be personal* – Personal stories can evoke the past and help the audience relate to the story on an emotional level; 2) *Be informal but expert* – Overly technical and academic language can put people off, but stories shouldn't be impoverished; 3) *Tell those hidden stories* – Giving visibility to inaccessible heritage and stories that have not yet been told by involving the public and creating a sense of community, identity and shared history; 4) *Illustrate your points* –How visuals and text work together in the stories; 5) *Signpost your journey* – Digital storytelling requires having a clear sense of the narrative and its structure, by directing attention from beginning to end; 6) *Be specific* – It often works best to move from specific details and topics and progress to the big picture; 7) *Be evocative* – It is possible to enrich stories through poetic, descriptive and evocative images and approaches, to make them more captivating and engage people. The sample highlights 43 good examples of digital tools and resources produced from cultural heritage collections. In their analysis, the experts considered specific storytelling characteristics focused on the narrative approach, such as the type of narrator, genre, and narrative style. But they also highlight the way they seek to involve the audience, namely how the resource is navigated and what is asked of the user, depending on the type of target audience, including co-creation features.

In both surveys [1, 2], there was still limited user participation, particularly in terms of content contribution, despite some story creation features being explored and the possibility of users creating curations based on objects from the collections. In the samples of both studies, most cases were relatively conventional and somewhat lacking innovative approaches, both in terms of interface proposals, visualization and storytelling, and in terms of participation and co-creation features, which continue to provide low autonomy and have little impact on the content being presented. In addition to the apparent gap in terms of collaborative storytelling, these cases also take little advantage of current advances in Artificial Intelligence (AI) in creative areas, whether at a generative level or in its potential to assist in the curation of content and stories, that could benefit from more powerful processing and semantic correlation.

Considering this framework, the paper is structured around the data collection methodology and results from a systematic literature review and focus groups. It culminates with the discussion and highlighting of the main insights and future steps regarding prototype development and evaluation.

2 Methodology

The research adopts a Grounded Theory methodology [3] and a UCD approach [4] relying on mixed methods. This paper presents the qualitative results gathered from a systematic literature review and focus groups carried out with experts to collect opinions and systematize requirements to develop a functional prototype of a participatory platform.

2.1 Literature Review

Objectives. The research question "What platforms, approaches and functionalities are used in the context of heritage and cultural events, based on storytelling and social enrichment by users?" guided the literature review with the aim to: i) Identify contexts using digital storytelling and co-creation linked to shared experiences and cultural heritage; ii) Identify strategies to enrich and give more visibility to resources and collections of museums and archives through community participation; iii) Identify user participation features in prototypes.

Protocol. The research was assisted by two queries, targeted at publications from the last 5 years (2019–2023) indexed in the SCOPUS database and using a combination of keywords related to collaborative storytelling within the scope of cultural heritage experiences and collective memories. Query 1 included a variation of keywords regarding contexts ("cultural event"; "cultural heritage"; "natural heritage"; "digital collection"; "museum"), audiences ("collective memory"; "digital experience"; "user-generated"; "citizen engagement"; "co-creation"; "community-driven"; "collaborative stories"), technology ("digital platform"; "mobile application") and features ("image curation"; "metadata aggregation"; "storytelling"; "visualizations"). Query 2 focused on the mobile and social aspects to complement the previous results, through the combination of the keywords "mobile app", "storytelling" and "collaborative". The eligibility criterion for the sample was the focus on prototypes, whose application context encompasses collective cultural experiences and incorporates social features of participation and/or co-creation by users, particularly regarding visual and locative storytelling. In the screening of the results, a total of 79 papers were found, of which 17 cases were considered for analysis: 60 were obtained in Query 1, of which 14 were considered; and 19 were obtained in Query 2, with 3 duplicates excluded and 3 papers selected based on the eligibility criterion.

Sample Characterization. The sample is composed of 17 cases (see Table 1), 14 of them referring to implemented prototypes and 3 papers referring to prototype conceptualization stages (Q1_31; Q1_40; Q2_16). One of these papers (Q1_40) was authored by our team members, and focused on preliminary research for the Polariscope project, but was considered in the sample as it was covered by the eligibility criterion. Table 1 also presents a classification of the degree of participation allowed to users, considering the ability of users to contribute with content. This classification does not apply to the three papers focused on prototypes not implemented.

Most of the cases in the sample are funded projects, lasting between 1 and 3 years (some extending this duration), with 7 projects financed by European funds and the others financed by entities such as UNESCO, or by national and private funds to support the collaboration between educational institutions and cultural entities, such as libraries, archives, museums, and sites of heritage interest.

Table 1. Sample of cases of the literature review (n = 17).

*	Paper ID	Prototype name	Year	Country
◉	Q1_05 [5]	*Laboratory of Stories - #dolomitesmuseum[a]*	2023	Italy
◕	Q1_10 [6]	*Momentus[b]*	2023	Australia
◕	Q1_11 [7]	*InCulture[c]*	2022	Greece
◉	Q1_20 [8]	*Pssst! Not on everybody's Lips*	2022	Italy
◕	Q1_21 [9]	*STEAM Stories[d]*	2022	Austria
◕	Q1_23 [10]	*Shangai Memory: A Journey from Wakag Road[e]*	2021	China
●	Q1_24 [11]	*CuRe – Culture and Rememberance[f]*	2021	Greece
◉	Q1_25 [12]	*Spotlight Heritage Timisoana[g]*	2021	Romania
◕	Q1_31 [13]	*MEMEX - MEMories and EXperiences for inclusive digital storytelling[h]*	2021	Portugal
●	Q1_34 [14]	*Crowdheritage[i]*	2021	Greece
◔	Q1_40 [15]	*Polariscope*	2021	Portugal
◕	Q1_45 [16]	*The COVID-19 Memorial Archive[j]*	2020	China & USA
◕	Q1_48 [17]	*youARhere – Seeing and feeling change[j]*	2020	USA
◕	Q1_49 [18]	*Narralive*	2019	Greece
●	Q2_02 [19]	*Triangolazione[l]*	2022	Italy
◕	Q2_12 [20]	*CAST – Context-Aware Collaborative Story-telling Platform*	2022	USA
◔	Q2_16 [21]	*Heritage trail mobile app*	2019	Ireland

* Users content contribution: ◉ Open   ◕ Mediated   ● None   ◔ Not applicable

[a] https://museodolom.it/en/exhibitions

[b] https://momentous.nma.gov.au

[c] https://explore.inculture-project.gr

[d] https://minkt-stories-lungau.zgis.at; https://ideas-lab.at

[e] http://wkl.library.sh.cn

[f] https://explore.cure-project.gr

[g] https://spotlight-timisoara.eu

[h] https://memexproject.eu/en

[i] https://crowdheritage.eu/en

[j] https://arcg.is/1OLGz1

[k] http://youarhere.org

[l] https://www.triangolazioni.unito.it

2.2 Focus Groups

Objectives and Protocol. After the literature review the following stage was to systematize personas and use scenarios to design a User eXperience (UX) flow through low-fidelity mockups (see the following section), which were presented in the focus groups with experts, to gather insights to inform further stages of the prototyping process. The qualitative approach of focus groups was adopted since it allows faster and richer access to information in collective sessions, based on the discussion of different points of view [22]. The content analysis was based on the dimensions of analysis defined in the semi-structured script, focused on features, and use scenarios. Usage flows were presented along with the discussion about the proposed features, during 90-min sessions with 3 to 5 participants. The participants were encouraged to freely express themselves during the sessions and give opinions and suggestions. The data collected through the focus groups was coded and analysed using the NVivo software. Following the qualitative method of content analysis [23], the dimensions defined in the script were subsequently recoded and regrouped after reading the full transcripts.

Sample Characterization. The sample consisted of 20 participants, 13 female and 7 male, experts in the fields of archives, museology, cultural mediation, and community projects. These participants constitute specialized profiles of users as academics, technicians and promoters of digital archives and cultural events, that can provide insights regarding digital archives management and curation. The participants were sorted into three groups, according to their professional area and institutional affiliation: Group 1 (G1) is composed of 11 history researchers, experts in life testimonials and community archives; Group 2 (G2) gathers 4 academics and experts in ethnography, multimedia archives and cultural mediation; and Group 3 (G3) comprises 5 experts from a city council, working on library, historical archives, museums, and tourism services.

3   The Concept of an AI-Assisted Collaborative Storytelling Platform

Polariscope is being designed as a collaborative storytelling platform, supported by AI, to showcase and connect institutional collections and content shared by users. In this sense, it constitutes an online community that promotes digital experiences about diverse heritage and cultural events that bring together collective memories (e.g.: national memorial events; local traditions and festivities; and routes through historical and natural heritage; among others) presenting them from multiple perspectives through multimedia visualizations, stories, and curations to collect, preserve and activate these memories. As shown in Fig. 1, which exemplifies a project regarding the Portuguese Carnation Revolution, the platform is organized around three main features: Projects, Polaris, Capsules, and Challenges. The Projects are sections that can be created in the platform to share content around a significant cultural event, generating multimedia storytelling visualizations that correlate resources from a living archive comprising institutional collections and user-generated content. The Polaris corresponds to AI-powered visualizations automatically generated using the Project's living archive. The archive can also be explored by themes that reflect the evolution of this communal media repository. The Capsules are collaborative narrative curations created by users and may incorporate social mechanisms to boost participation (Challenges).

In the ideation phase of the prototype, two main types of user profiles were considered: the regular user, who views and enriches projects; and the promoters, who can create and manage projects. Other profiles and corresponding personas and their motivations for using the Polariscope platform were also mentioned during the focus groups to explain specific features, such as: the "challenger", applicable to teachers or educational service facilitators who can explore Challenges with groups; the "prosumer"

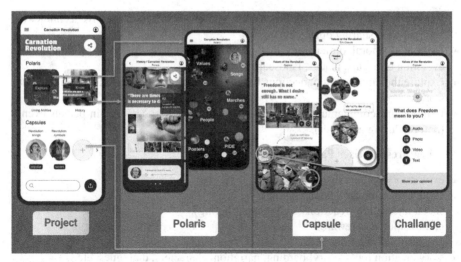

Fig. 1. Example of a Polariscope Project and its corresponding Polaris, a Capsule and a Challenge integrated into that curation.

profile linked with younger generations with higher digital literacy; and the "nostalgic" profile related with older generations who may share first-person testimonies about their experiences of historical events that evoke collective memories.

4   Results and Discussion of the Literature Review

The results from the analysis of the sample prototypes (see Table) are systematized into three axes corresponding to the stated objectives:

4.1   Use Contexts Resorting on Digital Storytelling and Co-creation Linked to Shared Experiences and Cultural Heritage

- digital and augmented reality experiences in cultural spaces activating digital collections.
- routes in historical, artistic, or natural sites of relevance.
- collections management tools mainly for institutional uses, which allow the generation of multimedia presentations (e.g.: stories, virtual exhibitions, etc.) and sometimes contributions from users.
- open-source tools for mapping, storytelling, creating stories, and multimedia presentations that can be shared on other platforms.

4.2   Strategies to Enrich and Give More Visibility to Resources and Collections of Museums and Archives Through Community Participation

- Promote co-creation laboratories and workshops that bring together specialists and non-specialists with an exploratory attitude, for creating and sharing content using digital storytelling tools.

- Explore spatial/geographical dimensions, taking advantage of locative technologies and real-time sharing during events.
- Explore temporal dimensions that allow measuring the passage of time and/or evolution of events, places, landscapes, etc.
- Explore the emotional connections between cultural heritage artefacts and personal stories.
- Explore the complementarity between digital experiences and in-person events (before, during and after).

4.3 Features for User Participation

- exploratory content discovery.
- content enrichment (social tagging).
- social interaction (reactions, comments, sharing).
- gamification and rewards.
- personalized curations.
- story creation tools (storyboarding, narration, characters, dialogues, etc.).
- camera and audio recording on mobile devices.
- georeferencing tools for mapping, route creation and augmented reality.

5 Results and Discussion of the Focus Groups

The focus group results are systematized into five axes corresponding to the topics, usage flows and features presented and discussed in the sessions, namely regarding open participation, content discovery and co-creation features using collaborative curations to produce multimedia storytelling presentations, either generated by the system or created by users.

5.1 Motivations of the Target Audience

Adoption Cost. The resistance to migrating or dedicating time to a new platform with no wide reach like the competition (e.g.: reputable and specialized platforms such as Europeana where institutions can upload their collections, and the informal groups on social media in which users already have a loyal community of followers and can freely interact and share content).

Reaching New Audiences. Captivating audiences that institutions usually do not have access to and giving them autonomy to participate (which frees up the effort of human resources) was indicated in G3 as the main competitive advantage of this platform. This allows making available user-generated content but also displaying digital content about artefacts that may not be physically accessible in institutions (either due to limited space in exhibitions or because it is restricted to the public).

Accessibility and Promotion of Digital Literacy. Since many institutions do not yet have their content accessible to a diversity of audiences, G1 suggested investing in multimedia accessibility, taking advantage of AI technologies to generate descriptions and captions for images and videos, generating summaries of denser scientific content with more accessible language, converting text-to-speech and vice versa, etc. These options could be activated according to the users' needs. Additionally, the provision of resources such as tutorials, didactic activities, and in-app tips were also suggested.

User Segments. In G2, participants mentioned that it is preferable to specialize in audiences and not try to reach everyone, highlighting age differences: if the platform is aimed at young people, it should take advantage of the complementarity with social media in which interactions could be carried out because users are already in those communities; aimed at seniors, it would involve face-to-face mediation associated with ethnographic testimonials; aimed at educational contexts, it would have to integrate specific features. However, in G1 and G3, participants highlighted the potential for intergenerational dynamics, on the one hand, to bring young people closer to archives and older people's life stories and, on the other hand, for younger people to help promote digital literacy among older adults. G1 mentioned that researchers would be a relevant target audience and highlighted the platform's potential for promoting partnerships, increasing their credibility when contacting people using the snowball method. Some participants of G1 already use informal groups and social media to source and curate content for their studies.

5.2 Creating and Managing Projects

Creation Process. Participants from all groups mentioned that, based on the prototype, the advantage of creating a Project needed to be clarified. Nevertheless, the form to create new Projects (Fig. 2) was unanimously considered easy and intuitive. G3 participants advised that importing content directly from open-access institutional repositories should be possible because manually uploading it would take considerable effort. Participants in G3 also questioned whether institutions must actively create Projects or should be the platform to create them and automatically aggregate content from multiple institutions relevant to those Projects.

Who Can Create. There was no consensus on whether, in addition to institutions, ordinary users can also create Projects, which implies their management. In this regard, G1 participants mentioned that users could suggest the platform to create a Project and find promoters. Despite that, all participants valued horizontal participation without "institutionalizing" the platform. The focus on collaboration led G1 participants to suggest using collective profiles for the consortium of institutions managing a Project and even suggested the rule of requiring more than one entity to avoid monopoly and involving citizens from the community, which was also mentioned as good practice by G2 participants. In G1, it was noted that users should be able to ask Project promoters to become collaborators, and the platform could make suggestions for collaborators based on their active participation.

Content Moderation and Validation. This was the most recurrent topic, especially in G1 and G3, due to the increased responsibility when institutions are involved. In G3, participants highlighted the need to make the authorship of who publishes very explicit to avoid confusing content shared by institutions and by users. In all groups, there was consensus on the existence of a peer reporting mechanism regarding inappropriate content and making clear in the terms and conditions of the platform that users are legally responsible for holding the copyrights of what they publish. In G3, participants agreed that Project promoters should have access to optional moderation and validation mechanisms, namely, to validate or make minor corrections to the automatic story generated

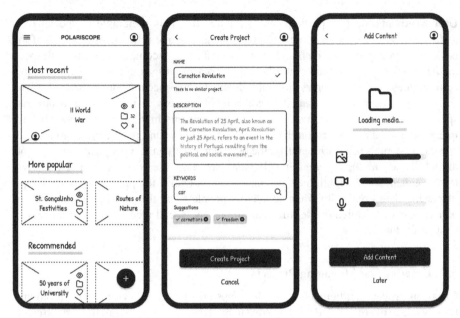

Fig. 2. The process of creating a Project: [left] The "Create new" button in the Polariscope homepage; [center] New Project form; [right] Add content to the Project.

by the system. In this group, all participants agreed that validating everything before becoming public would not be reasonable or desirable.

Fragmentation or Aggregating Projects. This was a non-consensual topic. Although the form for creating a new Project (Fig. 2) indicates when there are related Projects to be able to suggest to join them, G1 and G3 participants criticized the dispersion of efforts in creating similar Projects instead of promoting collaboration in larger ones that gather more users. A G2 participant expressed that more global Projects would appeal to younger audiences while older people would value local specificities instead of more generic Projects that could be perceived as impersonal. A participant from G1 mentioned that fragmentation is interesting but that it would be helpful to have a tree visualization of related projects to grasp diversity. On the other hand, G3 participants mentioned that the titles of the Projects can be misleading and that the same name of an event (e.g.: traditional celebrations of patron saints) has very different manifestations in different territories. At this level, another G3 participant mentioned the possibility of a title disambiguation system. In all groups, participants were divided between investing in more aggregating Projects or giving the freedom to create Projects even about smaller scope events. At this level, a G1 participant suggested that Projects could be classified by scope: global; national; and local. This participant also suggested that Projects could be explored through time (e.g.: the evolution of a tradition over the years) and space (e.g.: its manifestation in various locations) to provide broader views, but also to be able to navigate through more specific content feeds. A G1 participant mentioned that Projects were unnecessary and the system should be able to semantically aggregate and correlate institutional collections, user stories and individual content by thematic clusters, taking advantage of a single shared repository where everything is connectable.

5.3 Machine-Driven Visualizations of a Community Archive

Dynamism and Ephemerality of Automatic Visualizations. Exploring the Project's living archive through automatic visualizations (Polaris), either by emerging themes or in the daily generated story mode, was considered interesting and innovative by all participants. In G3, some participants highlighted the fact that being automatic constitutes an agile solution in terms of maintenance for Project promoters. The proposal for a story generated from collectively shared content was understood in G1 as a good strategy to convey that the History of humanity is dynamic and made up of transversal facts around which more personal and subjective connections and parallel stories gravitate. A G1 participant was very sceptical regarding the quality of the stories that will be generated by AI, noting that although this is a powerful tool for semantic correlation, the technology still has limitations in developing more engaging content from a narrative point of view. Given the ephemerality of this automatic story, some G1 and G3 participants mentioned the possibility of users being able to save the story to view it again. One of the G2 participants highlighted that it is a good strategy to fragment the story into chapters and focus on non-linear and shorter content because it is presently very difficult to capture and maintain people's attention to view it entirely (Fig. 3).

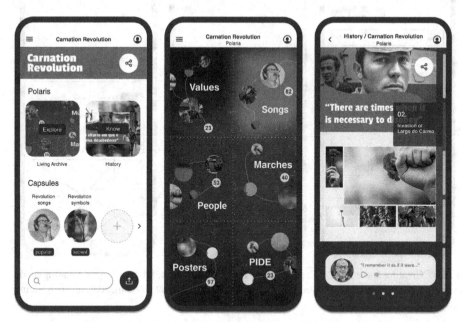

Fig. 3. Exploring a Project's AI-generated visualizations (Polaris): [left] Project homepage; [center] Free exploration of the Living Archive by themes; [right] Guided narrative visualization (Capsule).

Collaborative Enrichment of the Automatic Story. G1 participants mentioned Wikipedia's collaborative editing system as a good example. In G2 and G3, participants again highlighted the need to make the users accountable for what they publish, otherwise, it dissuades the institutions' interest in joining the platform. G1 participants found it interesting that users could add new chapters to the automatic story, which should have a permanent structure based on facts proposed by the system and validated by the promoters, allowing connections with peripheral and personal stories. Additionally, participants from G1 and G3 remained divided regarding the immediate publication of content uploaded by users, suggesting that it should only be public after validation from the promoters but could appear visible in the story only for that user as an immediate reward for participating. Once again, the topic of validation emerged, although being considered in theory as non-desirable. In G3, participants also suggested the optional possibility for promoters to validate the automatic story generated by the system to avoid publishing incorrect information.

5.4   Human-Driven curations with AI support and calls-to-action

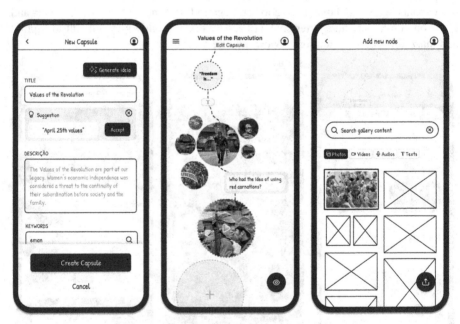

Fig. 4. Creating and editing a Capsule: [left] New Capsule form; [center] Capsule editing mode using storyline connections between content nodes; [right] Content recommendation when adding a new node.

Creation Process. The form for creating a new Capsule was considered unanimously clear. However, some G1 participants suggested that it could be presented in blocks and follow a sequence of steps, for example, starting with keywords, then providing a

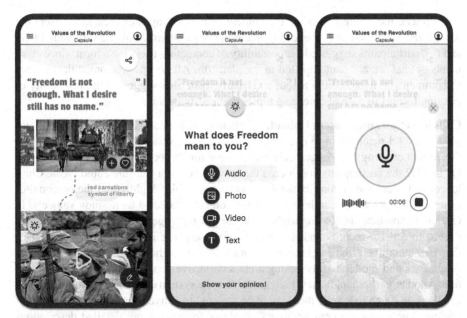

Fig. 5. Viewing and enriching a Capsule: [left] Capsule view mode displaying a Challenge on a content; [center] Challenge call to action; [right] Recording testimony in reply to a Challenge.

structure to fill with content, and allowing to choose templates. A G1 participant mentioned that the Polaris automatic story would not have to be formally different from the Capsules, and these could also have chapters. The same participant mentioned that if the platform provided support to create curations through templates to help a specialist create step-by-step multimedia stories, suggesting narrative structures and recommending content, the platform would be an appealing and differentiating product in itself. The content recommendation was also considered very useful by all groups, and G1 and G3 participants also suggested recommending related Capsules. A G3 participant considered the Capsules a very interesting way to create digital exhibitions without space limitations and even for showing material that cannot always be physically displayed. As a representative of an institution, this participant mentioned that there are fixed narratives supported by facts that they must follow. Still, the possibility of having several Capsules created by people allows to show diversity of perspectives, even if they present contradictory views, but avoiding the conflicts often associated with social media comments (Figs. 4 and 5).

Collaborative Enrichment of Users' Curations. A participant from G3 made an immediate analogy between the Polaris story and the Capsules with Spotify playlists that are generated either by the system or by people, and sometimes created in groups with shared authorship but identifying the content added by each user. In all groups, it was taken as logical that the creators could decide if their Capsules are public or private, as well as if they are open or not to other users' contributions, being able to moderate them. However, the platform should always encourage the users to make Capsules public and open. Despite that, some G3 participants expressed reluctance that, as promoters of a Project, they cannot validate the content of public Capsules created by users but recognized that a system for reporting inappropriate content should be sufficient. In G1 and G3, participants suggested the possibility of contacting users via a form, since comments or chat are not contemplated in the platform. All groups welcomed the absence of comments to avoid conflicts, but a G1 participant also suggested the possibility of creating forums in case of emerging topics that justify debate.

Calls to Action and Content Upload. Challenges were unanimously considered a simple and useful mechanism to encourage participation. Although G3 participants mentioned that creating Challenges only made sense for Project promoters or teachers, in G1 and G2 the participants considered that any author of a Capsule could create Challenges to foster guided contributions. G1 participants also highlighted the potential of using Challenges by researchers to call for content related to their study subjects. In G3, another participant also highlighted the use of Challenges associated with in-person events, to call for records and testimonies of those participating. One of the G1 participants mentioned that in classroom dynamics, the teacher should be able to create Challenges and moderate them using a class collective profile for students' participation. Another participant from G1 suggested that the system could also generate targeted Challenges. As an example, these could be targeted to active users who upload a lot of content, suggesting the creation of a Capsule or fostering more detailed descriptions about that content. A G2 participant considered that the platform facilitates content upload but valued in-person mediation with older people and audiences with low digital literacy. G1 participants also mentioned that content upload should contemplate the optional insertion of advanced metadata so that the platform could be referenced as a robust source.

5.5 Innovation and Foreseen Acceptance as a Future Product

All participants considered the platform an innovative future product and had curiosity about using it. The main strengths and innovative factors, as well as the weaknesses to be taken into consideration for the prototype iteration, are highlighted below:

Strengths and Innovative Factors

- Facilitated maintenance through the automatic generation of dynamic content (curations).
- The ability to provide unexpected connections between content and diversity of perspectives amplified by AI (human and machine-driven).
- The ability to bring archives to life through social dynamics and visual storytelling.
- The support for open, non-hierarchical, and collaborative participation that provides autonomy and supports participation step-by-step.
- The potential for documenting and studying contemporaneity and the evolution of cultural traditions by encouraging the sharing of memories but also current experiences.

Weaknesses

- Resistance to migrate from other platforms and groups with more reach.
- The complexity and unfamiliarity of the features.
- The possible inhibition of users' participation due to institutions being involved (but for some users may increase the perception of credibility).
- The possible inhibition of institutions' participation because of the lack of control over what is published.
- Loss of relevance due to lack of participation.

6 Final Considerations and Future Work

This paper focuses on the methodology applied in the development of a collaborative storytelling platform to enrich digital cultural heritage archives and collective memory. In addition to an overview of relevant studies and aggregating portals in the sector of cultural heritage digital platforms, a systematic literature review on related projects and focus groups with experts were carried out for further data collection and validation of the platform's concept and features.

From the systematic literature review of prototype-based research projects two relevant aspects stood out: first, there is a clear promotion of participatory approaches with audiences and there is an adoption of digital storytelling strategies to empower the sector; second, there is a lack of platforms embracing more open-ended participation that can transform users from crowd-contributors to co-creators.

These aspects tuned the research focus of the platform towards collaborative storytelling supported by AI as a differentiating factor, by proposing a new digital experience for showing and telling correlated stories, boosted by records of digital heritage enriched by people. To this end, it was important to consider the power of data processing and content recommendations supported by AI, combined with the social dynamics within a digital community that connects resources from institutions with content shared by users, who enrich this living archive with content contribution, appropriation, and remix. Therefore, content discovery and co-creation are the platform's core, materialized through narrative visualizations that semantically correlate multimedia resources through digital storytelling, challenging how we currently relate to cultural archives.

Promoting focus groups with experts in the fields of archives, museology, cultural mediation, and community projects appeared to be the most advantageous method to probe the acceptability of the platform and to gather opinions about this disruptive proposal at an ideation and low-fidelity prototyping stage. This empirical study included the design process of developing user stories, journey maps and low-fidelity mockups to present in the focus groups the concept and main features of the collaborative storytelling mobile application.

The qualitative analysis and the systematization into recommendations of the experts' contributions informed the subsequent stage of the medium-fidelity prototype, which will be tested in a laboratory setting with users. In addition to gathering opinions and validating the concept and functionalities with a sample including non-specialists, the tests in the laboratory aim to evaluate the UX of a semi-functional prototype resulting from the improvements provided by the focus group's insights. This version of the prototype will integrate stories generated by AI and request users to perform tasks such as creating projects, creating curations, and uploading content, allowing a more comprehensive evaluation of the UX, including usability, emotional and aesthetic reactions to the interface, navigation and content presentation and interaction.

Acknowledgments. This work is financially supported by National Funds through FCT – Fundação para a Ciência e a Tecnologia, I.P., under the project 2022.04424.PTDC.

References

1. Windhager, F., et al.: Visualization of cultural heritage collection data: state of the art and future challenges. IEEE Trans. Visual. Comput. Graph. **25**(6), 2311–2330 (2019). https://doi.org/10.1109/TVCG.2018.2830759
2. Europeana. Europeana as A Powerful Platform for Storytelling Task Force - Report and Recommendations. Europeana Network Association (2021). https://pro.europeana.eu/files/Europeana_Professional/Europeana_Network/Europeana_Network_Task_Forces/Final_reports/EuropeanaasaPowerfulPlatformforStorytellingReport.pdf
3. Glaser, B.G., Strauss, A.L.: The discovery of Grounded Theory - strategies for qualitative research. Routledge, London, New York (2017)
4. Lowdermilk, T.: User-centered design. A developer's guide to building user-friendly applications. O'Reilly Media, USA (2013)
5. Lacedelli, S.Z., Fazzi, F., Zanetti, C., Pompanin, G.: From "exhibition" to "laboratory": rethinking curatorial practices through a digital experimental project. the case study of #dolomitesmuseum - laboratory of storieS. Herança **6**(1), 143–168 (2023). https://doi.org/10.52152/heranca.v6i1.680
6. Davies, K.M.: Crowd coaxing and citizen storytelling in archives of crisis. Life Writ. **20**(2), 351–365 (2023). https://doi.org/10.1080/14484528.2022.2106611
7. Mathioudakis, G., et al.: InCulture: a collaborative platform for intangible cultural heritage narratives. Heritage **5**(4), 2881–2903 (2022). https://doi.org/10.3390/heritage5040149
8. Bollini, L., Facchini, C.: I wish you were here. designing a geostorytelling ecosystem for enhancing the small heritages' experience. In: Gervasi, O., Murgante, B., Misra, S., Ana, M.A., Rocha, C., Garau, C. (eds.) Computational science and its applications – ICCSA 2022 workshops: Malaga, Spain, July 4–7, 2022, Proceedings, Part II, pp. 457–472. Springer International Publishing, Cham (2022). https://doi.org/10.1007/978-3-031-10562-3_32
9. Zorenböhmer, C., Steinbacher, E.-M., Jeremias, P.M., Öttl, U.F.J., Resch, B.: STEAM stories: a co-creation approach to building STEAM skills through stories of personal interest. GI-Forum J. 135–149 (2022). https://doi.org/10.1553/giscience2022_01_s135
10. Cuijuan, X., Lihua, W., Wei, L.: Shanghai memory as a digital humanities platform to rebuild the history of the city. Dig. Scholarship Human. **36**(4), 841–857 (2021). https://doi.org/10.1093/llc/fqab023
11. Mathioudakis, G., et al.: Supporting online and on-site digital diverse travels. Heritage **4**(4), 4558–4577 (2021). https://doi.org/10.3390/heritage4040251
12. Vert, S., et al.: User evaluation of a multi-platform digital storytelling concept for cultural heritage. Mathematics **9**(21), 2678 (2021). https://doi.org/10.3390/math9212678
13. Nisi, V., Bostock, H., Cesário, V., Acedo, A., Nunes, N.: Impalpable Narratives: How to capture intangible cultural heritage of migrant communities. In: Proceedings of the 10th international conference on communities & technologies - wicked problems in the age of

tech (C&T 2021), pp. 109–120. ACM, New York, NY, USA (2021). https://doi.org/10.1145/3461564.3461575

14. Kaldeli, E., Menis-Mastromichalakis, O., Bekiaris, S., Ralli, M., Tzouvaras, V., Stamou, G.: CrowdHeritage: crowdsourcing for improving the quality of cultural heritage metadata. Information **12**(2), 64 (2021). https://doi.org/10.3390/info12020064

15. Velhinho, A., Almeida, P.: Sharing and visualizing collective memories – contexts and strategies for a participatory platform. In: Abásolo, M.J., Abreu, J., Almeida, P., Silva, T. (eds.) Applications and usability of interactive TV: 9th iberoamerican conference, jAUTI 2020, Aveiro, Portugal, December 18, 2020, Revised Selected Papers, pp. 3–14. Springer International Publishing, Cham (2021). https://doi.org/10.1007/978-3-030-81996-5_1

16. Bacon, B.L., Xu, W.: Memory, storytelling and gis digital archive: introducing the COVID-19 memory archival project. The Coronavirus. Palgrave Macmillan, Singapore (2020). https://doi.org/10.1007/978-981-15-9362-8_2

17. Taylor, M., Orland, B., Li, J., Berry, S., Welch-Devine, M.: Crowdsourcing environmental narratives of coastal Georgia using mobile augmented reality and data collection. J. Dig. Landscape Architect. **5**, 140–149 (2020). https://doi.org/10.14627/537690015

18. Vrettakis, E., Kourtis, V., Katifori, A., Karvounis, M., Lougiakis, C., Ioannidis, Y.: Narralive – creating and experiencing mobile digital storytelling in cultural heritage. Dig. Appl. Archaeol. Cult. Heritage **15**, e00114 (2019). https://doi.org/10.1016/j.daach.2019.e00114

19. Mauro, N., Cossatin, A.G., Cravero, E., Ardissono, L., Magnano, G., Giardino, M.: Exploring semantically interlaced cultural heritage narratives. In: Proceedings of the 33rd ACM conference on hypertext and social media (HT 2022), pp. 192–197. ACM, New York, NY, USA (2022). https://doi.org/10.1145/3511095.3536366

20. Caniglia, G.: Cast: a context-aware collaborative storytelling platform. In: Extended abstracts of the 2020 CHI conference on human factors in computing systems (CHI EA 2020), pp. 1–7. ACM, New York, NY, USA (2020). https://doi.org/10.1145/3334480.3382966

21. Basaraba, B., Conlan, O., Edmond, J., Arnds, P.: Digital narrative conventions in heritage trail mobile apps. New Rev. Hypermedia Multimedia **251–252**, 1–30 (2019). https://doi.org/10.1080/13614568.2019.1642963

22. Kruger, R.A., Casey, M.A.: Focus Groups. A Practical Guide for Applied Research. Sage, USA (2015)

23. Bardin, L.: Análise de Conteúdo. São Paulo: Edições 70, Almedina Brasil (2011)

Designing Interactive Infographics for Traditional Culture: An Exploration of Interaction Patterns

Ying Zhang, DanDan Yu$^{(\boxtimes)}$, and LiMin Wang

Art and Design Academy, Beijing City University, Beijing, China
1594425232@qq.com

Abstract. Information graphics, or infographics, combine elements of date visualization with design and have become an increasingly popular mean for disseminating information. In traditional media, the lack of interactivity in static infographics imposes limitations on information capacity, display space and user perspectives. When dealing with a large or complex amount of information, readability and comprehension can become challenging. However, due to the vast amount of information embedded in traditional cultures, it is challenging to fully showcase on a limited screen space. Therefore, adopting interactive infographics proves to be an effective method for inheriting and promoting traditional cultures. By employing various interactive modes, it presents the diversity and essence of cultures, allowing audiences to intuitively grasp historical and cultural information. This study, based on indepth interactive design methods, delineates eight types of infographics and potential interactive modes. Through concrete design practices and test evaluations, it empirically supports the exploration of interactive modes. The research aims to enhance user engagement, optimize information communication, and adapt to user needs and habits, thereby fostering a broader application of information graphics in cultural heritage.

Keywords: Traditional culture · Infographic Design · Interactive Pattern · Interaction Design · Data Visualization

1 Introduction

The introduction of infographics was an important advancement in information visualisation, rendering abstract data or textual descriptions in a manner that can be more easily understood. Due to technological advancements and the development of networks, real-time and dynamic interactive forms of information visualisation mean that information can be more readily analysed and processed than ever before. Currently, information visualisation can be divided into three categories according to its motion state, [1] static visualisation, dynamic visualisation, and interactivity information visualization [2]. Interactive data visualisation pertains to dynamic visualisation, with the addition of buttons, guided tours, and other interactive methods. As a result, data and user interaction have become a trend in the research, development, and application of visualisation design in recent years [3].

A. Marcus et al. (Eds.): HCII 2024, LNCS 14712, pp. 160–174, 2024.
https://doi.org/10.1007/978-3-031-61351-7_11

Traditional culture is inherently derived from and employed by people, whether through information visualisation methods to achieve "through the object to see the people" information understanding or for the digital protection of traditional cultural heritage to safeguard and open up new possibilities for future generations [4]. Contemporary society is in a period of rapid development; as a result, the traditional cultures of countries globally are inevitably impacted, with many traditional values gradually being forgotten. To continue the value advantage of their traditional culture, it is necessary to inform the public about cultural heritage and disseminate its value. However, the sheer volume of information that has emerged in the course of history has made it difficult for people to understand it. Moreover, it is difficult to fully comprehend the meaning of the huge "information map", which creates challenges in designing a more efficient way to preserve and promote traditional culture. With this in mind, interactive infographic design makes up for this deficiency, allowing users to more efficiently and quickly access information.

As a new type of traditional cultural heritage display combining graphics and text, infographics can facilitate two-way interaction between users and information to achieve optimal collaboration between humans and machines [5]. On this basis, there is much scope for exploration in the research on this topic. To be precise, this in clouds, traditional culture in the field of infographic interaction design and the effect of output results on the future of digital traditional culture dissemination, which will provide a new path to strengthen the propaganda of intangible cultural heritage.

2   Research Context and Concepts

The present work is a postgraduate project for the Digital Media Art program at Beijing City University. It adopts the Beijing Central Axis as the theme and displays its related history and culture in an interactive information visualisation. To do so, the relevant cultural characteristics and technical means were researched before initiating the project. Notably, the Beijing central axis, featuring ancient buildings from the Yuan dynasty capital to the Ming and Qing dynasties in different periods, has witnessed Beijing's historical development. In 2018, 14 places were identified as ancient architectural cultural heritage sites, such as Yong ding men, all of which are included in the World Cultural Heritage preparatory list [6]. At present, the pace of digital exploration of ancient architectural cultural heritage in China cannot keep pace with the development of the information age. Moreover, the protection of ancient architectural cultural heritage and the inheritance of history and culture need to be further explored to find new empowerment.

2.1   Characteristics and Ways of Traditional Cultural Information Dissemination

The diversity of traditional culture and science and technological progress have yielded a wealth of innovative methods that can be deployed to promote traditional culture [10]. In recent years, the Beijing Central Axis has become an example of how cultural heritage dissemination can be achieved through the use of new media resources and innovative forms of expression, allowing cultural heritage to be handed down across time and space to the present day. Through this process, this cultural heritage has been revitalised and invigorated in the new era, perceived, needed and loved by the public, and expanded the consumer market and cultural product groups [7].

First, the design and promotion of cultural and creative products constitute an important link between traditional culture and the needs of modern society. Secondly, the bulk of digital dissemination takes place through the establishment of a multi-level Internet platform. The official website enables the public and foreign tourists with a convent means to view heritage resources online. The Beijing Axis Line also promotes the dissemination of both historical knowledge and the image of the Axis Line on social media. However, problems persist in information dissemination, such as the relatively homogenous content and poor interactivity with social media users. Most publicity simply introduces and displays the central axis in a manner that leaves the audience unable to delve deeply into its connotation. Interactive infographics can play an effective role in shaping Beijing's image and conveying cultural information.

In this way, from online to offline, the Beijing Axis Line uses various cutting-edge technologies to communicate in different forms, adhering to the concept of "letting cultural heritage come alive" and arousing the audience's passion for history and culture.

2.2   Status and Characteristics of Traditional Cultural Information Design

In the information design field, the presentation of traditional culture-based information covers a number of dimensions, including interactive visualisations, infographics in printed books, and graphic-type infographic posters shared online [10].

According to the research on the infographics used in traditional books and print posters, the infographics presenting information on traditional culture exhibit the following characteristics: First, the visual presentation intuitively displays the cultural content through the use of images, symbols, and colours to enhance the user's perception of the content. Second, the theme is clear and typically centers on a specific cultural idea or field, such as traditional Chinese festivals or national costumes. Third, the charts incorporate many cultural elements, using rich traditional cultural elements, such as traditional patterns, colours, and fonts to reflect national characteristics. Fourth, the infographics analyse culture in depth, going beyond the simple display of culture to undertake an in-depth analysis of culture through data and charts, thereby revealing its inner laws and characteristics. Fifth, cultural infographics are of educational significance, helping to educate and publicise the value of traditional culture and heighten the public's awareness and understanding of traditional culture.

2.3   Characteristics of Interactive Visualisation

Regarding interactive infographic visualisation, it has several main distinguishing features, including tactile, experiential, communicative, interactive and emotional elements [11]. Therefore, interactive infographics can be seen to possess the following characteristics:

1. Interactive infographics aim to enhance the user's sense of participation and the enjoyment they derive from reading the chart. Through clever guidance and design, users can interact with the information more autonomously, thereby realising the

"effective interaction" between humans and machines [12]. Such interaction enhances the user's experience, stimulates the reader's desire to explore, and renders the reading of charts and graphs a more interesting process [9].

2. Interactive infographics improve the sense of order in how the information is presented to the viewer. By establishing folded and hidden layers of information, users can independently browse according to their personal interests, avoiding the problem of visual fatigue stemming from information overload [12]. Users can go deeper layer by layer using the touchscreen interface, providing more flexibility in the interactive experience. As an example in Fig. 1, the University of Washington studied "Lunar cycles & sleep patterns interactive infographic", putting forward results on how sleep quality is affected by lunar cycles. Through this infographic, users can explore the average time individuals go to sleep and the length of time they sleep in each part of the cycle. Additionally, by hovering over the sleep density circle (radial cycle), users can view the data, with the linear cycle graph providing a view of the contextual patterns starting at the new moon (day 15 of the lunar cycle).

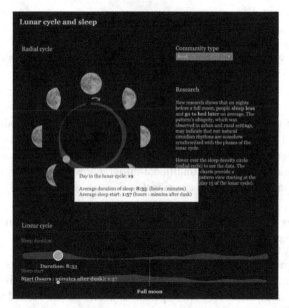

Fig. 1. Interactive infographic of 'Lunar cycle and sleep' (Picture source: https://tableau.was hington.edu/views/LunarCycleandSleep/LunarCycle?%3AisGuestRedirectFromVizportal=y&% 3Aembed=y)

3. Interaction infographics are conducive to the effective communication of complex information with greater coherence. Compared to the layout limitations that traditional infographic design is subject to, interactive displays can create multiple information hierarchies. In addition, different colour shades can be used to differentiate various information types, whilst colour shades can indicate the progressive relationship between information hierarchies [13]. As shown in Fig. 2, an interactive infographic about the global environment of plastic pollution is presented. The user

can control the presentation of the Earth in 3D by touching the infographic bar with different coloured regions positioned on the right-hand side to view where global marine pollution has accumulated over time. Users are able to select the information they are interested in and personalise it to achieve the desired message.

Fig. 2. 'The Seas of Plastic' (Picture source: https://www.cleverclip.ch/en/blog/the-best-interactive-infographics-2020)

4. Interaction infographics enhance emotional communication. By introducing a broader range of visual elements and interactive methods, designers can better express information and generate an emotionally resonant experience for users. This helps to break the single expression of traditional infographics and renders the information communication more vivid and emotional.

2.4   Advantages of Interactive Infographics in Traditional Cultural Communication

Interaction design is a central aspect of information visualisation charts. In the interactive process, users change from passively accepting information to active participation, alleviating the contradiction between large amounts of data and limited screen size to a certain extent. Through this interactive approach, the data can be better matched with human cognition, reasoning, and decision-making mental models, effectively improving user insights and elevating the user experience [13].

Humans can visually process images 6,000 times faster than text, which is a huge advantage in the age of time constraints. Interactive infographics typically entail user participation such as scrolling, clicking, and tapping to produce some of the effects. Such interactivity is able to attract and maintain the attention of the target audience and will express the communication power of the message more effectively [13].

3 Interactive Mode of Cultural Infographics

In the field of traditional culture, to discern how to better present information, the author conducted an in-depth study of nearly 10 infographic books on traditional culture themes and nearly 50 infographic poster works. From this, it was found that there are eight types of chart designs that are commonly used in traditional cultural presentations. Besides, through the design of effective interactive charts, the interaction modes suitable for each information chart were summarized (see Fig. 1). These eight types include Timeline infographics, Map Infographics, Process Infographics, Informative Infographics, Hierarchical Infographics, List Infographics, Data Visualization Infographics, and Comparison Infographics. It should be stressed that each type has interaction modes that are designed to attend to different purposes and needs (Table 1).

In summary, by collating and summarising traditional culture infographics from multiple sources such as books, posters, and interactional infographics, this approach lays the groundwork for a more targeted approach to proposing interaction patterns that correspond to the eight infographic types highlighted above. These research and informational data tables form the foundation for the further exploration of the potential applications of infographics in the field of traditional culture and will support future design innovation and research.

3.1 Timeline Infographics

Timeline infographics are the optimal form of infographics for visualising the development and evolution of historical events, allowing the viewer to better understand the development of history. Specifically, this type of infographics assists with understanding the sequence, duration and relationship of a series of events in a more intuitive way.

In terms of interaction modes, timeline infographics can fully exploit a variety of interaction modes to enhance the user experience and information conveyance effect. First, form interaction can be deployed to enable users to enter specific time points or event information by filling out a form, thereby helping to keep the information in order. Second, drag-and-drop functionality allows users to flexibly move, adjust or add events to the timeline, enhancing user interaction and operational flexibility. Third, the preview mode is both a simple display of information and a user-friendly aid. In this way, users can ensure that the sequence of events and the temporal relationship meet their expectations, helping to improve their comprehension of the entire timeline.

3.2 Map Infographics

Interactive maps are popular for communicating spatial information to viewers by presenting information in geospatial space through graphical representations. Such charts are designed to effectively communicate geographic locations, spatial relationships and territorial data, and clearly and intuitively present geographic information.

In the interaction mode, the user's interactive experience needs to be fully considered when determining how to clearly present geographic information and related data. When designing the interaction mode, the first consideration is the navigation tab mode, which allows the user to easily switch between different tabs to navigate to different areas or

Table 1. Summary of traditional cultural information graphics and interactive models

Chart	Quantity	Category Name	Interactive mode
Timeline infographic	7	1. Calligraphy culture 2. Gong Fan Culture 3. Dun huang Culture 4. History of perfume evolution 5. Ancient pet raising 6. Chinese Spring Festival 7. Brief history of Liang Liang	Form interaction Drag and dropfunction Preview mode
Map infographic	4	1. Customs of China's 56 ethnic groups 2. "African" continent 3. Famous scenic spots in Jiangxi 4. Shandong Province intangible cultural	Navigation TABmode Image zoommode Preview mode Modaframe mode
Process infographic	3	1. Dali Bai Tie-dye 2. Shui Xi Culture 3. Comparison China and the West	Touch navigation The node information popup Step navigation
Informational infographic	4	1. Big Wild Goose Pagoda in Xi'an 2. Terracotta Warriors 3. Dou Gong of Fo guang Temple 4. Agricultural tools	Timeline prompt Adaptive view pattern Paging mode Categorize patterns
Hierarchical Infographics	2	1. Time change of Macau Historical City 2. Temple of Heaven Building	Hierarchy mode Fold or unfold
List Infographics	1	1. Chinese imperial examinations	Row pattern Linkage mode
Data Visualization Infographics	3	1. Song Ci culture 2. Origin and development of tea culture 3. Intangible Shadow Play	Animation Interactive axis Interactive legend mode
Comparison Infographics	2	1. Gu qin art 2. Tang Palace Ladies Picture	The mode of multi-dimensional comparison The node information popup

information categories on the map. In addition, an image zoom mode that allows the user to zoom in and out of an image on the map through gestures can be incorporated to view more detailed images or information. Moreover, interactive map infographics require the use of preview modes: where the chart is too small to be easily read on the screen, it is common to imply that the user is viewing the chart in full screen, with navigation or other elements automatically restored when the user turns back to the device. The final mode to consider is the modal box mode, which enables the user to navigate and view specific areas or specific information within the modal box. For example, in Fig. 3, The Guardian's interactive map on women's rights allows viewers to access information by region, time period, or by right (voting, right to run, elected). More detailed information can then be accessed by clicking on a country.

Fig. 3. Interactive map chart of 'Women's Political Rights Around the World' (Picture source: https://www.columnfivemedia.com/101-fantastic-interactive-infographics-youll-love/)

3.3 Process Infographics

Flow-based infographics are intended to graphically display and explain processes, procedures or workflows. The purpose of this is to simplify complex processes so that viewers can clearly and quickly understand the relationships, sequences, and interactions between the various steps.

With regard to the different interaction modes, users can select touch navigation on the screen for horizontal or vertical navigation. Subsequently, through the inclusion of node information pop-ups, the user can click on a node which will display an information box pop to present detailed information about the node, including descriptions and key data. Clear step-by-step navigation is thoughtfully designed to display both the total number of steps and the step the user is currently in, giving the user visibility of the current display and what they will move on to next [14]. Furthermore, by means of timeline hints, a simple hint is included at the bottom or side of the chart to show the entire timeline of the whole process, thereby facilitating an understanding of the temporal relationship.

3.4 Informative Infographics

Informative infographics, which focus more on providing comprehensive and specific information, aim to visually convey in-depth knowledge. In the design of such charts, various graphical elements such as charts, graphs, labels and text are carefully selected and positioned to ensure the accuracy and legibility of the information.

In terms of interaction modes, as large volumes of content are typically included in infographics, adaptive view modes, which can change in real-time according to the amount of content in the interface, and pagination modes, which are suitable for displaying large amounts of information, can be selected during the design process in light of the content in question. Moreover, a compartmentalised mode can be integrated to organise information by category (see Fig. 4).

Fig. 4. Interactive infographic of 'Xi'an Big Wild Goose Pagoda' (Picture source: https://www. xiaohongshu.com/explore/654c4b170000000032004280?m_source=pinpai)

3.5 Hierarchical Infographics

Hierarchical infographics present information through a hierarchical or layered structure to assist viewers in understanding the organisation of information and its hierarchical structure. This kind of diagram differentiates between different levels of information by using various visuals and elements, such as icons, colours, shapes, and lines.

In the interactive mode, the first action that should be selected is to jump directly to a specific part of the hierarchical schema. Hierarchical charts that include a greater number of hierarchical relationships offer users the flexibility to use collapsed or expanded hierarchies, thus providing a more flexible viewing experience.

3.6 List Infographics

A list infographic is a graphical representation tool presenting data, information, or elements in a list format. By presenting information in an ordered list, users can readily easily identify and understand individual tasks. It should be highlighted that with this type of infographic, users can often sort or filter the list as needed to meet their individual viewing requirements.

Regarding interaction modes, the expandable row mode is incorporated to allow users to click on a row in the list to expand the information in more detail or switch the expansion state by clicking or sliding. In the combination of charts, the linkage mode between the list and the chart is highlighted by clicking on the list item, and marking and highlighting the relevant data in the chart accordingly.

3.7 Data Visualisation Infographics

Data visualisation is the process of presenting complex statistical data in an intuitive, easy-to-understand form through graphs and charts. Statistical charts are more inclined to transform abstract figures into intuitive images, facilitating the easy comprehension of vital information. For example, when in data trend analysis, the use of trend lines, curves and bar charts as a trend of data changes, allows for large volumes of data and data change processes to be readily understood.

In the interactive mode, animations can be used for time series or dynamic data to express the trend of the data. Due to the multiplicity of data, it is not possible to display all the information on one screen. Through the use of interactive technology, users can access interactive axes to allow the range to be adjusted and better control the display of data. The use of the interactive legend mode allows users to selectively show or hide specific data, thereby allowing them to control the complexity of the chart to suit their needs. Figure 5 (below) is an example of an interactive data visualisation infographic.

3.8 Comparison Infographics

Comparative infographics are a visualisation tool specifically designed to compare the differences and similarities between different data sets. Such an approach facilitates the comparisons of data at a glance through clever graphical design.

There is no single "best" mode of interaction, as it depends on the specific needs and user groups. In the comparison chart, a multi-dimensional comparison mode can be adopted: stacked charts, radar charts, or parallel coordinate charts can be considered to discern how to best convey the relationship between different dimensions. Secondly, through the form of node information pop-ups, the user can click a node to trigger an information box offering further details about the node.

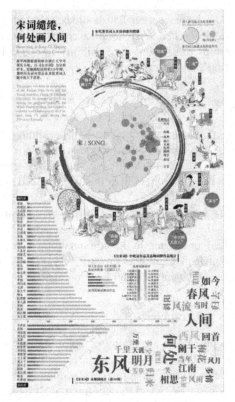

Fig. 5. Interactive Song Dynasty data visualisation charts (Picture source: https://www.xiaoho ngshu.com/explore/65831f6f000000003403c545?m_source=pinpai)

To sum up, different types of charts are suitable for different data analysis and display needs pertaining to traditional culture. Crucially, different interaction modes can improve user experience and efficiency. When designers design interactive information charts, they must reflect on what are the most appropriate chart types and interaction modes based on the context and information at hand in order to achieve the optimal information transmission effect.

4   Interactive Infographic Design for Beijing Axis Culture

This project aims to innovatively present this rich and unique cultural heritage by designing an interactive infographic on the culture of Beijing's central axis. Through the thoughtful deployment of interactive infographic design, users can obtain an in-depth understanding of the historical, geographical and cultural characteristics of the central axis.

As a symbol of China's ancient capital, the central axis is imbued with a rich history and culture, tying together important cultural sites such as the Temple of Heaven, the Forbidden City, and Yong dingmen, all of which have witnessed the glory of China's emperors, political changes and cultural inheritance over the centuries. The Central Axis, with its unique architectural style and traditional culture of cultural lineage, is a monument of the rich heritage of Chinese civilisation.

The interactive infographic is expected to be presented through a mobile application, communicating multi-dimensional, large-volume data in a single-screen interface to achieve the goal of "a picture is worth a thousand words". Importantly, the design will take into account both timeline, information and list types. Using a range of chart types not only increases the complexity of the project, but also meets the user's desire for a more comprehensive understanding of the in-depth culture of the Central Axis.

4.1 Timeline Infographics

Figure 6 follows the overall design of the timeline infographic process layout, covering 14 heritage sites along the Beijing Central Axis running from south to north, including the Temple of Heaven, Tiananmen Square, the Imperial Ancestral Temple, the Forbidden City, and the Bell Tower. With this in mind, the "Leap" design theme is utilised to make users feel as if they are experiencing the magnificent scene of stepping on the central axis and moving along it from south to north. Meanwhile, users can interact with the characters by clicking on them to trigger corresponding actions and sounds. Simultaneously, clicking on the buttons in the title can provide in-depth information about the building (see Fig. 6).

4.2 Informative Infographics

Figure 7, which focuses on the information design of the Temple of Heaven, is laid out according to the flow of informative infographics. The historical majesty of the central axis is felt in the first screen of the Flying Central Axis, which then leads on to the following secondary interface.

Users can view the dynamic change of information using buttons and access detailed scientific information by touching various features of the building. At the same time, the user can use the click functionalist to zoom in for a thumbnail view, rotating can be used to observe different angles of the beasts, and double-clicking on the roof beasts opens up related videos. These interaction modes are designed to engage users, enhance their interests, and stimulate their curiosity and exploration spirit (see Fig. 7).

4.3 Process Infographics

Figure 8 is laid out and designed according to the flow infographic, which introduces information about the design of the Temple of Heaven. By following the flow, users can read the information more clearly and enjoy an orderly, logical viewing experience. From the timeline information, users can expand and collapse the information as they see fit, as well as observe the dynamic changes of the building (see Fig. 8).

Fig. 6. The Flying Centreline interactive timeline infographic design (Picture source: Author's drawing)

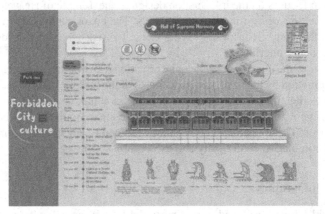

Fig. 7. Hall of Supreme Harmony interactive and informative infographic design (Picture source: Author's drawing)

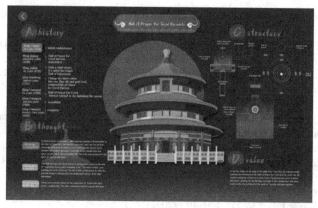

Fig. 8. Temple of Heaven interactive process infographic design (Picture source: Author's drawing)

5 Conclusion

This paper summarizes the results of the interaction research on eight types of infographics that contain different elements. Choosing the appropriate type of infographic can effectively highlight the focus of the information, leaving a deep impression on the user. [14] The aim of this study is to successfully identify the types of infographics and their basic elements, and propose applicable interaction patterns to improve the interactivity and interest between users and infographics. Furthermore, the study also considered how to better present complex data information on mobile devices.

In summary, interaction is an integral aspect of infographic design. On this basis, in the process of designing works, designers should focus on the user's operating experience, and the interaction mode is the core element [15]. This study has much reference value for the interactive design of infographics. With the continuous progress of technology, designers can continue to improve and explore the potential of design. As a result, interactive infographic design will become mainstream and in doing so, maximize the promotion and dissemination of traditional culture.

References

1. Zhu, Y.H.: Research on visual representation based on knowledge classification. Nanjing Normal University (2014)
2. Sun, Y., Wen, Z., Xu, R., et al.: An overview of data visualisation design for novel coronavirus pneumonia outbreak. Pack. Eng. **41**(08), 51–62 (2020). https://doi.org/10.19554/j.cnki.1001-3563.2020.08.008
3. Zhou, G.: Research on the design of NBA game data visualisation based on cognitive theory. Shandong University (2021). https://doi.org/10.27272/d.cnki.gshdu.2021.002502
4. Qin, J.: Research on information visualisation design methods in cultural heritage protection. Tsinghua University (2008)
5. Qi, S.: Exploration of interactivity in infographic design. Yiyuan **05**, 6–8 (2018)

6. Zhou, C., Zhang, X.: Research on visualisation design of cultural heritage information of Beijing central axis line. Art Technol. **35**(14), 96–98 (2022)

7. Wang, C.: Communication innovation of cultural heritage in the era of integrated media-taking the palace museum as an example. Media **08**, 66–69 (2020)

8. Song, F., Liu, Y.: Digital protection and inheritance strategy of intangible cultural heritage under the perspective of cultural industry. Shandong Soc. Sci. **02**, 83–87 (2015). https://doi.org/10.14112/j.cnki.37-1053/c.2015.02.015

9. Dur, B.İU., Filipczak-Bialkowska, A., Bresciani, S., et al.: Interactive infographics on the internet. Online J. Art Design **2**(4), 1–14 (2014)

10. Luo, Y., Jiang, S.: Cultural genetic restructuring in the digital era-current situation and future development of digitisation of china's cultural heritage. Sci. Technol. Progress Countermeas. **09**, 55–57 (2004)

11. Dou, X.: Research on the design method of infographics in the information age. Inform. Comput. (Theor. Edn.) **34**(21), 190–193 (2022)

12. Bao, Y., Qi, S.: Analysis of the characteristics of interactive infographic design in the information age. Popular Literat. Art **19**, 51–52 (2018)

13. Min, L., et al.: Exploring visual information flow in infographics. In: Proceedings of the 2020 CHI conference on human factors in computing systems (CHI 2020), pp. 1–12. Association for Computing Machinery, New York, NY, USA (2020). https://doi.org/10.1145/3313831.3376263

14. Shi, X., Ji, N.: Research on interaction design of information visualisation charts in the context of Internet B. Internet Weekly **09**, 94–96 (2023)

15. Yi, L.: Research on the interaction mode of mobile application. J. Beijing Inst. Print. **21**(05), 78–79 (2013). https://doi.org/10.19461/j.cnki.1004-8626.2013.05.020

16. Wang, W., Zhang, H., Chen, G.: Research on the future development trend of digital interaction design mode. Internet Weekly **2023**(19), 30–32 (2023)

The Effect of Color on Responsiveness in the Interactive Interface of the Space Station Alerting Task (SSAT)

Liangliang Zhao[1,3], Ao Jiang[1,2,3(✉)], Yan Zhao[4], Hao Fan[5], and Kun Yu[6]

[1] Nanjing University of Aeronautics and Astronautics, Nanjing, China
aojiang@nuaa.edu.cn
[2] Imperial College London, London, UK
[3] EuroMoonMars, ILEWG ESA, Wageningen, Netherlands
[4] The School of Mechatronical Engineering, Advanced Innovation Center for Intelligent Robots and Systems, Key Laboratory of Biomimetic Robots and Systems of Chinese Ministry of Education, Beijing Institute of Technology, Beijing, China
[5] Southeast University, Nanjing, China
[6] China Ship Development and Design Center, Beijing, China

Abstract. This study evaluates the effect of warning colors of different hues, brightness, and saturation on human color perception performance by conducting a space system fault alarm color keystroke experiment with 80 subjects and testing 30 warning color samples with reaction time and correctness as the interactive interface color perception performance evaluation indices. The results showed that the individual independent variables (hue, brightness, saturation) all had significant effects on the subjects' reaction time (p = 0.000 < 0. 05), and there was no significant effect on the accuracy rate; in the multiple comparisons by hue, there was a significant difference in the comparison of reaction time between the hues H = 0 and H = 20, and between the hues H = 20 and H = 340; in the multiple comparisons by brightness, there were significant differences; and in saturation, significant differences were observed between all three saturation levels (40%, 70%, and 100%). In conclusion, this study provides information for the color design of interactive interfaces for future spacecraft such as space stations.

Keywords: Emergency Alarm and Fault interface · Warning Colors · Visual Perception · Color Performance

1 Introduction

With the rapid development of China's space industry, space tasks are gradually becoming more diverse and challenging. For example, astronauts are essential for tasks such as on-orbit assembly, space vehicle maintenance, satellite recovery, and space science experiments. The spacecraft's human-computer interface (HCI) system, as a critical component of human-computer interaction, plays a pivotal role in ensuring the efficiency and proper functioning of spaceflight activities [1]. The design of colors for emergency

© The Author(s), under exclusive license to Springer Nature Switzerland AG 2024
A. Marcus et al. (Eds.): HCII 2024, LNCS 14712, pp. 175–186, 2024.
https://doi.org/10.1007/978-3-031-61351-7_12

alarm and fault interfaces significantly impacts the crew. In previous spacecraft, HCI design interface decisions were primarily driven by engineering considerations, with little regard for the influence of color factors on human performance [2]. The interface on the International Space Station (ISS) primarily presents data information, with minimal use of color for organizing and planning information on the operational interface [3]. However, the current spacecraft HCI presents challenges with an abundance of information, limited color variation, and a complex interaction structure. The alarm mission interface, a crucial part of the human-computer interaction system, is designed with such complexity that it can overwhelm astronauts in processing visual information, potentially leading to risks like mission operation errors, misinterpretations, and delayed responses.

Color elements play an important role in space missions due to their impact on human physiological parameters, cognitive and decision-making abilities, and human psychology [4]. An important challenge in the development of task-centric spacecraft alerting task-based interaction systems is efficient HCI design. The process of alerting task-centric design means that designers mimic the behavioral descriptions of real-world tasks that people perform, use them to select the task functionalities that should be supported by the system, and in the alert task-oriented process, analyze and build an interface system that meets the requirements [5]. This means that not only the coupling of the whole system and the comprehensiveness of the hierarchical system are ensured in the construction of the system, but also the hierarchical system should be combined with elements such as information layout and colors for an astronaut-centered design. Color is an effective way to establish a correct and efficient interaction between astronauts and the mission warning interface, and it is also an important means to enhance the aesthetic experience of the warning interface. For example, NASA has developed the Mission Control Center Managed Astronaut Work/Life Schedule Management System (MPI System), which not only highlights astronaut task sequences in a color-coded manner to provide visual cues during task viewing and rescheduling activities, but also provides a viable solution to the impending communication delays that can occur during long-duration spaceflight [6]. In addition, color has an impact on perception and objective criteria. The use of color as data visualization is one of the most common and important operations, Aritra Dasgupta analyzed the effect of hue and brightness values on subjective user performance metrics such as user confidence, perceived accuracy, preference, and familiarity with the use of different color scales, and the results showed that color contributes to the performance accuracy of climate modeling tasks [7]. Therefore, color, as an important component of the mission information interaction interface, is one of the most important factors affecting the performance of astronauts on space missions.

Color, as the human visual senses' response to light emitted or reflected from an object, permeates the human perceptual channel extensively. Color vision encompasses three key characteristics: hue, brightness, and saturation. Each attribute can be quantified objectively and described based on the observer's senses. Effective color design not only reinforces the conveyed information's meaning but also exerts a moderating influence on individuals' negative emotions, subsequently shaping their behavioral actions. Color represents a pervasive perceptual experience.In task-oriented systems, red, often employed as a warning color, is strongly linked with the risk of failure, prompting avoidance [8]. Research indicates that colors with longer wavelengths induce euphoria, while those with shorter wavelengths evoke feelings of depression. This phenomenon extends to astronaut reactivity. For instance, in the Lunar Exploration Augmented Reality System developed by Lea S. Miller for NASA SUITS (Space Suit User Interface Technology for Students), the warning color red serves as a visual aid. During the execution of a mission selection module, the highlighted mission flashes in red until the bumper is pressed. Once pressed, the user is notified that the mission is now highlighted in red. This component, utilizing colored warning signals to assist astronauts, requires only two navigation buttons and no additional controls. It also facilitates navigation through various guidance pages [9]. However, current research on red warning colors primarily focuses on the psychological aspect of attention, with limited exploration of the impact and connection between red attributes (hue, brightness, saturation) and people's behavior.

Therefore, this study aims to investigate how changes in warning color values on the display interface affect astronauts' responsiveness under space warning conditions. It experiments to evaluate differences in color performance, considering variations in hue, brightness, and saturation of warning colors under simulated conditions. The objective is to provide insights for future human-computer interfaces that support astronauts' activities in space.

2   Method

2.1 Participants

The formal experimental participants comprised undergraduate and graduate students from various universities, totaling 80 individuals. The gender distribution was evenly balanced, with a 1:1 ratio of males to females (40 males and 40 females). The age range of the participants was 18 to 26 years, with a mean age of 21.14 ± 2.38 years. Before the commencement of the formal experimental test, all participants underwent the Ishihara online color blindness test, achieving 100% accuracy and demonstrating no color blindness. Additionally, they exhibited normal or corrected-to-normal visual acuity. Participants were queried about their physical well-being before engaging in the formal experiment, and none reported a history of cardiac or cerebrovascular disease or psychiatric disorders. None of the participants had been exposed to the test materials used in this experiment before its initiation. Detailed explanations of the experimental procedures were provided to all participants before the start of the experiment, and each participant signed an informed consent form indicating their agreement to participate in the study.

2.2 Equipment

This experiment involves a color button response task, with the experimental procedure programmed using the psychological experiment design software E-prime. The alarm task interface was inspired by materials related to the International Space Station, the TianGong Space Station, and other relevant film and television sources.

For this study, 27 red warning color samples were selected as test stimuli, representing various combinations of hue, brightness, and saturation (3 hue * 3 brightness * 3 saturation). To prevent participants from developing a rhythmic response pattern, a green sample was introduced into the program as an interference stimulus.Participants were instructed to identify the color of the alarm pop-up window and respond accordingly by pressing the keys. Considering the impact of stimulus probability on human reaction time and accuracy, the experimental program limited the probability of red and green stimuli appearing. The two color pop-ups appeared randomly within the time frame of "500 to 1000 ms."

2.3 Warning Color Samples

The color mode utilized in this study is HSB (Hue, Saturation, Brightness). HSB controls color through three parameters: H (Hue), S (Saturation), and B (Brightness). The Hue value ranges from 0 to 360 degrees, representing the angle at the center of the color ring. Saturation and Brightness values range from 0 to 100%. The HSB color mode aligns closely with human visual perception, describing color in terms of hue, brightness, and saturation. This approach expands the concept of color based on the human brain's interpretation of "brightness and darkness," providing a more intuitive understanding of color [11]. Given the extensive angular range of the warning color red on the hue ring, this study focuses on the primary hue with an H value of 0%, corresponding to positive red. Additionally, an orange-red (warmer) hue with an H value of 20%, shifted 20 degrees to the right on the hue ring, and a fuchsia (cooler) hue with an H value of 340%, shifted 20 degrees to the left, was selected as the other two test hues. To examine the impact of changes in brightness and saturation on information recognition performance, each of the three hues varied in brightness and saturation from 0 to 100% of their volume fraction [12]. To ensure visual clarity among the test colors, dark colors in brightness and excessively light colors in saturation were excluded. Three Brightness levels (100%, 80%, and 60%) and three saturation levels (100%, 70%, and 40%) were determined to enhance visual variability. Ultimately, 27 warning color samples were selected (Fig. 1).

Fig. 1. A figure shows a sample of the red warning test color. (Color figure online)

2.4 Procedures

This experiment employed a three-factor within-subjects design, incorporating hue, brightness, and saturation as independent variables in the color of the system fault alarm pop-up window. The study aimed to assess subjects' reaction time and accuracy in discerning different colored warning pop-up windows. Participants were tasked with identifying the color of the system fault alarm pop-up window, determining whether it signaled a red or green alert, and responding by pressing the F key for a red pop-up window and the J key for a green pop-up window. The test program automatically recorded reaction times and the correctness of the warning pop-up window identification, with keystrokes scored as 1 for correct and 0 for incorrect inputs. To enhance the simulation of space emergencies, the research team decided to incorporate warning audio sourced from the Internet into the test program.

The formal experiment unfolded in three stages: the initial stage involved the original color vision test; the second stage encompassed the experimental test procedure practice; and the third stage constituted the formal experimental test.

The experimental test procedure comprised three main segments. The first part involved providing experimental instructions to guide subjects through the operational details, ensuring their understanding of the basic experiment procedures. The second part was a practice phase where subjects familiarized themselves with the color-key correspondences, preventing errors due to unfamiliarity with the experimental operation. During this phase, subjects were informed of the correctness of their key responses. Reaction times were automatically recorded by the program but were not subjected to statistical analysis. The third part constituted the formal test procedure, during which test results were not disclosed, and the next color pop-up window immediately followed the testing of each color until all color samples were assessed.

During the formal testing procedure, the researcher is required to sequentially assign numbers to and record each participant involved in the formal experiment. Participants are instructed to read the experimental guidelines, and upon completion, they should press the Q key to transition to the practice phase of the experiment. After completing the practice phase, participants are instructed to press the Q key again to initiate the formal test program. The test interface will become visible 30 s after the activation of an alarm audio, followed by the appearance of a "+" sign denoting an attention point. Subsequently, a warning pop-up window stimulus appears randomly at intervals of 500–1000 ms. Participants are tasked with determining the color of the warning pop-up window and responding by pressing the corresponding key based on the experimental requirements. After making the judgment, the "+" attention point reappears, signaling the readiness for the next pop-up window stimulus, which again appears at random intervals of 500–1000 ms. Participants repeat this process for each subsequent pop-up window stimulus until all color samples have been tested (Fig. 2).

3 Results

3.1 Results of Reaction Time Analysis

Initially, a repeated-measures ANOVA was conducted on the experimental data concerning reaction time. This analysis focused on exploring variations in the reaction time among the 80 subjects across different hue, brightness, and saturation conditions. Additionally, the study examined the interaction effects among these three factors, considering both significant and non-significant differences.

Fig. 2. Experimental Flowchart

The ANOVA results for the reaction time of the 80 subjects revealed that the individual independent variables—hue, brightness, and saturation of the color samples—exerted significant effects on the subjects' reaction time under conditions of correct responses. Notably, no significant differences were observed between the two-factor combinations of brightness, saturation, and brightness. Furthermore, the three-factor interaction (brightness*saturation) did not demonstrate a significant impact on reaction time (Table 1).

Table 1. Analysis Results of the ANOVA on reaction time

Source of effect	Degree of freedom	Mean square	F	Significance
hue	1.901	12471.106	15.593	<0.001***
brightness	1.954	2817.121	3.469	0.035*
saturation	2.0	0.375	23.413	<0.001***
hue*brightness	3.750	1093.912	1.911	0.113
hue*saturation	3.795	1437.714	2.053	0.091
brightness*saturation	3.678	262.321	0.382	0.806
hue*rightness*saturation	8.0	0.124	1.276	0.270

Therefore, according to the results of the ANOVA on reaction time, there was a significant difference between the hue, brightness, and saturation variations of the 27 warning color samples on the subjects' reaction time. It indicates that under the conditions of this experiment, the subjects' reaction time is strongly related to all three attributes of hue, brightness, and saturation of the warning colors, but the specific relationship between reaction time and these three attributes needs to be analyzed by multiple comparisons of the data between each attribute to further derive the intrinsic influence law of hue, brightness, and saturation of the warning colors on reaction time.

3.2 Hue-Reaction Time Multiple Comparison Results

According to the results of the multiple comparisons of the three hues, there is a significant main effect of hue in the color samples of this experiment: there is a significant difference between hue H = 0 and H = 20, with a difference of less than 0.001; there is a non-significant difference between hue H = 0 and H = 340; and there is also a significant difference between hue H = 20 and H = 340, with a p-value of 0.004 (Table 2).

Table 2. Analysis Results of Multiple Comparisons of Hues

(I) Hue	(J) Hue	Significance
H = 0	H = 20	<0.001***
	H = 340	0.087
H = 20	H = 0	<0.001***
	H = 340	0.004**
H = 340	H = 0	0.087
	H = 20	0.004**

Combining the results of the estimated marginal means of hue reaction time, hue H = 0 has the shortest reaction time, H = 20 has the longest reaction time, and H = 340 has the middle reaction time. There is a significant difference between hue H = 0 and H = 20, and the mean value of reaction time for hue H = 0 is the lowest, lower than the mean value of H = 20 and H = 340, which indicates that people react the fastest at hue attribute H = 0. There's a significant difference between hue H = 20 and H = 340, and the mean value of reaction time for H = 340 is smaller than that of H = 20, which indicates that people's reactions are faster and have a shorter reaction time than H = 20 [10] (Fig. 3).

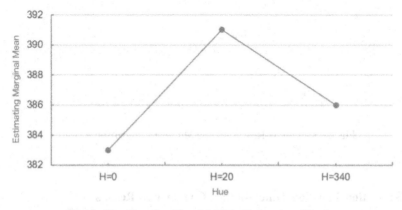

Fig. 3. Hue-Reaction Time Multiple Comparison Results

3.3 Brightness-Reaction Time Multiple Comparison Results

According to the results of the data analysis of brightness, the main effect of brightness in the color samples of this experiment was significant: there was a significant difference between 80% and 100% brightness, with a p-value of 0.025; and there was no significant difference between 60% and 80% and 60% and 100% brightness (Table 3).

Table 3. Analysis Results of Multiple Comparisons of Brightness

(I) Brightness	(J) Brightness	Significance
B = 60%	B = 80%	0.505
	B = 100%	0.097
B = 80%	B = 60%	0.505
	B = 100%	0.025*
B = 100%	B = 60%	0.097
	B = 80%	0.025*

Combining the results of the estimated marginal mean of brightness reaction time shows that brightness is significant between 80% and 100% and that the reaction time for brightness 80% is lower than 100%, indicating that in terms of brightness, the reaction time of people with brightness values around 80% is the shortest and that the reaction time of subjects increases instead of decreases when brightness rises to 100% (Fig. 4).

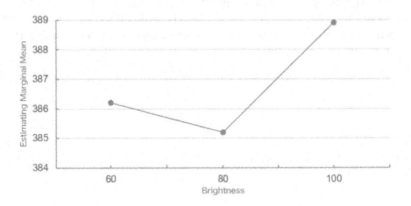

Fig. 4. Brightness-Reaction Time Multiple Comparison Results

3.4 Saturation-Reaction Time Multiple Comparison Results

According to the results of the data analysis of saturation, the main effect of saturation in the color samples of this experiment was significant: there was a significant difference between 40% and 70% saturation, with a p-value of 0.001; between 40% and 100% saturation, with a p-value of less than 0.001; and between 70% and 100% saturation, which also showed a significant difference, with a p-value of 0.015 (Table 4).

Table 4. Analysis Results of Multiple Comparisons of Saturation

(I) Saturation	(J) Saturation	Significance
S = 40%	S = 70%	0.001**
	S = 100%	<0.001***
S = 70%	S = 40%	0.001**
	S = 100%	0.015*
S = 100%	S = 40%	<0.001***
	S = 70%	0.015*

As can be seen from the figure, the pattern of change of saturation-response time in this experiment is significant, and when the saturation degree changes from 40% to 100%, the average value of the subjects' response time gradually decreases, and there are significant differences between the response times of all three saturation. Therefore, the basic law between reaction time and saturation can be drawn through this experiment: that is, the higher the saturation, the shorter the subjects' reaction time, and the higher the color perception performance (Fig. 5).

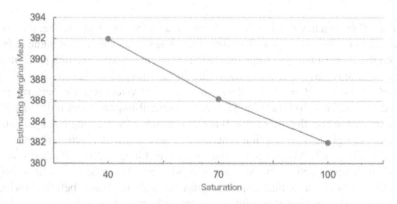

Fig. 5. Saturation-Reaction Time Multiple Comparison Results

3.5 Results of Correctness Analysis

Another important index of this experiment is the correct response rate of the 27 color samples and a repeated-measures ANOVA was conducted to analyze the correct response rate of 80 subjects. According to the test results, the effect of the single independent variables of hue, brightness, and saturation of the color samples of this experiment on the correct rate of the subjects in the correct response condition was not significant; the effects of hue*saturation, hue*brightness, brightness*saturation, and hue*saturation were also not significant; and the effect of hue*saturation, hue*brightness, brightness*saturation, and hue*saturation interaction was also not significant. The interaction of brightness*saturation was also not significant. This indicates that the subjects in this experiment all correctly recognized the alarm color signals (Fig. 6).

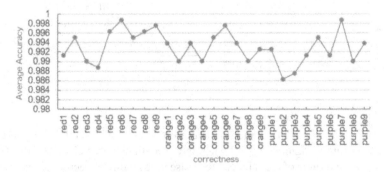

Fig. 6. Results of correctness analysis

4   Discussion

The subjects' emergency reaction time was influenced by three factors: hue, brightness, and saturation of the color signal. The analysis of hue revealed that a hue value of H = 0 exhibited the shortest reaction time, indicating the highest visual reaction performance, aligning with previous experiences regarding color perception's danger level [6]. Following closely is hue H = 340 (cooler), while the least visual reaction performance is observed for hue H = 20 (warmer). Hence, for optimal improvement in human visual response performance, the use of H = 0 is recommended for warning hue applications. The impact of lightness on reaction time is more specific, with reaction times ranging from 80%, 60%, to 100%, in order from shortest to longest. The estimated marginal mean of brightness reaction time suggests a non-linear relationship, wherein as brightness continues to increase, human reaction time initially decreases before showing an upward trend. This implies a non-linear change in brightness reaction time, and there might be a brightness value of around 80% that characterizes the highest performance. Consequently, when employing red as a warning color, it is suggested that the brightness value not be pushed to the highest level, but instead optimized around 80%. The influence of saturation on reaction time is evident, with significant differences observed in the comparison between three saturation levels. Reaction time decreases as the saturation value increases, indicating that higher saturation leads to better human reaction performance.

In summary, the warning color of the space station alarm mission interface needs to be selected by considering the three factors of hue, brightness, and saturation of the warning color, and it is necessary to carry out the simulated human factors ergonomics test in microgravity environment for the warning color value in the design scheme, to further explore the influence law of the color and the human response performance, and finally to determine the optimal color value of the color response performance.

5   Conclusion

In this study, we investigated the impact of alterations in the hue, brightness, and saturation of the warning color red on astronauts' reaction time and response accuracy. This was accomplished by simulating a spacecraft system fault alert task using the color key response method. Subsequent multiple comparisons of the three color attributes in this experiment yielded the following conclusions:

1. Reaction time demonstrated a significant correlation with the hue, lightness, and saturation attributes of the warning color. However, all three attributes had minimal impact on the accuracy of color recognition [13–16].
2. Concerning hue, human reaction time was found to be shortest when hue $H = 0$, indicating that individuals exhibit the highest level of alertness and visual perception efficiency for the warning color with a hue value of 0.
3. Participants in this experiment displayed the highest visual perception efficiency for colors with a hue value of 80%. In terms of hue, humans exhibited optimal color recognition performance and the most effective warning effect when the hue value was 80%.
4. The observed pattern in terms of saturation revealed that higher saturation corresponded to shorter human reaction times, indicating that human color recognition performance was at its peak, and the warning effect was most effective under conditions of increased saturation [17–20].

In conclusion, a specific analysis of the color values of the experimental samples highlighted that the visual response performance of the Red4 sample ($H = 0$, $B = 80\%$, $S = 100\%$) was superior, showcasing the highest warning effect and visual response efficiency [21].

References

1. Zhou, Q.: Research on human-machine interface design method for manned spacecraft. Shanghai Aerosp. **2002**(03), 39–41+52 (2002)
2. Maria, D., Favata, P.: Color considerations for the design of space habitats. In: AIAA space 2003 conference & exposition (2003)
3. Weiss, H., Liu, A., Byon, A., Blossom, J., Stirling, L.: Comparison of display modality and human-in-the-loop presence for on-orbit inspection of spacecraft. Hum. Factors **65**(6), 1059–1073 (2023)
4. Jiang, A., Yao, X., Foing, B., Westland, S., Hemingray, C., Mu, S.: Integrating human factors into the colour design of human-machine interfaces for spatial habitat, EGU General Assembly 2022, Vienna, Austria, 23–27 May 2022, EGU22-622

5. Nilgün, C., Yener, C., Güvenç, D.: Effects of hue, saturation, and brightness: Part 2: Attention. Color Research & Application: Endorsed by Inter-Society Color Council, The Colour Group (Great Britain), Canadian Society for Color, Color Science Association of Japan, Dutch Society for the Study of Color, The Swedish Colour Centre Foundation, Colour Society of Australia, Centre Français de la Couleur, vol. 29.1, pp. 20–28 (2007)

6. Elliot, A.J., Maier, M.A., Moller, A.C., Friedman, R., Meinhardt, J.: Color and psychological functioning: the effect of red on performance attainment. J. Exp. Psychol. Gen. 136(1), 154–168 (2007)

7. Dasgupta, A., Poco, J., Rogowitz, B., Han, K., Bertini, E., Silva, C.T.: The effect of color scales on climate scientists' objective and subjective performance in spatial data analysis tasks. IEEE Trans. Visual. Comput. Graph. 26(3), 1577–1591

8. Baltrusaitis, M., Feigh, K.: The development of a user interface for mixed-initiative plan management for human spaceflight. In: 2019 IEEE aerospace conference, pp. 1–9. Big Sky, MT, USA (2019)

9. Miller, L.S., Fornito, M.J., Flanagan, R., Kobrick, R.L.: Development of an augmented reality interface to aid astronauts in extravehicular activities. In: 2021 IEEE aerospace conference (50100), pp. 1–12. Big Sky, MT, USA (2021)

10. Jiang, A.O.: Effects of colour environment on spaceflight cognitive abilities during short-term simulations of three gravity states. University of Leeds (2022)

11. Küller, R., Ballal, S., Laike, T., Mikellides, B., Tonello, G.: The impact of light and colour on psychological mood: a cross-cultural study of indoor work environments. Ergonomics 49(14), 1496–1507 (2006)

12. Effects of nine monochromatic office interior colors on clerical tasks and worker mood Color Res. Appl. 21(6), 448–458 (1996)

13. Jiang, A., Foing, B.H., Schlacht, I.L., Yao, X., Cheung, V., Rhodes, P.A.: Colour schemes to reduce stress response in the hygiene area of a space station: a Delphi study. Appl. Ergon. 98, 103573 (2022)

14. Jiang, A., et al.: The effect of colour environments on visual tracking and visual strain during short-term simulation of three gravity states. Appl. Ergon. 110, 103994 (2023)

15. Yu, K., Jiang, A., Wang, J., Zeng, X., Yao, X., Chen, Y.: Construction of crew visual behaviour mechanism in ship centralized control cabin. In: Stanton, N. (eds.) Advances in human aspects of transportation. AHFE 2021. LNNS, vol. 270. Springer, Cham (2021). https://doi.org/10.1007/978-3-030-80012-3_58

16. Jiang, A., et al.: Space habitat astronautics: multicolour lighting psychology in a 7-day simulated habitat. Space: Sci. Technol. (2022)

17. Jiang, A., et al.: Short-term virtual reality simulation of the effects of space station colour and microgravity and lunar gravity on cognitive task performance and emotion. Build. Environ. 227, 109789 (2023)

18. Jiang, A., Yao, X., Westland, S., Hemingray, C., Foing, B., Lin, J.: The effect of correlated colour temperature on physiological, emotional and subjective satisfaction in the hygiene area of a space station. Int. J. Environ. Res. Public Health 19(15), 9090 (2022)

19. Jiang, A., Zhu, Y., Yao, X., Foing, B.H., Westland, S., Hemingray, C.: The effect of three body positions on colour preference: an exploration of microgravity and lunar gravity simulations. Acta Astronaut. 204, 1–10 (2023)

20. Huang, Z., Wang, S., Jiang, A., Hemingray, C., Westland, S.: Gender preference differences in color temperature associated with LED light sources in the autopilot cabin. In: Krömker, H. (eds.) HCI in mobility, transport, and automotive systems. HCII 2022. LNCS, vol. 13335. Springer, Cham (2022). https://doi.org/10.1007/978-3-031-04987-3_10

21. Jiang, A., Yao, X., Hemingray, C., Westland, S.: Young people's colour preference and the arousal level of small apartments. Color. Res. Appl. 47(3), 783–795 (2022)

Usability Testing and User Experience Evaluation

Workshop DUXAIT: Conducting Efficient Heuristic Evaluations with the Duxait-Ng Tool. A Case Study

Joel Aguirre[(✉)] [iD], Adrian Lecaros[iD], Carlos Ramos[iD], Fiorella Falconi[iD], Arturo Moquillaza[iD], and Freddy Paz[iD]

Pontificia Universidad Católica del Perú, Universitaria 1801, San Miguel, Lima 32, Lima, Peru

{aguirre.joel,adrian.lecaros,carlos.ramosp,ffalconit}@pucp.edu.pe,
{amoquillaza,fpaz}@pucp.pe

Abstract. In the context of Covid-19 pandemic, conducting a user experience evaluation has become more. For example, Heuristic Evaluation, is manual task-dependent, does not have a standardized way, and data processing costs valuable time. This context made heuristic evaluations even more difficult. Without specialized software, the tasks of a heuristic evaluation were manual and processing the final results was a burden to the researchers. There were attempts to standardize this method, for example, the software proposed by Lecaros, A. Another method is Tree Testing, for which Tapia A. proposed software to support the evaluation process. However, both the Tapia, A. software and Lecaros, A. software, were designed specifically for the evaluations they support. These studies served as a base so the authors could propose a software that aids UX enthusiasts conduct Heuristic Evaluations, and other types of usability evaluations, more efficiently. This software, named DUXAIT-NG, supports various evaluations and reduces the time for processing the final results, even when having a large group of participants. The article describes how to conduct a workshop, and what was learned by analyzing the results and experiences of all the participants. This article is organized as follows: the first section, tells the motivations of the study. The second section seeks to clarify theoretical concepts used throughout the article. The third section describes in detail the workshop. The fourth section describes the results of the participant's experience. Finally, the article ends with the conclusions and future work that the authors have planned for DUXAIT-NG.

Keywords: workshop · training · heuristic evaluation · usability evaluation · user satisfaction · user perception · human computer interaction · questionnaire · survey

1   Introduction

In the context of the COVID-19 pandemic, conducting a user experience evaluation became more tedious than it used to be. This is mainly because UX evaluations were characterized by user interaction with the evaluated system and this is usually performed in face-to-face settings, e.g., an HCI lab. Additionally, several user experience evaluation methods are usually heavily burdened with manual activities, both in execution and data analysis and there is usually no single standardized way of how to execute them. For example, Heuristic Evaluation, being the most widely used usability inspection method, is manually loaded, does not have a standardized way and data processing costs valuable time to the executors.

In this sense, in previous works, standardized processes were proposed to carry out heuristic evaluations in generic contexts, taking as a first reference the proposal of Paz, F [1]. Even having processes, carrying out a Heuristic Evaluation was still a manual task, therefore, Lecaros A. proposed in 2022 [2] a web software that supports the phases proposed in the methodology of Paz, F. This software reduces the manual tasks in the process and reduces the time to obtain the final results, being generated immediately when having all the answers of the participants. In addition to the methodology of Paz, F. there is the proposal of Granoller, T. [3] who proposed a Heuristic Evaluation process based on the fulfillment of general sub-heuristics that would apply to various types of software; unfortunately, the software of Lecaros, A. does not support this second standardization proposal.

Another method widely used in the design and evaluation of user experience is Tree Testing, for which Tapia A. [4] proposed a software to support the evaluation process, facilitating the execution of the evaluations and reducing the logistical costs involved in getting the evaluation to the participants. Unlike the Heuristic Evaluation that is usually carried out with HCI experts, Tree Testing looks for end users and needs a significant number of participants to have better results [5]. However, both the Tapia, A. and Lecaros, A. software were designed specifically for the evaluations they support.

In this sense, the authors proposed a standardized process [6] that allows the inclusion of any usability evaluation process, factoring common activities, such as planning, training of participants and analysis of results. This process would initially have the activities of the three proposals mentioned above, but with the particularity that it would allow the incorporation of any other usability evaluation method. This process led to the development of a web software called DUXAIT-NG [7], which is deployed and released for use at www.duxait-ng.net. In previous studies [8], duxait-ng was used in the heuristic evaluation of a web site, proving its usefulness over a formal process executed manually.

The above reasons motivated the authors to continue experimenting with the software tool, and as part of its dissemination phase, the organization of a workshop was ideal to convene a large group of participants. In order to carry out a successful implementation of the software, it was necessary to train the participants in the use of the tool and, above all, to teach the necessary concepts of HCI so that all participants were at the same level of understanding. For this purpose, it was necessary to plan two sessions, one to serve as a teaching class and the second to put into practice what was learned.

During the workshop, the authors played the role of presenters/trainers; the first training session was conducted virtually and the second practical session was face-to-face for pedagogical reasons, but it was not a necessity for the tool. The training session was planned to last two hours and addressed conceptual issues, definitions of terms necessary for the participants to have the same level of understanding. The second session, which would be face-to-face, was planned to last a maximum of six hours, in which a practical session was held where the DUXAIT-NG tool was used to perform a heuristic evaluation. This last session was held in a convention hall with sufficient capacity to accommodate the participants and to be able to support everyone.

In this article we will describe the 'DUXAIT Workshop 2023', how it was organized, the way in which we executed the sessions and the evaluation of the participants' experience. The article is organized as follows, the second section seeks to clarify theoretical concepts used throughout the case study. The third section describes in detail the workshop, from its planning and organization to the execution of the virtual and face-to-face sessions, until the end of the event. The fourth section describes the results of the participant's experience in the workshop and using the software. Finally, the article ends with the conclusions and future work that the authors have planned for DUXAIT-NG.

2   Background

In this section, we describe five terms that are mandatory to understand the case study and to know what we tried to perform during the workshop.

2.1   Workshop

A classic definition of a workshop is to see it as a space for discussion, debate or practical work, where participants share knowledge and compare experiences [9]. Although a workshop can deal with any topic, in the field of user experience, it is a tool that generates new ideas and democratizes learning [10].

2.2   NPS

Net Promoter Score, or simply 'NPS', is a tool for high-level diagnostic, the improvements are understood as a positive performance; whereas, a declining score means emerging problems, akin to 'measuring the temperature' of a product or brand [11].

NPS surveys are widely used across industries and could include specific questions to capture additional data on a specific domain [12]. To calculate NPS score, the survied is asked to rate a service on ascale of 1 to 10 where results between 9 and 10 categorize the customer as a promoter. Results between 7 and 8 classify the customer as neutral and a result less than or equal to 6 classify the customer as a detractor [13].

2.3   SUS

System Usability Scale, or simply SUS, created by John Brooke in 1986, is based on a 10-question questionnaire (alternating positive and negative aspects) that provides a value between 0 and 100 indicating how usable an interface has been for a given user. This value, not to be confused with a percentage, actually measures emotional aspects of the user, since the answers are totally emotionally drive [14].

2.4   TAM2

TAM2 is a questionnaire used to measure the perceived usefulness (four items), perceived ease of use (four items), intention to use (two items), subjective norm (two items), job relevance (two items), output quality (two items), voluntariness (three items), image (three items), and result demonstrability (four items), 26 items within a 1–7 scale, where one means disagreement and 7 an strong agreement [15].

2.5   Heuristic Evaluation

According to Nielsen, Heuristic Evaluation is a usability inspection method which is widely used as an informal approach. This method evaluates positive and negative aspects and requires the expertise of usability professionals who can assess whether the elements of dialogue or other interactive software components adhere to established usability principles or heuristics [16].

In order to define a formal approach, Paz, F. proposed a process based on the analysis of different case studies and established five phases for its execution, (1) planning, (2) training, (3) evaluation, (4) discussion, and (5) Report [17].

2.6   Tree Testing

Tree Testing is defined as the process for manual application of the Card-Based Evaluation Classification technique [18]. It is a quick way to evaluate the architecture of information without generating additional costs. Its central objective is to be able to solve the central problem of non-detection or late detection of errors within the information architecture [4].

3   Case Study DUXAIT Workshop 2023

3.1   Conducting the Workshop

This section details how we executed the duxait 2023 workshop, starting with the organization of the event. To do so, we defined the terms and conditions of the call, although it would be open, it would have a target audience, mainly developers from the financial sector. The participants filled out a form answering

Fig. 1. Workshop DUXAIT 2023 Poster - Open Invitation

questions about their previous experience and field of interest. Figure 1 shows the call published in several academic communication portals.

Once we received the applications from the interested parties, we had to make an initial filter, cleaning data from some applications that were not properly completed or did not comply with the rules. We were able to elaborate profiles according to the answers, to know if they work or not, their level of experience in HCI and UX.

Having the participants registered and knowing their profiles, we were able to start the virtual session, for which a video call tool was used. For the face-to-face session, we estimated the attendance of the same participants of the virtual session, thus having an estimated capacity for the room where the practice would take place.

More details of both sessions are given below.

3.2 Virtual Session

In this virtual session, we schedule participants for a two-hour workshop. At the beginning, we introduced the HCI-DUXAIT PUCP research group and each member. The topics covered were basic concepts of usability, the most used methods to evaluate usability, the benefits of heuristic evaluation as the most used method and examples of heuristic evaluations. For this examples, we detailed examples for each Nielsen's Heuristics [16]; as an example, Fig. 2 shows examples for the first two Nielsen's heuristics shown during the virtual session.

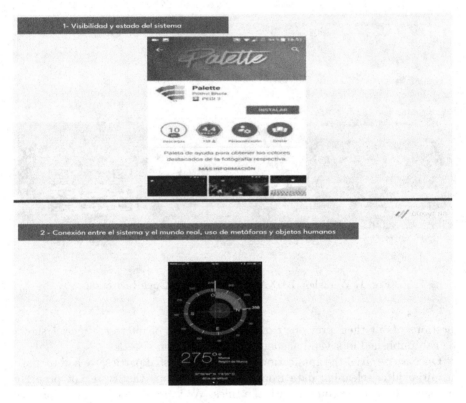

Fig. 2. Examples of heuristic principle used in Heuristic Evaluations

After having exemplified the heuristics used in the evaluations, we proceeded to explain the evaluation process. At the beginning, the explanation was theoretical, specifically explaining the method of T. Granollers [3] and the calculation of the final usability scores. This theory was supported by examples of the fifteen heuristic principles used.

This theory was necessary to finally show the stellar software. The participants had access to a DUXAIT-NG Demo, where a heuristic evaluation was performed following the method of T. Granollers. In Fig. 3, we see the answer section of the 15 heuristic principles, where the user must select if the evaluated software complies or not with the principle.

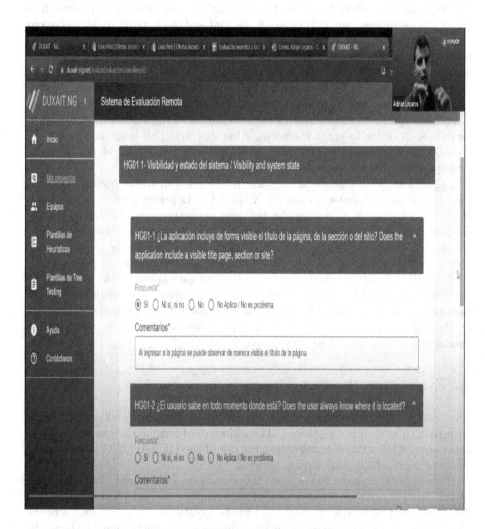

Fig. 3. Demo of DUXAIT-NG during virtual session

The final objective was showing the workshop participants a first encounter with DUXAIT-NG and the concepts of Heuristic Evaluation and Usability. So, in the second session they started with a better know-how and thus be able to present the case for the next session as a homework assignment. In addition, all the participants who registered in the initial call assisted to the first virtual session.

3.3 Practical Session

This second session of the workshop was held two days after the virtual session. Participants were scheduled for a six-hour session where the topics presented in the first session were put into practice. To that end, each participant was asked to attend with a laptop that could be connected to Wi-Fi. Attendees at the face-to-face session were the same as in the virtual session, so the capacity was within the expected range.

First, the room was set up, preparing a reception area where it was verified that the attendee actually belonged to the workshop. According to the order of arrival, the informed consent forms were presented to the attendees, who had to sign them in order to enter the room. After the first half hour and having all the attendees in the room, the session began with a reminder of the heuristic principles that would be applied in the evaluations.

Figure 4 shows a picture of the face-to-face session, where each participant used his or her computer to use DUXAIT-NG. As an exercise, a project was created from scratch, following the heuristic evaluation process and using the Granollers method. The project consisted of evaluating a governmental web page. During the execution of the case study, the authors played the assistant role, giving technical support and clarified doubts about the evaluation process.

Once the heuristic evaluation was finished, we gave space for the attendees to participate in a coffee break. During this time, the answers of all the evaluators were processed. After the coffee break, the final results were presented, processed by the software and graphed on screen. Finally, we explained how to export the results and proceeded to the survey phase.

4 Evaluating the Experience

This section details the phase of surveys and questionnaires conducted to workshop participants in both sessions. The objective of this phase was to know the experience of the attendees regarding the use of the DUXAIT-NG platform and the experience of the workshop in general.

This post-test phase starts from the virtual session, where attendees completed an NPS survey. Out of a total of 21 attendees, we had 18 promoters, zero detractors, but three who were passive to the questions. This gave us a score of 85.71 entering the 'word class' zone according to the metrics. Figure 5 shows the NPS 'thermometer', where 'world class' is a score greater than 75.

For the post-test phase of the practical session, participants began a SUS questionnaire focused on the use of DUXAIT-NG. Out of the twenty attendees of the practical session and with a total of ten questions, a SUS score of 75 was

Fig. 4. Workshop DUXAIT Second Day. Practice Session

calculated, entering the threshold of 'Good'. According to Fig. 6, from 68 to 80.3 means a good level of usability.

The second questionnaire proposed to the attendees was the TAM2, also focused on the use of the DUXAIT-NG platform, but in this case, it would be a use outside the workshop or recommendation to other people.

On a scale of 1 to 7, where 1 meant disagree and 7 meant strongly agree, the majority agreed that the use of DUXAIT-NG would be beneficial and would use it again to improve performance on their projects and jobs.

Finally, we closed the post-test with a second NPS survey focused on the Duxait workshop and the DUXAIT-NG platform, where eleven promoters, two detractors, and seven passives were found. This resulted in an NPS score of 54.90, meaning an 'Excellent' rating.

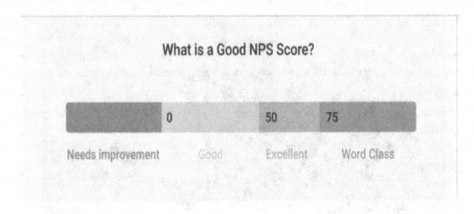

Fig. 5. NPS Score Termometer

SUS Score	Grade	Adjective Rating
> 80.3	A	Excellent
68 – 80.3	B	Good
68	C	Okay
51 – 68	D	Poor
< 51	F	Awful

Fig. 6. SUS Score table [14]

5   Conclusions and Future Works

Finally, after processing the results of the post-test phase, we were able to demonstrate that DUXAIT-NG is a stable platform, which allows us to perform heuristic evaluations in a standardized way, automating steps and reducing time for the executors.

As a research group, it was a challenge to organize both sessions of the workshop. From the promotion and visibility of the open invitation, to the logistics necessary to carry out the face-to-face session. Therefore, we highlight having a virtual training session. This saved time in the face-to-face session and we recommend that future workshops follow this organization to level the knowledge of the participants.

DUXAIT-NG proved to be easy to handle and understandable; however, at the time of the workshop it still had technical limitations that affected the perception of the system's speed. For this reason, for future opportunities, we will have more control over the number of simultaneous requests made to the server. In spite of the inconveniences, the surveys showed that DUXAIT-NG has enough usability level to generate a good experience and be recommended to other people.

In this workshop we used the Granollers subheuristics method, but DUXAIT-NG is capable of supporting other methods. As future work we plan to execute the other process already implemented, proposed by Paz, F. Additionally, we plan to start with case studies of the Tree Testing evaluation method.

Acknowledgments. This work is part of the research project "Virtualización del proceso de evaluación de experiencia de usuario de productos de software para escenarios de no presencialidad" (virtualization of the user experience evaluation process of software products for non-presential scenarios), developed by HCI-DUXAIT research group. HCI-DUXAIT is a research group that belongs to the PUCP (Pontificia Universidad Católica del Perú). This work was funded by the Dirección de Fomento a la Investigación at the PUCP through grant 2021-C-0023.

Disclosure of Interests. The authors declare there are no interest conflicts.

References

1. Paz, F., Paz, F.A., Pow-Sang, J.A., Collazos, C.: A formal protocol to conduct usability heuristic evaluations in the context of the software development process. Inter. J. Eng. Technol. **7**, 10-19 (2018). https://doi.org/10.14419/IJET.V7I2.28.12874
2. Lecaros, A.: Implementación de una aplicación web de soporte al proceso formal de evaluaciones heurísticas. Pontificia Universidad Católica del Perú. Departamento de Ingeniería (2022). https://tesis.pucp.edu.pe/repositorio/handle/20.500.12404/22388
3. Granollers, T.: Experimental validation of a set of heuristics for user experience evaluations in e-commerce websites. In: 2016 IEEE 11th Colombian Computing Conference, CCC 2016 - Conference Proceedings, pp. 27-34 (2016). https://doi.org/10.1109/COLUMBIANCC.2016.7750783

4. Tapia, A., Moquillaza, A., Aguirre, J., Falconi, F., Lecaros, A., Paz, F.: A Process to Support the Remote Tree Testing Technique for Evaluating the Information Architecture of User Interfaces in Software Projects. LNCS, vol. 13321, pp. 75-92 (2022). https://doi.org/10.1007/978-3-031-05897-4_6

5. Arslan, H., Yüksek, A.G., Elyakan, M.L., Canay, Ö.: Usability and quality tests in software products to oriented of user experience. Online J. Quality Higher Educ. **5**, 79 (2018)

6. Paz, F., Lecaros, A., Falconi, F., Tapia, A., Aguirre, J., Moquillaza, A.: A Process to Support Heuristic Evaluation and Tree Testing from a UX Integrated Perspective, pp. 369-377 (2023). https://doi.org/10.1007/978-3-031-28332-1_42

7. Aguirre, J., Lecaros, A., Ramos, C., Falconi, F., Moquillaza, A., Paz, F.: DUXAIT NG: a Software for the Planning and Execution of User Experience Evaluations and Experiments (2023). [unpublished]

8. Lecaros, A., Moquillaza, A., Falconi, F., Aguirre, J., Ramos, C., Paz, F.: Automation of Granollers Heuristic Evaluation Method Using a Developed Support System: A Case Study (2023). [unpublished]

9. Collins Dictionary: Workshop. Collins Dictionary Online (n.d.). https://www.collinsdictionary.com/us/dictionary/english/workshop

10. Moquillaza, A., Falconi, F., Aguirre, J., Lecaros, A., Tapia, A., Paz, F.: Using remote workshops to promote collaborative work in the context of a UX process improvement. In: Marcus, A., Rosenzweig, E., Soares, M.M. (eds.) Design, User Experience, and Usability. HCII 2023. LNCS, vol. 14030. Springer, Cham (2023). https://doi.org/10.1007/978-3-031-35699-5_19

11. Baehre S., O'Dwyer M., O'Malley L., Lee N.: The use of Net promoter score (NPS) to predict sales growth: insights from an empirical investigation. J. Acad. Marketing Sci. **50**(1), 67-84 (2022a). https://doi.org/10.1007/s11747-021-00790-2

12. Baehre, S.: From Research to action: enhancing net promoter score utilization in managerial practice. Inter. J. Market Res. (2023). https://doi.org/10.1177/14707853231209893

13. Moquillaza, A., Falconi, F., Aguirre, J., Paz, F.: Using verbatims as a basis for building a customer journey map: a case study. In: Stephanidis, C., Antona, M., Ntoa, S. (eds.) HCI International 2021 - Late Breaking Posters. HCII 2021. CCIS, vol. 1498. Springer, Cham (2021). https://doi.org/10.1007/978-3-030-90176-9_7

14. Granollers, T.: System Usability Scale (SUS) en el s. XXI. Curso de Interacción Persona-Ordenador (2015). https://mpiua.invid.udl.cat/system-usability-scale-sus-en-el-s-xxi/

15. De Angelis, G., Brosseau, L., Davies, B., King, J., Wells, G.A.: The use of information and communication technologies by arthritis health professionals to disseminate a self-management program to patients: a pilot randomized controlled trial protocol. Digital Health **4**, 205520761881957 (2018). https://doi.org/10.1177/2055207618819571

16. Nielsen, J.: Usability inspection methods. In: Conference Companion on Human Factors in Computing Systems, pp. 413-414 (1994)

17. Lecaros, A., Moquillaza, A., Falconi, F., Aguirre, J., Tapia, A., Paz, F.: A comparison between performing a heuristic evaluation based on a formal process using a system and the traditional way: a case study. In: Marcus, A., Rosenzweig, E., Soares, M.M. (eds.) Design, User Experience, and Usability. HCII 2023. LNCS, vol. 14032. Springer, Cham (2023). https://doi.org/10.1007/978-3-031-35702-2_2

18. Spencer, D.: Card-Based Classification Evaluation. Boxes and Arrows (2003). https://boxesandarrows.com/card-based-classification-evaluation/

A Study of the Usability and Experience of Public Space in Rural Watershed Environments

Yali Chen[✉] and Xin Tu

South China University of Technology, Guangzhou 510006, China
chenyali@scut.edu.cn

Abstract. As a place frequently accessed by residents and tourists, the public space of rural watershed environment, with its good performance of availability and service experience, is conducive to the adaptation of the countryside to the development needs of the new era. In this study, a typical water village in Lingnan region is selected as a sample, and the rural spatial form and spatial nodes are analyzed, and it is proposed that there are problems such as weak service function and lack of coordination of landscape effect in the current rural water public space. The study combines the theories related to service experience and usability of public space, establishes a service experience perception model for rural public space, and explores the optimization path of rural water public space to enhance the perception and applicability of rural experience users. The study shows that measures such as street optimization, spatial node planning, and overall landscape transformation of buildings can effectively improve the safety, comfort, and pleasure indicators of rural waterfront space. Improving the service function and landscape visual effect of rural water public space can further enhance the usability and user experience of public space in water network villages.

Keywords: Aquatic Environments · Public Spaces · Experientiality · Usability

1 Introduction

Rural public space witnesses the development and change of rural society, which is reflected in the whole process of rural public participation. Previous research on rural public space focuses on the morphological characteristics, protection and renewal, and evolution and reconstruction of space [1], but in recent years, relevant research has focused on the excavation of cultural attributes of rural public space [2], the composite characteristics of spatial ternary attributes [3], and the relationship between space and people [4], etc., so as to explore the issue of rural public space with a more diversified theoretical framework.

Regarding the research related to spatial experience and perception, there is no lack of scholars who start from the perspective of embodied perceptual experience of space, and take the interconnection of body, emotion and space as the elements to explore the problem of human experience and behavior in space, as shown in the Fig. 1. Xiaodong

Li analyzed the embodied experience of urban residents' participation in community sports from three dimensions, including body, emotion and space, aiming to improve the quality of residents' community sports participation from a diversified perspective [5]. Yirui Wang et al. classified six types of urban space under the perspective of subjective experience, in order to provide a reference for the creation of "high perception" cities, and to meet the public's spiritual and cultural perception needs in the experience era [6]. Bin Liu et al. explored the deeper connotation and value of the popularized phenomenon of elderly people's "sojourn" by improving the research framework of tourists' embodied experience [7].

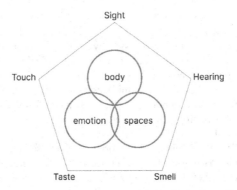

Fig. 1. Constituent elements of embodied perception.

Under the background of rural revitalization, there is an increasing trend of rural renovation towards diversified subjects, and focusing on the construction of livable environment and tourism development has become one of the main directions of rural development in the future. The natural landscape with water as the core is the typical landscape style of Lingnan water village, the water network of the Lingnan region is crisscrossed in the historical development period, and the hills and terraces are scattered as the geographic environment for the emergence of settlements, and in the development and change of urban and rural structure, the public space in the rural water environment is often associated with the hydrophilic attribute, which becomes a part of the villagers' emotional memory of the space.

As the rural public space becomes an important carrier for the continuation of rural culture, behind the construction of rural public space is the contemplation of its own future development and the inheritance of the core values of the countryside [8]. The public space of rural water environment in the Pearl River basin is an important space type of water-friendly environment in Lingnan water town. Publicity and service are the basic attributes of public space, human activities rely on the space carrier, and there is an interactive relationship between behavior and space. In promoting the urbanization process today, from the single physical environment to the human experience in space has become a shift in the direction of research, and the spatial human experience has become a key concept [9]. One-sided static optimization of village space can not inherit the regional culture of the village, and will reduce the availability of village space and the experience of villagers and tourists. To improve the service experience and usability of public space, we should start from user behavior and optimize the place where the behavior occurs.

2 Literature Review

Through a large number of field research and literature research, this study summarizes the current situation of planning and construction of rural public space and the existing problems with generality, which will be explained in the following with the actual situation of different villages.

The atrophy of the vitality of the village public space and the lack of organizing coherence between spatial nodes. In the process of social change in China's villages, the evolution of village public space can be divided into two stages, the first stage shows the general trend of formal public space tends to shrink and informal public space is becoming more and more prominent [10], and the second stage is to build a large number of formal public space with external intervention, but the lack of spatial vitality, which is due to the neglect of the traditions, habits and real needs of the village interior [11]. The new public space in the countryside under blind intervention has problems such as insufficient vitality of facilities, poor spatial quality of highly utilized places, and lack of coherence between spatial nodes. In this study, Mishi Village in Paitan Town, Zengcheng District, Guangzhou City, is one of the typical representatives of Lingnan waterside villages, with small streams trickling in the village, and water environment resources such as Shimalong Wetland Park and Baishui Zhai within a 5-km radius. Thanks to the advantages of natural resources, Mishi Village, like other villages in Lingnan Watershed, is rich in agricultural products, and the economic development of village industries makes full use of water resources, and the tourism space is also effectively combined with the water network space. Mishi Village has established a number of cultural theme attractions related to persimmon as its leading industries, with the guesthouse "Sushanfang" as the centerpiece of the village. However, the original village road is difficult to lead as many tourists as possible to the internal resources. There is an urgent need to create a combination of short and long tours in the village, connecting the rural landscape nodes, including the guesthouse, to enhance the comprehensive development of cultural and tourism industry in the village of Mishi, as shown in the Fig. 2.

The fragmentation of the spatial landscape has resulted in a yet uncoordinated landscape effect. In those villages with a long history in the waters of Lingnan, affected by the rapid development of urbanization in the Pearl River Delta, problems such as the degradation of the functions of the traditional residential buildings and the deterioration of the building façades have emerged in the traditional settlements, such as some of the building spaces being left unused, the building façades of the residential buildings along the streets of the alleys on both sides of the streets not being repaired for a long period of time, the styles of the building façade walls not being unified and the building façades being exposed at the damaged places and lacking in visual aesthetics, and so on. Qiangang Village, located in Taiping Town, Conghua District, Guangzhou, Guangdong Province, has undergone rapid changes in the historical process of the Pearl River Delta, and although public activity spaces such as the Guangyu Ancestral Hall have been better repaired, the presence of damaged and collapsed building facades, as shown in the Fig. 3,

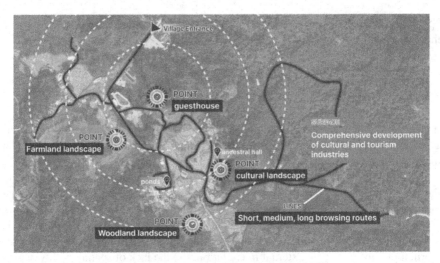

Fig. 2. Distribution of spatial nodes in Mishi Village.

was still found when visiting through the ancient village, and the deficient facade gives a sense of shabbiness and insecurity compared to the intact one, and it should be improved on the basis of maintaining the architectural style.

Fig. 3. Building elevations in Qiangang Village.

Poor interaction between people living in the countryside and the space. In the hydrophilic space of Lingnan waterside countryside, there are also common problems such as cracking of hydrophilic space and weakening of spatial connectivity between people and water environment. People have hydrophilic characteristics and will have the tendency to approach the water environment, and the rural waterside environment provides a good opportunity for the interaction between people and the environment. During the fieldwork, it was found that the existing public space of the aquatic environment lacks a platform for interaction between people and water, and the construction of water-friendly spatial services is difficult to meet people's daily expectations. Chatang

Village in Gaoyao City, Guangdong Province, was built in the Qing Dynasty, Guangxu 22nd year, the main entrance is located in the front plaza, the plaza on one side facing the water and the other side facing the residential area, the village square is more open, is an important place for residents and tourists activities, as shown in the Fig. 4. The half-moon pond on the side of the village square has not been well developed, and its interaction with people is weak. Consideration should be given to increasing water-friendly facilities, in order to improve the water-friendly experience of villagers and tourists and enhance the usability of water-friendly platforms.

Fig. 4. Half Moon Reservoir in front of the village in Chatang Village.

In summary, although rural public space has been renewed and improved to a certain extent under the background of rapid urbanization, the construction of public space under external intervention has not taken into account the relationship between the demand and the supply of space within the village, which makes it difficult to further enhance people's experience of living in the countryside and visiting the countryside. Exploring the scenarios under the nodes, landscapes and interactive behaviors of rural public space can help to balance the relationship between the supply of rural public space and the social demand inside and outside the village, with a view to improving the usability and service experience of rural public space.

3   Research Method

Theories such as embodied experience and spatial perception can be used to explain people's cognitive and feedback behaviors about the environment they are in. The body produces emotions in the environment and has a range of emotional associations with the space, which are linked to personal experience, social status, and individual differentiation. However, in the same environment, people's surface perception of the environment tends to be similar, and space is perceived through sensory channels, giving people a first impression.

In the study of traditional villages in Lingnan water towns, spatial perception is often based on the feelings gained from human sensory channels, centered on the individual's perception of the surrounding environment, and forming a cognition of the countryside environment in which it is situated through the comprehensive feelings of multiple senses. Among the five sensory channels, human visual perception is the most prominent, which affects the user's perception of the environment they are in to a large extent, for example, pavement materials, architectural style, and color of facilities are all elements that are directly seen by people. Everything that people can perceive, most of which is seen by the eyes, this information is brought together to become people's perceptual experience of space. Yuhong Gao et al. believe that when people enter traditional villages, they use physical perception as a starting point for behavioral experience and produce emotional cognition and the construction of imagery of the place [12]. Factors such as the width of streets and lanes and the size of space in different villages will bring people different perceptions of places, and different people's perceptions of the same village will also be different. In the Lingnan traditional water village settlement, by analyzing the ratio D/H of the width and height of the streets and alleys, it can be visualized that the difference in the scale of the streets and alleys will bring different spatial feelings to the experiencers. As shown in the Fig. 5, the width to height ratio of public waterfront space is 0.90, which gives people a feeling of openness and comfort, and people are willing to stay here for a long time, whereas in the width-restricted longitudinal and transverse streets, the width to height ratio of the streets is 0.7 or even 0.4, which makes people feel constrained and tense, and they will choose to stay for a short period of time or even pass through quickly in this kind of space. When people's perception of the environment is processed by the brain, different cognitions and responses will be generated, and a variety of interactive behaviors in the space will be created.

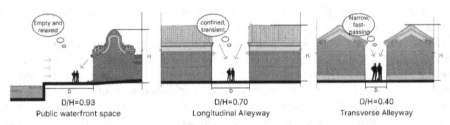

Fig. 5. Street aspect ratios and user perceptions of public waterfront spaces in Lingnan waterfront areas.

Based on the above theories, and on the basis of combining the related theories of spatial behavior, this study establishes a perception model of the degree of experience of rural public space services, including three dimensions of spatial place, spatial behavior and perceived experience, as shown in the Fig. 6. Spatial place and spatial behavior jointly affect the results of perceived experience, and different behaviors occurring in different places will produce different perceptions. Under the model construction, different point-like perceptual experiences together form the perceptual experience layer of rural public space, in which different slope perceptions of the perceptual experience layer are selected for analysis and intervention. For good perceptual outcomes, we consider adding more exciting perceptual experiences, and for poorer perceptions, we attempt to enhance the perceptual experience. The transformation and optimization of different strategy layers are carried out through emotional perception, which in turn improves the usability and service experience degree of rural public space from the perspective of the dual dimensions of human behavior and spatial perception.

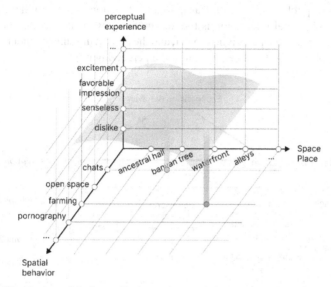

Fig. 6. A model of perceived experience of rural public space services.

4 Data Collection and Analysis

Rural public space uses the medium of spatial behavioral interaction and physical perception to enable people to produce spatial experience. Space is the place where behavior occurs, and to a certain extent, it is the carrier that provides services for people, so the spatial service experience is also an important content of spatial experience degree. In traditional villages, the settlement space is the home that villagers rely on for survival, the wide and narrow alleys and the ear protection walls on both sides can resist most of the heat, the water system flowing through the village provides villagers with the convenience and interest of life, and the lush old trees are the first choice for villagers to take a cool place. The villagers, with their wisdom of construction, make their home environment into an ideal pattern and enjoy the service experience provided by the space continuously. There are also public service facilities guided by external factors, such as fitness places and pavilions, all of which are designed to enhance the usability and user experience of the limited space on the basis of ensuring the internal needs of the village.

Perceiving subject, perceiving object and perceiving behavior constitute the three elements of the rural public space perception model. As shown in the Fig. 7, the main body of perception experience is mainly composed of residents and tourists, who can be called "experiencers", interacting and perceiving with the perception object through complex behaviors in the space. The object of perception is the rural public space, which can be divided into public activity space, public interaction space and public transportation space, in addition to formal and informal space. The public activity space includes ancestral halls and temples, the public interaction space includes places with high social frequency such as ancient wells and shady trees, and the public transportation space mainly refers to public spaces with transportation functions such as village entrances and bridges. Behavioral interaction is the intermediary of the connection between the perceiving subject and the perceiving object, and the perceiving subject under behavioral interaction generates the local perception of the perceiving object.

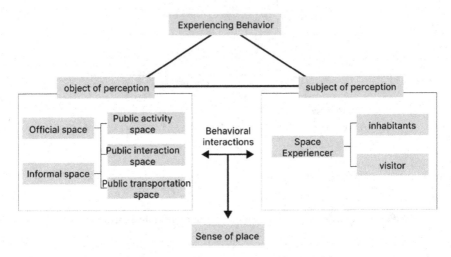

Fig. 7. Rural Public Space Perception Model.

To enhance the usability and service experience of public space in the rural watershed environment, it is necessary to find the opportunities in the interaction between space and behavior, analyze the balance between the existing public space and the internal needs of the village and make reasonable interventions. In our study, we set up the rural space of Lingnan waters as a circle structure, as shown in the Fig. 8, we can see that in the rural circle structure, the ancestral halls and temples, as the public activity space, are located in the core of the village's many public spaces. In the village public space, nodes such as ancestral halls, ancient banyan trees, and ponds have a high density of foot traffic, and they are the main public places where behaviors occur in the village. In the Pearl River Delta region, ancestral halls are the materialized manifestation of clan power and strength, and major events, such as clan organization and deliberation, festivals and ritual practices, often take place in ancestral halls. In addition, in the villages under the functional and bloodline organizations, the ancestral hall leads the village pattern and is in the leading position, and it is also the necessary way for villagers to enter and leave the village. The important position of the ancestral hall in the settlement space continues to this day as a place for villagers to rest and socialize, as well as a way for visitors to learn about the history of the village. Other public interaction spaces, such as the ancient banyan, are typical Lingnan vegetation, and their shade is a place for villagers and tourists to rest. Waterfront spaces not only have functional uses, but also carry significance beyond the mundane. Public transportation spaces such as streets, alleys, and bridges are also an important place for behaviors to take place in the village, where villagers engage in daily conversations.

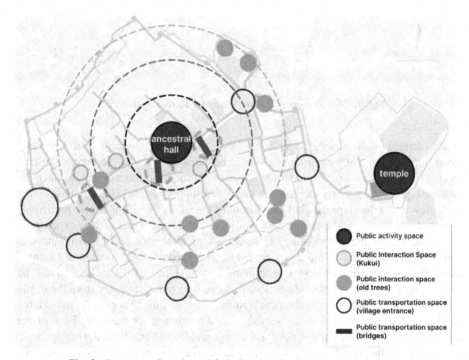

Fig. 8. Structure of rural spatial circles and distribution of public space.

Statistics on the travel density of villagers and tourists in public space found that 9:00–12:00 in the morning and 15:00–17:00 in the afternoon are the time periods with the highest crowd density in rural public space, and the travel density of tourists and villagers in these two time periods have reached the two peaks of the day (see Fig. 9). The travel density largely affects the behavioral density of the perceiving subject in the perceived object, and the experiential behavior then brings about the user's local perception, and the multidimensional relationship between behavior and space, behavior and time jointly determines the effect of the usability of the rural public space and the degree of service experience.

5   Discussion

5.1   Public Space Optimization Content and Experience Enhancement

The perceiving subject obtains the corresponding perceptual experience through behavioral interaction in the space, and the place and time of behavioral occurrence are very closely related to the results of public space experience perception. After researching the behaviours and perception subjects in the space, based on the experience perception

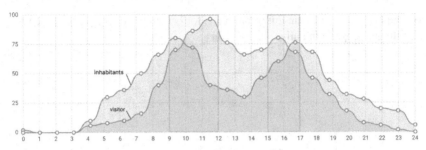

Fig. 9. Distribution of Travel Density for Rural Experiencers.

model of rural public space, the author believes that the transformation of the public space in rural watershed environment should be carried out under the premise of preserving the traditional spatial undertones. The transformation can not only balance the relationship between user experience demand and supply of rural space in the context of the new era of development, but also stimulate the subject's willingness to participate in spatial interaction, and enhance the usability of public space and service experience.

At the same time, we continue to select a typical sample of Lingnan waterside villages that are linked to the water environment - Jiexiazhuang, located in Doumen Town, Doumen District, Zhuhai. Jiexiazhuang has a long history dating back to the end of the Song Dynasty, and the village is surrounded by a moat, far away from the hustle and bustle of the world. During the development process of the historical period, a large number of villagers moved to the south-east and south-west of the same bank of the river to the external new village, but a few villagers still live here. With the precipitation of time, Jiexiazhuang village has accumulated a large number of cultural monuments, and then by virtue of the geographical location of Zhuhai City, attracting a large number of foreign tourists to visit. Jiexiazhuang has a beautiful environment, the existence of a large number of ecological farms with idyllic flavor, providing visitors with self-help picking and other idyllic experience activities, is a typical water ecological environment and cultural flavor of the village.

In the preliminary research, it was found that the public space status quo problems in Jiexiazhuang exist in most of the water towns in the Lingnan region. Jiexia Zhuang waterfront area near the Zhuang River waterfront vitality shrinkage, building facades on both sides of the street in disrepair, and residents, tourists and the interaction of public space is weak. In view of the deficiencies in the construction of public space in the ancient village of Jiexiazhuang, the renovation project is based on the positioning of the two themes of ecology and culture and tourism, and optimizes the landscape around the water environment of the Nguzhuang River. The optimization is carried out in several aspects: village street space, node space and building facade.

The spatial layout of the entrance street of Jiexiazhuang is shown in the Fig. 10. There is a suspension bridge at the entrance of the village to guide people to cross the river and enter the village, there are detached villas on one side of the entrance, and the other side of the entrance road is adjacent to the river, which is a common street scenario of the spatial pattern of the Lingnan water village. In the entrance space, the village residents and tourists will have the need to rest and buy and sell, but the existing space lacks facilities such as stone benches, which cannot carry more experience needs in the village. The vegetation on both sides of the original road is single and non-hierarchical, and the damaged façade of the building is exposed on both sides of the street, which visually lacks guidance and aesthetics. After optimization, public facilities are added to meet the spatial needs of experiencers, and at the same time, the vegetation on both sides of the road is enriched to enhance the visual guidance of the entrance road, and a large visual space is left for the water surface of the moat.

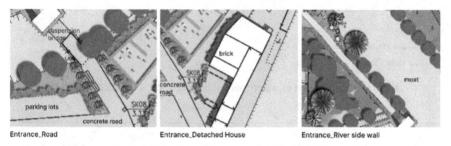

Entrance_Road   Entrance_Detached House   Entrance_River side wall

Fig. 10. Spatial layout of the entrance street of Jiexiazhuang.

In terms of nodes, the focus is on the design of water-friendly space along the river tour route. Considering that Jiexiazhuang is surrounded by the river, the village is rich in water resources, which can be utilized to strengthen the interaction between the experience subject and water, and at the same time, enhance the availability of space and service experience. The renovation plan integrates the element of "water" into the behavioral activities of the experiencers, and adds water-friendly platforms, stone benches, pavilions and other village service facilities along the water according to the key elements and interactive behaviors of the nodes in the waterfront area (see Fig. 11). By adding facilities such as water-friendly platforms, villagers and tourists can not only walk on the water-friendly platforms to have a close contact with the river, but also be able to rest on the stone benches and pavilions, resulting in a better sense of spatial experience in the watershed.

Building facade renovation, the main sightseeing routes in Jiexia Zhuang along the street facade dilapidated degree varies, some buildings wall weathering is serious, the damage is more serious, and some buildings are still inhabited by residents. The renovation is based on the preliminary field inspection of eight major buildings along the street, and the facade remediation program is determined on the basis of retaining the traditional elements (see Fig. 12). The remediation is carried out by means of facade repair, wall painting, clearing of debris, vegetation screening, and unification of door and window styles to achieve a visually uniform and beautiful effect of the building facades along the street. In traditional villages, the facade of the building contains many patterns and motifs symbolizing traditional elements, and all these traditional elements are mediums for conveying cultural and emotional experiences to the experiencers, which can build effective paths between history and reality, physical space and psychological space [13], and should be inherited and preserved.

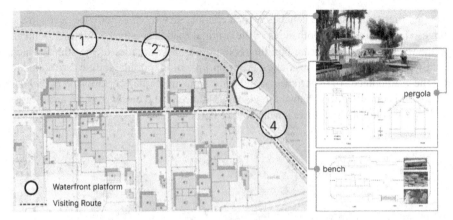

Fig. 11. Optimization of waterfront public space nodes in Jiexia Village.

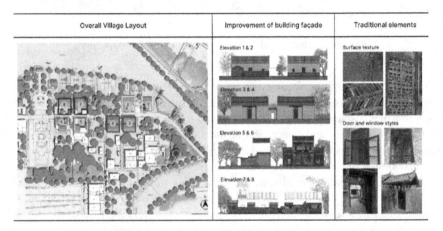

Fig. 12. Jiexiazhuang Building Facade Improvement.

5.2 Optimization Strategies for Experience Enhancement in Public Spaces

In the public space of rural waterside environment, the interaction behavior between people and space is more complex, the interaction opportunity is more diverse, the interaction relationship is more close, the usability of waterside environment space and user experience will largely affect people's overall experience of the village. However, there are still deficiencies in the construction of water environment public space, and problems such as insufficient node space connectivity, lack of landscape coordination, and weak interaction between people and space exist widely. Enhancing the usability and experience of rural waterside environment public space should start from the interactive behavior of people and space, and fully consider the spatial human nature experience. Optimization can be carried out from the perspectives of alleyway reconstruction, landscape optimization, interactive platforms, etc., to redesign and plan the streets, nodes, and building facades in the villages in order to provide a better experience to meet the needs of users.

Based on the problems existing in the public space of the rural water environment, from the perspective of spatial usability and user experience, the public space transformation is carried out in three aspects: streets, nodes and facades. The optimization is based on the actual needs of the users, focusing on the experience of the local residents of the villages and the tourists. On the basis of retaining the traditional spatial elements, the spatial transformation increases or optimizes the scenes of interaction between people and space, in order to promote the behavior of user participation in space, and to improve spatial usability and user experience (see Fig. 13).

Fig. 13. Optimization Strategies for Usability and Experience of Public Space in Lingnan Rural Watersheds.

After the implementation of the renovation plan, through the collection of public opinion data and on-site experience conclusions, the optimized public space of the waterside environment is evaluated in terms of performance, three primary indicators of safety, comfort, and pleasure and nine secondary indicators are selected for the evaluation, and the score of the public space indicators of the waterfront area of the Lingnan countryside is calculated and obtained (see Table 1). Through the data, it can be found that the value of spatial safety in the second-level indicators increased from the original 4.8 to 4.9 after effectively utilizing the waterfront boundary, and the climate protection performance score increased from 4.35 to 4.43, so the public space of the watershed has been improved in general in terms of first-level indicators of safety. Secondly, at the comfort indicator level, among the four secondary indicators, the environmental landscape is improved from 4.11 to 4.54 after effective control of the landscape view corridor, the accessibility is enhanced after the adjustment of the road system in the village is increased from 4.52 to 4.53, the spatial layout after the adjustment of the functional space, the indicator is improved from 3.74 to 3.89, and the public facilities are implanted into the public space, the indicator is improved from 4.4 to 4.68, indicating that the relevant measures have significantly improved the comfort of residents and outsiders' experience of rural public space. The results show that the transformation of streets, nodes and building facades of public spaces in the waterside environment can effectively enhance spatial vitality and improve the spatial perception experience of users.

Table 1. Indicator Score for Public Space in Lingnan Waterfront Spaces.

Tier 1 indicators	Tier 2 indicators	Score before promotion	Score after promotion
safety	Space security	4.80	4.90
	weather protection	4.35	4.43
comfortableness	environmental landscape	4.11	4.54
	accessibility	4.52	4.53
	space layout	3.74	3.89
	public facilities	4.40	4.68
cheerfulness	Street Scale	4.32	4.36
	Traditional Cultural Elements	4.79	4.80
	Frequency of activities	3.86	4.23

6 Conclusion

In the context of accelerated urbanization, the availability of rural public space and service experience is an important evaluation index that affects the experience of the village experience subject. Rural public space service is the service provided to the subject of space experience after transformation, and balancing the supply and demand relationship between the space and the internal demand of the village is crucial for improving the availability and service experience of rural public space. Public space is an important place for villagers and tourists' daily behavior, carrying people's emotions and memories of village life. Public space in traditional villages is often associated with several nodes: ancestral halls, ancient banyans, streets and alleys, etc., and there is coherence between user behaviors and nodes, and the overall pattern of the village and the daily habits of the residents echo each other. As an important element of traditional villages in the Lingnan region, "water" has not only become a necessary condition for the production and life of local villagers, but has also been given a connotation beyond the secular symbol. Activities related to water are carried out in the water environment, and folk festivals and rituals are all linked to water, which are passed down from generation to generation. This study first examines the current situation of public space services in rural water environments, analyzes the relationship between experiential behaviors and spatial places, and proposes optimization strategies. The study includes the following conclusions.

At present, there are problems of shrinking spatial vitality in the public space of rural watershed environments, a lack of coherence in the organization of nodal spaces, uncoordinated landscapes and styles, and weak interaction between people and the environment. Since the acceleration of the rural construction process, the proportion of formal public space in traditional settlements has gradually increased, but top-down blind planning cannot consider the balance between demand and space supply in the village, resulting in the construction effect falling short of expectations. At the same time, due to one-sided planning of the village landscape, the coherence between nodes in traditional villages lacks a sense of wholeness, and the correlation between spaces is poor. In villages with a long history, some of the building facades are seriously damaged, which not only lacks safety considerations, but also is not conducive to the coordination and unity of the overall landscape effect. In addition, the interaction between people and space in rural space is not strong, and many environmental resources have not been developed to a large extent, which makes it difficult to further enhance the availability of spatial services and user experience.

The research found that in the public space of rural water environment, public activity space such as ancestral halls and ancient trees, public transportation space such as streets and alleys, and public interaction space such as waterfront areas are intensive places where residents' and visitors' behaviors occur, and there is a higher degree of interaction between people and space. Within the scope of the activity circle centered on public activity space, there exists the possibility of more interactive behaviors occurring. On the other hand, in the time distribution of spatial behaviors, tourists and residents, as the common village environment experience subjects, have the same distribution trend of behavioral frequency, with higher behavioral density at 9:00–12:00 a.m. and 15:00–17:00 p.m., and the reliance on the spatial carriers, and the interaction with the space will be relatively stronger.

Aiming at the problems existing in the public space of rural water environment and the experience of rural environment, the study takes Jiexiazhuang in Doumen Town, Doumen District, Zhuhai as an example. Study starts from the spatial places in the countryside where people's behaviors occur more frequently, and optimizes the alleys, node spaces and building elevations in the area. The optimization is based on the principles of preserving the traditional background, promoting the interaction between people and the environment, and enhancing the spatial service experience, and different targeted optimization strategies are proposed for the existing problems on the basis of the perception model of the service experience degree of the rural public space. The results found that through the transformation of rural water environment public space, the public space performance score increased, effectively improving the water environment public space usability and service experience.

Acknowledgments. This study was funded by Humanities and Social Sciences Project Planning Fund of the Ministry of Education (grant number 23YJAZH013). This research was funded by Guangdong Provincial Philosophy and Social Sciences "14th Five-Year Plan" Fund (grant number GD22CYS23).

Disclosure of Interests. The authors have no competing interests to declare that are relevant to the content of this article.

References

1. Jin, L., Zegang, X., Hui, C.: Research review of rural public space in China based on CiteSpace. South Architect. **02**, 11–21 (2022)
2. Longfei, Y., Renhua, S.: The shaping of contemporary rural public cultural space in a society of emotional and ritual interaction. Fujian Tribune **04**, 26–34 (2023)

3. Ping, W., Baogang, L., Xiaorui, Z.: Study on the rural public space production research of the relocation and combination-oriented rural based on spatial trialetics: a case study of shibianyu Village in Xi'an area. Mode. Urban Res. **05**, 64–69 (2022)

4. Huiyuan, B., Hui, T., Meiyi, G., et al.: The Impact mechanism and construction strategy of attachment to public places in rural areas-taking qiu village in Yingde City as the example. Chin. Landscape Architect. **38**(S2), 58–62 (2022)

5. Xiaodong, L.: Physical, emotional and spatial reconstruction: the embodied experience of urban residents participating in community sports-fieldwork based on 6 urban communities. J. Sports Res. **37**(04), 87–98 (2023)

6. Yirui, W., Qinghua, Z., Xiaodan, Y., et al.: Discussion on urban space types based on perception. Planners **38**(07), 135–140 (2022)

7. Bin, L., Zhao, Y., Yongting, L., et al.: Body, emotion and space: the embodied experience of leisure sojourn for the elderly. Hum. Geogr. **38**(01), 169–180 (2023)

8. Mengxi, S., Weiyu, T.: The logic and mechanism of rural public aesthetic space based on the practice of "art intervention in the countryside." Ethnic Art Studies **36**(01), 136–143 (2023)

9. Jiaojiao, S., Yingzhi, G.: Research on spatial humanistic experience of the urban tourists: structural dimension, scale development and validity test. Hum. Geogr. **38**(05), 162–171 (2023)

10. Hailin, C.: Village public space in rural social change–an empirical study examining the reconstruction of village order in the case of kiln village in Northern Jiangsu Province. China Rural Survey **06**, 61–73 (2005)

11. Zhen, Z., Yingqiu, X., Hao, W.: Beautiful countryside and reconstruction of rural public space. Mod. Urban Res. **08**, 106–109 (2022)

12. Yuhong, G., Lanlin, X.: A study on the placemaking of rural lodging in traditional villages from an embodied perspective. In: Annual National Planning Conference 2022/2023, Urban Planning Society of China, Rural Planning, vol. 16, pp. 1200–1209. CNKI, Wuhan (2023)

13. Jiali, Z., Huiping, W.: Connotation construction and value realization of linguistic landscape of culture and tourism in traditional villages of Guangzhou. J. Huaqiao Univ. (Philos. Soc. Sci.) **06**, 81–93 (2023)

Optimization of Display Content Switching Under Multiple Large-Screen Displays: A Multi-channel Interaction Usability Evaluation

Jialing Chen, Xiaoxi Du, Xinhao Guo, Xiaozhou Zhou, and Chengqi Xue[✉]

Southeast University, Nanjing 211189, China
ipd_xcq@seu.edu.cn

Abstract. Large displays offer enhanced information presentation, enriching the immersive interactive experience; however, their physical distance from users poses usability problems for human-computer interaction. In order to improve interaction experience and task performance on large displays, this study incorporates voice input technology and somatosensory input technology. Subsequently, an evaluation is conducted on the usability of voice interaction and somatosensory + voice interaction, focusing on the task of screen content switching. The results suggest that under ideal circumstances, the incorporation of somatosensory interaction significantly enhances the performance of switching screen content. Nevertheless, due to somatosensory technology recognition's instability and the switching costs between voice and somatosensory interaction, the amalgamation of somatosensory interaction and voice interaction fails to effectively improve interactive performance in content-switching tasks. Ultimately, voice interaction emerges as the more suitable choice for large display screen content-switching tasks.

Keywords: Large Displays · Somatosensory Interaction · Voice Interaction · Multichannel Interaction · Human-computer Interaction

1 Introduction

With the continuous advancement of manufacturing processes and the concurrent reduction in production costs, large display devices have become ubiquitous across various industries, including but not limited to traffic management, monitoring and command systems, education, medical training, leisure and entertainment, and office environments [1]. These large displays facilitate the simultaneous opening of multiple application windows, enhancing overall visibility and efficiency. The expansive screen size and high resolution empower information workers to access more comprehensive information and execute intricate multitasking operations.

The significance of large displays is particularly apparent in the environment of complex systems. They play a crucial role in the real-time display of equipment status

A. Marcus et al. (Eds.): HCII 2024, LNCS 14712, pp. 217–231, 2024.
https://doi.org/10.1007/978-3-031-61351-7_15

inspections, data inspection, production factual analysis, alarm fault discovery, and other pivotal content. By offering comprehensive and timely reference information, large displays support decision-makers in navigating complex scenarios. In order to synchronize the display of multiple aspects within a complex system, various application scenarios adopt a collaborative approach, combining several display panels into a multi-screen configuration.

The composition of such a large display system involves multiple displays, necessitating a thoughtful and rational design regarding the number of information displays to attach the best balance. An insufficient number of displays may impede the simultaneous presentation of multiple layers of information, thereby hindering the user's ability to access necessary data. Conversely, too many displays may impose an undue cognitive burden on operators, adversely affecting observation and operational efficiency.

To address this challenge, large displays are often equipped with a content-switching function, allowing users the flexibility to select display screen content as needed. This design meets the requirements of human factors ergonomics, but also effectively mitigates production costs. By avoiding the need to add additional displays, this approach achieves an optimal equilibrium between enhancing efficiency and maintaining technical economy.

Despite the empirically validated advantages of large displays as elucidated in research, there persist certain usability issues when employing large display systems in practical scenarios. For instance, users are obliged to maintain a certain distance to fully see and grasp the screen content, consequently limiting the application of conventional interaction methods such as touch. Consequently, there is an immediate imperative to devise an interaction methodology that ensures seamless and efficient interaction while facilitating users in clear and coherent reading of interface content.

This study amalgamates and deploys speech and somatosensory interaction technologies, specifically tailored for the task of content switching on a large display. And the usability evaluation tests have been meticulously designed to assess the influence of speech interaction and somatosensory + speech interaction technologies on interaction performance and user experience.

The primary objective of this paper is to ascertain the most suitable interaction method for tasks related to screen content switching in large display systems featuring multi-screen collaboration. Particular emphasis is placed on the integration of voice input and somatosensory + speech input, aiming to investigate how interaction channels can be judiciously chosen to enhance interaction efficiency and user experience on large displays.

2   Related Work

Desktop management systems offer various mechanisms for switching content between spatially overlapping applications and windows [2]. However, large displays, characterized by an expansive screen area in comparison to smaller counterparts, are predominantly utilized for information browsing and monitoring tasks rather than intricate editing or interaction. Consequently, application windows on large displays typically exhibit less overlap, often arranged side-by-side or in a grid-like configuration. Moreover, the increased display area and user control distance on large displays pose challenges for fine-grained operations. As a result, distinct interaction techniques for operation are imperative, diverging from the conventions of traditional desktop displays.

In the realm of large display interaction, frequently employed external interaction devices encompass keyboards, laser pointers, and smartphones. Keyboard interaction, exemplified by the Microsoft Windows desktop's Alt + Tab functionality, serves as a common method for interface switching and is renowned for its efficiency in personal computer usage. However, when applied to large displays, this approach appears less natural and intuitive. The necessity for users to shift their line of sight between the expansive display interface and the keyboard introduces an additional operational burden. Given that the display area and volume of information on large displays far surpass those on traditional screens, users face challenges in seamlessly executing tasks. Laser pointer interaction [3–5] involves the remote utilization of handheld devices equipped with lasers and keys to control the content of large displays. While this form of interaction facilitates more intricate operations, practical applications encounter several challenges. Firstly, users must familiarize themselves with the laser pointer's function buttons through pre-emptive learning and adaptation. Secondly, holding the laser pointer during interaction may lead to inconvenience. Prolonged use of this interaction method has the potential to induce user fatigue and limit free movement, thereby affecting the overall smoothness of the interaction experience. Smartwatch and cell phone input controls, as examined by Sharma et al., scrutinized the usability of input mechanisms employing smartwatches as large displays. Despite the novelty of this interaction type, their study revealed that inputting on-screen gestures from the watch to a large screen did not fulfill the criteria of an intuitive interaction mechanism, primarily due to the small size of the watch's interface [6]. Utilizing a smartphone as an input device similarly necessitates the occupation of the user's hand for operation. Concurrently, interaction accuracy proves insufficient when executing touch or keystroke operations on smaller surfaces intended for mapping to large displays.

With the evolution of interaction technology, multimodal and multichannel natural human-computer interaction techniques have been introduced to offer a broader spectrum of possibilities for switching screen content on large displays [7, 8]. Multichannel interaction strives to leverage multichannel information, encompassing speech, images, text, eye movement, and haptics, to facilitate information exchange between humans and computers [9]. The collaboration of multiple interaction channels serves to expedite the communication of interaction information between users and computers, thereby enhancing interaction efficiency. Employing multichannel interaction techniques for large display interaction entails the system capturing user interaction intent through information derived from the user's eyes, hands, head, and voice.

Eye-tracking-based interaction [10], while intuitive, necessitates the acquisition of eye video data and requires the camera to be close to the eyes. During large-screen interface operations, as users often need to focus their gaze on specific information locations, utilizing gaze information for interface operations simultaneously becomes challenging, with no guaranteed accuracy in human eye recognition. Speech recognition, providing a swift and efficient input method, is well-suited for remote control. Gesture interaction, although introducing novel interaction possibilities [11], may induce fatigue during prolonged use. For instance, Sharma's study identified that utilizing Leap Motion as a wristband device for gestures like grasping, swiping, clicking, and scrolling can lead to user fatigue due to the prolonged outward extension of both hands [6]. Somatosensory interactions, such as those facilitated by Kinect [12], enable remote manipulation through body postures but face limitations in supporting complex tasks due to restricted limb precision.

Human-computer interaction systems are ideally designed to closely emulate the easy and natural forms of interaction inherent in human daily life. Achieving this emulation becomes particularly potent when multiple interaction channels are combined, resulting in a more robust interface compared to the use of any single modality in isolation. A case in point is Krahnstoever's exploration of the combined interaction of voice commands and gesture interaction for large displays [13]. Nevertheless, somatosensory interaction stands out by being grounded in movements and actions that users are already familiar with, mirroring actual actions in their daily lives. This eliminates the need to memorize specific gestures, as required in gesture interaction, thereby reducing the learning curve and enhancing the overall natural and immersive quality of the interaction. Simultaneously, voice interaction ensures accurate information representation. Consequently, the integration of voice and somatosensory interaction exhibits distinct advantages in the realm of human-computer interaction, particularly when confronted with the intricacies of spatial representations.

3 Methods

We undertook a usability evaluation study to examine the efficacy of interaction channels, specifically comparing the use of voice-only interaction against multichannel interaction involving both voice and somatosensory input. This investigation focused on a large-display content-switching task, exploring the effects of diverse interaction operations on both task performance and user experience.

3.1 Participants

In this study, a cohort of 26 participants participated in the experiment, comprising 20 males and 6 females. The age range of the participants was between 21 and 29 years. While all participants had experience with voice interaction, their daily usage frequency was relatively low. Notably, only three participants had prior exposure to somatosensory interaction.

3.2 Experimental Facility

The experiment took place in a controlled laboratory setting equipped with three displays (left, center, and right), a Kinect somatosensory recognition device, a microphone, and a laptop. The arrangement of equipment is illustrated in Fig. 1. The utilized Kinect device (Azure Kinect DK) integrates a depth camera, a spatial microphone array, and an RGB camera, as illustrated in Fig. 2. It offers the flexibility to select different Software Development Kits (SDKs) based on specific task requirements. For this experiment, we predominantly employed the body tracking SDK, which leverages the RGB and infrared cameras of the Azure Kinect DK to capture images of the user's body poses. The motion positions of the user's joints were obtained using image segmentation and feature extraction algorithms. The recognition program interprets and captures the user's somatosensory input by comparing the similarity between the user's somatosensory movements and predefined movements, subsequently executing corresponding computer commands.

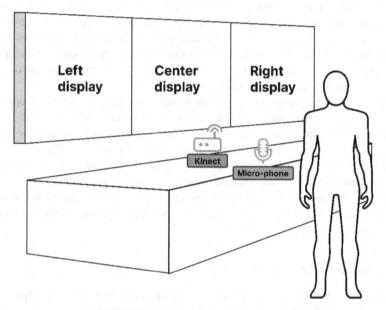

Fig. 1. Position of the Apparatus

Fig. 2. Kinect Product Appearance

3.3 Experimental Tasks

This experiment involves two distinct task types, wherein participants are tasked with switching interface content in the corresponding area of the large-screen display. The switch is achieved through either voice interaction or a combination of somatosensory and voice interaction, as dictated by task requirements. Figure 3 illustrates the comparative analysis of these interaction channels and encapsulates the four potential participant postures during the experiment.

In the voice interaction task, participants received experimental instructions and then depressed the space bar to transition the laptop interface to the task execution page. Subsequently, participants were obliged to articulate the switching instructions into the microphone, specifying the targeted area on the large-screen display and the specific content to be presented. Upon completing the instruction, participants pressed the space bar again to conclude the ongoing trial task.

In the somatosensory + voice interaction task, following the initiation command for the experiment, participants pressed the space bar to access the task execution page. Subsequently, participants were required to elevate their left arm to indicate the specific area on the large-screen display requiring switching and subsequently articulate the specific content of the presentation through the microphone. Following the completion of these operations, participants pressed the space bar again to conclude the trial task.

This experiment employed a between-participant design, where each participant was required to take part in 18 trials, 9 of which using voice interaction and the other 9 using somatosensory + voice interaction.

3.4 Experimental Procedures

Before the initiation of the experiment, participants completed a consent form and a questionnaire to gather essential user information. Subsequently, the experimenter elucidated the experiment's purpose, guided participants in acquainting themselves with the experimental procedure, and facilitated their comprehension of instructions. Additionally, participants were given a few minutes to practice the screen content-switching task using both input channels.

Throughout the formal experiment, each trial presented sequentially three task instructions through the laptop interface: (1) Instruction 1: " Please make the left display (center/right display) content switch to the data analysis interface (equipment monitoring interface/process planning interface/production live interface/workshop planning interface) by voice (somatosensory + voice) interaction and press the space bar to initiate…" (2) Instruction 2: "Voice (somatosensory + voice): left display (center/right display) presents the data analysis interface (equipment monitoring interface/process planning interface/production live interface/workshop planning interface) - press space-bar to complete the task…" (3) Instruction 3: "This trial finished; press space bar to proceed to the next trial…".

Instruction 1 serves to provide a concise overview of the task, encompassing the interaction required during formal operation and task operation specifics. Upon the user's initiation of the space bar and the appearance of Instruction 2 on the interface, the experiment software automatically records the ongoing operation time as the task

Comparison of the two groups of interactions

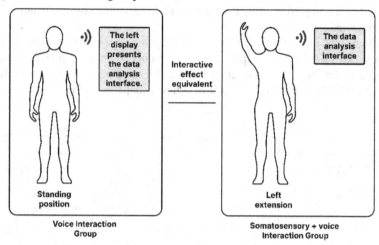

Participant body postures involved in the experiment

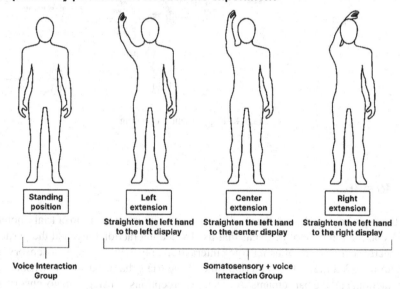

Fig. 3. Comparison of interaction tasks

execution start time for the trial. Instruction 2 serves as a reminder that the trial has officially commenced, and the user is expected to interact with the system as per its contents. Upon the user's completion of the operation and pressing the space bar, the Instruction 3 interface appears, and the experiment software automatically records the ongoing operation time as the task execution end time for the trial. The experiment computes the user's task completion time as the difference between the start and end times of task execution. When the Instruction 3 screen emerges, signifying the conclusion of the trial, participants can take a break or make adjustments. The device records the operator's task completion time. Participants had breaks between trials until all trials were completed.

Following the user study's conclusion, participants were invited to partake in a brief interview. During the interview, participants were queried about their preferred interaction modality for the content-switching task, and the reasons behind their preferences were explored. The entire experimental workflow is depicted in Fig. 4.

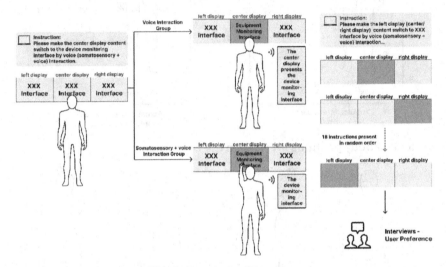

Fig. 4. Experimental Procedure

4   Results

In the experimental design, the results of the voice interaction group of trials included the task completion time of the trials that used voice interaction only, and the participants' subjective perceptions of using voice interaction only, while the somatosensory + voice group included the task completion time of the trials that used somatosensory + voice interaction, and the participants' subjective perceptions of using somatosensory + voice interaction. Therefore, the whole data analysis was conducted in two parts:

Part I: Task completion time analysis. Statistical tests were conducted on each of the two independent variables of this experiment to investigate whether the two interaction technologies would have a significant effect on the content-switching efficiency of large displays and to compare the interactive performance advantages and disadvantages of the two.

Part II: User Interviews. The user interviews of the voice interaction group and the somatosensory + voice interaction group were summarized and integrated to explore the effects of different interaction methods on the subjective experience of the participants.

4.1   Task Completion Time

This study used SPSS software to analyze users' task completion time data.

The data were filtered to exclude the data with serious faults in device recognition, and the data with completion times of 4480–13927 ms in the voice interaction group and 2608–52593 ms in the somatosensory + voice interaction group were retained for subsequent in-depth analyses.

First, the data were tested for normal distribution: given that the sample size was less than 50, the Shapiro-Wilk test was ultimately chosen. Using the normality test result in Table 1 and the normal Q-Q plots in Figs. 5 and 6, we found that the p-values for both groups were less than 0.05 and the distribution of data points on the Q-Q chart notably deviates from the anticipated range, which collectively suggests that the data are not normally distributed.

Table 1. Normality test result

	Group	Shapiro-Wilk		
		Statistics	Degree of freedom	Significance
Completion time	Voice interaction	.817	204	.000
	Somatosensory + Voice Interaction	.797	228	.000

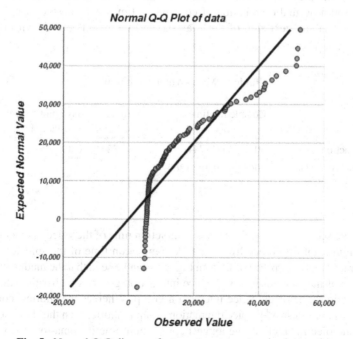

Fig. 5. Normal Q-Q diagram for somatosensory + voice interaction

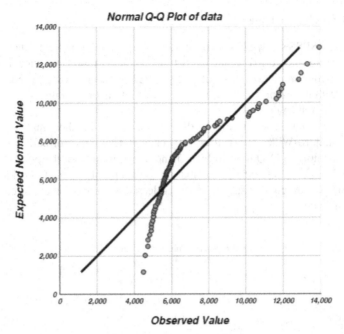

Fig. 6. Normal Q-Q diagram for voice interaction

Since neither the voice interaction group nor the somatosensory + voice interaction group showed a normal distribution of completion times, we chose to use the Mann-Whitney test for the next step of the analysis, and the results are shown in Table 2.

Table 2. Mann-Whitney test result

Group	Completion time	Z-value	Asymptotic significance (two-tailed)
Voice interaction	6032(5448^7744)	−8.432	.000
Somatosensory + Voice Interaction	10686.5(6080^21360)		

As can be seen from Table 2, the task completion time of the voice interaction group shows a significant difference from the task completion time of the somatosensory + voice interaction group ($p < 0.05$). From Fig. 7, it can be seen that the median task completion time of the somatosensory + voice interaction group is higher than the median task completion time of the voice interaction group. Whereas the shortest completion time in the somatosensory + voice interaction group is shorter than the shortest completion time in voice interaction, the longest completion time in soma-tosensory + voice interaction is longer than the longest task completion time in voice interaction. The

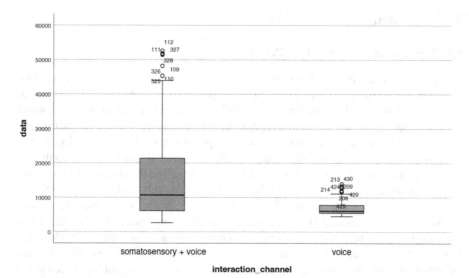

Fig. 7. Box plots of task completion time for voice interaction and somatosensory + voice interaction

range of data fluctuation of completion time in somatosensory + voice interaction is larger than the range of data fluctuation of completion time in the voice interaction task. From the overall view of the data, the time data of the voice interaction group in this experiment is more concentrated, indicating that the voice interaction is more stable, and at the same time, there is a significant decrease in the task completion time of the voice interaction group relative to that of the somatosen-sory + voice interaction group. This indicates that in this experiment, voice interaction is more suitable for the task of switching interface content on large displays.

4.2 User Interviews

In the voice interaction group, many users indicated that voice interaction was "stable and precise" for the screen content-switching task and that they were able to communicate task instructions more quickly, saving interaction input time. However, some participants reported that this mode of interaction "may be difficult to apply in noisy environments". Overall, the voice interaction group achieved higher user satisfaction due to its convenience.

In the somatosensory + voice interaction group, many users found it comfortable to interact with natural body movements, but because the somatosensory devices were "not very stable in recognizing them," this led to the negative emotion of "anxiety," and thus disliked the somatosensory + voice interaction. Other participants believed that somatosensory interaction requires users to continuously perform large body movements, which can cause arm pain after repeated operations, resulting in a poor operating experience.

In summary, users in the voice interaction group had a better subjective experience.

5 Discussion

5.1 Influencing Factors of Task Performance

Analyzing the trend of data distribution in in Fig. 7, it is easy to find that the top 25% of the somatosensory + voice interaction group presented a shorter task completion time than the voice interaction group as a whole. The reason for this may be that under the stable operation state of the Kinect device, somatosensory + voice interaction can further improve the interaction performance compared to voice interaction. However, in terms of average completion time, because the Kinect device is unstable in recognition, it requires participants to change their posture several times to achieve correct somatosensory recognition as well as command input, which ultimately leads to the completion performance of voice interaction being superior to somatosensory + voice interaction. On the other hand, since voice interaction only employs one interaction channel, while somatosensory + voice interaction employs a combination of two interaction channels, mobilizing the human hand channel and voice channel, bringing more physiological and cerebral load to the participant, which may bring additional cognitive burden to the user, resulting in a longer task completion time. Therefore, if it is hoped to improve the completion time of the task of switching content on a large display, the form of voice interaction can be considered; if the recognition of the Kinect device can achieve the desired stable recognition state, somatosensory + voice interaction can still be used as an effective interaction option. It should be noted that although somatosensory interaction is intuitive and easy to understand, it requires more physical movement from the user, which may be an aspect to keep in mind when considering this interaction mode.

5.2 Impact of Interaction Modality on User Experience

Participants in the interviews generally showed a strong usability preference for voice interaction. This may be attributed in part to the stability of the speech recognition and the fact that all participants had experience with voice interaction before the experiment. The ease of use of voice interaction mitigated the participants' difficulty in maneuvering. In terms of adaptability, participants perceived voice interaction as a better match to the screen content-switching task, providing a better user experience. On the other hand, since the naming of the sub-displays that make up the large display in this experiment was very concise based on placement, users were able to convey information more clearly through voice interaction, reducing misuse and increasing operational confidence. All in all, voice interaction maintains the consistency of the interaction operation, and its stable recognition performance also makes the user's behavior smoother and reduces the difficulty of learning and adaptation.

In the somatosensory + voice interaction group, interviews revealed that somatosensory interaction provided a novel and intuitive experience. In the experiment, participants simply raised their left arm naturally in the direction of the large display where the content needed to be switched, as required by the task. However, switching from somatosensory to voice interaction resulted in switching costs that additionally consumed the user's attention. At the same time, the unstable recognition of the somatosensory device resulted in the user repeatedly going through the process of waiting for the device to recognize and trying the operation again. This challenged the participants' patience level, which in turn also degraded the user's interaction experience. It was also observed that the efficiency of the Kinect device's somatosensory recognition varied depending on the participant's height, relative position to the device, and the angle at which the arm was raised, which is something that needs to be emphasized in the future development of the system to ensure the usability and user experience of the final system.

5.3 Limitations

In this paper, we conducted a study on the effects of different interaction modes in the task of switching content on a sub-display on a large display. The experiments focused on voice interaction and somatosensory interaction, but the overall interaction function of the system is not yet sufficient. Future related work can be improved in the following aspects:

Expanding the Sample Size. The sample size used in the experiment is small, which limits the generalization of the research results. Future studies should expand the participant sample size to obtain more representative data and conclusions.

Optimize Technical Equipment. Participants reported stability issues with the Kinect device. Therefore, subsequent studies should focus on the optimization of the recognition technology to reduce the impact of device errors on the experimental results.

Considering the Use Environment. The input modal design of large screen displays needs to fully consider their use in public or semi-public environments. Especially in noisy environments, speech recognition may be interfered with, which needs to be considered in future designs.

Multichannel Interaction Fusion. Considering that the Kinect development kit provides open-source code and application interfaces for human face-tracking technology, future research could explore the combined use of face recognition, gesture recognition, and somatosensory recognition technologies. This fusion may create more diverse forms of interaction and bring users a more personalized interaction experience.

6 Summary

Large displays offer the advantage of delivering vast amounts of information to users. However, the challenges arising from their large screen dimensions and the distance present intricacies in user interaction with the interface that merit careful consideration. Addressing this issue necessitates the formulation of specific interaction operations tailored to diverse scenarios. Conducting usability research with a focus on interactive operations holds substantial theoretical and practical significance.

Within the framework of this study, we amalgamate somatosensory interaction and voice interaction as an interactive input method for large displays, juxtaposed with the solo utilization of voice interaction. The outcomes elucidate that, in content-switching scenarios, voice interaction significantly outperforms the combined somatosensory and voice interaction method, demonstrating superior interaction efficiency and subjective experience.

Looking ahead, we posit that meticulous attention should be directed towards the following considerations in the realm of large display interaction research in the forthcoming years.

First and foremost, the evolving technological landscape will spawn an escalating array of information display scenarios necessitating large-screen displays. To enhance user performance and experience, a conscientious adherence to user interaction habits and information display modes is imperative, mandating the judicious design of large display interaction methods. Secondly, divergent interaction channels exhibit varying degrees of adaptability to distinct interaction tasks, thus necessitating a nuanced approach in selecting and combining modes in subsequent interaction designs based on specific application contexts, user demographics, and equipment constraints. In summary, the interaction design for large-screen displays ought to assimilate technological advancements and user requisites, thereby enhancing overall interaction efficacy and user experience through the deliberate crafting of judicious interaction methods.

Acknowledgments. This work was supported by the National Natural Science Foundation of China (grant numbers 72271053, 52275238).

Disclosure of Interests. The authors have no competing interests to declare that are relevant to the content of this article.

References

1. Bezerianos, A.: Using alternative views for layout, comparison and context switching tasks in wall displays. In: Proceedings of the 19th Australasian conference on Computer-Human Interaction: Entertaining User Interfaces, pp. 303–310. Association for Computing Machinery, New York (2007)
2. Bezerianos, A.: View and space management on large displays. IEEE Comput. Graphics Appl. **25**(4), 34–43 (2005)
3. Kim, N.W., Lee, S.J.: Vision based laser pointer interaction for flexible screens. In: Jacko, J.A. (ed.) Human-Computer Interaction. Interaction Platforms and Techniques 2007, LNCS, vol. 4551, pp. 845–853. Springer, Berlin, Heidelberg (2007). https://doi.org/10.1007/978-3-540-73107-8_93
4. Chittaro, L.: An electromyographic study of a laser pointer-style device vs. mouse and keyboard in an object arrangement task on a large screen. Inter. J. Hum.-Comput. Stud. **70**(3), 234–255 (2012)
5. Davis, J.: Lumipoint: multi-user laser-based interaction on large tiled displays. Displays **23**(5), 205–211 (2002)
6. Sharma, G., Radke, R.J.: Multi-person spatial interaction in a large immersive display using smartphones as touchpads. In: Arai, K., Kapoor, S., Bhatia, R. (eds.) Intelligent Systems and Applications 2021, LNCS, vol. 3, pp. 285–302. Springer International Publishing, Cham (2021). https://doi.org/1007/978-3-030-55190-2_22
7. Myers, B., et al.: Flexi-modal and multi-machine user interfaces. In: Proceedings. Fourth IEEE International Conference on Multimodal Interfaces, pp. 343–348 (2002)

8. Bernardos, A.M.: A multimodal interaction system for big displays. In: Proceedings of the 6th ACM International Symposium on Pervasive Displays, pp. 1–2. Association for Computing Machinery, New York (2017)

9. Tao, J.: A survey on multi-modal human-computer interaction. J. Image Graph. **27**(06), 1956–1987 (2022)

10. Zhu, A.: Eye Tracking and Gesture Based Interaction for Target Selection on Large Displays. In: Proceedings of the 2018 ACM International Joint Conference and 2018 International Symposium on Pervasive and Ubiquitous Computing and Wearable Computers, pp. 319–322. ACM, Singapore (2018)

11. Neto, A., Duarte, C.: Comparing Gestures and Traditional Interaction Modalities on Large Displays. In: Gross, T., Gulliksen, J., Kotzé, P., Oestreicher, L., Palanque, P., Prates, R.O., Winckler, M. (eds.): INTERACT 2009. LNCS, vol. 5726. Springer, Heidelberg (2009). https://doi.org/10.1007/978-3-642-03658-3_10

12. Qiao, C.: Research on human-computer interaction following motion based on kinect somatosensory sensor. In: 2022 IEEE 6th Information Technology and Mechatronics Engineering Conference (ITOEC), pp. 273–279. IEEE, Chongqing, China (2022)

13. Krahnstoever, N.: A real-time framework for natural multimodal interaction with large screen displays. In: Proceedings. Fourth IEEE International Conference on Multimodal Interfaces, pp. 349–354. IEEE Comput. Soc, Pittsburgh, PA, USA (2002)

Optimizing Information Seeking for Multi-person Collaboration: Evaluating the Influence of Various Zoom Centers and Interaction Modals

Xinhao Guo, Xiaoxi Du, Jialing Chen, Xiaozhou Zhou, and Chengqi Xue[✉]

Southeast University, Nanjing 211189, China
ipd_xcq@seu.edu.cn

Abstract. In collaborative multi-user environments, participants must often locate and assimilate information from specific screen regions swiftly and repeatedly. This necessity can engender operational redundancies that detrimentally impact the efficacy of collaborative efforts. To address this issue, the present study conceptualizes information-seeking behaviors as screen zoom actions and devises an experimental framework wherein the zoom center and the modality of interaction serve as independent variables. The objective is to ascertain which modal of interaction facilitates the most efficient information retrieval. The findings indicate that voice commands with clearly defined semantics significantly enhance information search efficiency. Conversely, the performance of traditional keyboard_mouse inputs and rudimentary voice commands is markedly diminished. Collectively, this research delineates the interaction dynamics elicited by diverse modalities within a singular task context, thereby offering novel insights for ameliorating operational redundancies in multi-user collaborative settings.

Keywords: CSCW · Information Seeking · Interaction Modal · User Experience

1 Introduction

As technology advances and society progresses, Computer Supported Cooperative Work (CSCW) has gained widespread acceptance and application across various industries [1]. Concurrently, extensive research has been conducted on collaboration tools tailored to CSCW [2]. Multi-person collaboration tasks, in contrast to typical single-user interactions, necessitate more complex information processing. This complexity demands that interactive interfaces not only present an increased volume of information but also dynamically adapt their layout to align with the evolving work progress and the collaborators' preferences. Despite the surge in research prompted by the advancement of XR technology for its integration into CSCW [3], the desktop screen remains the preeminent medium for interaction in commercial collaborative settings [4, 5]. In the current climate of rapid, real-time, multi-person collaboration, it is often necessary for users to swiftly redirect their focus to specific areas of information on the desktop screen to effectively

© The Author(s), under exclusive license to Springer Nature Switzerland AG 2024
A. Marcus et al. (Eds.): HCII 2024, LNCS 14712, pp. 232–247, 2024.
https://doi.org/10.1007/978-3-031-61351-7_16

assimilate and process information. This study presents a definition of the information-seeking process, which refers to the activities that users engage in to access and make use of relevant information. Specifically, the process entails identifying pertinent information at the outset and subsequently performing various operations to facilitate reading and other tasks.

Nevertheless, the intricacy of information inherent in collaborative tasks can significantly impede the collaborators' ability to efficiently process information, potentially diminishing work efficiency and jeopardizing the fulfillment of the primary task. While CSCW's multi-person collaboration mode has been proven to enhance work performance [1], the process of seeking information within such a context is frequently marred by operational redundancy, unlike in solitary tasks. This means that collaborative tasks necessitate a greater number of information-seeking actions than tasks completed independently by an individual. The repercussions of this redundancy on overall performance are substantial and cannot be overlooked. Prior studies have attempted to augment information retrieval efficiency by refining the design of collaborative interfaces [6, 7], however, these efforts have not fully addressed the issue. Consequently, the development of new interactive operations to streamline information-seeking and minimize operational redundancy has emerged as a pivotal area of research. The evolution of multimodal interaction technologies offers a broader scope for defining interactive operations, yet the suitability of different interaction modals varies across tasks. Selecting an appropriate modal of operation based on the nature of the interaction task is crucial to harnessing the strengths of various modalities, thereby enhancing task performance and user experience.

In essence, this study seeks to articulate and dissect the information-seeking task, taking into account the interactive nuances of such tasks to pair them with suitable interactive operations. We have developed and evaluated five distinct interaction operations to investigate the efficacy of information-seeking tasks and user satisfaction across these different modals. Through this investigation, this paper endeavors to identify a more universally efficient method of information search within the context of multi-person collaboration, aiming to curtail operational redundancy and, ultimately, elevate the overall efficiency of collaborative interactions.

2   Related Work

2.1   Multi-person Collaboration

The notion of multi-person collaboration originated from Computer-Supported Cooperative Work (CSCW), with early studies introducing a "spatio-temporal" matrix (see Fig. 1) to delineate and conceptualize this concept [8]. This matrix categorizes the pertinent patterns of CSCW into four quadrants, defined by whether collaborators engage in simultaneous cooperation (synchronous collaboration, asynchronous collaboration) or are physically located together (local collaboration, remote collaboration). Despite subsequent advancements in the exploration of more intricate and diverse patterns of multiplayer collaboration [9], the spatio-temporal matrix mentioned earlier continues to serve as the foundational framework for comprehending activities involving collaboration among multiple individuals.

	Synchronous (same time)	Asynchronous (different time)
Colocated (same place)	Face to face interactions	Continuous task
Remote (different place)	Remote interactions	Communication & Coordination

Fig. 1. CSCW "spatio-temporal" matrix

The multi-person collaboration mode examined in this study pertains to synchronous remote collaboration, situated in the bottom left corner of the collaboration quadrant. In recent investigations within this domain, whether implementing Extended Reality (XR) technology into the conventional office setting [10] or devising a novel collaboration system built on XR principles [11], the predominant focus has typically been on optimizing information layout within the spatial context or expanding the interaction space. The objective has been to enhance the efficiency of information search tasks during multi-person collaboration by incorporating additional layers of information.

While these studies on interaction space offer a more liberated and expanded environment for multi-person collaboration, they exhibit limited efficacy in addressing the inherent operational redundancy resulting from the information search process itself. In comparison, Feng et al. [12] introduced an Augmented Reality (AR) display tool in their research. This tool effectively highlights key information during collaborative assembly, resolves issues related to information occlusion in AR collaboration, and subsequently enhances the efficiency of collaborative assembly. Notably, this research not only spotlights the challenges of information-seeking in multi-person collaboration but also provides effective optimizations. However, akin to the majority of existing studies, Feng et al.'s work falls short of adequately tackling the intricacies of the information-seeking process itself. Consequently, while their research has proven effective in ameliorating the AR multi-person collaboration process, the impact of operational redundancy introduced by the high-frequency information search on overall collaboration efficiency has not been sufficiently mitigated.

In conclusion, enhancing the efficiency of multi-person collaboration necessitates attention not only to the development of new collaborative systems or the expansion of collaborative spaces but also to the intricacies of the information-seeking process itself. Recognizing the inevitability of information seeking, it becomes apparent that the complete elimination of operational redundancy is unattainable. However, an effective approach involves maximizing users' information-seeking efficiency to reduce operational redundancy, particularly when single-operator redundancy cannot be circumvented. This strategy could serve as a pragmatic method to streamline collaborative processes and optimize overall efficiency in multi-person collaboration contexts.

2.2 Information Seeking

The evolution of computer and display technology has indeed propelled electronic screens to the forefront of information acquisition, surpassing traditional paper media. Comparative studies analyzing the characteristics of information acquisition between these mediums have been conducted, highlighting the advantages and challenges inherent in each [13]. Despite the transition to electronic screens, users are encountering difficulties in navigating the increasing volume of displayed information.

Prior research has proposed various methods to address these challenges. One notable approach is user intention recognition-based screen information acquisition, which leverages technology to automatically present relevant information within the user's line of sight when they exhibit seeking behavior. This method enhances interaction performance and user satisfaction [14]. Additionally, studies focusing on visual information reading on web pages have demonstrated that employing appropriate interactive operations can significantly reduce the time required for extracting and comprehending information. This optimization enables users to conserve time and energy throughout the process of accessing data [15]. These findings underscore the critical importance of enhancing efficiency during the information-seeking phase, as it significantly impacts subsequent reading comprehension. Given these insights, minimizing redundant operational time by reducing search duration becomes imperative to enhance overall efficiency in multi-person collaboration scenarios.

In this study, the collaborators' information-seeking process was deconstructed into two well-defined parts, zooming in on specific areas of the screen to read content and relocating essential informational regions toward the center for improved visibility, which provides a structured approach to optimizing efficiency. Notably, the parts do not adhere to fixed temporal relations; instead, they can be executed sequentially or concurrently based on user preferences and task requirements.

3 Methods

To study the user's information-seeking process, and in conjunction with its dismantling above, this process can be abstracted into a simple screen manipulation task. Specifically, in the information-seeking process, the user will pan and zoom the information region of interest on the screen to adjust it to a state suitable for reading and understanding. This process can be simplified to the task of zooming a specified region within a screen and panning the corresponding region to the center of the screen. In this study, we designed experiments around this task, defined different screen zooming interactions, and investigated the effects of different interactions on the performance of the information-seeking task, to guide for optimizing the interaction performance and experience of the information-seeking process, and ultimately contribute to the improvement of the performance of multi-person collaboration.

The described screen operation task exhibits certain parallels with the interactive operation involved in web map tasks. Prior research emphasizes that the key determinants impacting the usability of the interactive modal in web map operation are the zoom center and translation methed [16]. Therefore, in this study, we designated two pivotal factors, namely zoom center and interaction modal, associated with information-seeking tasks as experimental independent variables for thorough investigation.

The zoom centers considered comprise the screen center, cursor center, and semantic center. Screen center zooming stands out as the most prevalent technique, extensively applied in image processing and mapping applications as a fundamental zooming interaction. Cursor center zoom empowers users to zoom around the cursor's position, enhancing operational flexibility and user autonomy. Semantic-centric zooming, exemplified by zooming into specific regions based on semantic commands (e.g., "zoom to region A"), embodies the interaction logic of high-level user interfaces. The system comprehends user semantic commands and executes corresponding actions, a feature particularly pertinent for natural language interactive applications.

Interaction modalities encompass speech interaction, keyboard_mouse interaction, and semantic interaction (pertaining to the semantic zoom task). Voice interaction stands as a pivotal component within contemporary interactive systems, offering users a more intuitive modal of interaction devoid of manual input. Meanwhile, keyboard_mouse interaction epitomizes the interaction paradigm prevalent in most desktop applications, serving as a familiar interface for the vast majority of users and thus representing a foundational variable in this study. Semantic interaction, on the other hand, aligns with semantic center scaling.

The experiment's dependent variables include task performance and user satisfaction. Task performance was assessed through task completion time, specifically denoting the temporal disparity between the initiation and conclusion of a singular zooming task. User satisfaction, conversely, was gauged via post-experiment interviews conducted with the subjects upon completion of the tasks.

3.1 Experimental Tasks

The experimental tasks were systematically categorized based on the zoom center into three distinct types: the screen center zoom task, the cursor center zoom task, and the semantic center zoom task. In each of these tasks, participants were required to manipulate the screen's zoom level and adjust its position to attain a predetermined zoom ratio in the center of the screen. To maintain consistency across the information search tasks, the ratio between the current zoom area and the target zoom area size remained constant for each task. This standardization ensured an equivalent level of complexity for all individual tasks, promoting a fair comparison across different interaction modalities. The area earmarked for scaling was chosen randomly on the screen, and the target zooming region is defined as the corresponding region in the center of the screen where the user can perceive the region to be zooming. For a visual representation and clarification of the three task categories, see Fig. 2, which likely provides a schematic diagram illustrating the specifics of each task.

Task 1: Screen Center Zoom Task. In this kind of task, the screen's zoom center is fixed at the center of the screen. Users are randomly permitted to zoom using either mouse or voice commands. Additionally, the screen can be shifted and dragged through both mouse and voice inputs. Each interaction modal is iterated 10 times, resulting in a total of 20 completed tasks. The specific area to be zoomed for each task is randomly determined within the map area.

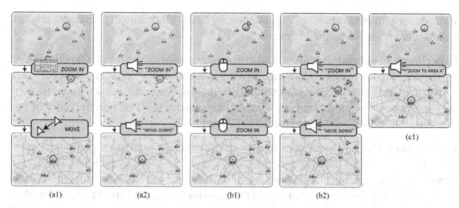

Fig. 2. The schematic diagram of the three types of tasks. Where (a1) and (a2) represent the keyboard_mouse interaction and voice interaction for the screen-centered zoom task, respectively, (b1) and (b2) represent the keyboard_mouse interaction and voice interaction for the cursor-centered zoom task, respectively, and (c1) represents the semantic interaction for the semantic-centered zoom task.

Task 2: Cursor Center Zoom Task. This task involves a dynamic zoom center linked to the cursor's position. Users can zoom the screen through keyboard_mouse interactions or speech commands. Each interaction method is repeated 10 times, totaling 20 tasks, and the zoom area for each task is randomly situated within the map area.

Task 3: Semantic Center Scaling Task. In this task variant, the screen's zoom center is determined by the semantics of the user's voice command. For instance, when the user issues a voice command like "zoom to region A," the system automatically scales the area corresponding to "Region A" and centers it on the screen. Users engage in semantic interactions to perform 10 repeated tasks, with the area to be zoomed randomly appearing within the screen area for each zooming task.

3.2   Experimental Setting

This experiment is conducted within the laboratories of the School of Mechanical Engineering at Southeast University, aiming to ensure that users can successfully execute experimental tasks in an optimally illuminated environment with minimal noise interference. The experimental setup comprises a high-performance computer, encompassing a computer mainframe and a 27-inch 2K resolution monitor, a trackball mouse, a keyboard, and a microphone. Preceding the experiment, meticulous equipment debugging is conducted to ascertain its proper functionality. Additionally, the user's seating arrangement is adjusted to ensure that they are positioned facing the center of the screen.

3.3   Experimental Procedure

The experiment comprises three blocks, with the initial two consisting of 20 trials each for specific screen center scaling and cursor center scaling, while the third block involves

10 trials for semantic center scaling, totaling 50 trials. The entire experimental process unfolds across the following stages:

Experiment Preparation Phase. The experimenter verifies the normal functioning of the experimental program and ensures that the interaction devices are operational. This is crucial to guarantee the smooth execution of the four interaction tasks. Subsequently, the experimenter employs the Latin square arrangement to determine the order of the experimental tasks for the participants.

Introductory Phase. Participants receive an introduction from the experimenter, covering the experiment's purpose, procedures, and any necessary precautions. Clear explanations of each experimental task are provided to ensure participants comprehend each phase. Following this, participants fill in the experimental record sheet and comfortably take their place in front of a single desk.

Experimental Phase. Once seated, participants are presented with an on-screen instruction: "What kind of zoom center task is carried out this time, please operate through what kind of interaction, if there is no doubt, you can press the space bar to continue." Upon pressing the space bar, the first task is displayed. After completion, participants continue to press space. The first block concludes after 10 or 20 repetitions of the task, and the subsequent block is introduced. The experimental phase concludes upon the completion of all three blocks. See Fig. 3 or a detailed schematic representation of a single experimental trial.

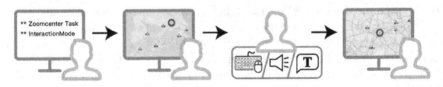

Fig. 3. Schematic flow diagram of a single experimental trial

Interview Phase. User interviews were conducted after subjects completed all trials to understand users' perceptions of the interactions of the different zoom centers.

3.4 Data Collection

A cohort of 24 participants, consisting of 14 males and 10 females, all Southeast University students, participated in this experiment. The age range of the participants was between 18 and 28 years, and they possessed a foundational understanding of the experimental system and its interactive functionalities. This ensured that the potential influence of the subjects' learning effects could be disregarded.

To mitigate the impact of the order effect on interaction performance, a Latin-square treatment was applied to determine the sequence of the three types of tasks. Each participant was assigned a specific order for the three types of experimental tasks.

Every participant completed the entire experiment, resulting in the collection of 50 task completion time data per participant, amounting to a total of 1200 task completion time data. Among these, 17 data points were excluded due to being either too short or too long resulting from participant misuse, and an additional 31 were eliminated due to system identification errors, leading to a total of 1152 valid data for analysis.

4 Data Analysis

The experimental design incorporated three different interaction conditions: screen center, cursor center, and semantic center. The screen center and cursor center conditions involved both keyboard_mouse and voice interactions, while the semantic center condition solely focused on semantic interactions. The subsequent data analysis was divided into two parts:

In part 1, independent one-way analyses were performed for each of the two independent variables: interaction modals (keyboard_mouse and voice interactions) and zoom centers (screen center, cursor center, and semantic center). The goal was to assess whether these factors had a significant impact on information-seeking task performance. This analysis allowed researchers to evaluate the individual effects of interaction modals and zoom centers on the dependent variable, which presumably measures the participants' performance in information-seeking tasks.

In part 2, a two-way analysis was conducted specifically on the data from the screen-center and cursor-center conditions. This analysis aimed to explore whether there were significant interactions between the two independent variables: interaction modals and zoom centers. By using a two-way ANOVA, researchers could examine not only the main effects of each independent variable but also whether there was a combined effect or interaction between them on information-seeking task performance.

4.1 One-Way Analysis

Firstly, the dataset underwent normality tests to inform subsequent method selection for data analysis. Specifically, the Shapiro-Wilk test was employed to assess the normality of each data group, complemented by visual inspection via QQ plots of the normal distribution. Adequate normality was indicated by a Shapiro-Wilk test p-value exceeding 0.05, accompanied by data points aligning closely with the QQ plot. Tables 1 and 2 present the test outcomes for data stratified by distinct interaction modals, while Figs. 4 and 5 depict the results for data segmented by various zoom centers.

The examination of data charts for the two grouping methods readily reveals that the p-values for each dataset do not align with the prescribed criteria. Furthermore, the distribution of data points on the QQ chart notably deviates from the anticipated range. Consequently, it can be concluded that the datasets corresponding to both the three interaction modalities and the three zoom centers fail to conform to the assumption of normality.

Subsequently, the aforementioned datasets underwent a homogeneity test of variance to evaluate the uniformity of variance within each group, employing Levene's test. The test outcomes for the two groups of data are presented in Table 3 below. Notably, the

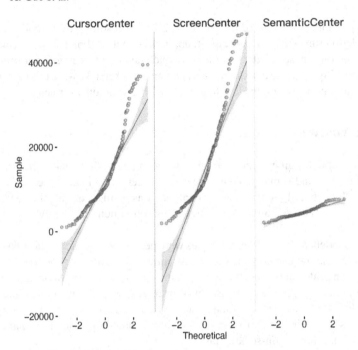

Fig. 4. Normal QQ plots of data grouped by zoom center

homogeneity test of variance indicates a lack of homogeneity in the variance across different levels of the independent variables for both datasets ($p < 0.05$). This indicates that the variance of the data corresponding to each level of the independent variables is not consistent.

In summarizing the two tests, it is evident that the data derived from this experiment did not adhere to the assumptions of normality and homogeneity, precluding the application of a conventional one-way ANOVA for analysis. Consequently, Welch's one-way test serves as a viable alternative to the standard one-way ANOVA, and Games-Howell post hoc tests facilitate the comparison of all conceivable combinations of group differences.

The outcomes of the Welch test, utilizing the interaction modal and zoom center as independent variables, are respectively detailed in Table 4. The results reveal that the two independent variables, interaction modal and zoom center, at different levels show significant distinction in task completion time ($p < ****$). This implies a significant main effect between the interaction modal, the zoom center, and task completion time. Subsequent to the Welch test, the Games-Howell post-hoc test results indicate a substantial variance in task completion time among the three interaction modals (****, ****, ****) (see Table 5). This signifies that keyboard_mouse, voice, and semantics, the three interaction modals, exert varying degrees of influence on users' task performance, with semantics interaction notably surpassing the other two (see Fig. 6). Additionally, a significant distinction in task completion times is also observed among the three zoom centers (***, ****, ****), underscoring the varying impact of screen-centered zoom, cursor-centered zoom, and semantic-centered zoom on user task performance (see Fig. 7). Specifically,

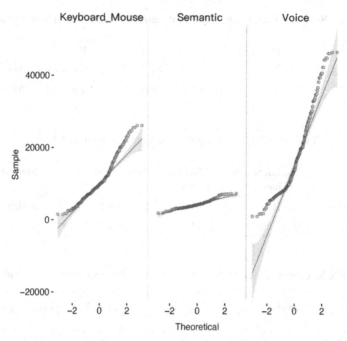

Fig. 5. Normal QQ plots of data grouped by interaction modal

Table 1. Results of normality tests grouped by interaction modal

InteractionModal	Variable	Statistic	P
Keyboard_mouse	TaskTime	0.944	3.55e−12(<0.0001)
Semantic	TaskTime	0.948	3.07e−7(<0.0001)
Voice	TaskTime	0.916	1.82e−15(<0.0001)

Table 2. Results of normality tests grouped by zoom center

ZoomCenter	Variable	Statistic	P
CursorCenter	TaskTime	0.880	1.36e−18(< 0.0001)
ScreenCenter	TaskTime	0.874	7.22e−19(< 0.0001)
SemanticCenter	TaskTime	0.948	3.07e−7(< 0.0001)

the performance of semantic-centered zoom significantly outshines that of the other two zoom centers.Two-way Analysis.

Upon visualizing and comprehensive description of the data (see Fig. 8), it can be inferred that there is a potential substantial main effect attributable to the interaction modal on task completion time. Furthermore, there appears to be a significant main effect

Table 3. Results of the homogeneity test of variance for data from different groups

	Df1	Df2	Statistic	P
InteractionModal	2	1149	81.5	7.64e−34(< 0.0001)
ZoomCenter	2	1149	181	4.66e−69(< 0.0001)

Table 4. Welch's test results for different subgroups of data

Independent variable	Dependent variable	N	Statistic	DFn	DFd	P	Method
InteractionModal	TaskTime	1152	658	2	685	(****)	Welch ANOVA
ZoomCenter	TaskTime		547		661	(****)	

Table 5. Games-Howell post-hoc test results for different subgroups of data

Independent variable	Level 1	Level 2	Conf. Low	Conf. High	p
InteractionModal	Keyboard_mouse	Semantic	−6860	−5724	****
InteractionModal	Keyboard_mouse	Voice	4693	7077	****
InteractionModal	Semantic	Voice	11099	13255	****
ZoomCenter	CursorCenter	ScreenCenter	921	3464	***
ZoomCenter	CursorCenter	SemanticCenter	−8997	−7348	****
ZoomCenter	ScreenCenter	SemanticCenter	−11367	−9364	****

associated with the zoom center on task completion time, albeit to a lesser degree than the interaction modal. While the figure suggests a modest interaction effect between the interaction modal and the zoom center, its significance remains uncertain. Consequently, a more rigorous statistical test is imperative to ascertain the validity of this interaction effect.

Given the non-conformity of this section of the data to normality and homogeneity of variance, the direct application of the standard two-factor ANOVA is precluded. Consequently, the Scheirer-Ray-Hare test based on rank order, which is an extension of the Kruskal-Wallis H-test, can be used as a nonparametric alternative to two-factor ANOVA.

The Scheirer-Ray-Hare test, applied to screen-center and cursor-center data re-vealed a statistically significant difference in task completion time across zoom centers (H = 12.908, p = 0.00033 < 0.05) and interaction modals (H = 85.519, p < 0.00000). Notably, there was no significant difference observed for the interaction effects between the zoom center and interaction modal on task completion time (H = 0.144, P = 0.7039 > 0.05)

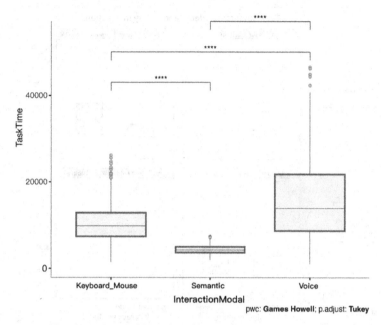

Fig. 6. Task completion time for different interaction modals

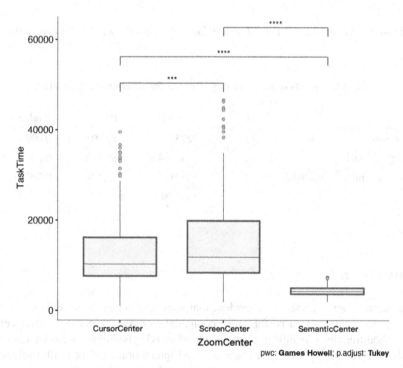

Fig. 7. Task completion time for different zoom centers

TaskTime: main effects and 2-way interactions

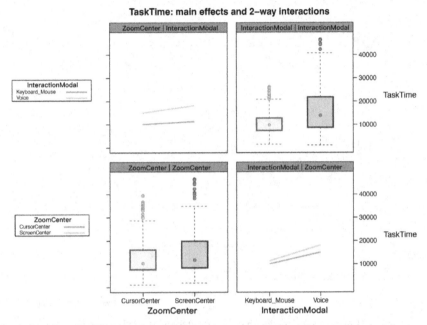

Fig. 8. Task completion time for different zoom centers and interaction modals

(see Table 6). Therefore, all the inferences described above were validated in the test results.

Table 6. Results of Schehrer-Ray-Hare test for different grouped data

	Df	Sum Sq	H	P.value
Zoomcenter	1	927339	12.908	0.00033
InteractionModal	1	6143914	85.519	0.00000
ZoomCenter:InteractionModal	1	10371	0.144	0.70399
Residuals	924	59515801		

5 Discussion

Based on the data analysis, it is evident that semantic center zoom exhibits significantly superior interaction performance compared to screen center and cursor center scaling. Additionally, semantic interaction outperforms keyboard_mouse as well as voice modals. The remaining two zoom schemes and interaction modals exhibit relatively minor discrepancies despite significant differences. Upon analysis, this outcome could be attributed to the increased number of steps required to execute tasks using the latter two modalities. Despite offering enhanced flexibility, rapid and precise localization of the target region is paramount for goal-oriented information-seeking tasks. Consequently, semantic interactions, with their notable temporal advantages, along with corresponding semantic center zoom strategies, merit further refinement and development.

Considering the interaction modals, voice interaction demonstrates inferior performance compared to traditional keyboard_mouse interaction. This discrepancy may stem from the frequent inability of ordinary voice interaction to accurately interpret user commands during experimental procedures. While semantic interaction also encounters similar challenges voice interaction entails repeated voice commands, thereby exacerbating the adverse effects of system recognition errors on overall task interaction performance. In contrast, although keyboard_mouse interaction also involve multiple steps, they are relatively immune to system recognition errors and exhibit high stability. Consequently, among the three interaction modals, voice interaction records the longest task completion time.

In the context of zoom centers, a comparative analysis between cursor-centered and screen-centered zoom reveals that the time required to accomplish tasks using cursor-centered zoom is notably shorter than that with screen-centered zoom, irrespective of whether the interaction involves keyboard_mouse or voice commands. Additionally, this time disparity is marginally exacerbated in voice interactions albeit insignificantly. An examination of the interaction process suggests that this discrepancy may stem from the prolonged duration required for voice interactions to execute the complete screen movement during center-focused zooming, as opposed to the more efficient keyboard_mouse interactions. Consequently, this temporal difference becomes compounded with the inherent divergence in zoom centers, yielding the aforementioned outcomes. Regarding the interaction modal itself, cursor-centered zooming facilitates concentrated attention on the operational center and enhances eye-hand coordination. In contrast, the screen-centered zoom task necessitates a division of attention when utilizing a keyboard and mouse, leading to increased operational demands and consequently influencing the user's overall interaction performance.

In addition, it is notable that the observation of users experiences a brief period of confusion about the current screen after an operation in these interaction modals. This confusion negatively impacts the users' ability to assess the interaction state post-operation, thereby influencing the overall user experience and the continuity of interaction, particularly pronounced in semantic interaction. The similar phenomenon has been identified in previous studies and defined as "lost in zoom" [17]. The explanation for this is perhaps because the semantic interaction is the most direct and discontinuous among the interaction modals in the study. While semantic interaction demonstrates better performance, it also increases the likelihood of users being unfamiliar with the screen after completing an operation.

This above-mentioned insight emphasizes the importance of considering not only the efficiency of interaction methods but also their impact on users' understanding and comfort during and after the interaction. Addressing the "lost in zoom" issue should be a focal point in further studies or related research, to refine interaction methods to mitigate the disorientation effect and enhance the overall user experience in zooming scenarios.

6   Conclusion

In this study, we explore the impact of varying zoom centers and diverse interaction modals on the performance of information-seeking tasks within a multi-person collaborative system through experimental analysis. Ultimately, semantic interaction emerges as the optimal choice due to its simplicity and efficiency, offering superior performance in meeting the demands of information-seeking tasks compared to the conventional keyboard_mouse interaction. This underscores the significance of considering semantic interaction for the application and enhancement development of multi-person collaborative systems. From an experimental perspective, semantic interaction excels in performance owing to the adaptability of its interaction modal to the task and the convenience of speech. However, it is essential to note its susceptibility to environmental interference during application. On the contrary, while the widely employed desktop-centric keyboard_mouse interaction may exhibit a slightly lower efficacy in terms of interaction performance, it remains the predominant choice in desktop collaboration systems due to its remarkable adaptability across diverse scenarios.

Expanding the scope from the current experiment to the evolution of collaborative interaction systems, the progression of various advanced technologies has significantly reduced the barrier to the development of interaction technology. This reduction has notably facilitated the utilization of multiple interaction modals either individually or in tandem within a unified collaborative system. This versatility opens avenues for more adaptable, natural, and efficient interactions within collaborative systems. Nevertheless, it is imperative not to overlook the adaptability of different modals to the interaction environment, task dynamics, as well as the user's cognitive processes and behavior in the development of interaction systems.

The integration of user cognition and behavior becomes pivotal in this context. The judicious selection and development of interaction modals that align with the inherent characteristics of the interaction environment and the specific task are crucial elements. This strategic approach serves as the linchpin for ensuring optimal user experience and task performance, thereby establishing the foundational requirement for the effective application of interaction technologies.

Acknowledgments. This work was supported jointly by the National Natural Science Foundation of China (grant numbers 72271053, 52275238).

Disclosure of Interests. The authors have no competing interests to declare that are relevant to the content of this article.

References

1. Ens, B.: Revisiting collaboration through mixed reality: the evolution of groupware. Inter. J. Hum.-Comput. Stud. **131**(SI), 81–98 (2019)
2. Hu, Y.: Hand-Eye Collaborative interaction design of virtual object in mixed reality sand table. Packaging Eng. **43**(6), 1–10 (2022)
3. Lee, B.: Shared surfaces and spaces: collaborative data visualisation in a co-located immersive environment. IEEE Trans. Visualizat. Comput. Graph. **27**(2), 1171–1181 (2021)

4. Madni, T.M.: Usability evaluation of orientation techniques for medical image analysis using tabletop system. In: 2016 3rd International Conference on Computer and Information Sciences (ICCOINS), pp. 477–482. IEEE, Kuala Lumpur (2016)

5. Forlines, C.: DTLens: multi-user tabletop spatial data exploration. In: Proceedings of the 18th Annual ACM Symposium on User Interface Software and Technology, pp. 119–122. Association for Computing Machinery, New York (2005)

6. Yuill, N.: Mechanisms for collaboration: A design and evaluation framework for multi-user interfaces. ACM Trans. Comput.-Hum. Interact. 19(1), 1–25 (2012)

7. Song, T.: Augmented reality collaborative medical displays (ARC-MeDs) for multi-user surgical planning and intra-operative communication. Comput. Methods Biomech. Biomed. Eng. Imaging & Visualizat. 11(4), 1042–1049 (2023)

8. Johansen, R.: GroupWare: Computer Support for Business Teams. The Free Press, USA (1988)

9. Du, X., Jia, L.: Trackable and Personalized Shortcut Menu Supporting Multi-user Collaboration. In: Kurosu, M. (ed.) Human-Computer Interaction. Technological Innovation 2022, LNCS, vol. 13303, pp. 28–41. Springer, Heidelberg (2022). https://doi.org/10.1007/978-3-031-05409-9_3

10. Speicher, M.: 360Anywhere: mobile Ad-hoc collaboration in any environment using 360 video and augmented reality. In: Proceedings of ACM Human-Computer Interaction, vol. 2(EICS), pp. 1–20 (2018)

11. Piumsomboon, T.: CoVAR: a collaborative virtual and augmented reality system for remote collaboration. In: SIGGRAPH Asia 2017 Emerging Technologies, pp. 1–2. Association for Computing Machinery, New York (2017)

12. Feng, S.: ARCoA: Using the AR-assisted cooperative assembly system to visualize key information about the occluded partner. Inter. J. Hum.-Comput. Interact. 39(18), 3556–3566 (2023)

13. Kong, Y.: Comparison of reading performance on screen and on paper: A meta-analysis. Comput. Educ. 123, 138–149 (2018)

14. Jin, H., David, B.: Exploring initiative interactions on a proxemic and ambient public screen. In: Kurosu, M. (ed.) Human-Computer Interaction. Advanced Interaction Modalities and Techniques 2014, LNCS, vol. 8511, pp. 567–577. Springer, Heidelberg (2014). https://doi.org/10.1007/978-3-319-07230-2_54

15. Sharif, A.: VoxLens: Making online data visualizations accessible with an interactive javascript plug-in. In: Proceedings of the 2022 CHI Conference on Human Factors in Computing Systems, pp. 1–19. Association for Computing Machinery, New York (2022)

16. Manlai, Y.: A usability evaluation of web map zoom and pan functions. Inter. J. Design 1(1), (2007)

17. Touya, G.: Please, Help Me! I Am Lost in Zoom. In: Proceedings of the International Cartographic Association, pp. 1–4. Copernicus Publications, Florence (2021)

Building the User Experience Evaluation Model of Bank Outlets by Service Design

Manhai Li[1(✉)] and Yixuan Liu[2]

[1] Chongqing University of Posts and Telecommunications, Chongqing 400065, China
limh@cqupt.edu.cn
[2] Sichuan Fine Arts Institute, Chongqing 401331, China

Abstract. The existing customer satisfaction evaluation model has three major problems in the data collection and evaluation methods: non-automation, non-sustainability, and imbalance. The same problems exist in bank outlets because they use traditional satisfaction evaluation methods. This study studies the service quality evaluation system and constructs an offline user experience evaluation index system of banks that scientifically quantifies the service experience to solve the three major problems. Taking the offline service of banks as the research object, based on *Scene* theory, the "DEPTH" experience evaluation index system was constructed, including five dimensions and 20 secondary indicators, which have three advantages: automaticity, sustainability, and compatibility. The data management and evaluation of service products are helpful to ensure the quality of service and provide a clear direction for subsequent service improvement and decision management.

Keywords: User experience · Service design · Experience evaluation model

1 Introduction

1.1 Customer Satisfaction of Bank Outlets

In the field of customer satisfaction evaluation models, the Sweden Customer Satisfaction Barometer was the earliest customer satisfaction index model in 1989 [1]. On this basis, Dr. Fornell of the University of Michigan and others further improved the Swedish SCSB model and created the American Customer Satisfaction Index (ACSI) [2]. Subsequently, European countries successively established customer satisfaction index models that suit their national conditions. There are also different experience evaluation models within major enterprises, such as the e-commerce platform PULSE model, Alipay PTECH model, Alibaba Cloud UES model, Google HEART model, Ali PTECH 1.0 model, and so on.

The data sources of the above customer satisfaction evaluation model can be divided into two categories: offline field research and online data collection. Offline field research often requires a lot of personnel energy. For example, the ACSI needs to be obtained by offline field visits, and researchers need to exert their subjective initiative to refine

© The Author(s), under exclusive license to Springer Nature Switzerland AG 2024
A. Marcus et al. (Eds.): HCII 2024, LNCS 14712, pp. 248–258, 2024.
https://doi.org/10.1007/978-3-031-61351-7_17

and summarize. Online data collection mostly relies on Internet platforms to obtain user online behavior data, but the way of collecting information and data is relatively limited, which cannot understand the user's true inner feelings, and it cannot be both functional and experiential. When banks conduct customer satisfaction surveys, traditional research methods and models are often used, so the same problems exist in customer satisfaction surveys of banks [3].

In summary, the data collection and evaluation methods of the existing customer satisfaction evaluation model of banks have three major problems: non-automation, non-sustainability, and imbalance. Given these three types of problems, we rely on scene theory and scene data collection systems and establish a corresponding experience index evaluation system for banks. The research results help reduce the uncertainty in user experience of banks and provide a reference value for the establishment of a data-based user experience evaluation system.

1.2 Service Design Method

As an emerging discipline, service design has an immature theoretical system and theory, and there are many uncertainties in the existing service design practice. Many factors will lead to changes in service experiences, such as participants' personal factors, physics environments, and human interaction forms [4]. At the same time, there are "tangible parts" and "intangible parts" in service products. So, it is difficult to judge the quality of services and produce a standard evaluation system due to uncertainty and intangibility [5]. Therefore, how to use scientific quantification of services has become a challenge for contemporary service design researchers.

Service design is a professional field with an interdisciplinary nature such as marketing, management, engineering, and service studies. Service design has a wealth of design methods and tools [6]. Although the original service design methods can ensure the availability of products, it is difficult to ensure the quality of the service experience enjoyed by each customer.

In service design, the scene can be a specific environment for purchasing, experiencing and displaying service [7], and scenario-based service design can help enterprises grasp the immediate needs of users, to improve user experience and improve management efficiency.

The word "scene" was born out of the term "scenario" in the field of drama [8]. In the 1960s, American communication scholar Erving Goffman introduced the dramatic analogy into sociology. Goffman's scene theory points out that the scene has the effect of influencing and changing people's behavior [9]. Philip Kotler, the father of modern marketing, realized the importance of scene atmosphere in the 1970s. He thought visual factors, auditory factors, olfactory factors, haptic factors, and other factors would affect the user's scene experience [10]. In the 1990s, Bitner first proposed the term "servicescape" and summarized it into three dimensions: environmental conditions, space, and function, guiding signs and decorations [11]. In 2014, Robert Scoble and Shell Israel proposed in *Age of Context: Mobile, Sensors, Data and the Future of Privacy* that there are five technical support methods for scenarios: mobile devices, social media, big data, sensors, and positioning systems, which can provide users with more convenient, efficient, and accurate services [12].

The term "scene" originally belonged to the field of drama, and scholars in different fields combined scenes with theories such as sociology and psychology. At the same time, with economic development and technological change, scene theory is gradually applied to the business field, and the "scene" has become one of the basic elements of service design, to facilitate enterprises to understand user needs from the perspective of the scene.

Data acquisition and processing system needs to comprehensively use four major information technologies: sensor technology, information processing technology, communication technology, and computer technology [13]. Data is obtained by sensors, cameras, and other intelligent terminals that automatically collect signals, pictures, or videos, and then analyze, filter, and store data through data processing mechanisms. Data acquisition system was first used in the American military field in the 1950s. Data acquisition equipment was introduced in China in the late 1960s. In the 1970s, the development of microcomputer technology led to the further development of acquisition systems, and acquisition systems are used in industry. In the 1980s, thanks to the rapid improvement of computer technology, the data acquisition system has been developed by leaps and bounds and put into the market. In the 1990s, monolithically integrated miniature data acquisition system enabled faster data acquisition response, higher accuracy, greater storage, and higher integration [14].

In recent years, Chinese design scholars and enterprises have been actively exploring new design models under data management [15]. If the data in the service scenario can be quantitatively managed and the corresponding index evaluation system can be established, it can undoubtedly help enterprises further understand the patterns of user behavior, ensure service quality, and discover operation management problems.

2   Build the User Experience Evaluation Model

2.1   Draw the User Journey Map

Based on behavioral economics theory and international experience scale, this research deeply investigates the service contacts of Ping An Bank's customers in the process of handling offline business, obtains the service needs of customers, and attempts to construct scientific, professional, and technical experience evaluation indicators, which aims to help enterprises objectively and quantitatively evaluate the customer experience of offline outlets, to improve user satisfaction and product loyalty.

In the research stage, we investigated the service touchpoints of Ping An Bank's customers in the process of handling equity business, from five aspects: decoration, engagement, performance, task success, and happiness.

According to the observation of the behavior process of customers handling business in the bank, we interviewed customers to obtain their inner needs and emotional experience and called back to users one month after using the bank's equity credit card. We sorted out the service contact points in the process of customer rights and interests business, combined user behavior with emotional experience, analyzed and summarized different stages of user behavior, and completed the drawing of the offline user experience map, as shown in Figs. 1 and 2.

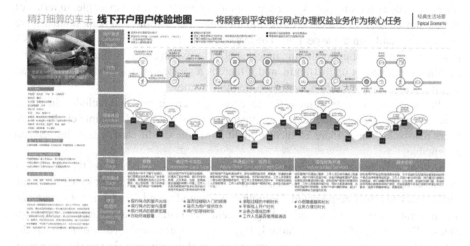

Fig. 1. Offline user experience map-male.

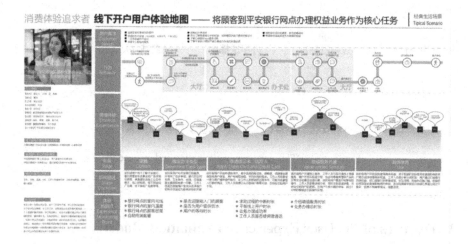

Fig. 2. Offline user experience map-female.

2.2 Build the Experience Evaluation Index

The survey found that users ranked the index elements of offline rights and interests business of banks in order of importance: performance, engagement, task success, decoration, and happiness. The reason why performance and engagement are so important is because customers of the bank want to be able to handle business quickly, the faster the speed, the higher the customer satisfaction, moreover, the professional ability and service attitude of the staff directly affect whether the user can handle the business smoothly, the smoother the process, the better the customer experience. At the same time, we obtained reference values for specific experience evaluation indicators. For example, in terms of "Customer density", customers think that less than 10 customers in bank branches are more comfortable; in the aspect of "The average length of time it takes to do business", customers can accept up to 30 min, in terms of "The average time in line for a number", customers can accept up to 10 min, and if there is a service interruption, customers can accept up to 1 min of waiting, and no more than 3 times.

In the aspect of rights, some users hope to have a credit card that includes the rights to eat, drinking, travel, and medical treatment, to avoid the use of multiple credit cards, users also said that if there is such a credit card, the credit card fees is higher and acceptable.

Referring to general experience evaluation points and interviews on the process of customer handling rights and interests, the experience evaluation index system of bank offline branches was constructed, including five latitudes and 20 secondary indicators. The five dimensions are Decoration, Engagement, Performance, Task-Success, and Happiness. The initials of these five latitude English words are combined, referred to as the "DEPTH" experience evaluation index system, as shown in Fig. 3. The 20 secondary indicators as shown in Form 1.

Fig. 3. "DEPTH" experience evaluation index system.

3   Features of the User Experience Evaluation Model

3.1   Automaticity

The data collection and evaluation methods of the existing customer satisfaction evaluation have the problem of non-automation, while the "DEPTH" experience evaluation index system relies on smart wearable devices with embedded UWB tags, high-definition cameras, temperature sensors, light sensors, noise sensors, infrared imaging sensors, and other devices to automatically obtain various real-time data in bank branch scenarios, such as user behavior trajectory data, temperature data, light data, sound data, user heart rate data, etc., and presents them in real-time in the form of information visualization through algorithm calculation and big data analysis, as shown in Figs. 4 and 5. At the same time, the data will be stored in the database for regular statistics, like the data

Table 1. "DEPTH" experience evaluation index system with 20 secondary indicators

Level 1 indicators	Level 2 indicators	Algorithm
Decoration	Indoor temperature	represents the temperature information returned by the sensor, and is the temperature weight of the region where the sensor is located
	Indoor light	represents the illuminance information returned by the sensor, and is the illuminance weight of the area where the sensor is located
	Indoor noise	represents the noise information returned by the sensor, and is the noise weight of the region where the sensor is located
	Customer density	represents the density information returned by the thermal imaging sensor, is the area occupied by the portrait in the image transmitted by the thermal imaging sensor, is the area of the detection area of the thermal imaging sensor, and is the density weight of the area where the thermal imaging sensor is located
Engagement	The number of responses during the call for help	is the number of times customer i responded during the request for help
	The number of interruptions during the call for help	is the number of times customer i was interrupted during the call for help
	The length of the interruption during the call for help	The total length of the interruption during the call for help is the length of time that customer i was interrupted during the call for help
	Number of errors in electronic terminals	The number of errors is counted by the terminal background software
Performance	The average length of time it takes to do business	is the total time that customer i spends before and after the transaction
	The average time in line for a number	is the total time that customer i spends before and after queuing to get his number

(*continued*)

Table 1. (*continued*)

Level 1 indicators	Level 2 indicators	Algorithm
	The average length of business help	is the total length of time Customer i spends during the help-seeking process
	The average time it takes to process value-added	Use the difference between the total service time and the time required for his own business to obtain the time spent on value-added business
Task-Success	Average business success rate	Through the algorithm of data analysis, the statistics of the success rate of business handling can be completed
	Successful problem solving at the first time	It can be found in the background records of customer transactions at bank branches
	Identity review task success rat	Through the algorithm of data analysis, statistical analysis of the business background database can be carried out
	Effectiveness of electronic terminal assistance	
Happiness	The customer's voice is gentle and steady	Multimodal fusion can be performed through sound and video data, and CNN neural networks can be used for emotion recognition
	Customers' mood swings are normal	Multimodal fusion can be carried out through voice, video, heart rate data, etc., and CNN neural networks and rules can be used to identify whether physiological indicators are normal
	Customers are orderly and quiet at bank branches	The thermal imaging data obtained by multiple sensors can be calculated uniformly to obtain the movement trajectory of customers at bank branches, and then through background calculation, analyze whether customers are anxious
	Successful enjoyment of the benefits of customers	Through the algorithm of data analysis, statistical analysis of the business background database can be carried out

changes in the "Performance" of a certain bank branch within a week, and the data collection technology and data analysis technology can be used to quantitatively manage the data in the service scenario to avoid repeated investment in a large number of manual research costs.

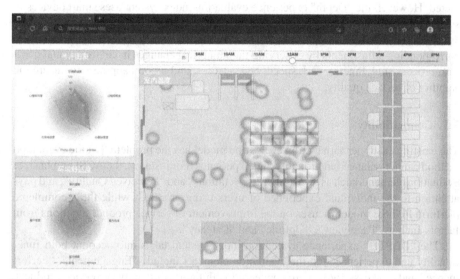

Fig. 4. Experience data visualization of "Depth" experience evaluation index system–indoor temperature

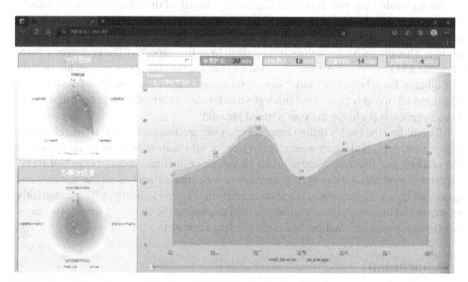

Fig. 5. Experience data visualization of "Depth" experience evaluation index system–the average length of time it takes to do business.

3.2 Sustainability

The data collection of the existing customer satisfaction evaluation model has the problem of non-sustainability; it is difficult for designers to know whether there are new changes in user behavior experience in the same scenario after the design project is completed. However, the "Depth" experience evaluation index system uses smart devices to sustainably obtain data from offline scenarios and establishes a database for data management, and managers and designers can continuously survey data changes, and make corresponding adjustments by observing the numerical changes in environmental comfort, process smoothness, work speed, task success, and mood happiness to ensure the stability of service quality.

3.3 Compatibility

The existing customer satisfaction evaluation model has the problem that the evaluation method cannot balance functionality and experience. For instance, the ACSI emphasizes evaluation elements such as "Customer Expectations" and "Perceived Quality", and pays attention to the individual experience of users using products, while the e-commerce platform PULSE model focuses on the improvement of service product functions from factors such as "Page view", "Uptime" and "Latency".

The "DEPTH" experience evaluation index system takes into account both functionality and experience, and the evaluation elements include "Engagement", "Performance" and "Success" which are concerned with the functionality of service products, while "Decoration" and "Happiness" belong to the grasp of the experience of service products. For example, in the detection method of "Performance", comprehensive calculations are made from four aspects: "The average length of time it takes to do business", "The average time in line for a number", "The average length of business help", and "The average time it takes to process value-added"; In the detection method of "Happiness", the user's happiness is comprehensively judged from four aspects: "The customer's voice is gentle and steady", "Customers' mood swings are normal", "Customers are orderly and quiet at bank branches" and "Successful enjoyment of the benefits of customers", Multi-modal fusion is carried out through sound, video, heart rate data, and action tracks to comprehensively judge the user's mood pleasure.

By building the bank's offline branch experience evaluation index system, relying on sensor equipment and smart wearable devices for information collection and algorithm calculation, and finally presenting data visualization and presentation, the "DEPTH" experience evaluation index system carries out data management of offline services and quantifies the invisible parts of the service scientifically and logically, which can greatly reduce the labor cost and time consumption of evaluating the quality of service products, help improve user satisfaction, maintain existing customers.

4 Conclusion

This study addresses the three major problems of existing customer satisfaction evaluation models: "non-automation", "non-sustainability", and "unable to balance functionality and experience". Based on scenario theory, we build an experience evaluation index system for offline service scenarios of banks and conduct data management and evaluation of service products.

Compared with the previous service quality evaluation model, the "DEPTH" experience evaluation index system has three advantages: automaticity, sustainability, and imbalance. On the one hand, data collection and data analysis technology can be used to continuously record scene data, and reduce uncertainty in the service process. On the other hand, it can also provide a clear direction for follow-up service improvement and decision-making management.

The final application of the experience evaluation index system needs to be adapted to local conditions, and the decision-makers should make appropriate adjustments to the service experience through the results presented by the data information to maximize the benefits as much as possible.

Acknowledgements. This work was supported by Doctoral startup fund and talent introduction fund project of Chongqing University of Posts and Telecommunications–Research on the cost and benefit distribution of big data productization (K2020–201) and Chongqing educational science planning project–Research on the talent training system of "social theme" in Colleges and Universities (2020-GX-284) and Research Center for network social development of Chongqing University of Posts and Telecommunications–Research on the cost of network big data production (2020SKJD06).

References

1. Fornell, C.: A national customer satisfaction barometer: the swedish experience. J. Marketing (1992)
2. Fornell, C., Johnson, M.D., Anderson, E.W., et al.: The American customer satisfaction index: Nature, purpose, and findings. J. Marketing (1996)
3. Yang, X.: The Evaluation and Research on the Personal Customers' Experience of Online Bank. Zhejiang Gongshang University (2014)
4. Xin, X., Xi, W.: Co-Creation and Uncertainties of Experiences in Service Design. ZhuangShi, (2018)
5. Liu, Y.: Research on the Service Design Method Based on Satisfaction Study: Case Study of Airport Service Design. ZhuangShi (2020)
6. Wang, P.: A review of the origin and development of service design. Design (2021)
7. Cao, J., Xin, X.: The five elements of service design: exploration based on the theory of dramatistic pentad. Creation and Design (2018)
8. Xin, Y.: New Retail Service Design Strategy Based on Scenario Theory. Jiangnan University (2020)
9. Goffman, E.: The Presentation of Self in Everyday Life. Peking University Press, China (2008)
10. Kotler, P.: Atmospherics as a Marketing Tool. J. Retailing (1973)
11. Bitner, M.J.: Servicescapes: the impact of physical surroundings on customers and employees. J. Marketing (1992)
12. Scoble, R., Israel, S.: Age of Context: Mobile. Beijing United Publishing Co., Ltd, Sensors, Data and the Future of Privacy, China (2014)
13. Liang, P.: Scheme Design and Implement of Real Time Data Acquisition System. Southwest University (2015)

14. Zhang, A.: Research on Data Perception Fusion and Visualization in Digital Workshop. Guizhou University (2019)
15. Yang, H.: The Integration of Data and Design: The Innovation Path Research of User Requirement Insight Through Big Data Analysis. ZhuangShi (2019)

Usability Testing for Electronic Remote Control Interaction Interface for Smart Home Products

Fanhao Li, Yonghong Liu, and Xiangtian Bai[✉]

School of Design, Hunan University, Changsha, Hunan, China
{liuyh,xtbai}@hnu.edu.cn

Abstract. The purpose of this study was to investigate the usability of three high-fidelity interactable prototypes with a stepper control, a slider control, and a picker control, and to suggest design improvements and recommendations. Participants used an Apple mobile phone to complete five tasks related to smart bed angle adjustment. A usability test was used to collect quantitative data (time to complete the tasks and SUS scores), and the results were tested using repeated measures one-way ANOVA. Users' subjective attitudes and user experiences of the different programmes were also collected through post-test interviews and observations of the experimenters. The final results showed that: (1) The use of shortcut input or one-button direct access in the angle adjustment control can significantly improve the efficiency of user adjustment. (2) Avoiding the display of too many numbers in the adjustment area can improve the intuition of user operation. (3) Introducing multimodal feedback in the process of angle adjustment can help to guide the user, convey key information and state changes, and further enhance the user experience.

Keywords: Stepper control · Slider control · Picker control · System usability scale (SUS) · Usability evaluation · Electronic control

1 Introduction

In recent years, the Internet of Things (IoT) has experienced rapid growth and has become an important trend-setting technology in the field of science and technology [1]. IoT refers to the connection of various objects through the Internet, enabling them to communicate and exchange data with each other. The rapid development of this technology is due to the wide application of IoT, covering a wide range of fields such as home, healthcare, industry and agriculture [2].

In the home sector, the popularity of smart home products has driven the development of IoT. From smart home appliances to smart security systems, users can remotely monitor and control devices in their homes through mobile phones or other devices, improving the convenience and comfort of life. In the medical field, IoT technology enables remote monitoring and data transmission of medical devices, providing more possibilities for medical services. The application of industrial IoT also provides a higher level of intelligence and automation to the production process, improving productivity [3].

A. Marcus et al. (Eds.): HCII 2024, LNCS 14712, pp. 259–267, 2024.
https://doi.org/10.1007/978-3-031-61351-7_18

In this process, smart home products are increasingly being controlled electronically, with different products of the same brand being integrated into one convenient application [4]. This integrated smart home system brings great convenience to users. Users can manage and control a variety of smart devices in their homes through a single platform without having to frequently switch between different apps, dramatically improving the convenience of integrating the entire home smart system. This integration allows users to easily understand and operate smart home devices through an intuitive user interface, which significantly improves the user experience [5].

However, in the electric smart bed industry, electronic control design has not yet reached a uniform standard, and different smart bed angle adjustment methods have not significantly improved user experience. In order to verify the impact of the details of the interaction design of different adjustment controls on user experience, we propose the use of usability testing to evaluate the user experience of different adjustment controls. The purpose of this study is to provide insights into the usability of different types of adjustment controls for the angle adjustment function of a smart bed and to suggest design improvements. The results of the study can be used as a reference for researchers and developers.

2 Materials

In this experiment, three high-fidelity prototypes of single-interface smart bed manipulation with different adjustment controls were designed and built by Protopie. All three prototypes can be independently adjusted to raise or lower the bed head or bed angle in the lift control function. The first prototype is a solution with "Stepper" controls. This solution replaces the Smart Bed lift control adjustment component with a stepper control. The stepper consists of an increase button, a decrease button, and an input box that is controlled by the buttons and displays a value. Each time the increase button (or decrease button) is clicked, the number of digits increases (or decreases) by a constant amount. If there is a need for a large adjustment of the value, it can be drastically and accurately changed in the input box using keyboard shortcuts. The area is divided into two parts, the left side for the head of the bed and the right side for the tail of the bed.

The second prototype is a solution with a "Slider" control. This solution replaces the smart bed elevation control with a slider control. The slider control consists of a track, a slider, a scale and a value controlled by the slider. The desired value is selected by dragging the slider left or right on the track, and the scale helps the user to select their desired value more accurately. The area is divided into two sections depending on the style of control, the top for the head of the bed and the bottom for the foot of the bed.

The third prototype is a solution with a "Picker" control. This solution replaces the smart bed lift control with a picker control. The selector consists of a items list and the current selection. By scrolling up and down the items list, the desired option will stay on the current selection to select the desired value. The area is also divided into left and right sections, with the head angle on the left and the tail angle on the right. The three programme interfaces are shown in Table 1.

Table 1. Three interactive high-fidelity prototype interfaces for this experiment

Iterface images	你的智能床 升降控制	你的智能床 升降控制	你的智能床 升降控制
Angle adjustment controls			
Basic adjustment controls	— 3 +		
Programme type	Programme 1: Stepper	Programme 2: Slider	Programme 3: Picker

3 Methods

The experiment was conducted with quantitative experiments as the primary experiment and qualitative experiments as the secondary experiment. The quantitative part included task performance analyses and System Usability Scale (SUS) questionnaires. The qualitative part consisted of post-experiment interviews and observations.

3.1 Participants, Experimental Tools, and Environment

A total of 20 participants (M = 24.7, SD = 1.98) were recruited for the experiment. They were all between 22 and 28 years old. The experimental period was from 9th January to 19th January 2024. Task operations were performed with an Apple 14Pro mobile phone. The experimental environment was a distraction-free, well-lit activity room. The experimental data were collected through the timing controls set up in the prototype of the programme and the screen recording function that comes with the Apple mobile phone.

3.2 Experimental Tasks

About the task design, the task design was based on the main adjustment functions of the smart bed in order to understand whether the user is able to operate the functions of the interface when operating the prototype of the programme. Finally, five tasks were planned for the experiment. The purpose and operation of the task design are as follows.

1. Task 1: Adjust the angle of the head of the bed to 15° while adjusting the angle of the tail of the bed to 10°. This angle is called "Zero Gravity", which is the first and the longest function used by the smart bed users after they go to bed.
2. Task 2: Adjust the angle of the head of the bed to 25°. Smart bed users usually adjust the angle of the head of the bed individually to meet individual needs such as reading or watching films.
3. Task 3: Adjust the angle of the tail of the bed to 5°. For long periods of rest, a specific bed angle can help alleviate some physical discomfort.
4. Task 4: Adjust the angle of the head of the bed to 40° while adjusting the angle of the tail of the bed to 0°. Adjusting the head of the bed to the proper angle can help the user get out of bed more easily or accommodate other user needs.
5. Task 5: Zero all head and tail of bed angles. When the user is away from the bed, it will level the smart bed for the next time they go to bed. The contents of the operation tasks are shown in Table 2

Table 2. Contents of the operation tasks.

Task	Content	Purpose
1	Adjust the angle of the head of the bed to 15° while adjusting the angle of the tail of the bed to 10°	This angle is called "Zero Gravity", which is the first and the longest function used by the smart bed users after they go to bed
2	Adjust the angle of the head of the bed to 25°	Smart bed users usually adjust the angle of the head of the bed individually to meet individual needs such as reading or watching films
3	Adjust the angle of the tail of the bed to 5°	For long periods of rest, a specific bed angle can help alleviate some physical discomfort
4	Adjust the angle of the head of the bed to 40° while adjusting the angle of the tail of the bed to 0°	Adjusting the head of the bed to the proper angle can help the user get out of bed more easily or accommodate other user needs
5	Zero all head and tail of bed angles	When the user is away from the bed, it will level the smart bed for the next time they go to bed

3.3 Testing Process Description

The testing process followed the generic usability testing guidelines. Each user was asked to complete all the user tasks described above and the testing process was recorded for further analysis. In order to simulate the real environment of smart bed control, a smart bed with adjustable head and leg angles was provided. During the test, the user was asked to lie flat on the smart bed, while the smart bed would adjust the angle to different degrees according to different tasks. To a certain extent, this reflects the challenges faced by the user in the real environment. Environment and test pose are shown in Fig. 1.

Fig. 1. Lying position, body naturally relaxed, holding according to personal habits

3.4 Statistical Tool and Questionnaire

As the participants operated the task, the researcher recorded the time it took them to complete the task. Upon completion of the manipulation, participants were asked to complete the System Usability Scale (SUS) questionnaire. The SUS was divided into ten questions, five positive and five negative, and used a five-point Likert scale design. A repeated measures one-way ANOVA was used to analyse the subjects' task completion times, and SUS records. As users manipulated the tasks, the researcher observed users' responses to each task and conducted post-experiment interviews with some users. The interviews were about task satisfaction with the experimental procedure and the strengths and weaknesses of the different programme prototypes. Participants were also encouraged to make suggestions for improving the functionality.

3.5 Procedure

The experimental design was a repeated measures one-way ANOVA design. The experimental equipment was an Apple 14Pro mobile phone, which was used to complete the tapping, swiping and typing operations. Each task was clearly described to the participants before the experiment. The researcher recorded the task completion time after the experiment by viewing the video recording of the experiment, and participants had to fill out the System Usability Scale (SUS) questionnaire after completing all the tasks. The experiment was designed in a balanced manner to avoid sequential and order effects. The order of the user interface was: Stepper 1, Slider 2, and Picker 3.The experimental procedures were 123, 132, 213, 231, 312, and 321 in that order. The data results were recorded and analysed using repeated measures one-way ANOVA.

4   First Section

4.1   The Results of Task Completion Time

The three programme prototypes showed significant differences in task completion times for all five tasks at the 0.05 level of significance (all p-values less than 0.05) as follows:

The results of the repeated measures one-way ANOVA in Task 1 showed a significant difference in task completion times for the three experimental prototypes ($F = 257.517$, $p = 0.00^* < 0.05$). Among them, the Programme 2: Slider ($M = 4.75$, $SD = 0.47$) and the Programme 3: Picker ($M = 5.39$, $SD = 0.37$) were significantly smaller than the Programme 1: Stepper ($M = 12.99$, $SD = 2.13$) in terms of time to complete Task 1.

Results of a one-way ANOVA with repeated measures in Task 2 showed a significant difference in task completion times between the three experimental prototypes ($F = 278.309$, $p = 0.00^* < 0.05$). In terms of post hoc comparisons of completion times, the Programme 3: Picker ($M = 2.48$, $SD = 0.3$) was significantly smaller than the Programme 2: Slider ($M = 3.06$, $SD = 0.31$) and significantly smaller than the Programme 1: Stepper ($M = 5.14$, $SD = 0.48$).

Results of a one-way ANOVA with repeated measures in Task 3 showed a significant difference in task completion times across the three experimental prototypes ($F = 38.947$, $p = 0.00^* < 0.05$). In terms of post-hoc comparisons of completion times, the Programme 3: Picker ($M = 2.3$, $SD = 0.28$) and the Programme 2: Slider ($M = 2.39$, $SD = 0.35$) were significantly smaller than the Programme 1: Stepper ($M = 3.21$, $SD = 0.43$).

Results of a one-way ANOVA with repeated measures in Task 4 showed a significant difference in task completion times across the three experimental prototypes ($F = 359.213$, $p = 0.00^* < 0.05$). In terms of post-hoc comparisons of completion times, the Programme 2: Slider ($M = 3.21$, $SD = 0.35$) was significantly smaller than the Programme 3: Picker ($M = 4.53$, $SD = 0.54$) was significantly smaller than the Programme 1: Stepper ($M = 10.34$, $SD = 1.41$).

Results of a one-way ANOVA with repeated measures in Task 5 showed a significant difference in task completion times across the three experimental prototypes ($F = 364.565$, $p = 0.00^* < 0.05$). In terms of post hoc comparisons of completion times, the Programme 2: Slider ($M = 1.97$, $SD = 0.15$) was significantly smaller than the Programme 1: Stepper ($M = 3.35$, $SD = 0.36$) significantly smaller than the Programme 3: Picker ($M = 4.7$, $SD = 0.48$). The results of the repeated measures one-way ANOVA for all five tasks are shown in Table 3.

Table 3. The repeated measures one-way ANOVA results of all five tasks (in second)

	Programme 1: Stepper M(SD)	Programme 2: Slider M(SD)	Programme 3: Picker M(SD)	F	P	Post Hoc(LSD)
Task 1	12.99 (2.13)	4.75 (0.47)	5.39 (0.37)	257.52	0.00^*	Slider=Picker<Stepper
Task 2	5.14 (0.48)	3.06 (0.31)	2.48 (0.3)	278.31	0.00^*	Picker<Slider<Stepper
Task 3	3.21 (0.43)	2.39 (0.35)	2.3 (0.28)	38.95	0.00^*	Picker=Slider<Stepper
Task 4	10.34 (1.41)	3.21 (0.35)	4.53 (0.54)	359.22	0.00^*	Slider<Picker<Stepper
Task 5	3.35 (0.36)	1.97 (0.15)	4.7 (0.48)	294.57	0.00^*	Slider<Stepper<Picker

4.2 SUS Result

SUS (System Usability Scale) is a commonly used scale for assessing system usability. Proposed by John Brooke in 1986, SUS contains a set of questionnaire consisting of 10 declarative questions which are divided into positive and negative directions [6]. Using a five-point Likert scale divided into five positive and five negative questions with scores ranging from 0–100, participants indicate their subjective views on the usability of the system by giving ratings from 1 to 5 to these questions. The SUS items were developed according to the ISO 9241-11 specification based on three main usability criteria: 1. Assessment of the user's ability to complete the task as well as the quality of the task output, i.e., the effectiveness of the system; 2. Examining the level of resources consumed by the user in performing the task, i.e., the efficiency of the system; and 3. Focusing on the user's subjective feedback while using the system, i.e., the user's satisfaction [7]. The results of the repeated measures one-way ANOVA are shown in Table 4. All three experimental prototypes showed significant differences in SUS scores at the 0.05 level of significance (F = 12.367, P = 0.00* < 0.05), and in terms of scores the Programme 1: Stepper (M = 73.5, SD = 3.28) and the Programme 3: Picker (M = 74.75, SD = 4.79) were not different and both were significantly smaller than the Programme 2: Slider (M = 79.5, SD = 3.86).

Table 4. The repeated measures one-way ANOVA results of SUS

	Programme 1: Stepper M(SD)	Programme 2: Slider M(SD)	Programme 3: Picker M(SD)	F	P
SUS	73.5(3.28)	79.5(3.86)	74.75(4.79)	12.37	0.00^*

5 Discussions

Based on the above quantitative data, combined with the researcher's observation and interview data, the findings are as follows.

1. In the experiments of the sliding selector and the selector, users tend to use the method of quickly sliding the slider or scrolling the list of options first when making large-range angle adjustments, and then adjusting the adjustment speed when the value is close to the target value to ensure that the adjustment is accurately made to the target value. However, the slider and selector list do not have a limit on sliding or scrolling, which may result in the final value not meeting the expectation due to too much sliding or scrolling. Therefore, an additional "correction" is required, where the user adjusts the value slowly after a quick adjustment to ensure the accuracy of the final value.
2. In the process of adjusting the angle of the smart bed, the user tends to imagine the maximum adjustment angle as a "pot of 100 energy". Manual adjustments tend to rely more on the individual's sense of releasing the energy of the can than on adjusting towards a specific numerical target. Stepper control and Picker control can cause the user to focus too much on how to adjust the number, and lose sight of the actual angle adjustment. This takes the user away from the original purpose of adjusting the angle in the first place, and the illogical visual design may cause distress to the user, necessitating a redesign to improve the user experience [8].
3. In contrast to the results of the previous four tasks, the Programme 1: Stepper performed more efficiently in Task 5. This is due to the fact that the Programme 1: Stepper provides the user with input boxes where the values can be modified directly. When users need to make a wide range of angle adjustments, they can choose to input the target values directly, thus completing the task more quickly. This approach embodies the principle of "variety" in UX design, ensuring that users are able to choose the most appropriate solution based on their personal preferences and abilities, thus enhancing the overall user experience.

6 Conclusion

In the above discussion, the significant findings of the research results indicate that the efficiency of user adjustment can be significantly improved by using shortcut input or one-button direct access in the angle adjustment control through UX design. In addition, avoiding the display of too many numbers in the adjustment area and simplifying the user interface can significantly improve the intuition of user operation. The introduction of multimodal feedback during angle adjustment helps to guide the user and convey key information and state changes to further enhance the user experience.

It is suggested for future research that prototypes with more sophisticated feedback mechanisms can be designed for experiments to explore in depth whether there are differences in user experience between the various adjustment control designs. By comparing the feedback mechanisms of different designs, a more comprehensive understanding of user perception and operation of the adjustment controls can be obtained. It is expected that these research results can provide a good design reference for the future application of smart bed angle adjustment controls.

References

1. Das, L., Chandan, R.R., Kaur, P., et al.: Advancements in wireless network technologies for enabling the (IoT): a comprehensive review. In: 2023 6th International Conference on Contemporary Computing and Informatics (IC3I), vol. 6, pp. 807–814 (2023)
2. Chataut, R., Phoummalayvane, A., Akl, R.: Unleashing the power of IoT: a comprehensive review of IoT applications and future prospects in healthcare, agriculture, smart homes, smart cities, and industry 4.0. Sensors 23(16), 7194 (2023)
3. Li, S., Da Xu, L., Zhao, S.: 5G internet of things: a survey. J. Ind. Inf. Integr. 10, 1–9 (2018)
4. Liu, C.Y., Lv, Q., Zhao, M.: Research on interaction design of smart home products based on the internet of things technology.In: 2023 International Seminar on Computer Science and Engineering Technology (SCSET), pp. 220–225 (2023)
5. Satheeskanth, N., Marasinghe, S.D., Rathnayaka, R.M.L.M.P., Kunaraj, A., Joy Mathavan, J.: IoT-based integrated smart home automation system. In: Karuppusamy, P., Perikos, I., García Márquez, F.P. (eds.) Ubiquitous Intelligent Systems. SIST, vol. 243, pp. 341–355. Springer, Singapore (2022). https://doi.org/10.1007/978-981-16-3675-2_26
6. Lewis, J.R.: The system usability scale: past, present, and future. Int. J. Hum.–Comput. Interact. 34(7), 577–590 (2018)
7. Borsci, S., Federici, S., Lauriola, M.: On the dimensionality of the system usability scale: a test of alternative measurement models. Cogn. Process. 10, 193–197 (2009)
8. Qi, W.Q., Xue, J.: Visual design of smartphone APP interface based on user experience. Comput. Aided. Des. Appl. 17, 89–99 (2020)

Public Transparency in Brazil: Evaluation of Transparency Websites and Portals of Local Governments with More Than 200 Thousand Inhabitants

João Marcelo Alves Macêdo[1]([email]) (iD), Valdecir Becker[2] (iD),
Felipe Melo Feliciano de Sá[2] (iD), Edvaldo Vasconcelos da Rocha Filho[3] (iD),
and Daniel de Queiroz Cavalcanti[2] (iD)

[1] Federal University of Paraíba (UFPB), Mamanguape, Paraíba, Brazil
joao.marcelo@academico.ufpb.br
[2] Federal University of Paraíba (UFPB), João Pessoa, Paraíba, Brazil
[3] Federal University of Paraíba (UFPB) and Technological Innovation Agency of the municipality of João Pessoa (InovatecJP), João Pessoa, Paraíba, Brazil

Abstract. Analyzing the usability of transparency websites and local government portals has been the subject of scientific discussion. Instead of discussing what was disclosed, research has focused on how attractive the government website is. In human-computer interaction, the evaluation of these environments has heuristic aspects, such as responsiveness in the migration between different types of devices, browsers, among others. In the Brazilian case, the type of connection and the user's familiarity have a relevant impact, especially when there are limitations. The Brazilian political environment still exerts control over the issue, since political decisions are involved. Thus, a deductive methodology with a theoretical-empirical basis and tests was used to analyze the transparency websites and portals of municipalities with 200,000 inhabitants. This test followed the following steps: first an evaluation based on heuristics, followed employing the Wave Evaluation Tool extension, known as WAVE, which is a tool capable of evaluating the accessibility of websites. Developed by WebAIM, an organization dedicated to web accessibility, WAVE helps designers and developers identify accessibility problems in their web pages. Finally, the data was processed using GNU PSPP 2.0 Statistical Software. The results strongly suggested that the majority of websites are responsive, but there are cases where they need to be improved or rebuilt. In this way, the lack of compatibility hinders the popularization of access, especially because it limits the population, especially in access mechanisms, or even when migrating between mobile devices.

Keywords: Usability · Public Transparency · Accessibility

1 Introduction

The scientific discussion on public transparency has focused on what was disclosed, but has recently moved on to analyze the usability of transparency websites and local government portals. Thus, instead of discussing what was disclosed, research has focused

A. Marcus et al. (Eds.): HCII 2024, LNCS 14712, pp. 268–284, 2024.
https://doi.org/10.1007/978-3-031-61351-7_19

on how attractive the government website is. There is an assessment that measures need to be taken to improve this environment to allow for greater transparency.

In Brazil, legislation on the subject of public transparency began with Complementary Law 101/2000 [1], establishing mechanisms for statements and reports to be presented, which were later reinforced by Complementary Law 131/2009 [2]. Finally, more recently, Law 12.527/2011 [3], known as the Access to Information Law (AIL), improved and consolidated access to public information. As a result, Brazilian public managers are striving to disseminate basic, standardized information. Secondly, it is possible to classify them as reactive, providing data and information relevant to the public, related to the bodies and their functioning, with the aim of avoiding punishment for not complying with them.

Dias et al. (2020) analyze the outsourcing of transparency portals to local governments in Brazil [4]. This has caused problems with public data not being updated or not being updated at all [4]. The authors found that the integration of the transparency portal with financial administration systems and the recording of budget events were decisive in preserving the updating of data on the portal of city halls after the period of increased scrutiny had ceased [4].

The issue of public transparency is encouraged by the Public Expenditure and Financial Accountability (PEFA) and the International Budget Partnership (IBP). These bodies promote the financial management processes and cycles of governments through their international initiatives. International initiatives to assess the level of transparency of countries generally focus on central government, such as the 2009 PEFA report [5] and the 2017 IBP report [6]. However, their scales and measures allow local governments to adopt widely recognized measures capable of increasing public transparency.

PEFA's vision enriches the debate as it seeks to identify the institutions that act effectively in public financial management (PFM). These institutions have a critical role to play in supporting the implementation of national development and poverty reduction policies (PEFA, 2011) [7]. Comprehensiveness and transparency analysis is characterized as verifying that budget and fiscal risk oversight is comprehensive and that fiscal and budget information is publicly accessible (PEFA, 2019) [8]. Verifying that PFM information is comprehensive, consistent, and accessible to users.

For Brazil, for example, the 2017 IBP report suggests increasing the detail of the government's financial position in the Budget Guidelines Law (LDO), extra-budgetary activities and resources, and expenditure estimates throughout the budget execution by government programs. With these actions, society's participation in the budget process has increased. These international monitoring initiatives consider "public information" to be information that is relevant and available free of charge on a government website, preferably in a timely manner.

In the political sphere, the relationship between voters and politicians, under the influence of digital technologies, has changed significantly, with the expansion of relationship and interaction channels (Barbosa et al., 2021) [10]. Although they are still widely used, one-way communication channels are limited, so the internet has emerged, which has a wide reach, offering new two-way communication channels, such as party websites, politicians' and voters' blogs, YouTube videos, and lives with the candidate, among other possibilities [10]. Despite these relationships, it is noticeable that e-gov has been increasingly present in mediating the relationship between citizens and the government, stimulating debates about the impact of design and usability on the population's dialog with the public administration [10]. Usability focuses on how a system is used, with the consequence of the user's characteristics, especially cognition, the ability to act and perceive responses [10].

The Transparent Brazil Scale—360° Evaluation, presented by the Office of the Comptroller General (CGU), is an innovation in the traditional methodology for evaluating public transparency adopted by the institution, and aims to cover both active and passive transparency, uniting the two lines of action (CGU, 2021) [11]. This debate, promoted by the CGU, aims to analyze the effectiveness of public transparency in Brazilian municipalities, corroborating the conclusion of Alves, Miranda, Teixeira, and Souza (2021) that the transparency of mandatory information is low. These findings justify the relevance of research into public transparency and its application, to verify whether the theory set out in the law is complied with in practice.

Transparency International Brazil [TIBR] (2023) [12] recently released the Transparency and Public Governance Index (2023). This edition aimed to analyze Brazil's sub-national powers, specifically the legislative assemblies of each state and the Federal District. Based on this analysis, a ranking is formed and scores between 0 and 100 points are assigned, with the objective assessment being that the higher the score, the better the transparency levels of that entity (TIBR, 2023) [12]. The results are worrying because they show that only four of the 27 (twenty-seven) are at the good level, compared to 12 at the regular level, eight at the bad level, and three at the terrible level [12].

Jácome Filho & Macêdo (2022) [13] discussed in their study the responsiveness of public transparency websites in Paraíba on mobile devices. In an exploratory and initial study, they concluded that the lack of this compatibility hinders the popularization of access to government information. The authors also found that this limitation impairs the population's access to public information, resulting in factors that hinder transparency, given that the majority of the population accesses this data via cell phones [13].

Macêdo, Becker and Sá (2023) [14] demonstrated this by comparing access via web and mobile browsers, using an experimental strategy, on the public transparency websites of local governments in the state of Paraíba. The authors found that the majority of websites are responsive, but there are cases where improvements or even rebuilding are necessary [14]. Thus, it can be inferred that the lack of this compatibility negatively affects the dissemination of access to public information, especially by restricting the population, which has reduced means of access, mainly due to limitations and excessive use of mobile devices [14].

In the Brazilian context, the type of connection and the familiarity of the user have a significant impact. The Brazilian political environment still has control over the issue, since the political decision is related to the debate and the choice of what will be disseminated, even though there is a legal basis that obliges this choice [15]. The ICT Households survey, carried out annually since 2005, aims to identify access to information technologies in the country's urban and rural households and the forms of use by people aged 10 and over [15]. This survey follows the principles of the multi-sectoral initiative Partnership on Measuring ICT for Development, coordinated by the International Telecommunication Union (ITU) [15]. The main reference for the indicators is the Manual for Measuring ICT Access and Use by Households and Individuals.

When we analyze the ICT Households survey, we see that 84% of homes in the country are connected to the network, which represents an increase of four percentage points compared to 2022 [15]. This indicator has been stable since 2020. The survey found that 84%, or around 156 million people, had accessed the internet in the three months before the survey, representing an increase compared to 2022 (81%) [15]. The majority (99%) of Brazilian Internet users over the age of 10 connected to the web via their cell phone, which continues to be the most used device for this purpose. In second place is the television (58%), a device that has been in increasing use for more than a decade. Connections using a computer remained stable at 42% [15]. Of the Brazilians who own a cell phone, 60% have a pre-paid plan, and 36% have a post-paid plan. In terms of connection, 97% of class A mobile Internet users have access to the Internet via both Wi-Fi and the mobile network. In classes D and E, 36% have access exclusively via Wi-Fi and 11% only via the mobile network [15].

The political situation in Brazil continues to influence this topic, as decisions are usually focused on the discussion and selection of media content, despite the existence of a legislative decision. Therefore, a deductive methodology based on a theoretical-empirical foundation and empirical tests was used to evaluate the transparency of the websites and portals of capital cities. This examination entails the subsequent procedures: a preliminary evaluation based on heuristics was conducted, followed by the implementation of the Wave Evaluation Tool extension, commonly referred to as WAVE [16].

2 Theoretical Reference

2.1 Public Management and Transparency

Public transparency was regulated by the 1988 Federal Constitution, which is still in force in Brazil [17]. This constitutional provision encourages public participation in drawing up public policies, monitoring the use of resources, and making the country's major decisions. It is known by scholars as the Citizen Constitution. The incentive for transparency is present in the principle of publicity, since the Federal Constitution ensures that any Brazilian citizen can obtain information of interest to them, except for information whose secrecy is indispensable for the security of society and the state (BRAZIL, 1988) [17].

Although the Federal Constitution supports these initiatives, two other complementary laws reinforce the normative framework that supports these initiatives: Complementary Law 131/2009 [2] (the Transparency Law) and Law 12.527/2011 [3] (the Access to Information Law). The first change to the original wording of the Fiscal Responsibility Law (LRF) concerns transparency in fiscal management. As such, the new text introduces innovations and requires detailed information to be made available on the budgetary and financial execution of the Union, the States, the Federal District, and the Municipalities. The second guarantee is that citizens will be able to request information from the public administration, with transparency being the rule and secrecy the exception.

The Technical Budget Manual [MTO] (2023) [18] states that one of the purposes of the budget principles is to establish fundamental rules, with the aim of ensuring rationality, effectiveness, and clarity in the procedures for drawing up, implementing, and controlling the public budget. They are valid for all public powers, including the Union, States, Federal Districts, and Municipalities, and are governed by constitutional and infra-constitutional rules and by doctrine. The discussion on transparency has focused on measurement initiatives, which generally capture a superficial aspect of disclosure, the normative [4]. In this way, they assess that the information and reports required by the legislation have been disclosed, which attests to fiscal transparency on the portals of agencies and governments [4]. Local governments in Brazil have opted to follow a standard checklist to comply with the legislation when adopting so-called transparency portals [4].

The government stimulates citizen participation by encouraging them to take part in its activities and actions through transparency, encouraging oversight, and, consequently, increasing citizen participation in the use of resources by their representatives [19]. To ensure effective social control and guarantee access to information, in accordance with legal precepts, public administrations must maintain transparency pages and other means of free access to information [19]. This participation is expected to result in the presence of society in the processes of implementing public policies [11]. Transparency is closely linked to democracy. O'Donnell (1994; 1999) apud Cunha Filho (2019) [20] classified Latin American democracies, which began in the 1970s, as merely "delegative democracies", giving citizens a single role in the political process, that of electing political representatives. Delegative democracies arise from the premise that the candidate who wins a presidential election is anointed to govern the country as he or she sees fit, and for as long as existing power allows, during the term of office for which he or she was elected. In this way, the President is the personification of the nation and the main guardian of the national interest, which he is responsible for defining. Thus, his government will not necessarily be what he said or promised during the election campaign, and he is authorized to govern as he sees fit [20].

In their studies, Machado, Nalini and Machado (2022) [21] proposed evaluating the impact of the AIL on the behavior of public inspection agents, using behavior analysis as a conceptual lens. In this way, there was a change in the behavior of professionals at the Municipal Audit Court of the Brazilian state of Goiás [21]. Thus, after the implementation of the law, there was a decrease in the number of cases, but the sanctions were more severe, both in terms of fines and debt collection [21]. Finally, the authors concluded that the AIL had an impact on the behavior of public inspection agents in relation to the application of sanctions, thus not refuting the research hypothesis [21].

In addition, it is important to assess the level of quality, usefulness, and sufficiency of what is available. Baldissera et al. (2019) [22] analyzed these criteria through the perceptions of members of non-governmental and non-profit public transparency organizations. Thus, the members of the Brazil Social Observatory (BSO) are aware that the quality of the information does not meet the objectives of the AIL [22]. In addition, they found that the information available in public transparency media is not sufficient to exercise social control, although they believe that public transparency tools have been useful in strengthening social control [22].

2.2 Evaluating Interfaces on Web and Mobile Devices for Heuristics

Among the various ways of evaluating the efficiency of using a program, we chose to work with Nielsen's heuristics [23, 24]. The heuristics and other methods aim to evaluate usability, accessibility and user experience, providing guidelines for collecting and analyzing data. The evaluator will select the method that best suits their evaluation needs and available resources. HCI evaluation methods can be divided into: investigations, user observations and inspection [10].

The aim of inspection is to predict user experiences and identify possible outcomes arising from that experience, as well as highlighting design flaws. Observation methods make it possible to analyze user data about situations that occur in a system, identifying real problems that users face during their experience of use. Thus, research methods employ interviews, field studies and the application of questionnaires, which gives the evaluator access to the user's opinions, expectations, and behavior in relation to the system.

Inspection procedures allow the evaluator to examine (or inspect) a solution to predict the possible consequences of certain design choices [10, 25]. As it does not involve users, this method seeks to identify possible drawbacks that may arise when using the system. By comparing different designs, it is possible to highlight problems and learn about possibilities for improving the product. When examining an interface, evaluators take on the role of a user with a specific profile, experienced in certain activities. The aim of this type of evaluation is to identify difficulties that the user may face when interacting with the system and what forms of support are available to help them overcome them.

Heuristic evaluation is a usability inspection technique that suggests that the evaluator navigates the system interface to investigate possible problems, based on various heuristics, such as those indicated by Nielsen [23, 24]. This type of evaluation is effective in identifying various usage deficiencies, and is a quick and low-cost option compared to empirical methods [10].

This evaluation technique is useful both for developing systems and for evaluating commercial systems with a view to improving them. When creating systems, it is important to evaluate how they are made, from the idea to the final version. When evaluating systems that are already in commercial use, the method aims to redesign the system, adding improvements in future versions.

Machado Neto and Pimentel [26] changed the rules suggested by Nielsen to work on mobile devices. This is shown in Table 1 and helps us understand how people use these devices.

Table 1. Heuristics for evaluating the usability of mobile device interfaces: second version.

Heuristic Mobile	Description
HM1 - Use of screen space	The interface should be designed so that the items are neither too distant, nor too stuck. Margin spaces may not be large in small screens to improve information visibility. The more related the components are, the closer they should appear on the screen. Interfaces ought to not be overwhelmed with a large number of items
HM2 - Consistency and standards	The application should maintain the components in the same place and look throughout the interaction, to facilitate learning and to stimulate the user's short-term memory. Similar functionalities ought to be performed by similar interactions. The metaphor of each component or feature ought to be unique throughout the application, to avoid misunderstanding
HM3 - Visibility and easy access to all information	All information ought to be visible and legible, both in portrait and in landscape. This also applies to media, which should be fully exhibited, unless the user opts to hide them. The elements on the screen ought to be adequately aligned and contrasted
HM4 - Adequacy of the component to its functionality	The user should know exactly which information to input in a component, without any ambiguities or doubts. Metaphors of features ought to be understood without difficulty
HM5 - Adequacy of the message to the functionality and to the user	The application should speak the user's language in a natural and non-invasive manner, so that the user does not feel under pressure. Instructions for performing the functionalities ought to be clear and objective
HM6 - Error prevention and rapid recovery to the last stable state	The system ought to be able to anticipate a situation that leads to an error by the user based on some activity already performed by the user [8]. When an error occurs, the application should quickly warn the user and return to the last stable state of the application. In cases in which a return to the last stable state is difficult, the system should transfer the control to the user, so that he decides what to do or where to go

(continued)

Table 1. (*continued*)

Heuristic Mobile	Description
HM7 - Ease of input	The way the user provides the data can be based on assistive technologies, but the application should always display the input data with readability, so that the user has full control of the situation. The user should be able to provide the required data in a practical way
HM8 - Ease of access to all functionalities	The main features of the application ought to be easily found by the user, preferably in a single interaction. Most-frequently-used functionalities may be performed by using shortcuts or alternative interactions. No functionality should be hard to find in the application interface. All input components should be easily assimilated
HM9 - Immediate and observable feedback	Feedback should be easily identified and understood, so that the user is aware of the system status. Local refreshments on the screen ought to be preferred over global ones, because those ones maintain the status of the interaction. The interface should give the user the choice to hide messages that appear repeatedly. Long tasks ought to provide the user a way to do other tasks concurrently to the task being processed. The feedback ought to have good tone and be positive and may not be redundant or obvious
HM10 - Help and documentation	The application should have a help option where common problems and ways to solve them are specified. The issues considered in this option should be easy to find
HM11 - Reduction of the user's memory load	The user should not have to remember information from one screen to another to complete a task. The information of the interface ought to be clear and sufficient for the user to complete the current task

Note. [26]

2.3 Site Evaluation by the WAVE Evaluation Tool Extension

The other analysis was based on the WAVE Evaluation Tool Extension as a tool for evaluating accessibility in web interfaces. Web Accessibility Evaluation (WAVE) is a web browser extension that helps identify accessibility problems, providing recommendations to improve the experience of users with disabilities [16]. This tool lists a diverse range of common accessibility challenges. Before starting the evaluations, the WAVE extension was configured according to the parameters needed to analyze accessibility [16].

The WAVE extension works by evaluating the structure of the page, identifying possible violations of accessibility standards, and marking them with suggestions for corrections. In this sense, various aspects were considered, such as HTML semantics, Accessible Rich Internet Applications (ARIA) attributes, color contrast, readability, keyboard navigation, among others. For the purposes of this research, the following issues were highlighted: errors, contrast problems, features, alerts, and ARIA.

When examining websites, especially analyzing their accessible interface for accessibility, it is crucial to ensure equal access to information, regardless of their physical disabilities and other possible limitations. In the study by Ahmi & Mohamad (2016) [27], AChecker and WAVE are used to evaluate accessibility. The results indicate a low level of compliance with the guidelines set out in WCAG 2.0 and Section 508 [27].

Among the points that should be considered are the provision of text alternatives for any non-textual content, keyboard accessibility and color contrast [27]. In addition, other issues such as adaptability, input assistance, compatibility, empty links and empty headers can be improved. Despite the low compliance, most of the sites integrated some accessibility features set out in Section 508 quite satisfactorily. Overall, this study provides relevant information, especially for website developers, aimed at better compliance with website development standards.

3   Methodology

This research used the experimental strategy, based on the deductive method, with exploratory and survey outlines, considering its representativeness. This examination entails the subsequent procedures: a preliminary evaluation based on heuristics was conducted, followed by the implementation of the Wave Evaluation Tool extension, commonly referred to as WAVE.

The study population is made up of cities with a total of 200,000 inhabitants, leaving a sample made up of 27 cities, i.e. 26 capitals and 1 Federal District. The official websites of these local governments were selected because they are references for their respective states. These choices were made to grasp the breadth of transparency and the impact of the vehicles that promote it.

To carry out the evaluation based on heuristics, we used the theoretical constructs of the original Nielsen's heuristics [23, 24] and the mobile version by Machado Neto and Pimentel (2013) [26].

The evaluation took place using the information available when accessing the site, particularly on the homepage of the respective institution. The responsiveness of the devices and browsers in the migration process was assessed by checking that they adjusted appropriately to the screen sizes.

Finally, the data from the heuristics was processed in the GNU PSPP 2.0 Statistical Software and the data obtained by Wave was tabulated and classified using specific guidelines from WCAG 2.2 (Web Content Accessibility Guidelines) [28]. According to the guidelines, websites need to meet Level A requirements to allow people with disabilities to use the sites. WCAG is based on 4 principles to consider good accessibility: perceivable, operable, understandable and robust.

4   Results

Firstly, an evaluation was carried out based on Nielsen's heuristics [9, 13] made up of 10 items, as shown in Table 2 below. The first heuristic aims to assess the user's knowledge, through responses to their actions, of how the system works and its status. In this way, the system should keep you informed about what is happening in a reasonable time. In this respect, the system worked correctly for all observations.

Table 2. Nielsen's Heuristics

Heuristics	Yes	%	No	%
Presents simple and natural dialog	27	100	-	-
Speaks in the user's language	27	100	-	-
Minimizes user memory load	15	55,6	12	44,4
It is consistent	26	96,3	1	3,7
Provides user feedback	25	92,6	2	7,4
It has clear and marked outputs	25	92,6	2	7,4
Provides shortcuts	24	88,9	3	11,1
Displays constructive and accurate error messages	26	96,3	1	3,7
Prevents user errors during navigation	23	85,2	4	14,8
They have good support, rescue and documentation	27	100	-	-

Note: Own elaboration, based on the research script

Table 2 also looked at whether the system used a language familiar to the user, avoiding technical and developer-specific terms. Moreover, whether the conventions of the real world were being met, where the appearance of the information should follow a natural and logical order, as expected by the users. What we found was that everyone followed this heuristic.

The biggest problem encountered was memory load, which is due to the excessive use of graphic elements and applications that consume an excessive amount of memory. In this respect, 44.4% overloaded the user's equipment. The system should minimize the user's memory load by making objects, actions, and options visible. The user should not have to remember information from one part of the dialog to another. The system's instructions for use should be visible or easily retrievable whenever appropriate.

It should be checked that the system offers an easily identifiable emergency exit, allowing the user to get out of the unwanted state without major difficulties. This prevents the user from thinking that different actions or situations mean the same thing. Or that the same element has different meanings in different situations. The conventions of the platform or computing environment must be followed. In these situations, no more than 11.5% was impacted.

On the other hand, the system should make it possible to optimize the experience for more experienced users. The use of irrelevant or unnecessary information on the screen should be avoided. It is essential to prevent errors from occurring. As well as using simple language to expose errors and suggest a solution. In these areas, the incidence of 3.7% to 14.8% remained low.

The Federal District, which includes Brasília, the federal capital, adopts a policy of creating several sub-sites to deal with each issue, which, in our opinion, deconstructs the logic of a government portal and transparency portal. This is even though the site even has a mobile version. We can list the https://www.transparencia.df.gov.br/- transparency portal, open data, http://dados.df.gov.br/ and participate, which is the passive transparency portal, at https://www.participa.df.gov.br/. Cuiabá and other cities have also adopted a separate transparency portal system, with a different look and design, giving the impression of different systems.

In the case of the Recife City Hall website, the work of the Municipal Information Technology Company (EMPREL) stands out. It is a public company, with legal personality under private law, its assets, administrative and financial autonomy, and is part of the Indirect Municipal Administration. Its work stands out strategically when it comes to planning and implementing Information and Communication Technology policy. The municipal government believes that such policies are necessary to standardize the bodies and entities of the direct and indirect administration of Recife City Hall. It is based on the Conecta Recife Portal, which is the User Services Charter for the Municipality of Recife and is in line with the requirements established in Law No. 13,460, of June 26, 2017 (Law for the Protection and Defense of Users of Public Services).

Table 3 shows the data perceived by the researchers about the heuristics in the mobile version when accessing the sites. The main finding is that all the sites had some observations, but all of them showed that the component and its functionality were appropriate. This clarifies it that there is a need to evolve for this type of device.

Table 3. Mobile Heuristics

Mobile Heuristics	Yes	%	No	%
Presents good use of screen space	26	96,3	1	3,7
Have consistency and standards of the interface	25	92,6	2	7,4
Visibility and easy access to all existing information	19	70,4	8	29,6
Suitability between the component and its functionality	27	100	-	-
Message adaptation to functionality and user	26	96,3	1	3,7
Error prevention and quick return to the last stable state	22	81,5	5	18,5
Easy data entry	24	88,9	3	11,1
Immediate and easy-to-notice feedback	25	92,6	2	7,4
Easy access to functionalities	23	85,2	4	14,8
Help and Documentation	23	85,2	4	14,8
Minimizing User Memory Load	19	70,4	8	29,6

Note: Own elaboration, based on the research script

The biggest impacts documented were in two checks, Visibility and easy access to all existing information and minimizing the user's memory load, where 29.6% of the sample were impacted. Ease of access to functionalities and Help and documentation were affected by 14.8% of the sample. Finally, we highlight the case of Ease of data entry, which was under performed by 11.1% of the sample.

Only the municipality of Vitória-ES has a mobile version of its website, something that is practically obsolete, but which generates an important impact and an experience beyond responsive, as it is fully adapted to the user's reality. Another finding is that only two sites use the transparency portal integrated with their municipal website. Thus, the others try to act with the look of a separate website, or even the strategy of a portal dedicated to public transparency, limiting performance and leaving the impression that it is a checklist for compliance with legislation and reducing the points for fines.

Evaluating the home pages of the town halls with WAVE, a total of 789 errors, 929 low-contrast problems, 1035 alerts, 1083 features and 1836 ARIA were found (Fig. 1). The average per home page was around: 29.22 errors, 34.4 contrast problems, 38.33 alerts, 40.11 features and 68 ARIA. This analysis indicates an inconsistency in accessibility standards between the different municipalities evaluated, with some demonstrating outstanding performance, while others face substantial challenges.

Some sites showed remarkable results. The Aracaju City Hall website had the highest number of errors obtained by WAVE, with a total of 124. The Maceió City Hall website had the highest number of contrast problems, with 153. The Aracaju City Hall website had a total of 106 alerts. And Belém City Hall obtained 329 ARIA elements. These discrepancies highlight the importance of a more comprehensive and uniform approach to digital accessibility.

It is noticeable that there are websites with very positive results, such as Belém, which had only 4 errors, 17 contrast problems, 19 features and 329 ARIA elements. Another great example is Cuiabá, which had no errors, only 4 contrast problems, 92 features and 52 ARIA elements. It is encouraging to note that some city halls, such as Belém and Cuiabá, have achieved remarkable results in terms of accessibility, with significantly fewer errors and contrast problems. These positive examples demonstrate that it is possible to achieve high standards of accessibility, even in the challenging context of government websites.

The three most abundant errors among the 27 sites evaluated were "Linked image without alternative text" with 287 errors, "Empty link" with 232 errors and "Missing alternative text" with 110 total errors. In terms of occurrence, i.e., errors that were most present among all the sites, were: "empty link" (20 sites), "Linked image without alternative text" (18 sites) and "Missing form label" (15 sites).

Looking at the most common errors, such as those mentioned, it is clear that special attention needs to be paid to these aspects during the development and maintenance of websites. Similarly, the frequency of features such as images linked with alternative text points to a recurring concern with the inclusion of image descriptions, although there is room for improvement in the quality of these descriptions.

The features with the highest number were "Image linked with alternative text" with 383 elements, "Null or empty alternative text" with 302 and 122 figures. In terms of occurrence, i.e., the features that were most present among all the sites, were: "Image

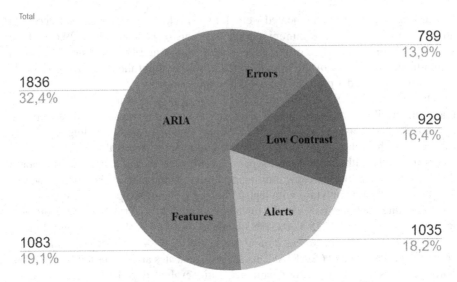

Fig. 1. Figure with the WAVE outputs from the research script.

linked with alternative text" (23 sites), "Alternative text" (22 sites) and "Language" (22 sites).

It is interesting to note that the biggest problems encountered coincide with the most frequent accessibility features. This pattern suggests a widespread awareness of the importance of these accessibility practices, but at the same time indicates a gap in the effective implementation of these features. This highlights the need not only to recognize the importance of accessibility, but also to ensure consistent, high-quality implementation to promote an inclusive and equitable experience for all users.

The evaluation of the accessibility of city hall homepages, conducted using the WAVE tool, revealed a comprehensive overview of the challenges faced by government websites in terms of digital accessibility. The results highlight the pressing need for significant improvements to ensure that these sites are accessible to all citizens, including those with disabilities.

Ultimately, digital accessibility is not just a question of compliance with regulations and guidelines, but also a question of inclusion and equity. Significant improvements in the accessibility of municipal websites are essential to ensure that all citizens have equitable access to government information and services online, thus promoting a more inclusive and participatory society.

Table 4 assesses whether the government website and the transparency website are accessible and provide a democratic space for the population to access information, with 85.2% agreeing and strongly agreeing.

After access via browse, we tried to assess access via mobile devices. The results are shown in Table 5, demonstrating whether the government website is accessible and promotes a democratic space for the population to access municipal data.

Table 4. Evaluation of whether the website and transparency services are accessible and provide a democratic space for the population to access information.

	Frequency	Percentage	Cumulative percentage
Indifferent (5)	1	3,7	3,7
Disagree more than Agree (6)	2	7,4	11,1
Agree more than Disagree(7)	1	3,7	14,8
Agree (8)	7	25,9	40,7
Strongly agree (9)	16	59,3	100,0
Total	27	100,00	

Note: Own elaboration, based on the research script

Table 5. After mobile access, the government website is accessible and provides a democratic space for the population to access municipal data.

	Frequency	Percentage	Cumulative percentage
Indifferent (5)	1	3,7	3,7
Disagree more than Agree (6)	0	0	3,7
Agree more than Disagree(7)	5	18,5	22,2
Agree (8)	9	33,3	55,6
Strongly agree (9)	12	44,4	100,0
Total	27	100,00	

Note: Own elaboration, based on the research script

5 Conclusion

The results of the study strongly suggested that the majority of websites are responsive, but there are cases where they need to be improved or rebuilt. In this way, the lack of compatibility hinders the popularization of access, especially because it limits the population, especially in access mechanisms, or even when migrating between mobile devices.

The second stage of the comprehensive analysis, focused on the accessibility of city hall homepages, conducted using the WAVE tool, offers a clear view of the challenges faced by government websites in terms of digital inclusion. The results reveal a significant disparity in levels of compliance with accessibility guidelines, highlighting the urgent need for substantial improvements to ensure that these sites are accessible to all citizens, regardless of their abilities. Although some municipalities have shown remarkable performance in terms of accessibility, it is clear that there are critical areas that require immediate attention.

The correlation between the most frequent problems and the most common accessibility features highlights a widespread awareness of the importance of these practices, but also points to a gap in effective implementation. The most common errors, such as linked images without alternative text and empty links, indicate the need for a more rigorous approach during the development and maintenance of websites. This underlines the importance not only of recognizing the need for accessibility, but also of ensuring consistent, high-quality implementation to promote an inclusive and equitable experience for all users.

Ultimately, digital accessibility is not just a matter of regulatory compliance, but also of justice and equality. Substantial improvements in the accessibility of municipal websites are essential to ensure that all citizens have equitable access to government information and services online, thus strengthening the fundamental principles of a democratic and inclusive society. Despite these findings, the final analysis government website and the transparency website are accessible and provide a democratic space for the population to access information, with 85.2% agreeing.

Acknowledgments. This work was funded by the Public Call n. 03 Produtividade em Pesquisa PROPESQ/PRPG/UFPB proposal code PVP13490-2020.

References

1. Complementary Law n.° 101, Of May 4, 2000 Establishes norms of public finances focused on responsibility in fiscal management and other provisions. https://www.planalto.gov.br/cci vil_03/leis/lcp/lcp101.htm. Accessed 21 Nov 2022
2. Complementary Law n.°131, Of May 27th, 2009. Adds provisions to the Complementary Law no. 101, of May 4, 2000, which establishes public finance norms aimed at fiscal management responsibility and other provisions, in order to determine the availability, in real time, of detailed information about the budgetary and financial execution of the Union, the States, the Federal District, and the Municipalities. https://www.planalto.gov.br/ccivil_03/leis/lcp/lcp131.htm. Accessed 21 Nov 2022
3. Law n.° 12.527, Of November 18, 2011. Regulates the access to information provided for in item XXXIII of art. 5, in item II of § 3 of art. 37 and in § 2 of art. 216 of the Federal Constitution; amends Law n.° 8112 of December 11, 1990; revokes Law No. 111 of May 5, 2005, and provisions of Law n.° 8159 of January 8, 1991; and makes other provisions. https://www.planalto.gov.br/ccivil_03/_ato2011-2014/2011/lei/l12527.htm. Accessed 21 Nov 2022
4. da Silva Dias, L.N., de Aquino, A.C.B., da Silva, P.B., dos Albuquerque, F.S.: Outsourcing of fiscal transparency portals by municipalities. J. Account. Organ. **14**, e164383 (2020). https://doi.org/10.11606/issn.1982-6486.rco.2020.164383. Accessed 19 Oct 2022
5. PEFA, Public Expenditure and Financial Accountability (n.d.). Recuperado em 20 de maio 2023, de https://www.pefa.org
6. IBP, International Budget Partnership (n.d.). Recuperado em 20 maio, 2020, em https://www.internationalbudget.org
7. Public Expenditure and Financial Accountability (PEFA). 2011 Public Finance Management - Performance Assessment Framework. https://www.pefa.org/sites/pefa/files/resources/downloads/PMF%20Portuguese_HGRFinal.pdf. Accessed 21 Nov 2022
8. Public Expenditure and Financial Accountability (PEFA). 2019 Global Report on Public Financial Management. https://www.pefa.org/sites/pefa/files/resources/downloads/2020002207PORpor002_Main%20text.pdf. Accessed 21 Nov 2022

9. International Budget Partnership (IBP). Open Budget Survey 2021. https://internationalbu dget.org/open-budget-survey/country-results/2021/brazil. Accessed 21 Nov 2022
10. Barbosa, S.D.J., Silva, B.D., Silveira, M.S., Gasparini, I., Darin, T., Barbosa, G.D.J.: Interação humano-computador e experiência do usuário. Auto publicação (2021)
11. Comptroller General of the Union (CGU). EBT Independent Assessments - 360° Assessment - 2nd Edition (2021). https://mbt.cgu.gov.br/publico/avaliacao/escala_brasil_transparente/66. Accessed 21 Dec 2023
12. Transparency International Brazil [TIBR]. Transparency and Public Governance Index (2023). https://indice.transparenciainternacional.org.br/. Accessed 21 Nov 2023
13. Jácome Filho, E.D.A., Macêdo, J.M.A.: Analysis of responsiveness and usability in websites serving public transparency in a mobile environment: case study in the state of Paraíba through heuristic evaluation. In: Kurosu, M. (eds.) HCII 2022, Part III. LNCS, vol. 13304, pp. 106–127. Springer, Cham (2022). https://doi.org/10.1007/978-3-031-05412-9_8
14. Macêdo, J.M.A., Becker, V., de Sá, F.M.F.: Heuristic-based evaluation of transparency web-sites of the municipal governments viewed on web and mobile browsers. In: Kurosu, M., Hashizume, A. (eds.) HCII 2023. LNCS, vol. 14012, pp. 434–454. Springer, Cham (2023). https://doi.org/10.1007/978-3-031-35599-8_29
15. Centro Regional de Estudos para o Desenvolvimento da Sociedade da Informação (Cetic.br). Classes C, D e E impulsionam crescimento da conectividade à Internet nos lares brasileiros, mostra TIC Domicílios 2023 (2023). https://cetic.br/pt/noticia/classes-c-e-de-impulsionam-crescimento-da-conectividade-a-internet-nos-lares-brasileiros-mostra-tic-domicilios-2023/. Accessed 20 Dec 2023
16. Institute for Disability Research, Policy & Practice. Web Accessibility Evaluation tool [Internet]. Logan, UT; 2024 [cited 2024 Jan 30] (2024). https://wave.webaim.org/
17. Brazil. Constitution of the Federative Republic of Brazil of 1988 (1988). http://www.planalto. gov.br/ccivil_03/Constituicao/Constituicao.htm. Accessed 29 Dec 2023
18. Federal Budget Secretariat (SOF) (2023). Technical Budget Manual - TBM 2023. https:// www1.siop.planejamento.gov.br/mto/doku.php/mto2023
19. de Sá Bartoluzzio, A.I.S., dos Anjos, L.C.M.: Análise de conglomerados do nível de transparência pública e indicadores socioeconômicos dos municípios pernambucanos. RACEF Revista de Administração Contabilidade e Economia da Fundace 11(2), 48–65 (2020). https://doi.org/10.13059/racef.v11i2.570
20. Cunha Filho, M.C.: Construção da transparência pública no Brasil: análise da elaboração e implementação da Lei de Acesso à Informação no Executivo Federal (2003–2019) (2019). https://repositorio.cgu.gov.br/handle/1/34839. Accessed 29 Dec 2023
21. Machado, L.D.S., Nalini, L.E.G., Machado, M.R.R.: Access to information law (AIL) and the behavior of audit agents of a court of auditors. Soc. Account. Manag. 17(1), 43–66
22. Baldissera, J.F., Walter, S.A., Fiirst, C., Asta, D.D.: The perception of social observatories on the quality, utility and sufficiency of public transparency of Brazilian municipalities. Soc. Account. Manag. 14(1), 113–134 (2019)
23. Nielsen, J.: Usability inspection methods. In: Conference Companion on Human Factors in Computing Systems, pp. 413–414 (1994)
24. Nielsen, J.: Severity ratings for usability problems. Papers Essays 54, 1–2 (1995)
25. Preece, J., Sharp, H., Rogers, Y.: Interaction Design: Beyond Human-Computer Interaction. Wiley, Hoboken (2015)
26. Machado Neto, O., Pimentel, M.D.G.: Heuristics for the assessment of interfaces of mobile devices. In: Proceedings of the 19th Brazilian Symposium on Multimedia and the Web, pp. 93–96 (2013). https://doi.org/10.1145/2526188.2526237

27. Ahmi, A., Mohamad, R.: Evaluating accessibility of Malaysian public universities websites using AChecker and WAVE. J. Inf. Commun. Technol. (2016). https://ssrn.com/abstract=355 0314

28. W3C. Web Content Accessibility Guidelines (WCAG) 2.2 [Internet]. [place unknown] (2023). https://www.w3.org/TR/WCAG22/#wcag-2-layers-of-guidance. Accessed 30 Jan 2024

DUXAIT-NG in Practice: Evaluating Usability on the Municipality of Lima Website

Arturo Moquillaza(✉) , Fiorella Falconi , Joel Aguirre , Adrian Lecaros ,
Carlos Ramos , and Freddy Paz

Pontificia Universidad Católica del Perú, Av. Universitaria 1801, San Miguel,
Lima 32, Lima, Perú
{amoquillaza,carlos.ramosp,fpaz}@pucp.pe, {ffalconit,
aguirre.joel,adrian.lecaros}@pucp.edu.pe

Abstract. Within the framework of a workshop held to present the DUXAIT-NG
platform, a heuristic evaluation with the approach proposed by Granollers was
carried out as a case study, with the participation of 20 participants with different
profiles and experience in usability and user experience. In this case study, the
Municipality's website was evaluated, specifically the Transportation section of
Metropolitan Lima. This experience allowed the participants to get in touch with
the DUXAIT-NG tool to carry out the entire evaluation, from planning to execution and reporting but also allowed to deepen the usability levels of the website in
question. Thanks to the qualitative and quantitative nature of Granollers' proposal,
the results showed a 48.39% usability percentage, which implies a medium-low
level of usability. The heuristics with the lowest levels were HG10 (Help and documentation), HG11 (Save the state and protect the work), and HG14 (Defaults).
The heuristics with the highest levels were HG02 (Connection between the system and the real world, metaphor usage, and human objects), HG05 (Recognition
rather than memory, learning, and anticipation), and HG04 (Consistency and standards). Likewise, the participants could leave their most relevant observations and
comments during the evaluation, which allowed for a qualitative deepening of
the results. In this sense, it was concluded that the Transport section's website
of the Municipality of Lima has many points for improvement, especially in the
heuristics mentioned above. This information is essential as a starting point for
redesign or continuous improvement processes and for improving the User Experience in general websites of other municipalities and the public sector. Finally,
the participants' positive reception of the DUXAIT-NG tool is worth mentioning.

Keywords: Human-Computer Interaction · Heuristic Evaluation · User
Experience · Usability · Electronic Government · Case Study

1 Introduction

There is a growing interest in usability and User Experience (UX) in all industries
and sectors, both private and governmental. In particular, in the Peruvian public sector,
there has been an increasing interest in measuring and improving the usability of web

A. Marcus et al. (Eds.): HCII 2024, LNCS 14712, pp. 285–299, 2024.
https://doi.org/10.1007/978-3-031-61351-7_20

systems, applications, and services delivered to citizens, especially efforts by academia [1, 2]. However, cases and experiences in the public sector are increasingly common [3, 4], as well as job applications in UX and HCI issues in the public sector, in addition to the increment of areas of Design and UX, and also calls for Design consultancies or UX Evaluation of digital products in the Peruvian state. This is related to the efforts that are evident (although not enough) from the Peruvian state itself to work on issues of digital transformation and improvement of the user experience [5, 6]. In concrete, in Peru, this interest has been manifested in the municipalities and the services and portals these institutions provide to the citizens of these territorial districts [7].

According to the above, there is an increasing interest in implementing and using applications, methodologies, and models to measure usability levels, among other facets of User Experience, in e-government websites in Peru [1, 2].

In this sense, as a contribution to this interest, a web tool has been implemented and released that allows evaluators, practitioners, and experts in HCI and UX to perform their usability evaluations using, among other techniques, heuristic evaluation. This tool is called DUXAIT-NG [8, 9].

Thus, in the framework of a hybrid workshop given to a group of students, professionals, and specialists in IT, UX, and HCI to present this tool, the heuristic evaluation of the web portal of the Municipality of Lima was proposed as an application case, using the Granollers approach. This paper reports on the realization of this evaluation, its planning, execution, and results.

The rest of the paper is organized as follows: Sect. 2 details the main concepts discussed in this paper and the local background on usability evaluations of Peruvian municipalities' websites and portals.

Section 3 details the case study, its planning and execution. Section 4 details the results of the evaluation, and finally, Sect. 5 details the conclusions of the evaluation as well as future research lines.

2 Background

This section details the main concepts and tools used, as well as the Peruvian background on the growing interest in usability evaluation of e-government websites, especially those of municipalities.

2.1 Usability and User Experience

While it is true that there are several definitions of Usability and User Experience, we will consider the definition of ISO 9241-11:2018, which indicates that Usability is the "extent to which a system, product or service can be used by specified users to achieve specified goals with effectiveness, efficiency, and satisfaction in a specified context of use." The same standard defines User Experience as "user's perceptions and responses that result from the use and/or anticipated use of a system, product or service" [10].

2.2   Usability Evaluation Methods

Over time, specialists and researchers have proposed, developed, adapted, and employed various methods focusing on measuring the User Experience and Usability of products and services [11].

According to Holzinger, there are two types of methods, depending on who performs such tests: Inspection methods, which are focused on experts, and testing methods, where end users are active participants in such evaluations [12]. Among the methods of the first group is heuristic evaluation.

2.3   Heuristic Evaluation

Heuristic evaluation was proposed by Nielsen and Molich in 1990 [13]. In general, it is an evaluation technique by inspection that is carried out by expert evaluators, where previously established and validated principles, known as Heuristics, are used [14].

2.4   Granollers Heuristic Evaluation

In 2018, Granollers proposed a heuristic evaluation method based on 15 heuristics resulting from the combination of Nielsen's heuristics and Tognazzini's design principles. These 15 new principles were broken down into 60 questions in order to make it easier for the evaluator to answer each question and find related usability issues. It also gives the heuristic evaluation a quantitative component, very much in line with current metric-based evaluation and comparison trends. The result of this evaluation is called Usability Percentage (UP) and is a scale ranging from 0 to 100 [15, 16].

2.5   DUXAIT-NG Platform

One of the main pain points of conducting usability evaluations (among them, heuristic evaluations) was the manual in planning, execution, and analysis. In addition, it often required the participants' physical presence [17]. These points, among others, led to the implementation of the DUXAIT-NG tool (https://www.duxait-ng.net/), which aims to support the entire process of usability evaluation, with emphasis on automation and virtuality, overcoming manual and physical distances [18]. Likewise, DUXAIT-NG is based on an integrated user experience evaluation process that allows evaluators and researchers of any level of expertise to perform evaluations in a systematized, guided, and tool-supported way [19, 20].

2.6   Background on Usability Evaluations in Municipalities in Peru

As mentioned in previous sections, several initiatives have been found in the literature that show the growing interest in measuring and improving the usability of e-government sites, especially those of municipalities in Peru from the Academia. As an example of this, we have the following works:

Olcay [1], in 2022, proposes to evaluate e-government sites in Peru. Likewise, Delgado [2] 2021 presents the implementation of an information system to measure the level of usability of web systems that provide e-government services, in this particular case, applying fuzzy logic algorithms.

Regarding specific measurement cases, we have the work of Becerra [21] in 2022, who evaluates the quality of the e-government service of the Municipality of Utcubamba in Peru, where he measures usability among different elements through questionnaires. Likewise, we have the work of Zevallos [22], who 2018 evaluated the usability of the Municipality of El Agustino website in Lima, Peru, using the Heuristic Evaluation technique, where he applied this technique manually.

Also reported is the work of Borjas [3], who, in 2022, carried out the evaluation of usability in various municipalities' websites in Peru based on the SQUARE ISO 25000 model.

Two additional cases should also be reported: Infante [23], who in 2022 conducted a usability evaluation of the transparency and participatory budget portal of the Municipality of Carmen de la Legua, also using questionnaires. Finally, the case of Allpas and Naucapoma [24], who in 2019 reported the usability and accessibility characteristics of the virtual platform of Miraflores in Lima for older adults. In that research, mixed techniques such as surveys and questionnaires were used.

In general, these studies evidenced that there are not only several usability problems and much to work on in this regard, but they also evidence both the interest and the need to carry out these evaluations for better citizen service.

2.7 Website of the Municipality of Lima

The website of the Municipality of Lima is a portal focused mainly on presenting information to citizens living in the territorial district of Metropolitan Lima on the various services offered by the municipality. Among the sections of this website is the Transportation section (http://www.gmu.munlima.gob.pe/index.php/es-es/). Figure 1 shows the first screen when accessing the website.

Fig. 1. First screen of the Transportation section of the Municipality of Lima (screenshot).

3 Case Study

The case study proposed to the workshop participants mentioned above was to evaluate the usability of the transportation section of the website of the Municipality of Lima, using the Heuristic Evaluation technique proposed by Granollers. The intention is to take this evaluation and its findings as a starting point for redesigning the abovementioned section.

As mentioned above, this case study was carried out simultaneously with a workshop open to professionals and academics to socialize and present the DUXAIT-NG tool. In the end, 20 evaluators participated in the study in a single group.

Now, why 20 evaluators? Although it is true that the use of 5 to 7 evaluators is well established in the practice of applying heuristic evaluations, especially in the study by Nielsen et al. [25], this value has been widely debated and depends on a number of factors. In that sense, at present, it is expected that there will be more evaluators [26, 27]. Finally, it is worth mentioning that Granollers proposal not only identifies usability problems but also intends to establish a quantitative value, called Usability Percentage, so the number of evaluators should also be higher.

The presentation of the problem was given as follows: *"The company where you work has assigned a new client to your UX team. The new client is THE MUNICIPALITY OF LIMA.The request: To redesign the transportation section of their website. They have received user comments indicating difficulty finding information and navigating.*

Your team has assigned you to perform a heuristic evaluation as a starting point for the redesign to show the client quantitative data; you have chosen the Granollers proposal.Objective: Identify web improvement opportunities based on heuristics.

Tool: DUXAIT- NG".

Based on the above information, the evaluation process was started, as the tool mentioned above supported. For this, the three main sub-processes were considered: Planning, Executing, and Reporting.

3.1 Planning

To carry out this first sub-process, in the case framework, the project was registered in the DUXAIT-NG platform with the participants, where information about the project was provided before registering the heuristic evaluation, as shown in Table 1.

Subsequently, the heuristic evaluation with the Granollers approach was registered, the evaluation was assigned to the evaluators, and the evaluation was sent to the evaluators by means of a personalized e-mail with a direct link to the evaluation.

It should be noted that this sub-process has the leading actor, the evaluation leader, as the evaluation planner; it starts with the registration of a new project and ends when the evaluation is sent to the previously assigned evaluators. Figure 2 shows the moment the case is presented to the evaluators and the planning is carried out together.

3.2 Executing

This second sub-process is the evaluation itself. Its main actors are the evaluators themselves. The leader planner also participates and can track the progress of the evaluations

Table 1. Data from the Municipality of Lima evaluation project, under the Transport section.

Step 1	General Information
Evaluation Name	Website evaluation - Municipality of Lima - Transportation
Objective	Identify problems and opportunities for improvement on the web-based on the heuristics of the Granollers method
Scope	Only points within the "Transportation" section will be evaluated
Software Product Name	Municipality of Lima - Transportation
URL Product	http://www.gmu.munlima.gob.pe/index.php/es-es/
Description of the Product	The Transportation Department of the Municipality of Lima is in charge of promoting and disseminating the use of bicycles as an alternative means of transportation through various sustainable programs
Step 2	Other Project Data
Problem Management	Internal
Limitations and Risks	- Limited time for evaluation - Limited access to actual website users - Budget constraints to implement significant changes
Estimated Cost	Time spent by the evaluation team
Estimated Time	2 h
Justification	Conducting the heuristic evaluation is essential to improve the user experience on the Municipality of Lima's transportation website. The heuristic evaluation, by identifying opportunities for improvement, will allow the Municipality of Lima to take steps to optimize the quality and effectiveness of the website. This, in turn, will improve the experience of users seeking transportation-related information in the city

by each evaluator, as well as provide an overview of the entire evaluation. This sub-process started when each evaluator accessed the link sent to their email, logged into the DUXAIT-NG platform, read the evaluation details, and started filling in the questions for each heuristic while browsing the website under evaluation. Figure 3 and Fig. 4 show the evaluators, as well as the support provided during the evaluation.

This sub-process ended when each evaluator completed their evaluation and submitted it through the tool. An advantage of the platform is that both quantitative data (each question in its respective scale) and qualitative data (evaluators' comments that could optionally be added for each question answered) could be captured.

It should also be noted that each evaluator completed a confidentiality agreement, according to the ethical guidelines for working with people, as well as a pretest as a screening.

Fig. 2. Presenting the case and planning the Evaluation.

Fig. 3. Support to Evaluations during the evaluation.

Fig. 4. Evaluators during the Evaluation experience.

3.3 Reporting

This sub-process is initiated when all evaluators have completed their evaluations. As shown in Fig. 5, the evaluation leader can access the results view once the evaluators finish their evaluations. In this view, the quantitative result of all the scores given by the evaluators can be observed in a cumulative way, as well as filtering them. Likewise, the results can be downloaded in PDF, where not only the same information is obtained but also the details of the answers and observations provided by the evaluators.

Figure 6 shows the presentation of the results and the analysis of the most relevant findings.

It can be observed, in general terms, that the results showed a 48.39% usability percentage (UP), which indicates that the website has a medium-low level of usability. The heuristics with the lowest levels were HG10 (Help and documentation), HG11 (Save the state and protect the work), and HG14 (Defaults). Likewise, the heuristics with the highest levels were HG02 (Connection between the system and the real world, metaphor usage, and human objects), HG05 (Recognition rather than memory, learning, and anticipation), and HG04 (Consistency and standards). We will discuss these results in the next section.

Fig. 5. Results section in the DUXAIT-NG platform.

4 Results

This section details the results on the characteristics of the participating evaluators and the findings after the heuristic evaluation.

4.1 About the Evaluators

As mentioned above, the evaluators completed a pretest as a screening. In this way, it is possible to obtain profiles of the evaluators who participated in the evaluation. Figure 7 shows that the vast majority of the evaluators work. Likewise, in Fig. 8, it can be seen that most evaluators have a complete or incomplete university level. Also, Fig. 9 shows that

Fig. 6. Presenting the reporting and analyzing results.

the age range of most evaluators was between 21 and 30 years old, and finally, Fig. 10 shows that their experience in HCI/UX issues is diverse.

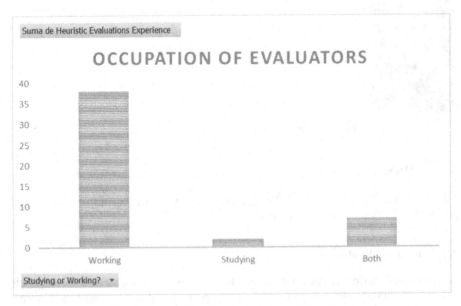

Fig. 7. Occupation of evaluators (own elaboration).

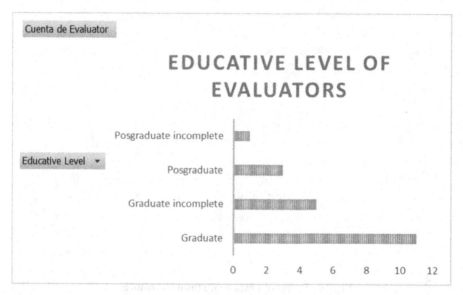

Fig. 8. Educative level of evaluators (own elaboration).

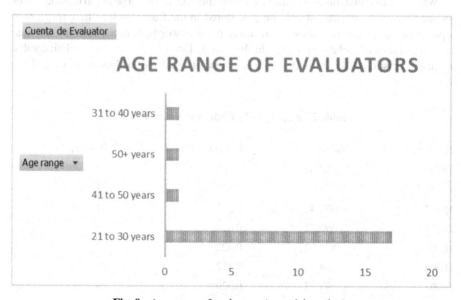

Fig. 9. Age range of evaluators (own elaboration).

4.2   About the Findings

As already mentioned, the overall UP delivered was 48.39%, which indicates a medium-low level of usability.

Fig. 10. Evaluator's experience (own elaboration).

While it is true that this closes the Granollers method, it should be noted that the scores obtained for each heuristic should be considered in the framework of how much they apply or not in the context of the application. In other words, not only take the absolute number but also the relative number. In this sense, Table 2 calculates the relative value of each heuristic, which provides a closer view of what the evaluators evaluated the website.

Table 2. Ranking of heuristics by relative values

Heuristic	Values	Relative Values	Ranking
HG01	2,80/4,64	0,603	4
HG02	2,45/3,73	0,657	1
HG03	1,28/2,41	0,531	7
HG04	3,59/5,77	0,622	3
HG05	3,00/4,82	0,622	2
HG06	2,18/4,18	0,522	8
HG07	1,44/2,77	0,520	9
HG08	0,92/1,86	0,495	11
HG09	2,11/3,95	0,534	6
HG10	0,22/2,32	0,095	14

In that sense, in the ranking of heuristics, the three with the highest values were HG02 (Connection between the system and the real world, metaphor usage, and human objects), HG05 (Recognition rather than memory, learning, and anticipation), and HG04 (Consistency and standards). Likewise, the three with the lowest values were HG10 (Help and documentation), HG11 (Save the state and protect the work), and HG14 (Defaults).

In addition, by delving into the comments and observations provided by the evaluators, which are available in the downloadable PDF, valuable insights can be obtained for the usability problems encountered, which can serve as a starting point for redesign processes in search of solutions.

It should be noted that these findings are in line with the background, where, in general, several usability problems are evident in this type of website.

5 Conclusions and Future Works

Regarding the evaluators, they had different profiles and levels of experience in heuristic evaluations, with a predominance of low experience. This was their first experience with this type of technique for many of them. However, this was not an obstacle to them satisfactorily completing their evaluations.

Regarding the results, the heuristics with the lowest levels were HG10, HG11, and HG14. Likewise, the heuristics resulting in the highest levels were HG02, HG05, and HG04. The in-depth comments and observations of the participants provided valuable information on the findings that the evaluators found in the platform. As has been evidenced in the past [28], the analysis of qualitative information greatly enriches any quantitative evaluation.

Regarding the support tool, it could be evidenced that it allowed an adequate application of the evaluation method, mainly because, as it was evidenced, the whole process could be carried out in two hours.

In future work, new case studies will continue to be applied using the platform, and the incorporation of new User Experience evaluation methods and techniques is in the platform's roadmap. Likewise, the heuristics ranking view by relative value has been included in the platform's backlog, as presented in Table 2.

Acknowledgments. This work is part of the research project "Virtualización del proceso de evaluación de experiencia de usuario de productos de software para escenarios de no presencialidad" (virtualization of the user experience evaluation process of software products for non-presential scenarios), developed by HCI-DUXAIT research group. HCI-DUXAIT is a research group that belongs to the PUCP (Pontificia Universidad Católica del Perú). This work was funded by the Dirección de Fomento a la Investigación at the PUCP through grant 2021-C-0023.

References

1. Espinoza Olcay, W.A.: Gobierno electrónico en el Perú: evaluación de los servicios. Escritura Y Pensamiento **21**(43), 175–190 (2022). https://doi.org/10.15381/escrypensam.v21i43.22792
2. Delgado, M.: Implementación de un sistema de información para medir el nivel de usabilidad de sistemas web que brindan servicios de gobierno electrónico usando lógica difusa (Tesis de grado). Facultad de Ingeniería. Pontificia Universidad Católica del Perú (2021). http://hdl.handle.net/20.500.12404/20874

3. Linares, F.: Optimización de la experiencia del ciudadano: UX en el sector público. Boletín Punto de Equilibro nro. 21. Universidad del Pacífico (2021). https://ciup.up.edu.pe/analisis/optimizacion-de-la-experiencia-del-ciudadano-ux-en-el-sector-publico/

4. Del Río, M., Linares, F.: UX Latam: historias sobre definición y diseño de servicios digitales. Fondo Editorial Universidad del Pacífico (2022). https://repositorio.up.edu.pe/handle/11354/3413

5. Gobierno del Perú: Desarrollo de competencias digitales avanzadas. Gob.Pe (n.d.). https://www.gob.pe/13806-desarrollo-de-competencias-digitales-avanzadas

6. Robles, C.: Día 2 - UX UI en el diseño de servicios digitales en el Estado. Secretaría de Gobierno Digital (Presidencia del Consejo de Ministros) (n.d.). https://cdn.www.gob.pe/uploads/document/file/1868766/Di%CC%81a%202%20-%20UX%20UI%20en%20el%20disen%CC%83o%20de%20servicios%20digitales%20en%20el%20Estado%20-%20C amila%20Robles.pdf

7. Borjas, L.: Evaluación de la usabilidad en los sitios web municipales del Perú teniendo como referencia el modelo SQUARE ISO/IEC 25000 (Tesis de grado). Universidad Nacional Agraria de la Selva (2022).https://hdl.handle.net/20.500.14292/2496

8. HCI-DUXAIT: DUXAIT-NG. DUXAIT Research Group. Pontificia Universidad Católica del Perú (2022). https://duxait-ng.net/

9. Aguirre, J., Lecaros, A., Ramos, C., Falconi, F., Moquillaza, A., Paz, F.: DUXAIT NG: a software for the planning and execution of user experience evaluations and experiments. In: Ruiz, P.H., Agredo-Delgado, V., Mon, A. (eds.) Human-Computer Interaction. HCI-COLLAB 2023. CCIS, vol. 1877, pp. 143–155. Springer, Cham (2024). https://doi.org/10.1007/978-3-031-57982-0_12

10. ISO: ISO 9241-11:2018. Ergonomics of human-system interaction—Part 11: Usability: Definitions and concepts. International Standards Organization (2018). https://www.iso.org/obp/ui/#iso:std:iso:9241:-11:ed-2:v1:en

11. Paz, F., Pow-Sang, J.A.: Usability evaluation methods for software development: a systematic mapping review. In: 2015 8th International Conference on Advanced Software Engineering and Its Applications (ASEA), Jeju, Korea (South), pp. 1–4 (2015). https://doi.org/10.1109/ASEA.2015.8

12. Andreas, H.: Usability engineering methods for software developers. Commun. ACM **48**, 1, 71–74 (2005). https://doi.org/10.1145/1039539.1039541

13. Nielsen, J., Molich, R.: Heuristic evaluation of user interfaces. In: Proceedings of the SIGCHI Conference on Human Factors in Computing Systems (CHI '90) , pp. 249–256. Association for Computing Machinery, New York, NY, USA (1990). https://doi.org/10.1145/97243.97281

14. Nielsen, J.: Finding usability problems through heuristic evaluation. In: Proceedings of the SIGCHI Conference on Human Factors in Computing Systems (CHI '92) , pp. 373–380. Association for Computing Machinery, New York, NY, USA (1992). https://doi.org/10.1145/142750.142834

15. Granollers, T.: Usability evaluation with heuristics, beyond nielsen's list. In: ACHI 2018: The Eleventh International Conference on Advances in Computer-Human Interactions. ARIA, 2018 (2018). https://www.thinkmind.org/articles/achi_2018_4_10_20055.pdf. ISBN 978-1-61208-616-3

16. Granollers, T.: Usability evaluation with heuristics. new proposal from integrating two trusted sources. In: Marcus, A., Wang, W. (eds.) DUXU 2018. LNCS, vol. 10918, pp. 396–405. Springer, Cham (2018). https://doi.org/10.1007/978-3-319-91797-9_28

17. Moquillaza, A., Falconi, F., Aguirre, J., Lecaros, A., Tapia, A., Paz, F.: Using remote workshops to promote collaborative work in the context of a UX process improvement. In: Marcus, A., Rosenzweig, E., Soares, M.M. (eds.) HCII 2023. LNCS, vol. 14030, pp. 254–266. Springer, Cham (2023). https://doi.org/10.1007/978-3-031-35699-5_19

18. Lecaros, A., Moquillaza, A. Falconi, F. Aguirre, J., Ramos, C., Paz, F.: Automation of granollers heuristic evaluation method using a developed support system: a case study. In: Ruiz,
P.H., Agredo-Delgado, V., Mon, A. (eds.) Human-Computer Interaction. HCI-COLLAB 2023.
CCIS, vol. 1877, pp. 93–108. Springer, Cham (2024). https://doi.org/10.1007/978-3-031-579
82-0_8

19. Lecaros, A., Moquillaza, A., Falconi, F., Aguirre, J., Tapia, A., Paz, F.: Selection and modeling
of a formal heuristic evaluation process through comparative analysis. In: Soares, M.M.,
Rosenzweig, E., Marcus, A. (eds.) HCII 2022. LNCS, vol. 13321, pp. 28–46. Springer, Cham
(2022). https://doi.org/10.1007/978-3-031-05897-4_3

20. Paz, F., Lecaros, A., Falconi, F., Tapia, A., Aguirre, J., Moquillaza, A.: A process to support
heuristic evaluation and tree testing from a UX integrated perspective. In: Latifi, S. (ed.) ITNG
2023. AISC, vol. 1445, pp. 367–377. Springer, Cham. (2023). https://doi.org/10.1007/978-3-
031-28332-1_42

21. Becerra, M.R.: Calidad del servicio de gobierno electrónico de la Municipalidad Provincial
de Utcubamba, región Amazonas 2021 (Tesis de licenciatura). Universidad Católica Santo
Toribio de Mogrovejo (2022). http://hdl.handle.net/20.500.12423/5549

22. Zevallos, K.: La usabilidad del sitio web de la Municipalidad de El Agustino: un aporte en la
mejora del proceso comunicacional, 2018 (Tesis de licenciatura). Universidad César Vallejo
(2018). https://hdl.handle.net/20.500.12692/48005

23. Infante, E.: Usabilidad del portal de transparencia y seguimiento del presupuesto participativo,
Municipalidad de Carmen de la Legua Reynoso, 2017–2020 (tesis de maestría). Universidad
César Vallejo (2022). https://hdl.handle.net/20.500.12692/82012

24. Allpas, C., Naucapoma, M.: Características de usabilidad y accesibilidad de la plataforma
virtual Miraflores es Único en adultos mayores 2019. Universidad Tecnológica del Perú
(2019). https://hdl.handle.net/20.500.12867/3330

25. Nielsen, J., Landauer, T.K.: A mathematical model of the finding of usability problems. In:
Proceedings of ACM INTERCHI'93 Conference, Amsterdam, The Netherlands, 24–29 April
1993, pp. 206–213 (1993). https://dl.acm.org/doi/10.1145/169059.169166

26. Zapata, C., Pow-Sang, J.A.: Sample size in a heuristic evaluation of usability. In: Software
Engineering: Methods, Modeling, and Teaching, Pontificia Universidad Católica del Perú,
vol. 37 (2012)

27. Alroobaea, R., Mayhew, P.J.: How many participants are really enough for usability studies?
In: 2014 Science and Information Conference, London, UK, pp. 48–56 (2014). https://doi.
org/10.1109/SAI.2014.6918171

28. Moquillaza, A., Falconi, F., Aguirre, J., Paz, F.: Using verbatims as a basis for building a
customer journey map: a case study. In: Stephanidis, C., Antona, M., Ntoa, S. (eds.) HCII
2021. CCIS, vol. 1498, pp. 44–50. Springer, Cham (2021). https://doi.org/10.1007/978-3-
030-90176-9_7

Proposal for Packaging Evaluation Methodology Based on Eye-Tracking and Affective Evaluation

Shuma Ohtsuka(✉), Naoya Kumagai, and Midori Sugaya

Shibaura Institute of Technology, 3-7-5 Toyosu, Kotoku 135-8548, Tokyo, Japan
{ma22029,ma23074,doly}@shibaura-it.ac.jp

Abstract. Package design plays an important role as a means of communicating product information and value. In terms of package design, knowledge is needed on how to visually convey the value of the contents to better show the value of the product. However, in previous studies, there has not been much research on which elements of the package are looked at and what impressions are made about each one. Therefore, the purpose of this research is to clarify exactly the elements of the package that affect kansei by investigating both gaze measurement and kansei evaluation. To achieve the purpose, we will evaluate the gaze time with kansei words and discuss the results.

Keywords: kansei · food · packaging

1 Introduction

1.1 Background

Consumers understand the value of a product and select a product through the impression they get when looking at a package design that integrates various elements. Therefore, package design plays an important role as a means of communicating product information and value. Food packaging is attracting attention as a means of conveying the impression of the contents to consumers. Meanwhile, in recent years, kansei value has been attracting attention when creating package designs. Kansei value is that realized by appealing to consumers' sensibilities and gaining emotion and empathy. By adding this kansei value, various effects such as increasing consumer awareness can be obtained [1]. For this reason, adding kansei value is important in package design. In contrast, in a previous study, Hagtvedt et al. pointed out that in addition to color and shape as package design elements, kansei design elements strengthen consumers' kansei connection to the product [2]. In addition, Yamamoto et al. conducted a study that focused on illustrations drawn on sweets' packages among other sensuous design elements [3]. Preference was evaluated. The results showed that "friendliness" and "apparent taste" differ depending on the illustration design [3]. However, these previous studies have not investigated exactly which package design elements respond to the sensibilities, So it was difficult to determine how it was induced. On the other hand, Asakawa et al. evaluated each element of food packaging using line-of-sight measurement. As a result, it was found that the award mark attracted the most attention among the chocolate package design elements [4].

© The Author(s), under exclusive license to Springer Nature Switzerland AG 2024
A. Marcus et al. (Eds.): HCII 2024, LNCS 14712, pp. 300–309, 2024.
https://doi.org/10.1007/978-3-031-61351-7_21

1.2 Challenges

However, although kansei value is important in package design, the evaluation of kansei value of each element of package design is not sufficient. The evaluation methods of Hagtvedt et al. [1] and Asakawa et al. [3] do not clarify which elements of a food package induce which kind of kansei. Therefore, it is difficult to develop a package design that objectively improves kansei value according to specific elements.

1.3 Objective and Proposal

Therefore, the purpose of this research is to clarify the exact elements of the package that affect sensibility by investigating both gaze measurement and sensibility evaluation (Fig. 1). We believe that this allows us to identify package design elements that are effective in increasing kansei value. To achieve the purpose, we evaluate the gaze time of the AOI (Area of Interest) and the related kansei words.

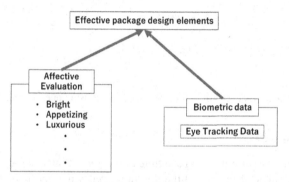

Fig. 1. Proposed Methodology

2 Experiment

2.1 Experimental Procedure

To begin, we will describe the experimental procedure. First, participants were asked to freely look at the package image for 3 s. Finally, participants were asked how they felt about the package image they saw earlier by responding to the six kansei words "bright", "warm", "unique"', "delicious", "luxury", and "familiar"; an example of which is shown in Fig. 3. Each of these emotions was evaluated on a five-point scale. This "process was repeated for 21 images. The reason for choosing these six kansei words is that, according to previous research, these six kansei words are important when looking at food packaging. The image used was the product package image of SB Foods Co., Ltd. [5] (Fig. 2). In addition, in the experiment, we selected images with high preference among images with some elements such as color and shape changed based on the results of a preliminary survey.

image 1   image 2   image 3   image 4   image 5   image 6   image 7

image 8   image 9   image 10   image 11   image 12   image 13   image 14

image 15   image 16   image 17   image 18   image 19   image 20   image 21

Fig. 2. Images used in the experiment.

Did you find the package to look "appetizing"? *

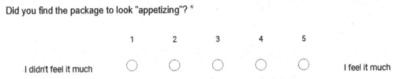

Fig. 3. Example of kansei word evaluation using questionnaire

2.2 Evaluation Index

As an evaluation index, we use the gaze time of the area of interest (AOI). This method calculates the number of times and the duration over which the line of sight enters a specific area and can tell you how much attention is paid to the area of interest. The reason for using AOI is that it has been used in previous research to evaluate what elements are being focused on in package images, so it was used in this evaluation. Six AOIs were set this time: "raw materials", "logo", "bottom pattern", "product photo", "product name", and "background" (Fig. 4). In addition, for the two images in Fig. 4, two AOIs were set: "NEW" and "Years" instead of "Logo".

Next, regarding kansei words, we set an index called kansei word score based on the results of the questionnaire. Regarding scoring, "I didn't feel it very much" was given 1 point, "I felt it very much" was given 5 points, and the numbers on a 5-point scale were used as scores from 1 to 5.

2.3 Analysis Method

In conducting the analysis, we established the following two hypotheses based on the results of previous research [4]:

1. Is there a significant difference in the gaze time for each AOI.
2. Differences in elements may cause significant differences in the gaze time of each AOI.

Fig. 4. AOI settings and "NEW "and "anniversary" settings

To prove these two hypotheses, we performed the following analysis:

1. Perform a one-way analysis of variance to clarify whether there is a main effect on the gaze duration of each AOI.
2. Perform a one-way analysis of variance to clarify whether there is a main effect on the gaze time of each AOI due to differences in factors.

2.4 Result

We conducted a one-way analysis of variance to clarify whether there was a main effect on the gaze time for each AOI. Figure 5 shows the results of the one-way analysis of variance.

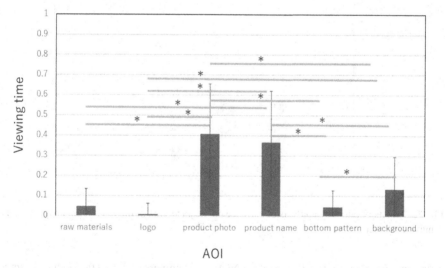

Fig. 5. Results of one-way analysis of variance for AOI fixation time

There was a significant difference in the gaze time for each AOI shown in Fig. 4. In addition, "Product photos" received the most attention, and a significant difference was seen in all gaze durations. In addition, the results showed that "raw materials", "logo", and "pattern underneath" received almost no attention. Next, Figs. 6 and 7 show the results of a one-way variance analysis of images with "NEW "and "anniversary" set.

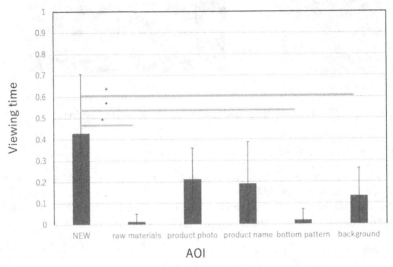

Fig. 6. Results of one-way analysis of variance for fixation time of AOI of images set to "NEW"

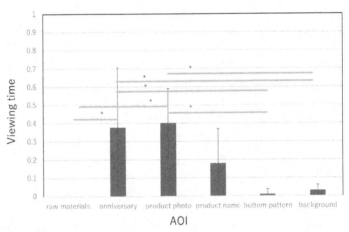

Fig. 7. Results of one-way analysis of variance on the gaze time of the AOI of the image with the "anniversary" set

From Figs. 6 and 7, the gaze time for NEW and anniversary was a factor that attracted attention for a longer time compared to product names. From the above results, it can be concluded that "product photo" and "product name" receive the most attention and adding new elements such as "NEW" and "years" increases the gaze time on those parts. It is also thought that the length of gaze time is proportional to the area occupied in the image. Afterwards, we performed a one-way analysis of variance to see if there was a significant difference for each kansei word score (Fig. 8).

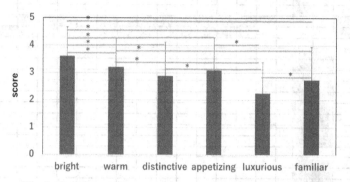

Fig. 8. One-way variance analysis results for kansei word scores

Figure 8 show that "bright" is the most easily felt sensibility depending on the element, and there is a significant difference from all other sensibility words. From these results, we believe that product photos are a package design element that influences the sensibility of "brightness".

Next, we conducted a one-way analysis of variance to find out whether there was an effect on gaze time due to differences in factors. Regarding the results, Table 1 shows the results for "lower pattern" where a significant difference was found. The numbers on the vertical and horizontal axes in the table represent the image numbers in Fig. 2, respectively, $\times$ indicates no significant difference, and $\bigcirc$ indicates $p < 0.05$ indicates a significant difference.

From the results in Table 1, there were no significant differences in the gaze time for anything other than the "bottom pattern" depending on the element. In addition, in images where the gaze time for the "bottom pattern" was long, we believe that if the bottom pattern changes to yellow, the bottom pattern is likely to attract attention. Next, we conducted a one-way analysis of variance to find out whether there was a main effect on Kansei word scores due to differences in factors. Regarding the results, Tables 2, 3, 4, 5 and 6 show the results for the five kansei words for which significant differences were found.

Tables 2, 3, 4, 5 and 6 show that there were significant differences in kansei word scores other than "familiar" depending on the element. In addition, "bright", images with high brightness are considered to have high scores. For "distinctive", images with a changed background color are considered to have high scores. For "looks delicious", red images that are like existing products have high scores. For "luxury", images with low brightness are considered to have high scores.

Table 1. One-way variance analysis results for the gaze time of "bottom pattern"

	1	2	3	4	5	6	7	8	9	10	11	12	13	14	15	16	17	18	19	20	21
1		×	×	○	×	×	×	×	×	×	×	×	×	×	×	×	×	×	×	×	×
2	×			○	×	×	×	×	×	×	×	×	×	×	×	×	×	×	×	×	×
3	×			×	×	○		○						○	×	○	○	○	×		○
4	○	○	×		×	○	○	○	○	○	○	○	○	○	×	○	○	○		○	○
5	×	×	×	×		×	×	×	×	×	×	×	×	×	×	×	×	×	×	×	×
6	×	×	○	○			×	×	×	×	×	×	×	×	×	×	×	×	×	×	×
7	×	×		○	×	×		×	×	×	×	×	×	×	×	×	×	×	×	×	×
8	×	×	○	○	×	×	×		×	×	×	×	×	×	×	×	×	×	×	×	×
9	×	×		○	×	×	×	×		×	×	×	×	×	×	×	×	×	×	×	×
10	×	×		○	×	×	×	×	×		×	×	×	×	×	×	×	×	×	×	×
11	×	×		○	×	×	×	×	×	×		×	×	×	×	×	×	×	×	×	×
12	×	×		○	×	×	×	×	×	×	×		×	×	×	×	×	×	×	×	×
13	×	×		○	×	×	×	×	×	×	×	×		×	×	×	×	×	×	×	×
14	×	×	○	○	×	×	×	×	×	×	×	×	×		×	×	×	×	×	×	×
15	×	×	×	×	×	×	×	×	×	×	×	×	×	×		×	×	×	×	×	×
16	×	×		○	×	×	×	×	×	×	×	×	×	×			×	×	×	×	×
17	×	×			×	×	×	×	×	×	×	×	×	×	×			×	×	×	×
18	×	×	○	○	×	×	×	×	×	×	×	×	×	×	×	×	×		×	×	×
19	×	×	×		×	×	×	×	×	×	×	×	×	×	×	×	×	×		×	×
20	×	×		○	×	×	×	×	×	×	×	×	×	×	×	×	×	×	×		×
21	×	×	○	○	×	×	×	×	×	×	×	×	×	×	×	×	×	×	×	×	

Table 2. Results of one-way analysis of variance for the "bright" kansei word score

	1	2	3	4	5	6	7	8	9	10	11	12	13	14	15	16	17	18	19	20	21
1		×	×	×	×	×	○	×	○	○	×	×	×	×	○	×			×	×	×
2	×		×	×	×	×	×	×	×	×	×	×	×	×	×	×	×	×	×	×	×
3	×	×			×	×	○	×	○	○	×	×	×	×	○	×	×		×	×	×
4	×	×	×		×	×	×	×	×	×	×	×	×	×	×	×	×	×	×	×	×
5	×	×	×	×		×	×	×	×	×	×	×	×	×	×	×	×	×	×	×	×
6	×	×	×	×	×		○	×	○		×	×	×	×	×	×	×	×	×	×	×
7	○	×	○	×	×	○			○	×	×	×	×	×	×	×	×	×	×	×	×
8	×	×	×	×	×	×	○		×	×	×	×	×	×	×	×	×	×	×	×	×
9	○	×	○	×	×	○	×	○		×	×	×	×	×	×	×	×	×	×		○
10	○	×	○	×	×		×		×		×	×	×	×	×	×	×	×	×	×	×
11	×	×	×	×	×	×	×	×	×			×	×	×	×	×	×	×	×	×	×
12	×	×	×	×	×	×	×	×	×	×			×	×	×	×	×	×	×	×	×
13	×	×	×	×	×	×	×	×	×	×	×	×		×	×	×	×	×	×	×	×
14	×	×	×	×	×	×	×	×		×	×	×	×		×	×	×	×	×	×	×
15	○	×	○	×	×	×	×	×	×	×	×	×	×	×		×	×	×	×	×	×
16	×	×	×	×	×	×	×	×	×	×	×	×	×	×			×	×	×	×	×
17	×	×	×	×	×	×	×	×	×	×	×	×	×	×	×	×		×	×	×	×
18	×	×	×	×	×	×	×	×	×	×	×	×	×	×	×	×	×		×	×	×
19	×	×	×	×	×	×	×	×	×	×	×	×	×	×	×	×	×	×		×	×
20	×	×	×	×	×	×	×	×	×	×	×	×	×	×	×	×	×	×	×		×

Table 3. Results of one-way analysis of variance for the "warm" kanseikansei word score

	1	2	3	4	5	6	7	8	9	10	11	12	13	14	15	16	17	18	19	20	21
1		×	×	×	×	×	×	×		×	×	×	×	×	×	×	×	×	×	×	×
2	×		×	×	×	×	×	×	×	×	×	×	×	×	×	×	×	×	×	×	×
3	×	×		×	×	×	×	×	×	×	×	×	×	×	×	×	×	×	×	×	×
4	×	×	×		×	×	×	×	×	×	×	×	×	×	×	×	×	×	×	×	×
5	×	×	×	×		×	×	×	○	×	×	×	×	×	×	×	×	×	×	×	×
6	×	×	×	×	×		×	×	×	×	×	×	×	×	×	×	×	×	×	×	×
7	×	×	×	×	×	×		×	×	×	×	×	×	×	×	×	×	×	×	×	×
8	×	×	×	×	×	×	×		×	×	×	×	×	×	×	×	×	×	×	×	×
9	×	×	×	×	○	×	×	×		×	×	×	×	×	×	×	×	×	×	×	×
10	×	×	×	×	×	×	×	×	×		×	×	×	×	×	×	×	×	×	×	×
11	×	×	×	×	×	×	×	×	×	×		×	×	×	×	×	×	×	×	×	×
12	×	×	×	×	×	×	×	×	×	×	×		×	×	×	×	×	×	×	×	×
13	×	×	×	×	×	×	×	×	×	×	×	×		×	×	×	×	×	×	×	×
14	×	×	×	×	×	×	×	×	×	×	×	×	×		×	×	×	×	×	×	×
15	×	×	×	×	×	×	×	×	×	×	×	×	×	×		×	×	×	×	×	×
16	×	×	×	×	×	×	×	×	×	×	×	×	×	×	×		×	×	×	×	×
17	×	×	×	×	×	×	×	×	×	×	×	×	×	×	×	×		×	×	×	×
18	×	×	×	×	×	×	×	×	×	×	×	×	×	×	×	×	×		×	×	×
19	×	×	×	×	×	×	×	×	×	×	×	×	×	×	×	×	×	×		×	×
20	×	×	×	×	×	×	×	×	×	×	×	×	×	×	×	×	×	×	×		×
21	×	×	×	×	×	×	×	×	×	×	×	×	×	×	×	×	×	×	×	×	

Table 4. Results of one-way analysis of variance for "distinctive" kansei word scores

	1	2	3	4	5	6	7	8	9	10	11	12	13	14	15	16	17	18	19	20	21
1		×	×	×	×	○	×	○	×	×	×	×	×	×	×	×	×	×	×	×	×
2	×		×	×	×	○	×	○	×	×	×	×	×	×	×	×	×	×	×	×	×
3	×	×		×	×	×	×	×	×	×	×	×	×	×	×	×	×	×	×	×	×
4	×	×	×		×	×	×	×	×	×	×	×	×	×	×	×	×	×	×	×	×
5	×	×	×	×		×	×	×	×	×	×	×	×	×	×	×	×	×	×	×	×
6	○	○	×	×	×		×	×	×	×	×	×	×	×	×	×	×	×	×	×	×
7	×	×	×	×	×	×		×	×	×	×	×	×	×	×	×	×	×	×	×	×
8	○	○	×	×	×	×	×		×	×	×	×	×	×	×	×	×	×	×	×	×
9	×	×	×	×	×	×	×	×		×	×	×	×	×	×	×	×	×	×	×	×
10	×	×	×	×	×	×	×	×	×		×	×	×	×	×	×	×	×	×	×	×
11	×	×	×	×	×	×	×	×	×	×		×	×	×	×	×	×	×	×	×	×
12	×	×	×	×	×	×	×	×	×	×	×		×	×	×	×	×	×	×	×	×
13	×	×	×	×	×	×	×	×	×	×	×	×		×	×	×	×	×	×	×	×
14	×	×	×	×	×	×	×	×	×	×	×	×	×		×	×	×	×	×	×	×
15	×	×	×	×	×	×	×	×	×	×	×	×	×	×		×	×	×	×	×	×
16	×	×	×	×	×	×	×	×	×	×	×	×	×	×	×		×	×	×	×	×
17	×	×	×	×	×	×	×	×	×	×	×	×	×	×	×	×		×	×	×	×
18	×	×	×	×	×	×	×	×	×	×	×	×	×	×	×	×	×		×	×	×
19	×	×	×	×	×	×	×	×	×	×	×	×	×	×	×	×	×	×		×	×
20	×	×	×	×	×	×	×	×	×	×	×	×	×	×	×	×	×	×	×		×
21	×	×	×	×	×	×	×	×	×	×	×	×	×	×	×	×	×	×	×	×	

Table 5. Results of one-way analysis of variance for "appetizing" kansei word scores

	1	2	3	4	5	6	7	8	9	10	11	12	13	14	15	16	17	18	19	20	21
1		×	×	×	×	×	×	×	×	×	×	×	×	×	×	×	×	×	×	×	×
2	×		×	×	×	×	×	×	×	×	×	×	×	×	×	×	×	×	×	×	×
3	×	×		×	×	×	×	×	×	×	×	×	×	×	×	×	×	×	×	×	×
4	×	×	×		×	×	×	×	×	×	×	×	×	×	×	×	×	×	×	×	×
5	×	×	×	×		×	×	×	○	×	×	×	×	×	×	×	×	×	×	×	×
6	×	×	×	×	×		×	×	×	×	×	×	×	×	×	×	×	×	×	×	×
7	×	×	×	×	×	×		×	×	×	×	×	×	×	×	×	×	×	×	×	×
8	×	×	×	×	×	×	×		×	×	×	×	×	×	×	×	×	×	×	×	×
9	×	×	×	×	○	×	×	×		○	○	×	×	×	×	×	×	×	○	×	○
10	×	×	×	×	×	×	×	×	○		×	×	×	×	×	×	×	×	×	×	×
11	×	×	×	×	×	×	×	×	○	×		×	×	×	×	×	×	×	×	×	×
12	×	×	×	×	×	×	×	×	×	×	×		×	×	×	×	×	×	×	×	×
13	×	×	×	×	×	×	×	×	×	×	×	×		×	×	×	×	×	×	×	×
14	×	×	×	×	×	×	×	×	×	×	×	×	×		×	×	×	×	×	×	×
15	×	×	×	×	×	×	×	×	×	×	×	×	×	×		×	×	×	×	×	×
16	×	×	×	×	×	×	×	×	×	×	×	×	×	×	×		×	×	×	×	×
17	×	×	×	×	×	×	×	×	×	×	×	×	×	×	×	×		×	×	×	×
18	×	×	×	×	×	×	×	×	×	×	×	×	×	×	×	×	×		×	×	×
19	×	×	×	×	×	×	×	×	○	×	×	×	×	×	×	×	×	×		×	×
20	×	×	×	×	×	×	×	×	×	×	×	×	×	×	×	×	×	×	×		×
21	×	×	×	×	×	×	×	×	○	×	×	×	×	×	×	×	×	×	×	×	

Table 6. Results of one-way analysis of variance for the "luxury" kansei word score

	1	2	3	4	5	6	7	8	9	10	11	12	13	14	15	16	17	18	19	20	21
1		×	×	×	×	×	×	×	×	×	×	×	×	×	×	×	×	×	×	×	×
2	×		×	×	×	×	×	×	×	×	×	×	×	×	×	×	×	×	×	×	×
3	×	×		×	×	×	×	×	×	×	○	×	×	×	×	×	×	×	×	×	×
4	×	×	×		×	×	×	×	×	×	○	×	×	×	×	×	×	×	×	×	×
5	×	×	×	×		×	×	×	×	×	×	×	×	×	×	×	×	×	×	×	×
6	×	×	×	×	×		×	×	×	×	○	×	×	×	×	×	○	×	×	×	×
7	×	×	×	×	×	×		×	×	×	×	×	×	×	×	×	×	×	×	×	×
8	×	×	×	×	×	×	×		×	○	○	×	×	×	×	×	○	×	×	×	×
9	×	×	×	×	×	×	×	×		×	○	×	×	×	×	×	×	×	×	×	×
10	×	×	×	×	×	○	×	○	×		×	×	×	×	×	×	×	×	×	×	×
11	×	×	○	○	×	○	×	○	○	×		×	×	×	×	×	×	×	×	×	×
12	×	×	×	×	×	×	×	×	×	×	×		×	×	×	×	×	×	×	×	×
13	×	×	×	×	×	×	×	×	×	×	×	×		×	×	×	×	×	×	×	×
14	×	×	×	×	×	×	×	×	×	×	×	×	×		×	×	×	×	×	×	×
15	×	×	×	×	×	×	×	×	×	×	×	×	×	×		×	×	×	×	×	×
16	×	×	×	×	×	×	×	×	×	×	×	×	×	×	×		×	×	×	×	×
17	×	×	×	×	×	○	×	○	×	×	×	×	×	×	×	×		×	×	×	×
18	×	×	×	×	×	×	×	×	×	×	×	×	×	×	×	×	×		×	×	×
19	×	×	×	×	×	×	×	×	×	×	×	×	×	×	×	×	×	×		×	×
20	×	×	×	×	×	×	×	×	×	×	×	×	×	×	×	×	×	×	×		×
21	×	×	×	×	×	×	×	×	×	×	×	×	×	×	×	×	×	×	×	×	

3 Summary and Future Challenges

This time, we aimed to clarify whether differences in factors affect gaze time and kansei word scores. We formulated the following two hypotheses for our purpose and conducted the following analysis:

1. Perform a one-way analysis of variance to clarify whether there is a main effect on the gaze duration of each AOI.

2. To clarify whether there is a main effect on the gaze time of each AOI and each kansei word score due to differences in factors.

The results revealed the following:

1. A main effect was found in the gaze duration of each AOI.
2. Significant differences were found in the gaze time of each AOI and each kansei word score depending on the element.

Based on the above results, it is thought that the difference in factors affects the gaze time and kansei word score. This time the discussion focused on one single flavor and did not investigate differences in taste, so this could be the topic of future research. Previous research has shown that the elements that attract attention change depending on taste. Therefore, we believe that it is necessary to evaluate not only the differences in elements but also the influence of differences in "taste" regarding gaze time and kansei word scores.

Acknowledgment. We would like to thank you for the valuable cooperation from Mr. Taketo Sagawa and Mr. Shunsaku Isaji of S&B Foods Co., Ltd. Mr. Kenichi Endo, Mr. Yusuke Okada, and Mr. Masayuki Omachi. They give us the variable advices including providing package design. Thank you for your cooperation in conducting the preliminary survey. Students from Shibaura Institute of Technology Junior and Senior High School, Prof. Ryo Iwata, I would like to thank you for the grate support.

References

1. Schifferstein, H.N.J., Howell, B.F.: Using color–odor correspondences for fragrance packaging design. Food Qual. Prefer. **46**, 17–25 (2015). (in Japanese)
2. Hagtvedt, H., Patrick, V.M.: The broad embrace of luxury: hedonic potential as a driver of brand extensibility. J. Consum. Psychol. **19**(4), 608–618 (2009)
3. Yamamoto, R., Yamada, H.: The impact of facial expressions in illustrations on product evaluation in package design. J. Jpn. Soc. Sens. Eng. (2022). (in Japanese)
4. Asakawa, M., Okano, M.: Elements of visual attention by consumers in food packaging: an analysis using eye-tracking. Glob. Bus. J. **7**(3), 21–29 (2021). (in Japanese)
5. S&B FOODS INC.: https://www.sbfoods.co.jp/. Accessed 20 June 2022. (in Japanese)

Qualitative and Quantitative Approaches to Conduct Heuristic Evaluations: A Comparison Study

Freddy Paz[1]([✉])[iD], Freddy-Asrael Paz-Sifuentes[2][iD], Arturo Moquillaza[1][iD],
Fiorella Falconi[1][iD], Joel Aguirre[1][iD], Adrian Lecaros[1][iD], and Carlos Ramos[1][iD]

[1] Pontificia Universidad Católica del Perú, San Miguel 15088, Peru
{fpaz,amoquillaza}@pucp.pe,
{ffalconit,aguirre.joel,adrian.lecaros,carlos.ramosp}@pucp.edu.pe
[2] Universidad Nacional Pedro Ruiz Gallo, Lambayeque, Peru
fpaz@unprg.edu.pe

Abstract. Heuristic evaluation has become one of the methods most used by specialists to measure the level of usability of software products. However, there are many differences between authors on how to execute this inspection process. From a systematic review of the literature carried out in a previous study, it was possible to identify the two most relevant approaches to carry out this evaluation process: the qualitative approach proposed by Nielsen and the quantitative approach established by Granollers. Although both proposals aim to identify design problems to be corrected subsequently to improve the level of usability, the quantitative proposal also establishes a mechanism to obtain a value between 0 and 100 on the level of usability of the product, system, or service. In this way, it is possible to make comparisons and identify the remaining percentage of a proposal to achieve an appropriate level of usability. In this study, the differences in the results obtained from applying both approaches for the usability evaluation of a publicly accessible website in Peru are analyzed. The purpose is for this research to serve as a guide for executing heuristic evaluations and used for specialists and development teams to choose the most appropriate approach in their business scenarios. The results show that although many findings are similar, both approaches have differences and specific advantages that are discussed in depth.

Keywords: Human-Computer Interaction · Graphical User Interfaces · Usability Evaluation · Quality Assessment · Software Development

1 Introduction

Heuristic evaluation has become a reference inspection method to evaluate the level of usability of software products [20]. According to a previous study [19], it is one of the most used and preferred methods by specialists and academics to quickly identify design problems that a graphical user interface may have. Likewise, ensuring that a software product is simultaneously easy to use and attractive is mandatory in a highly competitive market like today's [5]. For this reason, development teams and companies focus on ensuring that the interfaces of their systems are usable and that the interaction experience with them is satisfactory. Products, systems, and services must be understandable to users and conduct them intuitively towards achieving their objectives, those for which the artifacts are being used.

The methods that can be used to evaluate usability and user experience are diverse and involve different procedures. However, selecting the most appropriate one will depend on the scenario of each context. There is no one method better than the other. The fact is that all methods complement each other in one way or another in their findings [18]. Teams often decide to apply two or more usability evaluation methods to confirm or explain the results. Heuristic evaluation is one of scholars' most used and preferred methods due to its simplicity and the few resources it demands. The method involves identifying non-compliance with a particular set of guidelines, which are subsequently classified as design problems [14]. Likewise, this method is directed and executed by specialists in the area of Human-Computer Interaction, representing this approach's most challenging aspect since it is difficult to have the availability of these professionals. However, the literature has reported that this method is executed in multiple ways and that there are different perspectives on carrying out the evaluation process step by step [15]. There are differences in the type of professional who carries out the inspection, the number of participants that make up the evaluation team, the heuristics that are used, and how the results are established. Within the studies reviewed in a systematic review process, two perspectives stand out as the most cited and complete proposals: the qualitative approach and the quantitative approach, which the authors of this research have formalized in a single evaluation process [16]. This study analyzes the differences between both approaches and details the findings that can be identified with each proposal. This study is intended to serve as a guide both for the execution of the heuristic inspection method and to establish the considerations for academics and development teams to make the most appropriate decision regarding the approach to employ to evaluate the usability degree of a software product.

2   Theoretical Background

This section presents the concepts that have been required to develop this research. The purpose of this study was to compare the qualitative and quantitative approaches to carry out heuristic evaluations in a case study where the usability of a website is evaluated.

2.1   Heuristic Evaluation

Heuristic evaluation is one of the most used inspection methods to evaluate the degree of usability [10]. Likewise, it is an assessment process that is within the category of "inspection methods", which means that specialists with extensive experience in the field of Human-Computer Interaction must carry it out [6]. Unlike those methods where the participation of representative users of the product or system is required, only professionals with extensive experience carrying out usability evaluations participate in heuristic evaluation. For this reason, the precision of the results depends on the level of expertise possessed by those involved in the evaluation process.

According to Nielsen [14], the heuristic evaluation method consists of a group of specialists reviewing the graphical interfaces of the software product in search of non-compliance with a set of design guidelines. The number of evaluators that Nielsen recommends is 3 to 5 because this number of participants makes it possible to identify the highest percentage of usability problems presented by a graphical user interface [12]. As more evaluators join the evaluation group, it is possible to locate a more significant number of problems. However, the cost-benefit relationship decreases since the additional identified issues are less relevant than the cost required for additional professionals to participate. Likewise, the principles that are used are called "usability heuristics". These are considered good design practices that professionals have studied and validated after several case studies. For this reason, the design of interaction interfaces must follow these rules to ensure their ease of use.

Nielsen's ten usability principles are the authors' most used and cited heuristics [11]. These have been elaborated considering a large set of case studies whose purpose was to identify the aspects that the design of a graphical user interface must necessarily comply with. However, it is essential to highlight that heuristics are considered an instrument in the evaluation process. It is possible that the members of the evaluation team determine that Nielsen's heuristics, despite being widely referenced, are not the most appropriate to carry out the usability inspection [1]. This fact occurs because when evaluating specific category software products, it is necessary to consider additional aspects to those established by Nielsen, which also affect the interaction experience and, therefore, the ease of use of the product, system, or service.

In a previous study [19], through an exhaustive systematic review, it was possible to verify that academics and specialists carried out the heuristic evaluation process differently. In the literature, different procedures are reported concerning the tasks included in the assessment process. To formalize the heuristic evaluation process and provide a general framework that serves as a guide, the common characteristics in the different reported procedures were analyzed, and a formal proposal was developed [8]. Within this novel general framework [16], 5 subprocesses were defined in which most studies that report a heuristic evaluation can be framed: (1) Planning, (2) Training, (3) Evaluation, (4) Discussion and (5) Report. Figure 1 shows the complete heuristic evaluation process that has been formalized based on the review of scientific papers.

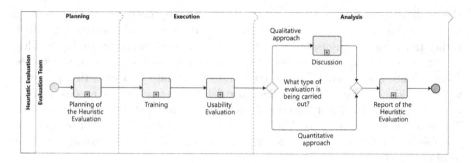

Fig. 1. Heuristic evaluation process

According to an analysis of existing usability evaluation methods [16], it was possible to identify that almost all of them can be framed into 3 phases: (1) Planning, (2) Execution, and (3) Analysis. The purpose of this structure is that more methods will subsequently be incorporated into the framework that is being proposed.

According to our proposal, before carrying out the heuristic evaluation, it is necessary to determine the software product to be evaluated, the members of the team of specialists, the scope of the inspection, the time, and the budget for the execution of the entire evaluation process. In this new approach, it is established to begin with a planning phase, in which the heuristics that must be used to carry out the evaluation will be selected, and the way of working will be defined, which can be face-to-face/virtual, synchronous/asynchronous, as well as to identify the most representative graphical interfaces of the system to carry out the evaluation. Subsequently, a training stage is executed. This part of the process allows all members to reinforce their knowledge of usability and user experience and examine the heuristics selected to execute the inspection.

As mentioned above, there are multiple ways to execute heuristic inspection. After an exhaustive analysis, it was possible to determine that there are two clearly defined approaches in the literature [16]. One proposal is the qualitative approach focused on identifying all the design problems that the interface has for their subsequent categorization based on their severity [13]. In addition, there is the quantitative approach, which, rather than finding all the possible design problems that the interface presents, aims to quantify the software product's usability level based on quite specific guidelines [3]. The execution of the evaluation process, which is the next sub-process established in the proposal, will depend on the selected approach. According to the characteristics of the scenario and the requirements, the team of specialists must determine the most appropriate approach to carry out the assessment.

If the evaluation team has opted for the qualitative approach, a discussion phase is carried out once the evaluation process has been completed. This process is not carried out if the approach used has been quantitative because the guidelines used in this case are more detailed than the general rules used in the qualitative case. Likewise, in the quantitative approach, the main objective is to establish a numerical value on the usability level of the software product rather than discuss the usability problems of graphical interfaces in depth. This fact does not mean that the usability problems identified in the quantitative approach are not analyzed. Both approaches culminate in a reporting phase in which the identified usability problems are detailed, as well as the process carried out and the improvement opportunities for the graphical interfaces examined. The evaluation process must have a constructive analysis in the sense that the possible modifications to be made must be highlighted to achieve an appropriate level of usability.

2.2   Qualitative Heuristic Evaluation

The qualitative approach has been proposed based on the analysis of several studies [7,9,17,21]. Considering the information reported in these works, it has been established that the evaluation process begins with an individual analysis where each team member independently inspects all the graphical interfaces that are part of the scope of the evaluation. During this inspection, evaluators must identify non-compliance with the heuristic principles that were selected in the planning stage. These non-compliances will later be classified as "usability problems". Likewise, the members must have previously defined a template to document each identified problem's details. This process can be carried out in person or virtually. Once all the evaluators have completed the inspection, the result will be a list of problems for each evaluation team member, which will later be discussed as a group to consolidate results and share opinions. Changes may be made to the findings since new problems could arise by sharing results, repeated ones could be eliminated, or some details of the graphical interfaces that were not completely clear could be clarified. The result will be a single list that consolidates all the usability problems presented by the software product's graphical interfaces. Subsequently, an individual activity is once more suggested in which each evaluator rates the severity and frequency of each problem reported in the final list. The individual rating will allow the evaluators to meet again later to discuss the values obtained independently for the last time. This previous activity will lead to the report being subsequently developed, documenting the problems and actions the designers should consider to solve them, ordered by severity and frequency. It is essential to indicate which critical issues require immediate attention by the development team or the company that has requested the heuristic evaluation.

2.3   Quantitative Heuristic Evaluation

The quantitative approach was proposed by Antoni Granollers [3,4]. This way of carrying out heuristic evaluation arises due to the need to obtain a numerical value that represents the software product's current usability level. Obtaining a numerical value offers some advantages, such as comparing two different proposals or knowing how far or close the graphical interface design is compared to the competition. To quantify the level of usability, Granollers proposes a scoring scheme that allows determining a numerical value between 0 and 100, where 0 means that the system does not comply with any usability guidelines and 100 means that the system is entirely usable. Likewise, Granollers proposes a very detailed checklist that evaluators should use to evaluate the system's graphical interfaces. This checklist consists of 60 statements that specialists must confirm or deny about the design under evaluation [4], which have been developed from an analysis of two highly relevant sources: 10 usability heuristics by Jakob Nielsen [11] and the interaction design principles established by Bruce Tognazzini [22].

Unlike Nielsen's heuristics, which are fairly general rules, Granollers proposes specific guidelines that can quickly be verified in the design of the graphical interface of the software product. Likewise, the guidelines are classified into 15 categories and there is an Excel template that allows specialists to carry out the evaluation in a simple way [2]. Table 1 shows the guidelines established by Granollers for the category entitled: (H1) "Visibility and system status". In this category, Granollers proposes a set of five guidelines as questions that must be answered after reviewing the graphical user interfaces. However, not all categories contain the same number of questions. In some cases, more aspects are proposed to be reviewed depending on what is relevant to analyze for that criterion.

Table 1. Guidelines of the first category (H1) "Visibility and system status"

ID	Guideline
H1.1	Does the application include a visible title page, section or site?
H1.2	Does the user always know where it is located?
H1.3	Does the user always know what the system or application is doing?
H1.4	Are the links clearly defined?
H1.5	Can all actions be visualized directly? (No other actions are required)

In this approach, each specialist individually must complete the template, reviewing all the graphical interfaces and indicating an answer for each question. Among the possible answers that exist are: (1) Yes, (0.5) Neither yes nor no, (0) No, and (NP) Does not apply. Each response has an associated score that will allow specialists to calculate the total value of the software product's usability level. If the graphical interface meets the guideline, the evaluators will answer affirmatively, adding 1 point to the total usability value. In the same way, if the graphical interface does not comply with the guideline, the answer will be negative, and no score will be added to the total for that evaluated aspect. If the graphical interface partially complies with the guideline, then the evaluator will respond with a "neither yes nor no" answer, and 0.5 or half a point will be added to the total score. Assuming the graphical interfaces meet all guidelines, the total should be 60 points, since 60 questions must be answered. Given this case, 60 points represent 100% of the usability level of the software product. However,

Granollers also offers the possibility that evaluators can indicate whether there are questions that do not apply to the usability evaluation of the product being analyzed. Those interrogations that do not apply must be subtracted from the total number of questions in the proposal when calculating the percentage of the usability level [3]. In this way, it will always be possible to reach 100% if all the aspects that do apply reach a positive response. Equation 1 shows how to calculate the percentage of usability of the graphical user interfaces of a software product. In this formula, x_{ji} is the score obtained by the evaluator j in question i, q_j is the number of questions that do not apply to the evaluator j, and m is the number of evaluators who are performing the heuristic inspection.

$$\text{Software product usability percentage} = \frac{\sum_{j=1}^{m} \left(\frac{\sum_{i=1}^{60} x_{ji}}{60 - q_j} \times 100 \right)}{m} \tag{1}$$

3   A Comparison Study

In this research, a comparative study was proposed to determine if using both approaches (the qualitative and quantitative proposal) it is possible to achieve similar results or if the findings are completely different. For this comparison, the web portal of a Peruvian public health institution dedicated to the treatment of mental illnesses was selected. The purpose of this evaluation was not only to identify the degree of usability of the web portal but also to know in a certain way if the institutions in Peru are currently offering quality websites, that are easy to navigate, and in which relevant information can be found quickly to proceed with booking an appointment and the subsequent outpatient care.

Fig. 2. Home page of the selected Peruvian public health institution

Figure 2 shows the main page of the web portal that was selected for this case study. The purpose of this web portal, in addition to providing relevant information about the public institution, is to provide a means by which patients can carry out basic procedures. On this website, it is possible to view information related to the creation of the health institution as well as its history and mission. It is also possible to identify the multiple specialties related to the area of mental health that provide medical services to insured people. Likewise, information is transmitted through the portal about the services offered by the institution, and the events that are being organized. Among the services available on this website are the possibility of booking a medical appointment, contacting the institution for any query, claim, or complaint, and accessing a document processing system to review files and send formal documents addressed to the institution.

The comparison was carried out using two different groups of evaluators but with similar characteristics to avoid bias. However, due to the team composition structure, some factors could have influenced the results. Each team was made up of three Computer Engineering graduates from the *Pontificia Universidad Católica del Perú* (PUCP) - Perú. All participants have the same academic training, graduated the same year, and have similar knowledge about usability, user experience, and evaluation methods. Likewise, it is important to highlight that everyone voluntarily agreed to take part in this research for academic purposes. All participants were informed of the purpose of the study and signed an informed consent approved by the ethics committee of our university.

Before starting the evaluation process, our research team met virtually with both groups through the Zoom platform to explain in detail both approaches (the qualitative and quantitative proposal) of the heuristic evaluation process of software products. At this meeting, doubts and questions regarding the inspection procedure were resolved. Likewise, each team was given an Excel template to record their findings on the usability problems of the web portal interfaces. In the case of the team that carried out the quantitative evaluation, they used the template established by Granollers [2]. In the case of the team that carried out the qualitative evaluation, they used a template developed by the HCI-DUXAIT research group that contains the following sections to document each of the problems found: ID, description, comments/explanation, examples of occurrence, unfulfilled heuristic and screenshots that evidence the issue.

The heuristic evaluation was conducted asynchronously within one week. All participants were asked to perform the inspection individually according to the type of approach that was assigned to their team and then coordinate to meet and consolidate results. Likewise, they were asked to email the results of both the individual and report phase. Once the results were available, the comparative analysis was carried out.

4   Analysis of Results

The results were analyzed from the reports sent by the specialists. The findings demonstrate that although there are similar results, some aspects have only been identified through the specific approaches. The team that used the qualitative approach to perform the heuristic evaluation identified 32 usability problems. Table 2 presents the sixteen most severe issues that have been determined with the qualitative approach. The heuristics that were used in this case were the ten principles established by Nielsen for the assessment of the web domain graphical interfaces [11]. In Table 2 it is possible to examine the heuristic principle that is being infringed in each scenario. The problems identified are focused mainly on the information architecture, the feedback from the system to the user, the inappropriate functioning of the web portal that delivers responses not expected by the users, the system's lack of efficiency, and the absence of mechanisms for help and support.

From the findings, it can be determined that the aspects have been identified are mostly related to the information architecture, and this situation is because the web portal has a more informative purpose than a transactional one. Although the application offers a documentary processing system, its main objective is to provide relevant information about the public health institution. Likewise, it can be seen that the qualitative approach is more focused on finding problems and offering a solution to them rather than identifying the percentage of compliance with the usability level of the applications.

Regarding the quantitative approach, the participants used the template and question-like guidelines established by Granollers [2]. The results are detailed in Table 3. The quantitative evaluation findings reveal that the web portal lacks usability in several aspects that were evaluated. Those categories that were rated remarkably negatively are related to the lack of mechanisms to undo changes, the absence of functionalities that allow speeding up actions or searching for relevant information, the lack of an aesthetic and minimalist design, the lack of help and documentation, the impossibility of customizing the graphical interfaces and the high degree of system latency. Below are those guidelines that obtained a low rating almost unanimously by the team of evaluators that conducted the qualitative approach:

- H1.3. The user always knows what the system or application is doing.
- H2.2. The design of the icons corresponds to everyday objects
- H2.3. Every icon does the action that users expect.
- H3.2. The functions "undo" and "re-do" are implemented.
- H5.2. It is easy to locate information that has already been searched before.
- H5.5. The information is organized according to logic familiar to the user.
- H6.1. There are keyboard shortcuts for common actions.
- H7.4. Codes are used to reference error messages.
- H8.3. The search engine tolerates typos and spelling errors.
- H9.1. The system has a design without redundancy of information.
- H9.2. The information is short, concise and accurate.
- H10.1. There is "help" option.
- H10.5. The help documentation is clear, with examples.
- H11.1. Users can continue from a previous state.
- H13.1. The system keeps the users informed of system status.
- H13.2. The system status is visible and updated.
- H14.2. The system clearly indicates the consequences of the actions.
- H15.1. The execution of heavy work is transparent to the users.

Table 2. More severe problems identified with the qualitative approach

ID	Description	Infringed heuristic
P01	Excessively long loading time on the system, displaying blank screens for prolonged periods	N1
P02	Non-standardized font sizes in the design of graphic interfaces. In some sections, the size is too small while in others it is too large	N4
P03	The icons used for some of the functionality are unrelated to the system's actions. For example, the icon associated with sending mail has the plus symbol (+) as an image	N2
P04	The vertical navigation of the main page is extensive, making it complex	N8
P05	The relevant information displayed in the graphical user interfaces is not properly organized by sections and categories	N8
P06	The sections that have been defined in the graphical interface do not have hierarchies and dependencies on each other	N4
P07	Some links open the content in a different browser window instead of redirecting to the selected section	N4
P08	There are sections of the web portal that do not maintain the same design format that has been used on the main page, in which for instance, the menu bar and system sections disappear	N4
P09	No login mechanism that allows users to quickly identify a history of the documents sent through the document processing system or the procedures carried out	N7
P10	No manual or online support mechanism can assist users of the web portal	N10
P11	There are broken links that redirect to non-existent web pages	N4
P12	Some sections of the system no longer allow users to go back to the previous view	N3
P13	Transactional forms allow incorrect data to be entered. Although error messages are displayed later, these actions could be avoided by preventing inappropriate characters from being entered for specific fields of the form	N5
P14	Some error messages displayed are unrelated to the error made by the user. For example, the message "field is required" is displayed when the error is due to entering letters instead of numbers in a form field	N9
P15	The graphical interface does not adapt to different screen resolutions or different types of devices	N4
P16	No breadcrumb navigation that allows users to notice the current location where they are and the possibility of returning to the sections that would enable them to access that location	N1

Table 3. Scores obtained by evaluators who used the qualitative approach

Category	E1	E2	E2
(H01) Visibility and system state	2.5/5.0	1.5/5.0	3.0/5.0
(H02) Connection between the system and the real world, metaphor usage and human objects	0.5/4.0	2.0/4.0	1.0/4.0
(H03) User control and freedom	0.0/3.0	1.0/3.0	0.5/3.0
(H04) Consistency and standards	4.0/6.0	4.5/6.0	3.0/6.0
(H05) Recognition rather than memory, learning and anticipation	2.5/5.0	2.0/5.0	3.0/5.0
(H06) Flexibility and efficiency of use	1.5/6.0	0.0/6.0	2.0/6.0
(H07) Help users recognize, diagnose and recover from errors	2.5/4.0	2.5/4.0	3.0/4.0
(H08) Preventing errors	1.5/3.0	2.5/3.0	2.0/3.0
(H09) Aesthetic and minimalist design	2.0/4.0	1.0/4.0	0.0/4.0
(H10) Help and documentation	0.0/5.0	1.5/5.0	1.0/5.0
(H11) Save the state and protect the work	0.5/3.0	0.0/3.0	1.0/3.0
(H12) Color and readability	2.5/4.0	3.0/4.0	3.0/4.0
(H13) Autonomy	0.5/3.0	1.5/3.0	1.0/3.0
(H14) Defaults	0.5/3.0	0.0/3.0	1.0/3.0
(H15) Latency reduction	0.5/2.0	1.0/2.0	0.0/2.0
TOTAL	**21.5/60.0**	**24.0/60.0**	**24.5/60.0**

The web portal fails to comply with all aspects that received a low rating. As can be seen, the findings coincide with the results obtained from the qualitative approach. However, there are other aspects that are also different and that were not taken into account during the qualitative evaluation. Likewise, it is highlighted that none of the evaluators have chosen to indicate that there are aspects that are not applicable. It could be that there is a tendency to evaluate all 60 aspects even though there may be the possibility of not examining all of them in case they are not relevant for this type of software product. Regarding the usability degree of the application, it can be seen that it is quite low and that despite being a web portal for informational purposes, it needs to be improved significantly. The values obtained by the evaluators were 35.83%, 40.00% and 40.83%, resulting in an average of 38.89%. This value is below half and means that many improvements must be made to reach an appropriate level. The web portal, despite belonging to a public health institution and having a high degree of relevance for citizens, is not understandable and lacks mechanisms that make it easy to use and interact.

5   Conclusions and Future Works

Usability continues to be an essential quality attribute that must be considered in the design of the graphical interfaces of a software product. For this reason, multiple evaluation methods allow the identification of the most critical usability problems, and in that way, the development team can later solve them. One of the most used methods is the heuristic evaluation; however, different procedures to carry out the inspection are reported in the literature. In a previous study, through a systematic review of the literature we identified that the reported procedures can be classified into two approaches: qualitative and quantitative.

The qualitative approach aims to identify all possible design problems present in a software product's graphical user interfaces (GUI). In contrast, the quantitative approach proposed by Granollers seeks to quantify the level of usability through a numerical value. The qualitative proposal has a problem-search and discussion component that allows us to identify, in more detail and without restrictions, the most significant number of design aspects that must be corrected to guarantee a pleasant interaction experience, unlike Granollers' approach, which was developed to compare and determine how differentiated a design proposal is compared to the leading competitors.

On the other hand, Granollers establishes a novel way of quantifying a software product's usability level by verifying a set of guidelines that must have been respected in the design of the graphical interfaces. The way to calculate a numerical value is based on the 60 specific guidelines (as questions) that have been proposed and the associated scores that each evaluator assigns to each of these guidelines. However, the possibility of exploring different response scales and other proposals of guidelines oriented to software domains of particular categories remains open.

In this study, a comparative study was carried out to determine the similarities and differences in the results obtained by both approaches. For this purpose, the support of six Computer Engineering graduates, who formed two homogeneous groups, was requested. Each group was assigned a different approach and instructed prior to the inspection. Likewise, the web portal of a public mental health institution was selected, given its importance for society and citizens. The inspection process was carried out under the same conditions, and an attempt was made to ensure that no external factors affected the evaluation results. The main objective of the web portal is to offer relevant information to users about all the services provided by the institution. Likewise, the web portal has a module for booking appointments, document management and monitoring the procedures carried out with the health institution.

The case study evidences that some results obtained by both approaches are similar, but there are also differences. The qualitative approach offers greater freedom for evaluators to identify design problems since the heuristics are generic and not specific. On the other hand, the quantitative approach allows specialists to obtain the percentage of usability of the software product based on highly defined guidelines that the evaluators can quickly verify. Likewise, concerning the level of usability identified by the evaluators of the public mental health institution in Peru, it is possible to mention that it is low and that many improvements are required to obtain a quality product. It is essential to mention that more studies are needed to determine the current state of applications in this domain. Likewise, it would be relevant to carry out more case studies to generalize the results obtained and guarantee the usefulness and relevance of all the evaluation instruments.

Acknowledgement. This study is highly supported by the *Section of Informatics Engineering* of the *Pontifical Catholic University of Peru* (PUCP) - Peru, and the "HCI, Design, User Experience, Accessibility & Innovation Technologies" Research Group (HCI-DUXAIT). HCI-DUXAIT is a research group of PUCP.

References

1. Díaz, J., Rusu, C., Collazos, C.A.: Experimental validation of a set of cultural-oriented usability heuristics: e-commerce websites evaluation. Comput. Stand. Interfaces **50**, 160–178 (2017). https://doi.org/10.1016/j.csi.2016.09.013
2. Granollers, A.: Usability evaluation template (2023). http://mpiua.invid.udl.cat/wp-content/uploads/2018/04/Evaluaci'on-Heuristica-v2018-OK.xlsx. Accessed 15 Jan 2024
3. Granollers, T.: Validación experimental de un conjunto heurístico para evaluaciones de ux de sitios web de comercio-e. In: 2016 IEEE 11th Colombian Computing Conference (CCC), pp. 1–8 (2016). https://doi.org/10.1109/ColumbianCC.2016.7750783
4. Granollers, T.: Usability evaluation with heuristics. new proposal from integrating two trusted sources. In: Marcus, A., Wang, W. (eds.) DUXU 2018. LNCS, vol. 10918, pp. 396–405. Springer, Cham (2018). https://doi.org/10.1007/978-3-319-91797-9_28
5. Heinemann, G.: Business systems and benchmarks in e-commerce. In: The New Online Trade, pp. 261–401. Springer, Wiesbaden (2023). https://doi.org/10.1007/978-3-658-40757-5_4
6. Holzinger, A.: Usability engineering methods for software developers. Commun. ACM **48**(1), 71–74 (2005). https://doi.org/10.1145/1039539.1039541
7. Inostroza, R., Rusu, C., Roncagliolo, S., Rusu, V., Collazos, C.A.: Developing smash: a set of smartphone's usability heuristics. Comput. Stand. Interfaces **43**, 40–52 (2016). https://doi.org/10.1016/j.csi.2015.08.007
8. Lecaros, A., Moquillaza, A., Falconi, F., Aguirre, J., Tapia, A., Paz, F.: Selection and modeling of a formal heuristic evaluation process through comparative analysis. In: Soares, M.M., Rosenzweig, E., Marcus, A. (eds.) Design, User Experience, and Usability: UX Research, Design, and Assessment, pp. 28–46. Springer, Cham (2022). https://doi.org/10.1007/978-3-031-05897-4_3
9. Moran, K., Gordon, K.: How to conduct a heuristic evaluation (2023). https://www.nngroup.com/articles/how-to-conduct-a-heuristic-evaluation/. Accessed 15 Jan 2024
10. Mozaffari, S., Hamidi, H.R.: Impacts of augmented reality on foreign language teaching: a case study of Persian language. Multimedia Tools Appl. **82**(3), 4735–4748 (2023). https://doi.org/10.1007/s11042-022-13370-5
11. Nielsen, J.: 10 usability heuristics for user interface design (1994). https://www.nngroup.com/articles/ten-usability-heuristics/. Accessed 15 Jan 2024

12. Nielsen, J.: The theory behind heuristic evaluations (1994). https://www. nngroup.com/articles/how-to-conduct-a-heuristic-evaluation/theory-heuristic-evaluations/. Accessed 15 Jan 2024
13. Nielsen, J.: Usability Engineering. Morgan Kaufmann Publishers Inc., San Francisco (1994)
14. Nielsen, J.: Usability inspection methods. In: Conference Companion on Human Factors in Computing Systems. CHI 1994, New York, NY, USA, pp. 413–414. Association for Computing Machinery (1994). https://doi.org/10.1145/259963.260531
15. Paz, F., Collazos, C., Pow-Sang, J.A.: Validation in the web domain of a formal process to evaluate the usability of software applications: an approach based on the heuristic inspection. Int. J. u- and e- Serv. Sci. Technol. **10**(7), 65–82 (2017). https://doi.org/10.14257/ijunesst.2017.10.7.07
16. Paz, F., Lecaros, A., Falconi, F., Tapia, A., Aguirre, J., Moquillaza, A.: A process to support heuristic evaluation and tree testing from a UX integrated perspective. In: Latifi, S. (ed.) ITNG 2023 20th International Conference on Information Technology-New Generations, pp. 369–377. Springer, Cham (2023). https://doi.org/10.1007/978-3-031-28332-1_42
17. Paz, F., Moquillaza, A., Lecaros, A., Falconi, F., Aguirre, J., Ramos, C.: Applying heuristic evaluation with different evaluator profiles: a comparative study between novice and expert specialists. In: Proceedings of the XI Latin American Conference on Human Computer Interaction. CLIHC '23, New York, NY, USA. Association for Computing Machinery (2024). https://doi.org/10.1145/3630970.3631063
18. Paz, F., Paz, F.A., Villanueva, D., Pow-Sang, J.A.: Heuristic evaluation as a complement to usability testing: A case study in web domain. In: 2015 12th International Conference on Information Technology - New Generations, pp. 546–551 (2015). https://doi.org/10.1109/ITNG.2015.92
19. Paz, F., Pow-Sang, J.A.: A systematic mapping review of usability evaluation methods for software development process. Int. J. Software Eng. Appl. **10**(1), 165–178 (2016). https://doi.org/10.14257/ijseia.2016.10.1.16
20. Quiñones, D., Rusu, C.: Applying a methodology to develop user experience heuristics. Comput. Stand. Interfaces **66**, 103345 (2019). https://doi.org/10.1016/j.csi.2019.04.004
21. Quiñones, D., Rusu, C., Rusu, V.: A methodology to develop usability/user experience heuristics. Comput. Stand. Interfaces **59**, 109–129 (2018). https://doi.org/10.1016/j.csi.2018.03.002
22. Tognazzini, B.: First principles of interaction design (revised & expanded) (2014). https://asktog.com/atc/principles-of-interaction-design/. Accessed 15 Jan 2024

A Checklist for the Usability Evaluation of Artificial Intelligence (AI) mHealth Applications Graphical User Interface

Chanjuan Tu[1]([✉]), Alessia Russo[2], and Ying Zhang[3]

[1] Department of Design, University of Gloucestershire, Changchun GL50 2RH, UK
chanjuantu@connect.glos.ac.uk
[2] School of Architecture and Built Environment, Queensland University of Technology, Brisbane, Australia
[3] College of Education, Northeast Normal University, Nanguan District, 5268 Renmin Avenue, Changchun, China

Abstract. The download rate of AI mobile health (mHealth) apps has increased rapidly, and there are many usability evaluation studies based on mobile apps, but few studies have been conducted on the usability of AI mHealth applications. This study aims to develop a task-based usability checklist based on heuristic evaluation based on the opinions of AI mobile health app user interface (UI) practitioners. This study was divided into two phases. The first phase of the study developed a hierarchical structure of graphical user interface design elements and usability principles related to AI mHealth applications, which used to develop the visual checklist for the usability evaluation. In order to demonstrate the practical effectiveness of the proposed checklist, the second phase of the study makes the usability evaluation with the checklist in AI m-Health application. Thirty user interface practitioners were recruited for this test, and they will use a visual checklist to evaluate the usability of AI GUIs in mHealth applications. The results showed that this usability checklist identified most of the usability issues and considerations that should be taken into account when developing AI mHealth, especially the usability of conversational AI and chatbot. This facilitates the study of potential ways to standardize AI GUIs to enhance the user experience in AI mHealth applications. The usability checklist proposed in this study is expected to be used quickly and effectively by usability practitioners for user interface evaluation during AI m-Health application development.

Keywords: Artificial Intelligence · Mobile Health (mHealth) · Chatbot · Graphical user interface · Usability · Evaluation

1 Introduction

In recent years, artificial intelligence (AI) and big data have been increasingly used in healthcare [1, 10, 27]. However, AI health applications (Apps) face challenges in terms of usability; several studies note the fundamentals and guidelines for implementing mobile health (mHealth) apps as well as in terms of quality, usability, user engagement and behavioral change [10]. While there is much research on the successful use of these AI technologies in human-machine interfaces (HMIs) and the provision of a high user experience, there is still little knowledge targeting usability factors in healthcare AI apps that are not well researched, and in particular, targeted how to optimize the usability of an AI chatbot in mHealth apps. To fill this gap of the usability of conversational AI in mHealth applications, several papers have provided design guidelines for the usability of AI-based mHealth apps [10]. From this point of view, this study investigates the usability of user interfaces for AI-based mHealth apps.

This study aims to develop usability checklist for the graphical user interface of the AI mHealth applications. The checklist is used to evaluate and identify usability problems in the user interface of an AI mHealth application and to analyze and determine whether the user interface in the AI mHealth application complies with the accepted usability principles in user interfaces. Also, the checklist allows for the collection of a hierarchy of user interface design elements in the mHealth application and usability principles of the AI design elements to establish consistency and standardization in the use of user interfaces for AI mHealth applications in order to prevent user confusion about the AI user interface functionality in the graphical user interface of the mHealth application [14]. The essential usability checklist developed in this study is primarily based on commonly used heuristics evaluation, which is each software user interface element from the mobile phone developer's perspective. In order to validate the effectiveness of the proposed usability checklist, we tested the Sensely App (one of AI mHealth and insurance assistant apps) using the established usability checklist. We compared the results with the proposed usability checklist.

Research Questions (RQs).

- What are the elements of the graphical user interface (GUI) of an AI mHealth application and what are the usability principles of the user interfaces for AI mHealth applications?
- How to develop of a usability checklist for the user interface in AI mHealth applications?
- What is the comparison between the usability principles of the AI mHealth application and the usability checklist? To what extent does the AI UI usability evaluation influence the graphical user interface and overall user experience of mHealth applications?

2   Related Research

Big Data and Artificial Intelligence (AI) have become increasingly prevalent in the healthcare industry in recent years. The fundamentals and guidelines for the implementation of mHealth applications, as well as the obstacles encountered with regard to quality, usability, user engagement, and behavioral modification, are discussed by Deniz-Garcia et al. [10]. Despite this, the Human Machine Interface (HMI) is crucial to effectively operating these AI technologies and delivering an exceptional user experience [30]. However, the usability of user interface considerations in AI applications for healthcare remains understudied. Several papers provide design guidelines for the usability of AI-based mHealth applications to address this deficiency [4, 18, 30]. This study investigates the usability of the user interfaces of AI mobile health (mHealth) applications.

Zhang and Adipat assert that appropriate research methodologies must be developed and implemented to assess the usability of mobile applications [33]. Multiple studies have developed usability evaluation checklists for mobile phone user interfaces in light of this perspective [14, 17, 29]. Utilizing task-based usability checklists, these studies assessed the usability of mobile phone user interfaces [6, 14]. Nonetheless, the visual checklist has certain constraints, mostly notably the insufficient details regarding the gravity of the identified usability issues. The precision of these visual checklists and the thoroughness of the usability evaluation criteria are both substandard when attempting to assess the usability of the user interface of an AI-powered mHealth application. To fill this research gap, the current study improves the checklist for the graphical user interface of AI-powered mHealth applications.

3   UI Elements in AI mHealth Application

To ascertain user interface components about mobile phone user interfaces, Ji et al. gathered and analyzed style guides provided by several mobile phone manufacturers, including SK Telecom, Nokia, Verizon, and Sprint. Following the classification of the analyzed data by the keywords in the style guide documents, 86 elements of the graphical user interface were gathered [14]. The structure of the style guide was established by classifying and assembling the elements examined in terms of their relationships [14]. This study collects and analyses, by the structure of this guide, the distinctive features of the user interface of mHealth applications powered by artificial intelligence (AI). During this study's preliminary phase of data collection, a compilation of the attributes of AI in mobile health (mHealth) applications was amassed (Table 1). The attributes of AI mHealth applications, including Sensely, WebMD, Noom, Youper, Beijing Spring Rain Software CO., LTD., and SkinVision, are detailed in Table 1. The elements that should be emphasized in the user interface of AI health applications are conversational AI functions (Table 1). For instance, the AI function in WebMD and Youper is chatbots, the most prominent feature of the user interface of AI mHealth applications. A visual checklist should include the visual elements of chatbots to illustrate their usability in the mHealth user interface. Brandtzaeg and Følstad state that the domain of human-computer interaction (HCI) continues to confront significant obstacles, including conversational user interfaces such as chatbots [5]. In addition to AI changing the interface between users and technology, chatbots are changing user behavior and usage patterns [5]. In order to enhance user experience and usability of user interfaces, the increased interactivity of conversational user interfaces such as chatbots presents a challenge; thus, several distinct usability questions of chatbots will be added to the visual checklist for developing mHealth applications for AI tailored explicitly for chatbots.

According to Pirrone et al., integrating linguistic and graphical modes in chatbots enables the development of systems featuring interfaces that can be reconfigured based on the particular application context [23]. Chatbot user interface is often chatbot software that mimics a conversation with a natural person via text or voice. The user interface

Table 1. The characteristics exhibited by these Artificial Intelligence (AI) mobile health (mHealth) applications.

Name	Category	Rating	Language	AI Function
Sensely	Medical	4.6	English, Arabic, Dutch, Japanese, Simplified Chinese, Traditional Chinese	Conversational AI
WebMD	Health	4.8	English, Spanish	AI Chatbots
Noom	Health Coaching	3.8	English, German, Korean, Spanish	AI Statistics
Youper	Health & Fitness	4.7	English	AI Chat-bot
Beijing Spring Rain Software CO., LTD	Medical	4.8	Simplified Chinese	Conversational AI
SkinVision	Medical	3.7	English, Dutch, French, German, Italian, Polish, Spanish	AI Algorithm

design of a chatbot application plays a vital role in providing users with a seamless and user-friendly experience. Simultaneously, the chatbot's elements involve designing the application's layout, navigation and visual elements to ensure easy interaction and understanding. The usability of the chatbot app's user interface should be intuitive, visually appealing and responsive to different devices. It should also include features such as chat logs, input fields and clear call-to-action phrase buttons. Designing an effective chatbot app user interface requires consideration of the target audience, the usability and the specific features it provides.

Consequently, there needs to be standardized tools to assess the usability of the user interface to improve user satisfaction with the experience of using chatbots and conversational agents. Borsci et al. developed two tools to test chatbots: (i) a diagnostic tool in the form of a checklist (BOT-Check) and (ii) a 15-item questionnaire [4]. This study will combine these two tools to build the usability checklist for AI mHealth applications user interface. Designers can use it to assess the usability of AI mHealth applications' user interface, thus creating an independent GUI database for future evaluations of their reliability, validity, and sensitivity.

4 Development of Usability Checklist in AI mHealth Application

During the initial stage, data was gathered and examined from prior research regarding usability principles and user interface components of AI mHealth applications. Section 3 notes that the user interface elements of AI mHealth applications placed greater emphasis on AI functionality than the user interfaces of mHealth applications. The chatbot component's usability is critical to user interface elements in AI mHealth applications.

In the second stage, the results of a literature review we conducted on usability issues were compiled into tenets of usability that are crucial to remember when designing the user interface for mobile phone software. Simultaneously, this usability study develops a checklist questionnaire about usability objectives, which encompass the following: ease of recall, usability, effectiveness, safety, usability, and good utility [19]. A meticulous process was employed to classify the compiled usability principles to select, eliminate, and incorporate them into a framework. Subsequently, a questionnaire checklist (Appendix A) about the corresponding usability principles was formulated for a user interface element in the AI mHealth app. The questionnaire checklist is designed to be comprehensible and functional for developers and usability experts.

4.1 Components of the Graphical User Interface for the AI mHealth Application

Product engineers must know the user interface components for the AI mHealth application before designing the interface of the mHealth prototype application. According to Al Kuwaiti et al., the functions of AI in health imaging and diagnostics, health research and drug delivery, rehabilitation, virtual patient care, patient engagement and compliance, and administrative applications are the functions of AI in healthcare [2]. Simultaneously, the necessity of considering the usability of the functionality of dialogue tools and chatbots is highlighted in relevant studies concerning the usability of the user interface of AI mHealth applications. Abashev et al. illustrate the chatbot system. By excluding the technical aspect of artificial intelligence from their investigation, they directed the usability assessment of the chatbot user interface towards the conversational chat button [1]. The study by Camargo et al. describes in great detail that building a visual checklist for graphical user interface (GUI) evaluation should be done from six elements: color, typography, UI, Layout, Pattern, and Component [6]. Based on these six elements, the study explores the GUI evaluation elements of the AI mHealth application user interface. Table 1 describes the AI mHealth application function as Conversational AI and Chatbots. Meanwhile, Janarthanam states that there are four elements that designers can utilize to create a good experience for the chatbot user interface: text, emoticons, video/images, and dialogue flow [13]. Therefore, the main direction in building a visual checklist for usability is to focus on the six elements of Conversational AI and Chatbots - Color, Typography, UI, Layout, Pattern, Component and the element of Conversation UI.

4.2 Usability Principles of AI mHealth Application

World Health Organization's core ethical principles for the use of artificial intelligence in medicine: Protect autonomy; promote human well-being, human safety, and the public interest; ensure transparency, explain ability, and intelligibility; Foster responsibility and accountability; ensure inclusiveness and equity; promote artificial intelligence that is responsive and sustainable. We explore the Usability principles of AI mHealth applications based on the above ethical principles.

Nielsen states 10 Usability Heuristics for User Interface Design: visibility, contextual relevance, user controllability, consistency, accessibility, error-proofing, efficiency and flexibility, beauty and simplicity, fault-tolerance, and human assistance [20]. These principles are mainly used to evaluate the good or bad user experience, whether product managers or designers can use these ten principles for self-checking. The ten guiding principles of usability cover topics such as visual design, readability and comprehensibility, navigation, feedback, notifications, help resources and troubleshooting, historical data, accessibility and app evaluation. The guidelines are intended to guide mHealth stakeholders in developing secure and intuitive applications while meeting the needs of the target user in a given usage environment.

Usability principles are not a panacea, but they can circumvent some of the apparent problems and assist us in creating designs that are more responsive to the user experience. There will be instances where multiple principles are used for cross-purposes in different scenarios. Therefore, usability principles should be analyzed on a case-by-case basis, and the results of a mixed-methods study by Liew et al. show that mHealth industry insiders and consumers agree in prioritizing several usability attributes, particularly satisfaction, learnability and efficiency of mHealth apps [16]. However, the level of concern for these attributes varies. The usability category in Table 2 will be referred to in constructing a visual checklist of usability issues so that the created checklist can be considered as a diagnostic tool for app user interface usability.

4.3 Usability Checklist of the AI mHealth Applications

The development of the AI mHealth applications visual checklist was primarily based on recommended usability heuristics [3, 9, 19, 20, 22] and basic visual design principles and elements [6, 12, 23]. In addition, seven relevant checklists [6, 14, 21, 22, 24, 29, 32] were referenced and analyzed during the development process, which helped to define the product's GUI usability criteria. The checklists should.

1. Assist in GUI usability evaluation, especially for conversational UI.
2. Be a useful and easy-to-use resource for the development team.
3. Provide control over activities and evaluations.
4. Apply to users of different ages and occupations.

The structure of the visual checklist in Appendix A starts with seven main topics, which are then subdivided into 47 validation items. Checkboxes border each item to allow the team to control the assessment process. The checklist is designed to assess desktop interfaces and should be used by professionals with a specific theoretical background. Ideally, the checklist should be used after the design of the GUI and before its implementation to prevent and correct errors (e.g., contrast problems, poor readability, metaphorical failures, standardization issues, lack of overall consistency and uniformity, etc.) before coding begins. We collected and analyzed information from previous studies on usability principles and user interface elements of the AI mHealth application, which focuses more on the AI function- chatbot than the mobile health application user interface. Therefore, the usability of the chatbot component is placed at the bottom of the checklist when building the hierarchy of user interface elements. At the same time, this usability study builds a checklist questionnaire for usability goals, including easy to remember how to use, efficient to use, practical to use, good utility, safe to use, and easy to learn.

5   Usability Evaluation with Usability Checklist in AI mHealth Applications

5.1   The Process of Usability Evaluation

A panel of evaluators will assess the user interface using a heuristic approach to determine its compliance with generally accepted usability principles. The six-step heuristic evaluation procedure is as follows:

1. Five online-enlisted evaluators were selected for their familiarity with user interfaces and practical experience with the product being assessed.
2. The user interface checklist for the AI mHealth application, developed in Sect. 4 (see appendix A), was employed to ascertain usability principles and compile a list of usability questions.
3. The evaluator conducts the assessment using the Sensely application, one of the AI mHealth applications.
4. The evaluator initiates the evaluation process and assesses each component of the evaluation object using the usability checklist (Appendix A) and their expertise and understanding. The evaluator then compiles a written report on the evaluation object.
5. Consolidate the findings and include them in Sect. 5.2.
6. Elucidate the significance of the usability checklist as delineated in Sect. 6. Generate a list of usability concerns, converse regarding said concerns, and suggest enhancement strategies.

5.2   Result

Many studies have shown that usability evaluations can identify design problems in healthcare information systems and applications. However, more research needs to be done on the usability of AI mHealth application user interfaces. Nielsen notes that the probability of identifying a significant usability problem is higher than the probability of identifying a minor problem in a heuristic evaluation [19]. In this study, five trained usability evaluators were invited to independently evaluate the usability of the user interface of the Sensely application, which is one of the AI mHealth applications, using a visual checklist (Appendix A). The evaluators consolidated the identified issues into a list and independently rated the severity of the problems. The severity of usability issues was categorized into five levels: No problem, Cosmetic, Minor, Major, and Catastrophe [3].

The severity of usability problems:

- 0 (No problem), I do not think it is a usability problem at all.
- 1(Cosmetic), just a surface problem: no need to fix it unless the project has extra time.
- 2(Minor), minor usability problem: fixing it is a low priority.
- 3(Major), serious usability problem: fixing it is a high priority.
- 4(Cosmetic), just a surface issue: it only needs to be addressed if the project has extra time.

As can be seen from the description in Table 2, the results of this illuminating evaluation indicate that a total of 10 usability problems were identified for the GUI of the AI mHealth APP and conversational AI features. The highest level of mismatch with usability principles was for chatbot usability (Severity of usability problems: 3), and the lowest was for 'colors and graphics' (Severity of usability problems: 0). The average severity of problems ranged from 0 (No problem) to 3 (Catastrophe) (Fig. 1).

Table 2. Identified usability problems of Heuristic evaluation by one of Artificial Intelligence (AI) mobile health (mHealth) applications.

Usability principles	Usability problem of user interface	Severity of usability problems
Usability	The functionality of screen of the task usability	2
User control and freedom	Users can easily undo, redo, cancel or exit the actions they have taken on the interface	1
Consistency and standards	The user interface has a consistent, easily identifiable 'look & feel'	2
Functionality	The functions of the interface are easily accessible, and the app plays a relatively minor role in the functional content of the consultation, according to the checklist	1
Flexibility and efficiency of use		2
Aesthetic and minimalist design	Visualization of important information requires further improvement There are optimization options for error-prone interfaces	1
Color & Graphics	Weak color combinations, inappropriate for elderly rural users	0
Layout	There is usability for Chinese rural users	1
Typeface	The size of the text difficult to read	1
Chatbot	Users notes that they did not know how to use the AI chatbot function	3

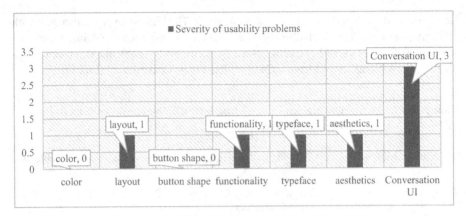

Fig. 1. Severity of usability problems of AI mHealth App (Sensely).

6 Discussion

Could the integration of conversational chatbots and the advent of AI technology eliminate the mHealth application's graphical user interface? Based on the existing user interface and checklist feedback of AI mHealth applications, it is evident that conversational AI and chatbots need to be fully capable of substituting other functional interfaces within the mHealth application, including those for product purchases, history management, advice seeking, and the primary focus of user interface usability research revolves around the interests and needs of the users. The most significant contribution we aim to make with this research is to optimize the user interface design of the application and improve the overall user experience via usability evaluation, which is made possible by the advancement of AI technology.

Previous research suggests that the human-machine interface (HMI) remains crucial for the effective operation of AI technologies and the delivery of an outstanding user experience. Therefore, to improve user experience, Sect. 3 examines the interface components of the graphical user interface (GUI) of the AI mHealth application. The usability checklist advances from precise and uniform user interface elements to the quality of speech and text in chatbot responses throughout the investigation (Appendix A). From the results of Sect. 5 via the checklist, it is clear that the graphical user interface has some degree of influence on the chatbot user experience. The latest advancements in artificial intelligence have made it possible to revive the conversational user interface of the AI mHealth app. The mHealth app with AI integrates conversational AI and AI chatbots, distinguishing it from traditional mHealth apps. Regardless of the evolution of AI technology, it is imperative that designers continually revise their graphical user interfaces in order to maximize the user experience.

This study uses a visual checklist to examine the usability of artificial intelligence graphical user interfaces (GUIs) in mobile healthcare applications. The checklist aims to assess the user interface elements of AI in mobile healthcare apps from a user-centered perspective and thoroughly evaluate possible usability concerns. The visual checklist assesses the graphical user interfaces (GUIs) of artificial intelligence in mobile healthcare applications. It establishes a hierarchical relationship among various design elements, including aesthetics, color, layout, typography, button shapes, navigation, and fonts. The second research phase determined that the visual inventory positively impacted identifying usability issues with AI GUIs in mobile healthcare apps and contributed to optimizing visual standards for AI user interfaces in mobile healthcare apps. This resource offers constructive recommendations for application developers in creating artificial intelligence graphical user interfaces (GUIs) within application prototypes.

7 Conclusion

The present study provides a synopsis of the UI Elements and Usability Principles of AI mHealth Applications. Furthermore, this research endeavors to create a task- and usability-based visual checklist (Appendix A). This checklist will enable a rapid and exhaustive assessment of the usability concerns of AI graphical user interfaces (GUIs) in mHealth applications. Its purpose is to analyze and ascertain whether the AI user interfaces in mHealth applications adhere to the established usability principles in user interfaces. In addition, this visual checklist can compile the usability principles and hierarchy of user interface design elements for AI innovative interface design elements in mHealth applications so that users are not confused by the AI user interface functionality in the graphical user interfaces of mHealth applications. This checklist will ensure consistency and standardization in user interfaces for AI mHealth applications. The primary foundation of the essential usability checklist formulated in this research is widely employed heuristics. Its objective is to evaluate every software user interface component of a mobile phone as perceived by the developer of said device. It is advisable that forthcoming research consistently revise the checklist to incorporate additional inquiries regarding the usability of chatbot user interface elements and conversational AI.

Appendix A

The Checklist for Graphical User interface (GUI) of AI mHealth application.
(Source: Developed by the authors, drawing on Microsoft Word, 2024)

Usability of mHealth App	Compliance			
	Always	Sometimes	Never	Notes
The app was easy to use				
I would need the assistance of a technical professional to use the App				
I felt very comfortable using the app				
I found the app to be somewhat cumbersome to use				
The user interface promotes clear and fast communication				

(*continued*)

(continued)

Usability of mHealth App	Compliance			
	Always	Sometimes	Never	Notes
Consistency	**Compliance**			
	Always	Sometimes	Never	Notes
The user interface has a consistent, easily identifiable 'look & feel'				
The graphical user interface effectively uses repeating visual themes to unify the app				
Even without graphics, it remains visually consistent				
Color	**Compliance**			
	Always	Sometimes	Never	Notes
I thought there was too much color inconsistency in this app				
I found the app's colors to be harsh				
I discovered that the app text color is inaccessible with a sufficient contrast ratio against the background color				
I found that the interface has an excessive amount of font/color variation				
Graphics	**Compliance**			
	Always	Sometimes	Never	Notes
All graphics are correctly aligned				
The graphics ensure that all command buttons are of similar size and shape, with the same font and font size				
Text wraps properly around images/graphics				
Even without graphics, it remains visually consistent				
Fonts	**Compliance**			
	Always	Sometimes	Never	Notes
All fonts should be the same				
All screen prompts are specified in the correct screen font				
If you need to return to a previous page, the content remains intact				
All text is properly aligned				
Conversational chatbot	**Compliance**			
	Always	Sometimes	Never	Notes
The chatbot can quickly respond to user queries				
The chatbot's conversational flow and coherence is very good				

(continued)

(continued)

Usability of mHealth App	Compliance			
	Always	Sometimes	Never	Notes
The chatbot displays a message of error				
The chatbot possessed a realistic and captivating personality				
Too robotic appeared the chatbot				
The chatbot effectively described its scope and function				
The chatbot goes by its script without listening to the user's responses, which seems rather ironic				
Graphical user interface of chatbot	**Compliance**			
	Always	Sometimes	Never	Notes
Good choice of calm and relaxing colors				
Friendly designs and cute characters				
Prioritizing user safety with elements such as emergency buttons				
Easy navigation between different features offered by the chatbot				
User journey focused on personalizing the experience				

References

1. Abashev, A., Grigoryev, R., Grigorian, K., Boyko, V.: Programming tools for messenger-based chatbot system organization: implication for outpatient and translational medicines. BioNanoScience 7(2), 403–407 (2017)
2. Al Kuwaiti, A., et al.: A review of the role of artificial intelligence in healthcare. J. Person. Med. 13(6), 951 (2023)
3. Atashi, A., Khajouei, R., Azizi, A., Dadashi, A.: User Interface problems of a nationwide inpatient information system: a heuristic evaluation. Appl. Clin. Inform. 7(01), 89–100 (2016)
4. Borsci, S., et al.: The Chatbot Usability Scale: the design and pilot of a usability scale for interaction with AI-based (2022)
5. Brandtzaeg, P.B., Følstad, A.: Chatbots: changing user needs and motivations. Interactions 25(5), 38–43 (2018)
6. Camargo, M.C., Barros, R.M., Barros, V.T.: Visual design checklist for graphical user interface (GUI) evaluation. In: Paper presented at the proceedings of the 33rd annual ACM symposium on applied computing (2018)
7. Choi, W., Tulu, B.: Effective use of user interface and user experience in an mHealth application (2017)
8. Costa, P., Paiva, A.C., Nabuco, M.: Pattern based GUI testing for mobile applications. In: Paper presented at the 2014 9th international conference on the quality of information and communications technology (2014)

9. de Lima Salgado, A., Freire, A.P.: Heuristic evaluation of mobile usability: A mapping study. In: Paper presented at the human-computer interaction. applications and services: 16th international conference, HCI international 2014, Heraklion, Crete, Greece, June 22–27, 2014, Proceedings, Part III 16 (2014)

10. Deniz-Garcia, A., et al.: Quality, usability, and effectiveness of mHealth apps and the role of artificial intelligence: current scenario and challenges. J. Med. Internet Res. **25**, e44030 (2023)

11. Holmes, S., Moorhead, A., Bond, R., Zheng, H., Coates, V., McTear, M.: Usability testing of a healthcare chatbot: Can we use conventional methods to assess conversational user interfaces? In: Paper presented at the proceedings of the 31st european conference on cognitive ergonomics (2019)

12. Issa, A., Sillito, J., Garousi, V.: Visual testing of graphical user interfaces: An exploratory study towards systematic definitions and approaches. In: Paper presented at the 2012 14th IEEE international symposium on web systems evolution (WSE) (2012)

13. Janarthanam, S.: Hands-on chatbots and conversational UI development: build chatbots and voice user interfaces with Chatfuel, Dialogflow, Microsoft Bot Framework, Twilio, and Alexa Skills: Packt Publishing Ltd. (2017)

14. Ji, Y.G., Park, J.H., Lee, C., Yun, M.H.: A usability checklist for the usability evaluation of mobile phone user interface. Int. J. Hum.-Comput. Interact. **20**(3), 207–231 (2006)

15. Kirkscey, R.: MHealth apps for older adults: a method for development and user experience design evaluation. J. Tech. Writ. Commun. **51**(2), 199–217 (2021). https://doi.org/10.1177/0047281620907939

16. Liew, M.S., Zhang, J., See, J., Ong, Y.L.: Usability challenges for health and wellness mobile apps: mixed-methods study among mHealth experts and consumers. JMIR Mhealth Uhealth **7**(1), e12160 (2019)

17. Mochammad Aldi, K., Harry Budi, S., Panca, O.H.P., Martin, S.: Evaluating user experience of a mobile health application 'Halodoc' using user experience questionnaire and usability testing. Jurnal Sistem Informasi **17**(1), 58–71 (2021). https://doi.org/10.21609/jsi.v17i1.1063

18. Mubeen, M., et al.: Usability evaluation of pandemic health care mobile applications. In: Paper presented at the IOP conference series: earth and environmental science (2021)

19. Nielsen, J.: Finding usability problems through heuristic evaluation. In: Paper presented at the Proceedings of the SIGCHI conference on Human factors in computing systemsv

20. Nielsen, J.: Enhancing the explanatory power of usability heuristics. In: Paper presented at the proceedings of the SIGCHI conference on human factors in computing systems (1994)

21. Petrovčič, A., Taipale, S., Rogelj, A., Dolničar, V.: Design of mobile phones for older adults: an empirical analysis of design guidelines and checklists for feature phones and smartphones. Int. J. Hum.-Comput. Interact. **34**(3), 251–264 (2018)

22. Pierotti, D.: Heuristic evaluation-a system checklist. Xerox Corporation 12 (1995)

23. Pirrone, R., Russo, G., Cannella, V., Peri, D.: GAIML: a new language for verbal and graphical interaction in chatbots. Mob. Inf. Syst. **4**(3), 195–209 (2008)

24. Richardson, B., Campbell-Yeo, M., Smit, M.: Mobile application user experience checklist: a tool to assess attention to core UX principles. Int. J. Hum.-Comput. Int. **37**(13), 1283–1290 (2021)

25. Ross, J., Gao, J.: Overcoming the language barrier in mobile user interface design: A case study on a mobile health app. arXiv preprint arXiv:1605.04693 (2016)

26. Schnall, R., et al.: A user-centered model for designing consumer mobile health (mHealth) applications (apps). J. Biomed. Inform. **60**, 243–251 (2016)

27. Shaban-Nejad, A., Michalowski, M., Buckeridge, D.L.: Health intelligence: how artificial intelligence transforms population and personalized health. NPJ Dig. Med. **1**(1), 53 (2018). https://doi.org/10.1038/s41746-018-0058-9

28. Sousa, P., Sabugueiro, D., Felizardo, V., Couto, R., Pires, I., Garcia, N.: mHealth sensors and applications for personal aid. Mobile Health: A Technology Road Map, 265–281 (2015)
29. Tu, C.J., Russo, A.: Visual design checklist for glucose monitor app user interface usability evaluation. In: Paper presented at the international conference on human-computer interaction (2023)
30. Wiebelitz, L., Schmid, P., Maier, T., Volkwein, M.: Designing user-friendly medical AI applications-methodical development of user-centered design guidelines. In: Paper presented at the 2022 IEEE international conference on digital health (ICDH) (2022)
31. Xu, J., Ding, X., Huang, K., Chen, G.: A pilot study of an inspection framework for automated usability guideline reviews of mobile health applications. In: Proceedings of the Wireless Health 2014 on National Institutes of Health, pp. 1–8 (2014)
32. Yazdanmehr, E., Shoghi, S.: Design and application of a 'Textbook visual effects' evaluation checklist. Theory Pract. Lang. Stud. **4**(3) (2014)
33. Zhang, D., Adipat, B.: Challenges, methodologies, and issues in the usability testing of mobile applications. Int. J. Hum.-Comput. Interact. **18**(3), 293–308 (2005)

Research on User Experience Evaluation System of Popular Science Games Based on Analytic Hierarchy Process

Yu Wan and Yide Zhou[✉]

Kunming University of Science and Technology, Kunming 650500, China
izyd@qq.com

Abstract. The main purpose of this study is to establish a systematic evaluation index system and conduct research on popular science games from the perspective of user experience. Firstly, the user experience index system of popular science games is established through a comprehensive literature analysis and the application of the Delphi method, informed by thorough research into the characteristics of these games. Subsequently, relevant data from experts are collected, and the weight coefficients for each index are determined using the analytic hierarchy process. Finally, we employ the evaluation index system to assess and discuss the design of Mortise and Tenon for popular science games. This paper presents a user experience evaluation index system for popular science games comprising four dimensions: sensory experience, learning experience, interactive experience, and emotional experience, encompassing a total of 20 evaluation indexes. The research findings indicate that the learning experience and emotional experience significantly influence users' experiences with popular science games, while sensory experiences and interactive experiences assume secondary roles. The proposed evaluation index system facilitates comprehensive and systematic evaluations of popular science games, offering theoretical references for design evaluations and iterative optimization.

Keywords: popular science game · user experience evaluation · AHP

1 Introduction

According to the 52nd Statistical Report on Internet Development in China, published by the China Internet Network Information Center (CNNIC) on August 28, 2023, the number of Internet users in China reached 1.079 billion as of June 2023. Among them, the number of online game users in China stands at 550 million, constituting 51.0% of the total Internet user population [1]. Online games have introduced a diverse array of virtual experiences to individuals and have gradually emerged as a primary form of entertainment in daily life. Concurrently, as the gaming industry has grown and expanded, various debates have arisen regarding its merits and drawbacks. This has prompted industry professionals and society at large to reflect on and explore the positive values associated with gaming. To fully leverage the societal value of games, popular science games have emerged as a burgeoning focal point within the domain of electronic gaming.

The popularization of science through gaming is an innovative approach in the digital and information age, where electronic games serve as a medium. This approach aims to disseminate scientific knowledge by utilizing popular science games as digital learning tools, providing an entertaining experience while fulfilling their scientific and functional goals. According to China's plan for the popularization of science and the enhancement of scientific quality, it is imperative to enhance the generation and dissemination of high-quality resources for science popularization, while intensifying efforts in diversifying novel forms of high-quality products for science popularization. Emerging as a novel facet of science outreach, popular science games, characterized by their capacity for media and boundary-free communication, play a pivotal role in bolstering public engagement and initiative. They contribute significantly to elevating public awareness and comprehension of scientific knowledge, thereby fostering an overall improvement in the scientific acumen of the populace. However, as a nascent form of business, popular science games still lack practical results and theoretical research to a certain extent. Simultaneously, they face the development dilemma of unbalanced knowledge and gameplay. The emphasis placed by popular science game designers and developers on disseminating and conceptualizing scientific content affects users' experience and learning enthusiasm in these games, making it challenging to achieve the desired product experience expectation. Consequently, designing high-quality popular science games that meet user needs while ensuring continued usage has become an urgent research focus for designers.

In the field of popular science game research, the predominant focus has been on technological development and theoretical investigations, with limited attention given to user perspectives [2–4]. Furthermore, there remains a dearth of empirical exploration concerning the evaluation of product design in popular science games, particularly lacking a systematic index system for guiding and assessing user experience. In the era of the experiential economy, satisfaction with functional requirements alone no longer suffices as an indicator for measuring product success. Instead, user experience has emerged as a crucial factor. By discussing user experience evaluation concerning popular science games, designers and developers can effectively enhance the quality of users' experiences while engaging in scientific learning activities. This can lead to increased retention rates and usage durations among users while subtly influencing their level of scientific literacy. Therefore, this paper aims to construct an index system for evaluating the user experience in popular science games based on their fundamental attributes while incorporating existing research findings on such games and established systems for evaluating user experience design. This evaluation index system will be applied to analyze the Mortise and Tenon Project's game offerings to identify shortcomings in current popular science game products and propose future development strategies.

2   Product Features and Elements

2.1   User Experience Characteristics of Popular Science Games

The concept of user experience was initially proposed by cognitive psychologist Don Norman at the 1995 International Conference on Human Factors in Computer Systems (CHI). Due to the inherent fuzziness and dynamic nature of user experience, there is no universally standardized definition or evaluation framework. The most widely accepted definition stems from the international standard ISO9241-210, which defines user experience as the perception and response elicited when using or anticipating the use of a product, system, or service. It emphasizes capturing users' holistic experiences before, during, and after usage encompassing emotions, beliefs, preferences, cognitive impressions, physiological and psychological responses, as well as behaviors and achievements [5]. The user experience evaluation of popular science games encompasses not only the assessment of their educational value but also a comprehensive examination of product usability, convenient and smooth operation modes, reasonable game mechanisms, enjoyable gaming experiences, and comfortable operational interfaces throughout all stages and processes. These comprehensive experiences are shaped by learners' perceptions of both rational elements (such as efficiency, usability, reliability, stability, and security closely related to the functionality and software performance) and emotional elements (including visual appeal, pleasure derived from flow experiences facilitated by popular science games, as well as embedded scientific content with goal-oriented values).

2.2   User Experience Elements of Popular Science Games

User Analysis of Popular Science Games. The target audience of popular science games is the general public, and the scientific information they encompass originates from various sources including government institutions, universities, research organizations, scientific communities, media outlets, and social organizations. As a form of science popularization, popular science games essentially serve as a means to transform the "private information" within the scientific community into "shared information" accessible by society at large. In other words, it facilitates top-down science education. Given that these games do not have explicit user restrictions and cater to user groups with shared interests in acquiring scientific knowledge, it becomes imperative to consider the cognitive abilities of different groups during their design phase. Gradually increasing the level of difficulty in knowledge presentation aligns with public cognitive logic while providing effective guidance and help documentation for novice players.

Product Analysis of Popular Science Games. Popular science games possess the dual attributes of scientific knowledge and entertainment, distinguishing them from conventional electronic games. The primary objective of popular science games is to enhance public scientific literacy by enabling individuals to acquire scientific and technological knowledge, develop scientific thinking skills, employ scientific methods, and embrace a scientific mindset through experiential learning. The development and design of popular science games should strike a balance, avoiding excessive prioritization of cognitive effects at the expense of gameplay design. Similarly, an exclusive pursuit of entertainment experience must not compromise the depth of educational content. It is imperative to provide users with an enjoyable learning experience by creating an effective gamified environment that fully engages participants in game-based learning processes while offering immersive gaming experiences. This transformation facilitates a shift from passive information reception to active input-driven modes of learning, subtly fostering the acquisition of knowledge, skills, intelligence, emotions, attitudes, as well as values within the realm of play. Flow is a psychological state characterized by intense concentration that arises spontaneously during engagement in an intrinsically interesting task. Psychologist Mihaly Csikszentmihalyi [6] delineates eight pivotal attributes of flow states: (1) tasks that are engaging and commensurate with individual skill levels; (2) intensified concentration and focus; (3) well-defined task objectives; (4) prompt feedback; (5) sense of mastery; (6) temporary relief from external concerns and worries; (7) attainment of self-transcendence, followed by reemergence of self-awareness upon completion; and (8) cognitive bias towards time. Norman [7] outlined the essential prerequisites for an effective learning environment as follows: (1) fostering a highly interactive and feedback-driven setting; (2) establishing clear objectives and predefined procedures; (3) implementing incentivization mechanisms; (4) maintaining a sense of continuous challenge; (5) reinforcing a sense of direct participation; (6) providing appropriate tools for task accomplishment; and (7) minimizing interference or disruptions that may impede the learner's experience. The ARCS motivation design model, proposed by American educator Keller [8], encompasses four fundamental strategies aimed at enhancing learning motivation: Attention, Relevance, Confidence, and Satisfaction. These strategies are respectively associated with the following elements: goal setting, challenging tasks, constructive feedback, and personal interest. In conclusion, there is a corresponding relationship between an effective learning environment and flow experience, and flow experience contains four basic elements to stimulate learning motivation. Therefore, creating an effective learning environment in popular science games can help users achieve immersive experiences through self-learning under internal drive while integrating popular science with entertainment.

Situational Analysis of Popular Science Games. The game contexts of popular science games should align with the scientific information objectives, tasks, and content requirements embedded within them. It is crucial to establish game tasks that cater to different types of knowledge while seamlessly integrating complex scientific principles and development processes into gameplay. Furthermore, various types of popular science games emphasize distinct aspects. Professional knowledge-based popular science games prioritize the professionalism and rigor of their content, whereas basic knowledge-oriented ones aim to enhance the public's comprehension of scientific knowledge by focusing on accessibility and product usability. And skill-based popular science games strive to cultivate practical scientific and technological skills among users, placing greater emphasis on immersive experiences and seamless interactions. Therefore, when designing and developing popular science games, it is essential to prioritize user experience factors that are suitable for each specific scenario.

3   Methodology

This research employs a combination of qualitative and quantitative methodologies. The user experience indicators of popular science games are derived through literature analysis and the Delphi method, followed by constructing a hierarchical architecture composed of these indicators. Finally, expert data is collected to establish a judgment matrix for determining the relative importance of each indicator and calculating their respective weight coefficients.

3.1   The Theoretical Basis for the Development of Standards

Research on user experience evaluation of popular science games can establish game design standards for popular science service institutions to enhance game quality and user experience, thereby supporting the development of a new popular science ecosystem. Popular science games, categorized as serious games, undergo evaluation through three main aspects: learning effects, technical dimensions (including usability, functionality, and interactivity), and simplified evaluation methods [9]. Additionally, the field of game evaluation research has witnessed the emergence of several mature evaluation systems such as the TEEM Teacher Evaluation Framework [10], Rubric for Assessing or Designing Digital Playful Learning Space [11], and Serious Educational Game Rubric [12], among others. These evaluation index systems offer comprehensive assessment criteria and design guidelines tailored for the application of popular science games.

3.2   Dimension Determination

The research on user experience evaluation of popular science games is still in its early stage, lacking substantial research findings and a unified and standardized evaluation framework. Synthesizing and scrutinizing relevant research findings on product user experience evaluation can provide valuable insights for determining the indices dimensions in this study. Hassenzahl et al. [13] conducted research on user experience from three dimensions: user needs, emotional experiences, and interactive products. Park et al. [14] highlighted that the elements of user experience encompass five aspects: availability, usefulness, ease of use, efficiency, and satisfaction. Garret [15] suggests that user experience includes users' perceptions of brand characteristics, information availability, functionality, and content. Schmitt [16] proposed a user experience system primarily composed of five experiences: sense, feel, think, act, and relate. Law [17] argues that the key components of user experience are perceived pleasure, enjoyment, sensory quality, functional aesthetics, and overall satisfaction. Ahmed et al. [18] divided the dimensions of learning information system user experience into attraction, efficiency, clarity, stimulation, reliability, and novelty. According to the findings of the literature research, despite the absence of a unified standard for evaluating user experience in existing product evaluation systems, research by foreign scholars predominantly focuses on exploring users' cognitive and emotional experiences. Furthermore, considering the dual nature of science popularization games as both educational tools and entertainment products, it is essential to consider their educational objectives and interactive gaming experiences. In summary, based on the literature review and the characteristics of popular science games, this study categorizes the dimensions for evaluating user experience in popular science games into three levels: sensory experience, learning experience, interactive experience, and emotional experience.

3.3 Index Determination

Sensory Experience. Sensory experience primarily refers to the direct physiological response elicited by a product through stimulation of an individual's sensory system, including vision, hearing, touch, taste, and smell. This encompasses the user's intuitive perception of the product's appearance, color, texture, and other attributes. In popular science games, the interface's color scheme significantly influences users' first impressions and their willingness to use it. Thus, ensuring coordinated color combinations is crucial. Additionally, the rational and orderly arrangement of functional blocks on the game interface can prevent interruptions in operation fluency while reducing the cognitive load that may affect user concentration. Finally, effective information transmission requires accurate and straightforward conveyance of information via text or multimedia carriers such as pictures or animations. Based on the aforementioned content, this paper presents a comprehensive analysis of specific indicators encompassing dimensions of sensory experience, including Color Style, Clear layout, and Clear message.

Learning Experience. The learning experience pertains to the process by which users acquire knowledge, skills, and understanding within the specific learning environment provided by popular science games, thereby reflecting the educational and scientific characteristics inherent in such games. During the design and development of popular science games, it is crucial to ensure congruence between game context, content, scientific objectives, and task requirements so that users can effectively apply acquired scientific knowledge to real-life situations. Furthermore, popular science games possess educational goals that should be centered around mechanics and storylines while ensuring clear communication of mission objectives to users along with a comprehensive grasp of conveyed scientific concepts throughout gameplay. Simultaneously, content should prioritize practical value alongside an appropriate increase in professional awareness to enable the effective enhancement of participants' scientific skills and knowledge. Considering the gradual process of public cognition, the content of popular science games needs to possess a comprehensive and coherent logical structure, progressively increasing task difficulty following user cognitive patterns while sequentially imparting relevant knowledge and skills. Furthermore, appropriate feedback should be provided during gameplay to enable users to perceive their knowledge absorption and skill enhancement. The content of popular science games must strictly adhere to scientific principles, avoiding any dissemination of misleading or inaccurate information that may misguide the public, thereby ensuring the accuracy and effectiveness of the final learning outcome. Lastly, adequate tools and comprehensive instructions should be provided within the game interface to prevent disruption in user experience caused by operational or cognitive difficulties as these tools serve as crucial incentives for enhancing persistence and playability. Therefore, this paper provides a comprehensive overview of the specific indicators on the dimension of the learning experience, encompassing Situational adaptability, Clear goal, Valuable content, Learning feedback, Content logicality, Rigorous content, and Instructional guidance.

Interactive Experience. The interactive experience is demonstrated through the interaction process between users and products, reflecting user feedback and perception regarding operational convenience, ease of learning, usability, and fluency when using products. A good interactive experience ensures the smooth completion of target tasks. As a software product, popular science games also require evaluation and analysis from a technical perspective. Usability researcher Nielsen [19] proposed heuristic usability principles, including system state visibility, alignment with users' real-world experiences, user controllability and freedom, consistency and standardization, error prevention measures, reduction of cognitive burden on users' memory, flexible and efficient design approaches, as well as concise and aesthetically pleasing designs. Additionally providing documentation and user manuals aids in error identification, judgment, and resolution for users. Therefore, based on the characteristics of popular science games and the principles of usability, this paper presents a comprehensive analysis of specific indicators about the dimensions of interactive experience, including ease of use, learnability, fluency, feedback, fault tolerance, and controllability.

Emotional Experience. Emotional experience refers to the user's feedback and psychological responses during product usage, resulting from the user's emotional communication with the product in a specific environment. For popular science games, the emotional experience encompasses feelings generated by users after engaging in-game entertainment experiences. Sweetser [20] proposed the GameFlow model based on flow experience in games, consisting of eight core elements: focus, challenge, skill, control, goal, feedback, immersion, and social interaction. Therefore, when designing popular science games four metrics should be considered: sense of achievement, immersion, sociability, and sense of challenge. Sense of achievement focuses on users' ability to achieve self-worth and recognition during gameplay. Immersion pertains to whether users can fully engage with products effectively improving learning outcomes through engagement with game tasks that lead to a state of flow. Sociability means players interact competitively or collaboratively meeting users' needs for community belongingness. The sense of challenge entails a perpetual endeavor to enhance and align one's abilities with the obstacles encountered within the game. Additionally, entertainment is an important indicator measuring emotional experiences within popular science games as it is one of their fundamental characteristics providing participants with enjoyable experiences.

3.4 Final Determination of the Evaluation Index System

After determining the evaluation indicators for sensory experience, learning experience, interactive experience, and emotional experience respectively, a panel of five experts was invited to reclassify and streamline these indicators using the Delphi survey method. Ultimately, four primary-level indicators and 20 secondary-level evaluation indicators were established, encompassing sensory experience, learning experience, interactive experience, and emotional experience as presented in Table 1.

3.5 Index Weight Calculation Based on the AHP Method

The procedure for calculating the weight value of an index based on AHP is outlined in detail below:

Table 1. User experience evaluation index system of popular science games

Dimension	Index	Description
Sensory experience (A)	Color Style (A1)	The color scheme of the interface is harmonized
	Clear layout (A2)	The layout is logical and the functions are organized systematically
	Clear message (A3)	The interface of the game effectively conveys accurate information
Learning experience (B)	Situational adaptability (B1)	The game situation aligns with the content and task requirements of the popular science game
	Clear goal (B2)	Users can easily comprehend the educational objectives of popular science games and fully grasp their content
	Valuable content (B3)	Games enable users to enhance their scientific skills and knowledge
	Content logicality (B4)	The logical structure of the game content is well-defined, with a gradual increase in difficulty that adheres to users' cognitive abilities
	Rigorous content (B5)	The game's content strictly adheres to scientific principles
	Instructional guidance (B6)	The game offers help and documentation for beginners
Interactive experience (C)	Ease of use (C1)	The product is user-friendly, reducing the learning curve
	Learnability (C2)	The operational logic is easily comprehensible and quickly graspable, alleviating the burden of memory
	Fluency (C3)	The system operates smoothly and reliably
	Feedback (C4)	Immediate feedback on product operation status is provided
	Fault tolerance (C5)	The product exhibits a robust fault tolerance for incorrect operations
	Controllability (C6)	Users have complete autonomy in the game and can control it according to their individual needs

(continued)

Table 1. (*continued*)

Dimension	Index	Description
Emotional experience (D)	Immersion (D1)	The product offers users an immersive experience
	Sense of achievement (D2)	Users can attain a sense of self-worth and recognition within the game
	Entertainment (D3)	Games provide entertainment and elicit pleasure for users
	Sociability (D4)	Through mutual communication, competition, and collaboration, users' need for a sense of community belonging can be fulfilled
	Sense of challenge (D5)	The game's abilities and obstacles are consistently elevated and harmonized, presenting an uninterrupted succession of challenges

- Construct the judgment matrix. To further analyze the significance of user experience indicators in popular science games, it is essential to gather expert opinions on various levels of indicators. For this study, a test group consisting of 5 experts was invited to construct a pairwise comparison judgment matrix. A 9-point scale method was employed, with ratings of 1, 3, 4, 7, and 9 denoting equal importance, slight importance, evident importance, strong importance, and extreme importance respectively. Ratings of 2, 4, 6, and 8 represented intermediate values accordingly. Questionnaires were collected through multiple rounds of discussion and analysis among experts until convergence was reached in their evaluations. Finally, a comprehensive judgment matrix was obtained as presented in Table 2, 3, 4, 5 and 6.

Table 2. Judgment matrix of first-level index

	A	B	C	D
A	1	1/3	1	1/3
B	3	1	2	2
C	1	1/2	1	1
D	3	1/2	1	1

- Calculate the relative weight value. The weight vector Wi of the judgment matrix is determined using the geometric average method and subsequently normalized, as depicted in formulas (1) and (2).

Table 3. Judgment matrix of the sensory experience

	A1	A2	A3
A1	1	1/3	1/3
A2	3	1	1
A3	3	1	1

Table 4. Judgment matrix of the learning experience

	B1	B2	B3	B4	B5	B6
B1	1	1	1/3	1/5	1/7	1/3
B2	1	1	1/3	1/5	1/5	1/3
B3	3	3	1	1/3	1/5	2
B4	5	5	3	1	1/3	3
B5	7	5	5	3	1	5
B6	3	3	1/2	1/3	1/5	1

Table 5. Judgment matrix of the interactive experience

	C1	C2	C3	C4	C5	C6
C1	1	1	1/3	1	3	3
C2	1	1	2	1	3	3
C3	3	1/2	1	1	3	5
C4	1	1	1	1	3	3
C5	1/3	1/3	1/3	1/3	1	1
C6	1/3	1/3	1/5	1/3	1	1

Table 6. Judgment matrix of the emotional experience

	D1	D2	D3	D4	D5
D1	1	1/3	1	3	3
D2	3	1	2	5	3
D3	1	1/2	1	3	1
D4	1/3	1/5	1/3	1	1
D5	1/3	1/3	1	1	1

$$W_i = \sqrt[n]{\prod_{j=1}^{n} x_{ij}}, \ i, \ j = 1, 2 \ldots, \ n \tag{1}$$

$$W_i^n = \frac{W_i}{\sum_{i=1}^{n} W_i} \tag{2}$$

The logical consistency of the judgment matrix requires a consistency test, as indicated by formulas (3) and (4).

$$CI = \frac{\lambda - n}{n - 1} \tag{3}$$

$$CR = \frac{CI}{RI} \tag{4}$$

Among them, CI is the consistency test index, CR is the consistency ratio, RI is the random consistency index, λ_{max} is the largest eigenvalue, and n is the matrix dimension. Table 7 presents the introduced random consistency index RI value for the judgment matrix. A CR value less than 0.1 indicates that matrix B satisfies the consistency condition and ensures effective weighting; otherwise, modifications should be made until a CR value less than 0.1 is achieved.

Table 7. Average random consistency index table

n	1	2	3	4	5	6	7	8
RI	0.00	0.00	0.58	0.90	1.12	1.24	1.32	1.41

4 Data Analysis

The weight coefficients of each index of user experience in popular science games were calculated and the results were integrated, as presented in Table 8.

Through the analysis of the user experience evaluation index system of popular science games, the following conclusions can be drawn:

- The weight data for sensory experience, learning experience, interactive experience, and emotional experience in the user experience evaluation index system of popular science games are 0.1316, 0.4243, 0.1917, and 0.2523 respectively. Learning experience and emotional experience dimensions hold a significant proportion while sensory experience and interactive experience dimensions exhibit relatively weaker influence. This indicates that user experience evaluation in popular science games emphasizes scientific objectives as well as emotional enjoyment aligning with the essential attributes of being both scientifically informative and entertaining.

Table 8. Popular science games user experience evaluation index weight

Dimension		weight	Index	Local Weight	Global Weight	Ranking
User Experience Evaluation System of Popular Science Games	Sensory experience (A)	0.1316	Color Style (A1)	0.1429	0.0188	18
			Clear layout (A2)	0.4286	0.0564	4
			Clear message (A3)	0.4286	0.0564	4
	Learning experience (B)	0.4243	Situational adaptability (B1)	0.0456	0.0194	17
			Clear goal (B2)	0.0482	0.0205	15
			Valuable content (B3)	0.1226	0.0520	7
			Content logicality (B4)	0.2443	0.1037	3
			Rigorous content (B5)	0.4419	0.1875	1
			Instructional guidance (B6)	0.0973	0.0413	11
	Interactive experience (C)	0.1917	Ease of use (C1)	0.1749	0.0335	13
			Learnability (C2)	0.2358	0.0452	10
			Fluency (C3)	0.2448	0.0469	8
			Feedback (C4)	0.2101	0.0403	12
			Fault tolerance (C5)	0.0700	0.0134	19
			Controllability (C6)	0.0643	0.0123	20
	Emotional experience (D)	0.2523	Immersion (D1)	0.2111	0.0533	6
			Sense of achievement (D2)	0.4168	0.1052	2
			Entertainment (D3)	0.1838	0.0464	9
			Sociability (D4)	0.0791	0.0200	16
			Sense of challenge (D5)	0.1092	0.0276	14

- Amongst the top ten secondary indicators, learning experiences and emotional experiences have three items each whereas sensory experiences and interactive experiences have two items each. This suggests that the primary indicators proposed in this article are reasonable for evaluating user experiences in popular science games covering most key aspects effectively. Notably, content rigor, content logic, and sense of achievement rank significantly higher than other indices with weights exceeding 0.1 indicating their prioritization within popular science games design considerations. These three indicators represent crucial factors to be emphasized in popular science game development. Additionally, the importance placed on clear layout and effective communication is also evident from their higher ranking among index weights highlighting emphasis on information structure effectiveness within popular science games.

In summary, contemporary experts prioritize the educational impact and emotional experience of players in the realm of popular science gaming. Emphasis should also be placed on factors such as sensory experience and interactive engagement.

5   Application

5.1   Project Background

Mortise and Tenon, a popular science game released in 2020, focuses on the Inheritance of traditional crafts. The game primarily simulates real-life mortise and tenon structure cutting and assembly to assess players' spatial thinking abilities and replicate the gameplay of tenon joints. Due to its significant recognition in the field of popular science games, this paper selects Mortise and Tenon as the subject for evaluation.

5.2   Project Method

Based on the user characteristics of popular science games, this study recruited 9 ordinary users with prior experience in using popular science games to evaluate the indicators based on their personal experiences and perceptions after playing the Mortise and Tenon games. Ratings were collected using a 5-point scale, ranging from 1 (lowest) to 5 (highest). Subsequently, by incorporating the weights assigned to each evaluation index within the system, an overall score of 3.6945 points was calculated for the game as presented in Table 9.

5.3   Result Analysis

As depicted in Table 9, the Mortise and Tenon game exhibits a high overall score. The design aspect of the learning experience has gained widespread recognition among users, encompassing clear goals, valuable content, and rigorous presentation. Furthermore, the actual gaming experience of users attests to the successful integration of traditional cultural knowledge into the game context for popular science education purposes. The interface color scheme is harmonious with a clear and logical layout that enhances usability while providing an entertaining experience with strong fault tolerance capabilities.

Table 9. User experience rating score of Mortise and Tenon

Index	Average score	Weighted score	Score
Color Style (A1)	4.1000	0.0771	3.6945
Clear layout (A2)	3.8000	0.2144	
Clear message (A3)	3.6000	0.2031	
Situational adaptability (B1)	3.7000	0.0716	
Clear goal (B2)	4.5000	0.0921	
Valuable content (B3)	4.2000	0.2186	
Content logicality (B4)	3.6000	0.3732	
Rigorous content (B5)	3.9000	0.7312	
Instructional guidance (B6)	3.2000	0.1322	
Ease of use (C1)	3.8000	0.1275	
Learnability (C2)	3.5000	0.1582	
Fluency (C3)	3.3000	0.1549	
Feedback (C4)	2.9000	0.1168	
Fault tolerance (C5)	3.9000	0.0524	
Controllability (C6)	3.3000	0.0407	
Immersion (D1)	3.6000	0.1917	
Sense of achievement (D2)	3.8000	0.3996	
Entertainment (D3)	3.6000	0.1669	
Sociability (D4)	3.8000	0.0759	
Sense of challenge (D5)	3.5000	0.0964	

However, there are some drawbacks in the interactive dimension of the Mortise and Tenon game where certain operational aspects perform poorly resulting in low scores for fluency, feedback provision, and sense of control. User feedback indicates a lack of an instant feedback mechanism and insufficient intuitiveness in teaching operation prompts which increases the cognitive load on players. Additionally, slow gameplay undermines user expectations leading to subpar emotional engagement during gaming experiences.

In conclusion, although Mortise and Tenon wood games fulfill requirements for popular science education and yield satisfactory overall experiential outcomes, iterative optimization is still necessary within the interactive dimension to enhance product usability design levels.

6   Conclusion

Popular science games are electronic games designed for science education. The user experience of popular science games, as the primary target audience, plays a pivotal role in determining their success or failure. Evaluating the user experience of popular science games holds significant importance for promoting and advancing their development. Commencing with the fundamental attributes of popular science games, this study systematically organizes and summarizes pertinent research findings, while employing an analytic hierarchy process to construct a relatively comprehensive user experience evaluation index system for popular science games from four perspectives: sensory experience, learning experience, interactive experience, and emotional experience. This evaluation system fills the research gap in understanding user experiences of popular science games and also serves as a reference point for optimizing such experiences.

References

1. CNNIC The 52nd Statistical Report on China's Internet Development. https://www.cnnic.net.cn/n4/2023/0828/c88-10829.html. Accessed 28 Aug 2023
2. Laine, T.H., Nygren, E., Dirin, A., Suk, H.J.: Science Spots AR: a platform for science learning games with augmented reality. Educ. Tech. Res. Dev. **64**, 507–531 (2016)
3. Lamb, R.L.: Examination of the effects of dimensionality on cognitive processing in science: a computational modeling experiment comparing online laboratory simulations and serious educational games. J. Sci. Educ. Technol. **25**, 1–15 (2016)
4. Jones, P.H., Demetriou, S., Bogacz, R., Yoo, J.H., Leonards, U.: Toward a science of learning games. Mind Brain Educ. **5**, 33–41 (2011)
5. Ergonomics of human-system interaction - Part 210: Human-centred design for interactive systems, ISO 9241-210:2010(en) (2020). https://www.iso.org/obp/ui/#iso:std:iso:9241:-210:ed-1:v1:en. Accessed 18 Jan 2024
6. Csikszentmihalyi, M.: Flow: The Psychology of Optimal Experience. Harper Perennial, New York (1990)
7. Rob, H., Scott, D.: Learning from games: seven principles of effective design. Tech. Commun. **45**(3), 319–329 (1998)
8. Keller, J.M.: Development and use of the ARCS model of instructional design. J. Instr. Dev. **10**, 2–10 (1987)
9. Garzotto, F.: Investigating the educational effectiveness of multiplayer online games for children. In: Proceedings of the 6th International Conference on Interaction Design and Children (Aalborg, Denmark) (IDC'07), New York. Association for Computing Machinery (2007)
10. McFarlane, A., Sparrowhawk, A., Heald, Y.: Report on the Educational Use of Games. TEEM (Teachers evaluating educational multimedia), Cambridge (2002)
11. Galvis, A., Moeller, B.: Rubric for Assessing or Designing Playful Learning Spaces. https://playspace.concord.org/Documents/Rubric%20for%20Playspaces.pdf. Accessed 20 Jan 2024
12. Annetta, L.A., Lamb, R., Stone, M.: Assessing serious educational games. In: Annetta, L., Bronack, S.C. (eds.) Serious Educational Game Assessment, pp. 75–93. Springer (2011). https://doi.org/10.1007/978-94-6091-329-7_5
13. Hassenzahl, M., Diefenbach, S., Goritz, A.: Needs, affect, and interactive products – facets of user experience. Interact. Comput. **22**(5), 353–362 (2010)
14. Park, J., Han, S.H., Kim, H.K., Oh, S., Moon, H.: Modeling user experience: a case study on a mobile device. Int. J. Ind. Ergon. **43**(2), 187–196 (2013)
15. Garrett, J.J.: The Elements of User Experience: User–Centered Design for the Web. New Riders, New York (2003)
16. Schmitt, B.H.: Experiential Marketing. Relate to Your Company and Brands. The Free Press, New York, How to Get Customers to Sense, Feel, Think, Act (1999)
17. Law, E.L.C., Schaik, P.V.: Modelling user experience – an agenda for research and practice. Interact. Comput. **22**(5), 313–322 (2010)

18. Ahmed, A.H., Rana, A., Bareep, A., Abdullah, A.S.: Student information system: investigating user experience (UX). Int. J. Adv. Comput. Sci. Appl. (IJACSA). **12**(2), 80–87 (2021)
19. Nielsen, J.: Usability Engineering. Morgan Kaufmann, San Francisco (1993)
20. Sweetser, P., Wyeth, P.: GameFlow: a model for evaluating player enjoyment in games. Comput. Entertainment. **3**(3), 3 (2005)

A Qualitative Study for Parametric Designed Custom-Fit Eyewear Frames: Fit Test Evaluation and User Insights

Yuanqing Tian$^{(\boxtimes)}$ [ID], Lingyu Li [ID], and Roger Ball [ID]

Georgia Institute of Technology, Atlanta, GA 30332, USA

{ytian303,lli653}@gatech.edu, roger.ball@design.gatech.edu

Abstract. Poor-fitting eyewear frames can lead to discomfort, inconvenience, or hazard for vision. Most eyeglasses are mass-produced in pre-defined sizes, resulting in improper fitting for a portion of the population. We previously developed a parametric algorithm to generate custom-fit eyewear frames based on individual 3D scanned data. In this study, we conducted a fit test study to evaluate the parametric algorithm on 10 subjects with 3D printed prototypes. Through a hybrid-approach user test including tasks, observations, surveys, and interviews, we summarized several findings that indicate the fit improvement on stability, security, and comfort. The test results also provided user-centric insights into the vanity aspect for further custom-fit eyewear design optimizations. This study validates the feasibility of using parametric design method as a powerful tool for custom-fit wearable products. Moreover, it presents a potential pathway to implement the Mass Customization service by flipping the traditional script of "user to fit product" into "product to fit user".

Keywords: Parametric design · 3D body scan · Fit test · Anthropometry · Ergonomics · Qualitative research methods · Mass Customization...

1 Introduction

People use eyewear products for different purposes and daily activities. Despite a professional optical prescription for vision correctness and protection, a poor-fitting eyewear frame can compromise the wearability, comfortableness, and wellness for users [18]. Typical issues of poor-fitting eyewear frames include improper sizes, nose bridge displacement, looseness, or tightness around ears, etc. [7]. These problematic fitting issues can result in long-term discomfort and inconvenience: pinching, headaches, dizziness, facial bruises, and sliding-off [6, 17]. The causes of these fit issues are multifaceted, including factors like conventional sizing systems [10, 11], human morphological variations, and obsolete handcrafted dispensing processes [7], etc.

Today, mass-produced eyewear frames use Annex A guidelines of three-dimensional sizing approach which defines frame size into arm length, nose bridge width, and lens cavity size [10, 11]. This relative arbitrary sizing approach produces most eyewear frames

A. Marcus et al. (Eds.): HCII 2024, LNCS 14712, pp. 354–370, 2024.
https://doi.org/10.1007/978-3-031-61351-7_25

in pre-defined incremental size segmentations, which can no longer accommodate the tremendous variations of facial morphologies within a grown and ever-changing population. When fitting issue appears, a handcrafted dispensing process is usually involved for form-fitting adjustments by heating and bending. For many users, the traditional sizing system and the time-consuming fitting process are often associated with dissatisfaction of undesirable appearances [7].

To address the improper fit issues and enhance user experience, we developed a parametric algorithm with Rhino3D software [14] and Grasshopper plug-in [9] to customize eyewear frames based on individual face-and-head profiles [22]. This algorithm requires acquiring 3D scan data of the user's head and importing the extracted anthropometric data into the Rhino and Grasshopper program for model generation. A detailed resource of the parametric algorithm development can be found in our previous paper [22].

In the study, we recruited 10 subjects, generated eyewear frames for each person and 3D printed frame prototypes to test the fit. The main goal is to assess the fit, comfort, security of the customized eyewear design and validate the usability of the parametric algorithm. We also collected subjects' opinions and feedback on material, style, and aesthetics of the eyewear frames. These results provided insights for further development of the eyewear design and optimization of the parametric algorithm. The study suggested broader and promising design opportunities towards the Mass Customization trend and parametric design applications around wearable products.

2 Preliminary Work

2.1 Development of the Parametric Algorithm

Prior to this study, we created the parametric algorithm with Rhino and Grasshopper software for a regular rectangle frame style. To generate a custom-fitted eyewear frame, we import 3D scanned head-and-face data of 32 landmarks and 7 dimensions into the Grasshopper program as inputs as shown in Fig. 1 (a) and (b) respectively. These human body data are correlated with eyewear components and dimensions, as defined "body-product relationship". 10 adjustive parameters can change different eyewear frame dimensions including vertex distance, arm breadth, nose bridge contour curvatures, frame edge radius, frame height, etc. as shown in Fig. 1(c) [13, 18, 19]. Figure 1 (d) illustrates the parametric algorithm on a mannequin head model in Rhino and Grasshopper software.

This parametric algorithm is technically applicable to everyone because the underlying body-product relationship regulates a consistent custom-fit modeling process for each profile. The required facial landmarks and dimensions are derived from anthropometric studies are defined as universal, as well as their identical correlations to the eyewear dimensions. While each individual has different head shapes and facial profiles, the spatial distribution of the landmarks can vary substantially, resulting in varied dimensions and contour curvatures. Thus, each individual's body data will affect the size, ratio, and dimension of their eyeglass frames (e.g., front face wrap angle, nose bridge contour, frame length, arm length, etc.).

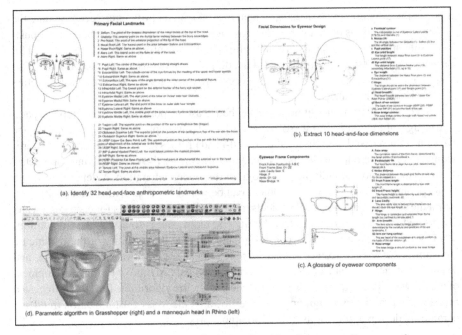

Fig. 1. Development of the parametric design algorithm for custom-fit eyewear frames.

2.2 Understanding Fit Factors

The parametric algorithm and its underlying "body product relationship" contains three important fit factors as pillars: Contact Fit, Interference Fit, and Ventilated Fit [3]. These three fit factors refer to combinations of different eyewear component dimensions as to guarantee a correct fit, comfort, and security. For example, Contact Fit mainly regulates the skin-contacting areas such as nose bridges and ear-hanging on the arms; Interference Fit guarantees a secure and stable wearing status to prevent potential looseness by providing a slightly "snug fit"; Ventilated Fit reserves necessary spaces in between the product and the skin, such as a proper Vertex Distance and face wrap angle, to avoid any irritations and uncomfortableness. These three fit factors associated with their corresponding eyewear components (as explained in Sect. 4) can indicate the three core aspects for the fit test assessments.

Another fit factor, the Vanity Fit, is also examined to acquire potential insights for future development on aesthetics. The current algorithm defines a classic rectangular-shaped eyewear frame style with several adjustable parameters to tune the style elements such as frame height, edge radius, and thickness. In the study, we investigated subjects' opinions on these aesthetic aspects with their vanity experience of the physical prototypes in terms of CFM (Color, Fabrication, Material).

3   Study Methods

3.1   Overview

We recruited a total of 10 subjects, ensuring a self-identified gender distribution of 5:5. Regarding ethnicity, our subjects predominantly represented Caucasian, East Asians, and South Asians, with a ratio of 4:4:2. In terms of eyewear use experience, 6 out of 10 subjects reported being experienced users who wore eyeglasses for vision correction on a daily basis. 2 out of 10 were intermediate level users who occasionally used eyewear products, and 2 subjects said they never or rarely worn eyeglasses.

3.2   Scan Data Collection and Prototyping

Prior to fit test, we utilized the Artec Eva scanner [1] and Artec Studio software [2] to collect digital head models from all subjects, as shown in Fig. 2(b). We used an eyeliner pencil to mark the pre-defined landmarks based on facial anatomy and anthropometry, as shown in Fig. 2(a). After cleaning up the raw scan data and digitalize the model and landmarks in Rhino 7 software, each model was re-positioned identically in world XYZ coordinate as shown in Fig. 2(c). This model was then brought into the parametric algorithm in Grasshopper platform. All landmarks coordinate values and facial dimensions were also entered as input parameters into the algorithm. A team member operated the algorithm to generate the customized eyewear frames for each subject profile, as shown in Fig. 2(d). Once the customized design is generated, the model can be saved into Rhino and patched to form a water-tight CAD model as shown in Fig. 2(e).

For 10 subjects, we generated the digital eyewear frame wireframes shown in Fig. 3(a). Figure 3 (b)(c)(d) display the 10 pairs of 3D printed prototypes in front, top, and side views.

3.3   Study Procedures and Approaches

Task Analysis and Observations. Subjects were invited to put on their eyewear prototype and examine themselves in a mirror. They were then informed about study content and encouraged to follow a "think-aloud" protocol [8] to express their feelings and experiences during the tests.

A proper-fitted pair of eyeglasses should enable the wearer to perform daily tasks with ease and safety. Task analysis and observation aims to record qualitative notes on these performances, such as the subject's body language, facial expressions, "think-aloud" quotes, and eyewear behaviors [15]. This approach help immerse subjects into real-world scenarios and examine the fit performances in an objective way Many fit evaluation studies used this approach, for example, A respirator study team asked subjects to complete different head movements (e.g., head up/down, shaking, etc.) to assess the respirator/mask security and leakage [12]. In our study, we decided on three parallel tasks based on daily eyewear use cases in real-life scenarios as listed below. We expected to observe fit-related performances of the subjects and the eyewear prototypes such as sliding-off, pushing back, swinging, etc. Figure 4 (a)(b)(c) exemplifies the three tasks performed by different subjects.

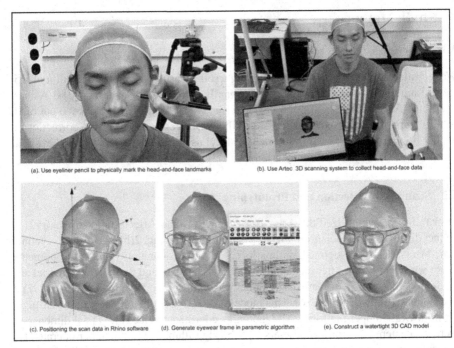

Fig. 2. Demonstration of the study process on one subject.

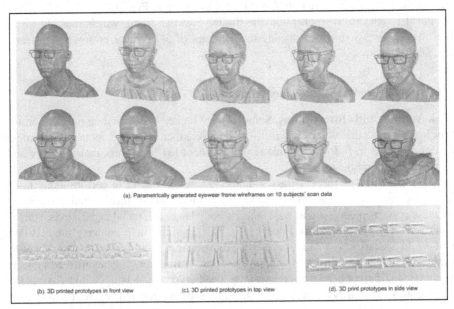

Fig. 3. All 3D printed prototypes of the custom-fit eyewear frames for 10 subjects.

- *Task 1. Walk around the table in the lab and squat / bend down to untie and tie up shoelaces.*
- *Task 2. Read a short article and fill out a reading quiz of 20 multiple choice questions.*
- *Task 3. Following a 2-min video to complete a lightweight exercise warm up and stretching routine.*

(a). Task 1: Tie up shoelaces.   (b). Task 2: Reading and quiz   (c). Task 3: Exercese

Fig. 4. Demonstration of the three task activities.

Self-reported Survey. Following the tasks, each subject completed a self-reported survey that collected quantitative data on size, fit, comfort, and aesthetics. The questionnaire format survey contains 13 Likert-scaled rating questions. These questions were created based on the fit factors and their respective eyewear components. The final three questions ask subjects to rate the current design's style, material, and aesthetics. All questions are graded on a 5-point scale, with 1 representing "Totally Disagree" and 5 representing "Totally Agree." Three questions (Q5,6, and 7) were asked in an opposite manner with the scores meaning reversed. Several questions were subconsciously repeatedly asked in different angles to ensure the validity and reliability of the survey [20]. Below list all questions with "*" indicating reversed questions.

1. Overall, I feel comfortable wearing this pair of eyewear frame prototypes.
2. The frame arm length is an appropriate length to sit on my ears.
3. I feel comfortable on the nose bridge area of the frame.
4. I feel comfortable around my ears regarding the ear-hang area on the frame arms.
5. *The nose bridge of the frame causes pressure, tightness, or pain around my nose area.
6. *The arms of the frame cause pressure, tightness, or pain around my ears.
7. *The frame would easily slide off or fall down frequently from my face.
8. The frame can securely and steadily stay on my face and ears.
9. The frame is at a proper distance from my eyes/face, without interfering with my eyebrows or eyelashes.
10. The frame width is appropriate and does not cause any pressure, tightness, or pain on my temples or side faces.
11. Overall, I think look good wearing this frame.

12. The material of the frame prototype is smooth and comfortable to wear.

13. I am satisfied with the style, shape, and material of this frame.

Interviews. The final session was an interview that collects additional qualitative and heuristic data. We asked the subjects to elaborate on their eyewear experiences regarding both usual and parametric-designed eyewear products. The interview was set up in a semi-structured format with a prepared script while allowing subjects to express additional stories. Throughout the discussion, we gained valuable insights on possible improvements for the parametric algorithm and customization design.

3.4 Data Analysis Methods

Triangulating analysis [4], referenced to Fig. 5(a), is a useful user research method that helps synthesis different data sources for enriched and profound findings from survey responses, subjects' comments, and observation notes. Affinity Diagraming helped us exploit the qualitative results into clear categorizations in Fig. 5(b) with "Top-to-Bottom" coding [21]. Starting with the top categories based on pre-defined eyewear components and fit factors, we examined down to observation notes and subjects' quotes and transcribed them into different codes, as shown in Fig. 5(c).

Fig. 5. Examples of data analysis process.

4   Results and Findings

According to eyewear components and their related questions, we classified fit factors with their indicating finding themes (with reversed questions corrected). Average scores for each classification are summarized and plotted as seen in Fig. 6 and Table 1. In this section, we will list prominent findings including positive achievements on fit and insights for further improvements. We will discuss and explain the findings with both survey results and qualitative data.

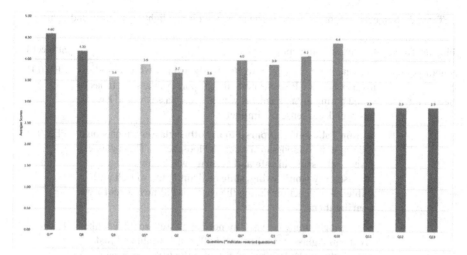

Fig. 6. Histogram plot of all questions' average scores.

Table 1. Average scores of fit factor and findings classification.

Fit Factors	Findings/Components	Questions	Average Score
Interference Fit	Stability & Security	Q7, 8	4.4/5.0
Contact Fit	Nose Bridge Fit	Q3, 5	3.8/5.0
	Arm Fit	Q2, 4, 6	3.8/5.0
Ventilated Fit	Overall Comfort	Q1, 9, 10	4.1/5.0
Vanity Fit	Aesthetics, CFM	Q11, 12, 13	2.9/5.0

4.1 Interference Fit: Enhanced Stability and Security

Two questions Q7 and Q8 are directly associated with Interference Fit, which indicates the stability and security level. They are rated highest average scores of 4.6 and 4.2 respectively. Both questions won highest frequencies with 8/10 people and 7/10 people rating a score 5 (Totally Agree) respectively. An overall average for this assessment is calculated 4.4/5.0, revealing a top positive improvement for the parametric eyewear fit. This means that the parametric designed eyewear satisfies a proper "snug fit" to prevent typical sliding and moving issues.

Furthermore, other qualitative data from subjects' comment and quotes reinforced this positive finding with implications of a non-compromised comfort along with such improved tightness. During activities or movements in the task session, the eyewear frames were unlikely to cause "impact," "swing," "slide," or "fall," from our observation. According to subjects, the personalized curvature and dimensions of the overall frame wrapping angle and width provided a stable support, making this parametrically designed eyewear rivaling to "sports eyewear" characteristics, as highlighted in Table 2.

Table 2. Subjects' feedback regarding Interference Fit highlighting stability and security.

Finding Theme	Quotes & Comments	Subject ID
Stability & Security	"I found these glasses are really **steady, won't swing or slide** as my usual ones…It seems more like a sport eyeglasses…It has no sound during my movements which usual glasses would have this sound and sense of "**impact.**"	PES-001
	"It **won't slide off compared to my other glasses** which would slide a lot due to long-term wear and looseness…These glasses gave me **the sense of safe and security** when I am doing exercise, they **won't swing, slide or drop. It fits so well and stable**, after sometime during the workout **I almost forgot I was wearing them.**"	PES-003
	"I'm trying to imagine what my normal glasses would feel like. My **normal glasses wouldn't slid off, but I would feel just a very slight tug slide forward because the little earpiece wouldn't be as well hooked on as this one (parametric one).**"	PES-005
	"These glasses **do not fall down like my current one** which forms my habit of holding up glasses frequently."	PES-006
	"I'm really happy with this frame that **it doesn't move on my face**. Because when it's really hot or sweaty, usual eyeglasses tends to move."	PES-007
	"They **did not bounce or slip, they were completely secure**. I did not even think about having to readjust the frames."	PES-008
	"I don't think they slide off at all. They seem to stay very well. I would say from a fit perspective, they fit and they stay on really well at the same time they're not like super tight. So normally when I wear glasses, they would bounce around. These frames **don't bounce around**. So I do like this part."	PES-009

4.2 Contact Fit: Minimal Pressure and "Imperceptibility" on Problematic Areas

Another prominent fit improvement is on Contact Fit, particularly addressing the typical problematic fit issues on nose bridge and ear-hanging of the arms. Q3 and Q5 directly assess the nose bridge fit, whereas Q2, 4 and 6 assess the eyewear arms. Both two sets of questions acquired high average scores of 3.8/5.0 and 3.9/5.0 respectively. Taken as an entire fit assessment for Contact Fit, the overall average score of 3.8/5.0 indicates a well-achieved comfortableness on the skin contacted areas.

This improvement is mainly explained by alleviated pressure. Because the contacting components of nose bridge and ear-hanging on arms were constructed based on individual facial contours, they can smoothly conform to the facial profiles. Compared to the mass-produced eyewear designs, the parametric algorithm can bridge the gap between the standardized component structure and the individual curvature nuances. This reduces the possible overly touches on skins and result in a minimized pressure level. We found most subjects frequently used keywords and phrases such as *"no pressure"*, *"less pressure"*, *"feel like nothing on face"*, or *"not noticing"* etc. We summarized this cluster of remarks into a feature of "imperceptibility". It indicated the minimal pressure, comfortableness, and ease of the skin-contact areas. Table 3 highlights several remarks from subjects.

Table 3. Subjects' feedback regarding Contact Fit on nose bridge and arms highlighting minimal pressure and imperceptibility.

Finding Theme	Quotes & Comments	Subject ID
Minimal Pressure & Imperceptibility	"The eyeglasses always leaves bruise/dent on my nose, especially those metal eyeglasses with silicone nose pads attached by screws. **I prefer this one-piece nose bridge that sits on my nose properly.**" "I feel like **the back of the ear is the best part of these glasses** while I was doing the reading and exercise tasks. Usually, my eyeglasses would come down like this (she put down the eyeglasses a little bit) but this one doesn't do that when I move my head."	PES-002
	"I didn't really notice the existence of wearing it…It felt nothing with no movements during my reading. It was very steady and didn't move much during the exercise and **there was not much pressure onto the face.**"	PES-004
	"Usually I get pressure. I have glasses where I get pressure pads. Like I get little spots here on the top of my nose where it's putting all the weight of the glasses and so I can feel that it's (the parametric eyewear) not doing that. There is **not much weight on the nose that causes pressure.**" "Um, **I actually like specifically around the ear. I don't even notice it.** I can tell that it's **gripping it really well, I can't even really feel it.**"	PES-005
	" I feel this is **quite comfortable with very little pressure on my face** compared to other eyeglasses. As you can see (he took off glasses and pointed onto his nose and tear ducts) my current glasses give me these hard bruises on tear ducts and temples…" "I quite **like the nose pad support** on this pair of glasses which is different from my current one. This one supports my nose a bit upper **with less pressure**, so it is **more comfortable for me.**"	PES-006
	"Ear blades are good, and they feel very secure. I normally have glasses sit crooked on my head due to my uneven ears, but this frame does not do that! "	PES-008

(continued)

Table 3. (*continued*)

Finding Theme	Quotes & Comments	Subject ID
	"Like the ears are a pretty good fit. They're not super long, which isn't really a problem for me because they just need to hook over a little bit. Traditional glasses, they usually come really far down. I'm not gonna lie, it's actually kind of steep and stupid. So I actually like that these are really short because it doesn't need to be that long. Also I don't want people to like look at the side of my head and see the glasses coming out that much. **So I like the way that you made them short and conforming the shape."**	PES-009
	"I didn't quite notice it while I was reading, it **just didn't cross my mind**, it's lightweight and **doesn't cause any pain."**	PES-010

4.3 Ventilated Fit: Overall Comfortableness and Satisfaction

When asked about the overall wearing experience in Q1 and two questions regarding Ventilated Fit in Q9 and 10. Several subjects described their initial impressions of distinct customization features with proper fit and comfort, as quoted in "Proper fit & Comfort" theme in Table 4. One subject PES-006 who self-identified as *"having a relatively wider face and flatter nose"*, the parametric eyewear frame provides an additional option that cares for his unique demands and saves extra efforts on size fitting. Another subject PES-007 reported herself as "having little eyewear experience" due to uncomfortableness and appraised the custom-fit eyewear frame that makes her "want to wear again".

4.4 Vanity Fit: Insights into Styles, Aesthetics, and CMF

Finally, we collected subjects' feedback on styles, aesthetics, and other CMF (Color, Material, Fabrication) factors for the parametric designed frames and prototypes, as summarized in Table 5.

1. Preferences on oversized frame style, organic curvatures, and slim details.
Several subjects admitted that they would prefer a larger frame cavity. It was also suggested that the frame shape be more rounded and organically curved, with larger radius fillets and thinner rim edges and hinges. Along with the trend of "oversized frame", slim and delicate detail design matches the tastes of the young generation. Subjects pointed out that the frame edges, nose bridge thickness, and hinge thickness can be further reduced to look more organic and exquisite. From a design perspective, we need to add adjustive parameters for reshaping the details and elaborate the modeling process; Plus, these remarks increased the scope for parametric design to accommodate a variety of aesthetics and fashion trends. For example, we can integrate more frame style options into the algorithm and adding more adjustable parameters for detail fine-tuning.

2. Polished material, texture, and more color options for high-finishing qualities.
We used FDM 3D print with white PLA filament in this study. This 3D printing method produced quick and economical prototypes for rapid testing. Yet its limited

Table 4. Subjects' feedback regarding overall fit and comfort

Finding Theme	Quotes & Comments	Subject ID
Proper fit & Comfort	"The major difference of this parametric frame glasses is that it looks very different in appearance compared to what we have in the market. **It has this strong vibe of "customization"** because it exactly matches my face. It fits smoothly and matches exactly onto my face."	PES-003
	" **So first notice immediately is that it's sort of slotted onto my ears correctly.** I've had glasses in the past that one of my ears is higher and one of the other ears is lower...and so that's always been an issue that my glasses - slide or be angled on my face. **So this automatically fits there perfectly.** And from what looks like in the mirror that it's, it's not skewed..." I think it just **removes the issue of uncomfortable fits. There is** always a problem is when you buy off a shelf or from one of those manufacturers who typically, you know, they have their sizing system, and if you don't fit that..."	PES-005
	" **It's always been challenging for me to find eyeglasses with suitable length and width.** Usually, I need to go to the store and let people help bend or adjust the eyeglasses for me...A good thing about these customized eyeglasses is that **I don't need those adjustments in store because they are already designed to fit my face size**...This frame overall fits me well: arm length, nose bridge width, and frame width are all fitting very well and matches my face shape, which most eyeglasses do not because my face is wide and nose bridge is relatively lower and wider."	PES-006
	"**Great Great work because you, you are making someone not wearing glasses want to wear glasses**...I didn't really find glasses that comfortable and that's why I didn't really wear my zero number glasses (non-prescription glasses)."	PES-007

color options and rough material finishings compromised the quality of the prototypes, which also affected subjects' experience on the overall fit. Because small burrs and noises remained after manual clean-up and sanding on PLA prototypes, several subjects reported feeling "sting" or "irritating" on skin-contacting areas. Subject PES -009 mentioned color bias and recommended using more neutral or translucent color options to avoid eyesight distraction and high contrast on skin tones. For the purpose of enhancing the textural quality of prototypes, more precise SLS 3D printing or digital CNC techniques can be implemented. In addition, superior material (Nylon or Alloy) in qualitative colorways and precise polishing and coating process can achieve with a finer finishing.

Table 5. Subjects' feedback regarding Vanity Fit

Finding Theme	Quotes & Comments	Subject ID
Frame Size and Styles	"For me, I would like the frame to **be larger, rounder and slimmer,** as well as the arms. I personally **prefer slim rim eyeglasses** however they are not that comfortable."	PES-001
	"I would like to have **larger size frame** to make my eyes look less baggy, the small frames leave shadow on face…I think I will keep the original shape of this frame but **make it more rounder and softer.** Also I would reduce the nose bridge size to be slimmer and less bulky."	PES-002
	"The sharp edges and angles in the inner lens could **be smoother and rounder.** The arch on the nose bridge could be smaller and more organic shaped. The hinge is a bit too bulky which **could be slimmer.**"	PES-005
	"Stylistically I tend to go slightly **larger frames overall.** I would like a **rounder frame and lens shape,** to look more neutral and **a slimmer nose bridge.**"	PES-010
CFM	"The material could be **smoother and lighter,** it is rough and irritates my skin."	PES-003
	"I can feel a bit sting on my nose skin, the material is bit rough with these **burrs** on nose pads."	PES-004
	"The overall frame looks good. I think it's (material) comfortable enough. It could definitely be smoother though. It's not like I'm not feeling any pinching or scraping or anything digging into my face really. I can just tell that it's a **little bit rough** since it's printed."	PES-005
	""I wonder if there's an opportunity for sort of **neutral color.** Or maybe make them **somewhat transparent** so that it would be less distracting on face."	PES-009

5   Discussion

5.1   Contributions and Significances

The fit test study verified the capabilities and usability of the parametric algorithm. Given the sample of 10 subjects varying in demographics and facial profiles, the algorithm was able to accommodate the variances among individuals. Results revealed to us that this method could overcome many current fitting issues in the market. For instance, mass-produced eyeglass frames are pre-defined in sizes that can theoretically fit regular face-and-head sizes but lack inclusivity and diversity for outliers. In this case, parametric algorithm allows to adjust univariate product dimensions on an individual basis, thus, provides flexible solutions to improve fit, comfort, security, and stability for various facial profiles. Furthermore, qualitative findings include valuable user-centric insights into further optimizations on multiple aspects such as style option expansion and CMF quality improvements. Overall, these findings corresponding with the positive fit test results implied an optimism towards the customization design. Therefore, we believe that this new method of parametric design can be applicable to a broader field of custom-fit wearable designs. Incorporated with 3D scanning technologies and digital-driven fabrication methods, parametric design will serve a powerful tool to implement the Mass Customization service.

In addition, methods and approaches utilized in this study formed a systematic framework for fit-related evaluations. Given the challenge of the complexity in fit assessments, the data collection and analysis procedures tried to encompass multi-perspective information by involving a hybrid of quantitative and qualitative data. Following the defined fit factors to construct fit assessment questions with specific product components helped us classify the fit test results; Using a triangulating analysis with affinity diagraming helped us organize the connections among heuristic data. Through this workflow, we acquired a comprehensive documentation to clarify findings. We hope that these methods can provide instructive references for other relevant studies of fit evaluation or human factor assessments.

5.2 Limitations and Challenges

Due to the study's main reliance on individual reports and qualitative data, the subjectivity was a significant limitation of this study. We used several interventions to counteract this subjectivity bias, such as the Likert-scale partitions in the survey and a third-party note-taking process during the observation. These approaches helped us quantify the data and analyze the results from an externally objective perspective. It is nondeniable that precisely measuring the "fit" and "comfort" remains a challenge for many wearable product evaluations. A few studies use sensor technologies (e.g., pressure or thermos-detection) to examine the skin-contact fitting results. However, a daily-use eyewear frame product has little affordance to compact such technologies and may even compromise the fit and comfort on the contrary. Besides, eyewear fitting has long been dependent on manual dispensing adjustments with little scientific quantified index or ranges for pressure or comfort references. This being said, more works and study opportunities await exploitation to understand fit and comfort with an integration of tech-oriented measuring process and human factor analysis.

Another limitation was the relatively small sample size of 10 subjects. Challenges included the limited resources for 3D printing and prototyping, efforts in developing, tuning, and operating the parametric algorithm, and time-consuming CAD modeling works, etc. Up to this stage, the 10 subjects share a variety of demographic backgrounds and cover a moderate range of face-and-head sizes and profiles. From this point, we have verified the current algorithm being able to output correct and proper models for each subject. However, if targeting on a more advanced statistical analysis and through investigation, at least over 30 subjects should be an ideal sample size for further development and test evaluations.

5.3 Future Work

Throughout the study, we identified opportunities for future work in both perspectives of parametric algorithm optimization and fit test evaluation.

Findings from the study implied a promising design space for the parametric algorithm to expand the customization compatibility on style options and aesthetic elements. One suggestion is to enlarge the overall frame size and reduce the bulky and rough details. On one hand, this requires us to further modify the adjustable parameters by offering higher thresholds and more delicate control points. On the other hand, we should refine the subsequent process of solid modeling construction and prototyping techniques. Considering the customization compatibility, we can also incorporate multiple eyewear styles (e.g., round Harry Potter style, oversized avatar shape, Cat-eye shape, etc.) into the algorithm with an arrangement of modularization. This will allow users to match their unique preferences beyond the custom-fit features.

As for the fit test evaluation, future work should address the current limitations of sample size and assessment subjectivity. One possible way is to establish a more rigorous recruitment standard and comprisable evaluation process. For example, we can recruit experienced eyewear users over 30 people and conduct an A/B test formatted study to compare between the customized eyewear frames and the regular off-the-shelf eyewear frames.

Finally, we intend to continue the parametric algorithm development towards an omni of Mass Customization service system. This requires integrating the algorithm with an interactive user interface that allows users to participate in their design decisions. Meanwhile, many peripheral developments await further exploring, such as data management for 3D scan, matched services for anthropometric data acquirement, and enhanced user experience design. The transformation of Mass Customization is on demand in many areas for many types of products and for a large portion of population. As we propose parametric design method as a useful technique for designers to start, more topics, issues, and services are opened for further research and studies.

6 Conclusion

This paper documents a qualitative study to validate the previously development parametric algorithm for custom-fit eyewear frames. The results demonstrated a satisfactory improvement on proper size, comfortableness, stability, and security of the parametric designed eyewear frames, as well as provided user-centric insights for further development and optimizations. Despite several limitations and challenges, the study validated the capability and potential of using parametric design tools to address the critical fit issues regarding ergonomics and user experience. A significant impact of this study demonstrates a new paradigm to impact user experience with the integration of CAD (parametric design), emerging technologies (3D scanning), and advanced digital fabrication methods (3D printing). This paradigm, including the approaches utilized in fit test evaluation, can be applied to a wide range of consumer products and wearable applications. In contrast to traditional Mass Production which requires "users to fit the (pre-defined) products", this study proposes to flip this script into a new one which allows "the products fit users", uncovering the discussion of the upcoming Mass Customization services.

Disclosure of Interests. The authors have no competing interests to declare that are relevant to the content of this article.

References

1. 3D Object Scanner Artec Eva, Best Structured-light 3D Scanning Device. https://www.artec3d.com/portable-3d-scanners/artec-eva. Accessed 11 Sept 2023
2. Artec Studio, Best 3D Scanning Software. https://www.artec3d.com/3d-software/artec-studio. Accessed 11 Sept 2023
3. Ball, R.: 15 - Headwear: designing headwear to fit the size and shape of Western and Asian populations. In: Faust, M.-E., Carrier, S. (eds.), Designing Apparel for Consumers, pp. 292–307. Woodhead Publishing (2014). https://doi.org/10.1533/9781782422150.2.292
4. Barnum, C.M.: 8—Analyzing the findings. In: Barnum, C.M. (ed.), Usability Testing Essentials, pp. 239–275. Morgan Kaufmann (2011). https://doi.org/10.1016/B978-0-12-375092-1.00008-8
5. Duarte, B. K., Pinto, J. (eds.): Mass Customization and Design Democratization. Routledge (2018). https://doi.org/10.4324/9781351117869
6. Evans, L.:5 signs your glasses don't fit. All About Vision (2019). https://www.allaboutvision.com/eyeglasses/wrong-size-glasses/. Accessed 11 Sept 2023
7. Eyewear Dispensing Guidelines for Eyewear Professionals. https://www.harisingh.com/DispensingGuidelines.htm#photo. Accessed 11 Sept 2023
8. Fonteyn, M.E., Kuipers, B., Grobe, S.J.: A description of think aloud method and protocol analysis. Qual. Health Res. **3**(4), 430–441 (1993). https://doi.org/10.1177/104973239300300403
9. Grasshopper—Algorithmic modeling for Rhino. https://www.grasshopper3d.com/. Accessed 18 Sept 2023
10. ISO 12870:2016(en). Ophthalmic optics—Spectacle frames—Requirements and test methods. (n.d.). https://www.iso.org/obp/ui/en/#iso:std:iso:12870:ed-4:v1:en. Accessed 11 Sept 2023
11. ISO 8624:2020(en), Ophthalmic optics—Spectacle frames—Measuring system and vocabulary. (n.d.). https://www.iso.org/obp/ui/en/#iso:std:iso:8624:ed-4:v1:en. Accessed 11 Sept 2023
12. Lin, Y.-C., Chen, C.-P.: Characterization of small-to-medium head-and-face dimensions for developing respirator fit test panels and evaluating fit of filtering facepiece respirators with different faceseal design. PLoS ONE **12**(11), e0188638 (2017). https://doi.org/10.1371/journal.pone.0188638
13. Mclean, K.: Lens Tips: The Possibilities of Wraps. Eyecare Business (2021). https://www.eyecarebusiness.com/issues/2012/april-2012/lens-tips. Accessed 11 Sept 2023
14. McNeel, R., et al.: Rhinoceros 3D. Robert McNeel & Associates, Seattle, WA. (2010). https://www.rhino3d.com/. Accessed 11 Sept 2023
15. Moreira, M., Peixoto, C.: Qualitative task analysis to enhance sports characterization: a surfing case study. J. Hum. Kinet. **42**, 245–257 (2014). https://doi.org/10.2478/hukin-2014-0078
16. Online Training Courses for Eyewear Professionals. Optical Course. https://www.harisingh.com/OpticalCourse.htm#gross. Accessed 11 Sept 2023
17. Optiks, A.: When Your Glasses Don't Fit: Signs You Have the Wrong Size Glasses. Art of Optiks (2023). https://artofoptiks.com/eyewear/2023/01/glasses-dont-fit-wrong-size-glasses. Accessed 11 Sept 2023

18. Santini, B.: Position of Wear. 20/20 (2011). https://www.2020mag.com/article/position-of-wear. Accessed 11 Sept 2023

19. Santini, B. : The Real Details of Vertex, Tilt and Wrap. 20/20 (2015). https://www.2020mag.com/ce/the-real-details-of-vertex-5E16F. Accessed 11 Sept 2023

20. Taherdoost, H.: Validity and Reliability of the Research Instrument; How to Test the Validation of a Questionnaire/Survey in a Research. SSRN Electronic Journal (2016). https://doi.org/10.2139/ssrn.3205040

21. Tech, V., Ave, J.: A Structured Process for Transforming Usability Data into Usability Information (2007). https://www.semanticscholar.org/paper/A-Structured-Process-for-Transforming-Usability-Tech-Ave/b665a84971820e28a4c22d4f970facd8de51fd4c

22. Tian, Y., Ball, R.: Parametric design for custom-fit eyewear frames. Heliyon, e19946 (2023). https://doi.org/10.1016/j.heliyon.2023.e19946

Quality Assessment of Interdisciplinary Virtual Simulation Comprehensive Practical Training Program for Economics and Management Based on Students' Experience

Jixu Zhu[1,2] and Xiaoshi Chen[1,2(✉)]

[1] Guangzhou City University of Technology, Guangzhou, China
601668750@qq.com
[2] SEGi University, Kota Damansara, Malaysia

Abstract. The assessment of the quality of the interdisciplinary virtual simulation Comprehensive training program of economics and management can effectively analyze and find out the problems in the process of cultivating talents in economics and management, and promote the improvement of the cultivation level of talents in economics and management in colleges and universities. In this study, we used the literature research method and the Delphi method to design a quality assessment index system for inter-disciplinary virtual simulation integrated training programs in economics and management based on students' experience, which contains 4 first-level indicators, 14 s-level indicators and 47 third-level indicators. Then the AHP method was used to evaluate the quality of the inter-disciplinary virtual simulation integrated training program of economics and management carried out by universities, and the results showed that there were 3 first-level indicators, 6 s-level indicators and 21 third-level indicators that had a greater impact on the quality of the program. Based on the assessment results, the study proposes quality improvement measures such as improving the project management mechanism, standardizing the practical training process, carrying out teaching reform and innovation, introducing experiential teaching mode, exploring diversified assessment methods, and constructing a collaborative and mutual-help learning platform, with a view to improving the quality and cultivation effect of the interdisciplinary virtual simulation integrated practical training program in economics and management.

Keywords: Student experience · Virtual simulation training · Quality assessment · AHP · Delphi

1 Introduction

The General Office of the Ministry of Education proposed in 2017 to carry out the planning work for the construction of demonstrative virtual simulation experimental projects, to deeply promote the deep integration of informatization and education and teaching, and to strive to improve the quality of experimental teaching and the teaching level in higher education [1]. With the rapid development of social economy, higher education is facing the pressure of transformation of talent training mode. In order to adapt to the economic needs, the economic and management majors need to reform and innovate to cultivate applied talents with compound ability and practical experience [2]. As a new talent cultivation mode, inter-professional virtual simulation comprehensive practical training has received increasing attention in universities in recent years. It builds simulation environments and scenarios, so that students of different specialities work together to complete practical training tasks, which can effectively improve students' hands-on ability, ability to solve complex problems, communication and collaboration ability, etc., and enhance their employment competitiveness [3]. Therefore, it is of great significance to carry out the quality assessment of the virtual simulation comprehensive practical training project to find out the existing problems and continuously optimize and perfect it to ensure the quality of talent cultivation.

In this study, we choose the virtual simulation integrated training program of economics and management carried out by universities in Guangdong, China, as the evaluation object. Interdisciplinary virtual simulation training is to build a virtual business operation environment through professional simulation software (VBSE), configuring students of different majors into virtual enterprises with different roles according to their professional backgrounds, such as production enterprises, trading enterprises, raw material supply enterprises, logistics enterprises, etc., and related public service institutions, such as industrial and commercial bureaus, tax bureaus, banks, talent centers, accounting firms, etc. According to their own professional knowledge, students in the virtual environment for role-playing and simulation of operations [4]. In the practical training through job simulation, simulation training of enterprise business management process, so that students in the virtual business environment to fully experience the job responsibilities, to develop students' comprehensive professionalism [5]. VBSE is a virtual simulation platform that has been adopted by many universities. The platform can build a simulation of the internal and external environments of manufacturing and service enterprises, and students can experience and understand the business linkages between different functional departments of the enterprise, as well as the business collaboration process between the enterprise and relevant government departments and external organizations in this virtual environment [6].

With the wide application of information technology in teaching, virtual simulation training has gradually become an important means in the training of economics and management majors. He et al. (2020) evaluated the quality of the virtual simulation inter-disciplinary comprehensive training platform from four dimensions: functionality, rationality, maintenance and effectiveness [7]. Zeng (2018) suggested the construction of an inter-disciplinary simulation integrated training platform from the aspects of practical training software platform, hardware facilities, faculty and teaching materials [8]. Li (2016) introduced the experimental teaching system of "core competence orientation + professional group leading entrepreneurial chain simulation" by utilizing real data cases of local economy, industry development and mass entrepreneurship [9]. Yang (2019) suggested building a national virtual simulation experimental teaching center for economics and management from the aspects of top-level design strategization, modularization of teaching system, the institutionalization of basic guarantee, synthesis of platform resources, echelon of teachers' equipping, standardization of management system, synergization of external cooperation, diversification of resource sharing, and socialization of construction results [10].

In summary, studies have proposed an analytical framework for the quality of virtual simulation programs from multiple perspectives, but fewer studies have systematically assessed the quality from the perspective of student experience, while combining multiple decision-making methods to determine the weights of indicators and scoring results. In order to ensure the training quality of virtual simulation programs, it is necessary to carry out quality assessment to improve and optimize them. Based on the results of previous researchers, this study aims to fill this gap and enrich the research in this field.

In order to comprehensively evaluate the implementation effect of the program, this study establishes an evaluation framework from the perspective of students' experience, selects system quality, information quality, service quality and other perspectives to design the evaluation indexes, and applies the hierarchical analysis method and the Delphi method to determine the indexes' weights and scores. The results of the evaluation can identify the problems of the program, provide the university with targeted suggestions for improvement, and also provide a reference for the design of similar programs. This study chooses student experience as the perspective of quality inspection, based on student needs, and conducts the quality assessment of virtual simulation programs, aiming to promote the program to better meet the needs of students and enhance the effect of talent cultivation.

2 Overview of the Delphi and AHP

2.1 Delphi

The Delphi Method, also known as the Expert Scoring Method or the Expert Opinion Method, is a forecasting and decision-making method that gradually reaches a consensus through multiple rounds of anonymous expert consultation surveys. It originated in the 1940s by Helm and Dalke, and was later developed by the RAND Corporation as a qualitative assessment method, initially used for technology forecasting and military program evaluation. Later, the Delphi method began to be widely used in governmental decision-making, social planning, economic forecasting and other fields [11]. Its basic steps include: the formation of a panel of experts who have extensive knowledge and experience in the problem area under discussion; and multiple rounds of anonymous surveys, the first of which is usually an open-ended question that allows experts to make predictions and give their opinions; feedback aggregation, in which the panel coordinator summarizes the results of the previous round and gives feedback to the experts for their reference; modification of the experts' opinions, according to the aggregated information, adjusting and amending their own opinions; and the survey, feedback, and modification process is repeated until the experts' opinions converge; and the formation of an expert consensus, which serves as the final prediction report. Repeat the process of investigation, feedback, and modification until the experts' opinions tend to stabilize and agree; form an expert consensus as the final prediction report [12].

2.2 AHP

Hierarchical analysis method (AHP) is a multi-criteria decision analysis method, proposed by American operations researcher Seyati in 1970, which is a systematic and hierarchical decision analysis method. It decomposes a complex decision-making problem into multiple levels and multiple factors, makes comparative judgments, and finally arrives at the optimal solution of the problem [13].

The basic steps of AHP include (1) hierarchization of decision-making problems: according to the decision-making objectives, the complex problem is decomposed into some levels and several factors. (2) Construct a judgment matrix: according to the hierarchical structure, compare the relative importance of each factor at the same level, and form a judgment matrix. (3) Calculate factor weights: Calculate the weight of each factor in each level by judgment matrix. (4) Integrate the weights: Combine the weights of the judgment matrices at each level to arrive at the final weights of each decision-making scheme. (5) Consistency test: the judgment matrix should meet the consistency requirements, or need to be adjusted. (6) Select the best program according to the results: the final weight of the largest is the best choice [14].

3 Construction of Quality Assessment System for Interdisciplinary Virtual Simulation Comprehensive Training Program

3.1 Determination of Assessment Indicators

In this paper, the literature research method and the Delphi method (also known as the experts grading method) were used to solicit experts to determine the indicators for assessing the quality of the program. In order to come up with a quality assessment system for the inter-disciplinary virtual simulation integrated training program, the opinions of 12 leaders and teachers who have presided over or participated in the work of the inter-disciplinary virtual simulation integrated training program for economics and management were solicited. In the process of collecting experts' opinions, the quality and quality of the indicators were continuously improved and optimized. In this process, the principles of merging indicators, deleting indicators, and adding and replacing indicators were emphasized, and the indicators were strictly screened, and through a series of indicator optimization processes, the completeness and operability of the indicators were sought. Four aspects, such as project organization and leadership, project concept and resource allocation, project teaching design and project teaching effect, are finally selected as the first-level indicators in the assessment system, 14 s-level indicators are set from different perspectives, and 47 third-level indicators are set based on hierarchical subdivision, which finally form the table of the quality assessment index system of the inter-disciplinary virtual simulation comprehensive training project of economics and management, as shown in Table 1.

Table 1. Construction of Quality Assessment Indicator System for Interdisciplinary Virtual Simulation Comprehensive Training Program in Economics and Management Based on Students' Experience

First-level indicators B	Second-level indicators C	Third-level indicators D
B1 Project organization and leadership	C1 Importance of the project	D1 Representing the school's level of practical training and teaching
		D2 Representing the quality of practical training and teaching in the school
		D3 Become a model for the school's practical training program
	C2 Division of labour among leaders	D4 Has a dean dedicated to the program
		D5 Have a faculty director in charge of the program
		D6 There is a teacher dedicated to the program
	C3 Organization and setting	D7 Establishment of a program team
		D8 Clear project implementation plan
		D9 Projects are followed up by full-time teachers
B2 Project concept and resource allocation	C4 Guiding ideology	D10 Having relevant policy documents to guide the project
		D11 With the guidance of good examples from sister colleges and universities
		D12 School philosophy
	C5 Participants	D13 School-Enterprise Joint Venture
		D14 Teacher Level
		D15 Student participation
	C6 Scale of the project	D16 Number of participating faculties
		D17 Number of participating leaders

(continued)

Table 1. (*continued*)

First-level indicators B	Second-level indicators C	Third-level indicators D
		D18 Number of participating teachers
		D19 Number of students participating
		D20 Project cycle
	C7 Financial support	D21 Strength of financial investment
		D22 Rationalization of the use of funds
		D23 Transparency in the use of funds
	C8 Faculty	D24 Academic leader
		D25 Innovative teaching staff
	C8 Faculty	D26 Teachers are experienced in teaching practical training
B3 Project teaching design	C9 Reforming the teaching method	D27 Experiential Learning
		D28 Increase on-campus simulation training opportunities
		D29 Enhanced awareness of innovation and entrepreneurship
		D30 Developing comprehensive application skills
	C10 Enriching the content of the course	D31 Adequate and reasonable arrangement of practice hours
		D32 More complete types of simulated industries
		D33 Organize thematic salon sharing sessions
		D34 Conducting professional skills competitions
		D35 Diversification of appraisal methods
	C11 Improvement of teaching standards	D36 Well-planned and structured classroom teaching

(*continued*)

Table 1. (*continued*)

First-level indicators B	Second-level indicators C	Third-level indicators D
		D37 The classroom's interactivity and inspiration
		D38 All aspects of instruction can be effectively organized and implemented
B4 Project teaching effect	C12 Student performance	D39 Degree of application of specialized knowledge
		D40 Change in perception of major
		D41 Enhanced ability of teamwork

3.2 Assignment of Quality Assessment Indicators for Interdisciplinary Virtual Simulation Comprehensive Training Program

This study adopts the AHP and expert grading method to determine the weights of evaluation indicators. First, the AHP is constructed, and the judgment matrix is determined by comparing the indicators two by two; then the consistency test is carried out and the weights of the indicators are calculated. In order to determine the relative weights of project quality evaluation indexes, this study invites a number of industry experts to conduct a questionnaire survey, and constructs a judgment matrix based on the results of the experts' ratings of the importance of each index, and carries out a consistency test on this basis. Accounted by yaahp software, the total ranking consistency ratio C.R. of each level is less than 0.1, which indicates that the judgment matrix passed the consistency test and ensures the reliability of the results. The judgment matrices of the first-level indicators and the weights of the quality assessment index system of the inter-disciplinary virtual simulation comprehensive training program in economics and management are shown in Tables 2 and 3.

Table 2. Judgment matrix for First-level indicators

A	B1	B2	B3	B4	Wi	C.R. = 0.02491
B1	1	5	3	7	0.57684	λmax = 4.06724
B2	1/5	1	1/2	3	0.13336	
B3	1/3	2	1	4	0.23028	
B4	1/7	1/3	1/4	1	0.05952	

Table 3. Assignment of weights in the quality assessment index system of the inter-disciplinary virtual simulation comprehensive training program for economics and management

First-level indicators and weights	Second-level indicators and weights	Third-level indicators and weights
B1 Project organization and leadership (0.57684)	**C1 Importance of the project(0.36053)**	**D1 Representing the school's level of practical training and teaching (0.19431)**
		D2 Representing the quality of practical training and teaching in the school (0.10717)
		D3 Become a model for the school's practical training program (0.05905)
	C2 Division of labour among leaders (0.13757)	**D4 Has a dean dedicated to the program(0.07423)**
		D5 Have a faculty director in charge of the program(0.04086)
		D6 There is a teacher dedicated to the program(0.02248)
	C3 Organization and setting (0.07874)	**D7 Establishment of a program team (0.04343)**
		D8 Clear project implementation plan (0.02341)
		D9 Projects are followed up by full-time teachers (0.01290)
B2 Project concept and resource allocation (0.13336)	**C4 Guiding ideology (0.05574)**	**D10 Having relevant policy documents to guide the project(0.03309)**
		D11 With the guidance of good examples from sister colleges and universities(0.00875)
		D12 School philosophy(0.01390)

(continued)

Table 3. (*continued*)

First-level indicators and weights	Second-level indicators and weights	Third-level indicators and weights
	C5 Participants (0.04235)	D13 School-Enterprise Joint Venture(0.00464)
		D14 Teacher Level (0.01309)
		D15 Student participation (0.02462)
	C6 Scale of the project (0.00620)	D16 Number of participating faculties(0.00034)
		D17 Number of participating leaders(0.00262)
		D18 Number of participating teachers(0.00167)
		D19 Number of students participating(0.00059)
		D20 Project cycle(0.00098)
	C7 Financial support (0.01950)	**D21 Strength of financial investment(0.01052)**
		D22 Rationalization of the use of funds(0.00580)
		D23 Transparency in the use of funds(0.00318)
	C8 Faculty (0.00957)	D24 Academic leader(0.00517)
		D25 Innovative teaching staff(0.00284)
		D26 Teachers are experienced in teaching practical training(0.00156)
B3 Project teaching design (0.23028)	**C9 Reforming the teaching method (0.14669)**	**D27 Experiential Learning(0.08926)**
		D28 Increase on-campus simulation training opportunities(0.03197)
		D29 Enhanced awareness of innovation and entrepreneurship(0.01769)
		D30 Developing comprehensive application skills(0.00777)

(*continued*)

Table 3. (*continued*)

First-level indicators and weights	Second-level indicators and weights	Third-level indicators and weights
	C10 Enriching the content of the course (0.05948)	**D31 Adequate and reasonable arrangement of practice hours(0.02486)**
		D32 More complete types of simulated industries(0.01889)
		D33 Organize thematic salon sharing sessions(0.00276)
		D34 Conducting professional skills competitions(0.00870)
		D35 Diversification of appraisal methods(0.00427)
	C11 Improvement of teaching standards (0.02411)	D36 Well-planned and structured classroom teaching (0.00554)
		D37 The classroom's interactivity and inspiration (0.01562)
		D38 All aspects of instruction can be effectively organized and implemented (0.00295)
B4 Project teaching effect (0.05952)	C12 Student performance (0.03208)	D39 Degree of application of specialized knowledge (0.00954)
		D40 Change in perception of major (0.00525)
		D41 Enhanced ability of teamwork (0.01729)
	C13 Teacher Evaluation (0.01769)	D42 Exchanging feedback with students during the teaching process (0.00194)
		D43 Grading of Student Practical Training Process (0.00547)
		D44 Scoring of students' practical training reports (0.01028)
	C14 Employer satisfaction (0.00975)	D45 Feedback on student internships (0.00102)

(*continued*)

Table 3. (*continued*)

First-level indicators and weights	Second-level indicators and weights	Third-level indicators and weights
		D46 Employment rate of students participating in the program (0.00621)
		D47 Business evaluation of talent quality (0.00252)

4 Analysis of Quality Assessment Results of Interdisciplinary Virtual Simulation Comprehensive Training Program

From the calculation results in Table 2 and Table 3, it can be seen that there are 3 first-level indicators, 6 s-level indicators, 21 third-level indicators and so on that have a greater impact on the quality assessment of the inter-professional virtual simulation integrated training program in economics and management. Weighted such as B1 project organization and leadership, B2 project concept and resource allocation, B3 project teaching design of the three first-level indicators; B4 project teaching effect due to the evaluation of inter-professional virtual simulation comprehensive practical training project teaching results performance, social benefits and other evaluation of the phenomenon of lagging influence. Therefore, B4 Program Teaching Effectiveness has a low weighting.

Sorting the results according to the weights of the second-level indicators, the six indicators with higher weights are: C1 Importance of the project (0.36053), C9 Reforming the teaching method (0.14669), C2 Division of labour among leaders (0.13757), C3 Organization and setting (0.07874), C10 Enriching the content of the course (0.05948), and C4 Guiding ideology (0.05574), as well as D1 Representing the school's level of practical training and teaching (0.19431), D2 Representing the quality of practical training and teaching in the school (0.10717), D27 Experiential learning (0.08926), D4 Has a dean dedicated to the program (0.07423), D3 Become a model for the school's practical training program (0.05905), D7 Establishment of a program team (0.04343), D5 Have a faculty director in charge of the program (0.04086), D10 Having relevant policy documents to guide the project (0.03309), D28 Increase on-campus simulation training opportunities (0.03197), D31 Adequate and reasonable arrangement of practice hours (0.02486), D15 Student participation (0.02462), D8 Clear project implementation plan (0.02341), D6 There is a teacher dedicated to the program (0.02248), D32 More complete types of simulated industries (0.01889), D29 Enhanced awareness of innovation and entrepreneurship (0.01769), D41 Enhanced ability of teamwork (0.01729), D37 The classroom's interactivity and inspiration (0.01562), D12 School philosophy (0.01390), D14 Teacher Level (0.01309), D21 Strength of financial investment (0.01052), D44 Scoring of students' practical training reports (0.01028), and 21 other third-level indicators.

The above 30 indicators have a greater impact on the quality of conducting inter-disciplinary virtual simulation integrated training programs in economics and management, and support in these areas should be strengthened in future work.

5 Summary and Recommendations

This study firstly adopts the literature research method and Delphi method, repeatedly consults the opinions of experts in the field, and constructs the quality assessment index system of inter-disciplinary virtual simulation comprehensive training program of economics and management, in which there are 4 first-level indexes B1-B4, 14 s-level indexes C1-C14, and 47 third-level indicators D1-D47. Then the AHP method is applied to calculate the weights of the indicators, and the assessment results show that the indicators that have a greater impact on the quality of the program include 3 first-level indicators, 6 s-level indicators and 21 third-level indicators. The assessment process is scientific and effective, and the indicator setting and weight calculation are in line with the reality of the practical training program. The finalized key indicator system can provide a reference for the quality control of this kind of program. In order to further improve the quality of the inter-disciplinary virtual simulation comprehensive practical training project of economics and management, the following suggestions are put forward.

1. Sound project management mechanism, standardize the process of practical training

In order to standardize the management of inter-professional comprehensive practical training project and improve the quality of the project, we should establish a perfect project organization and leadership system, implement the responsibility system of the project leader, set up a project leading group to determine the direction, project working group is responsible for the specific implementation of the project, and the project supervision team to follow up and check the project progress and effect. Formulate management methods suitable for the project, including fund management methods, quality management methods, etc., so that the project in the deployment of resources, process control, output assessment, etc., have rules to follow. In terms of project implementation monitoring, we can add a system that requires teachers to fill in work logs, recording in detail the problems and solutions that arise in the process of guiding practical training, as well as the whole process of tracking the project and quality control. Organize summary exchange meetings for teachers to review the operation process of the project, identify problems and make improvements. Through the establishment of project performance management mechanism, sound workflow, can effectively standardize the management of inter-disciplinary comprehensive practical training project, to ensure the quality of the project.

2. Teaching reform and innovation, the introduction of experiential teaching model

In order to further improve the teaching quality of inter-specialty virtual simulation training, we can consider reforming and innovating the teaching method and introducing experiential teaching mode. First, the application of scenario teaching should be increased. In the virtual environment, all kinds of real work scenarios are carefully set up, and students can perform various tasks in the simulated scenarios to fully experience the whole workflow. Second, project teaching should be organized. Design inter-disciplinary teamwork projects, so that students of different majors can experience the application of knowledge and accumulate experience in completing the projects. Projects such as new product development, activity planning, etc. can be set up. Third, carry out discussion teaching. Organize students to discuss the problems in the process of virtual training, which will stimulate their interest in learning and active thinking, so that students can gain from the discussion. Fourth, the application of case studies. Bring successful or failed practical training cases into the teaching, guide students to analyze the lessons learned in the cases and get valuable reference. Fifth, the use of game teaching. Convert the knowledge points into interesting games or simulation competition to improve the interest of learning. Sixth, the implementation of reflective teaching. Require students to write practical training learning experience, and organize exchanges, in order to deepen the understanding of knowledge and internalization.

3. Explore diversified assessment methods

The assessment methods include teacher's rating, enterprise simulation CEO's rating and team mutual evaluation, etc., which mainly assess the students' ability to improve the application of professional knowledge, teamwork and business negotiation ability. Specific initiatives are as follows: firstly, implement knowledge assessment, adopt written test or online test to check students' mastery of professional knowledge, examine the understanding of concepts, principles and other aspects, and lay the foundation for further ability assessment. Secondly, to set up skills assessment, students need to complete the actual operation in the virtual simulation environment to test the mastery of the process and application capabilities. Simulated task assessment and comprehensive project assessment can be adopted to examine the skill level. Once again, quality and ability assessment is carried out, and inter-professional groups are organized to complete the project to examine the comprehensive ability of teamwork, problem solving, organization and management, etc., and peer evaluation is also carried out. In addition, process evaluation is introduced to dynamically assess students' learning attitude, thinking quality and communication ability through practical training records, learning reports and teachers' observation. Finally, self-assessment of learning effect is carried out, so that students can make descriptive reflections on the improvement of their own abilities before and after the virtual training to stimulate active learning.

4. Build a cooperative and mutual learning platform

In order to comprehensively enhance the effect of inter-specialty virtual simulation comprehensive practical training, you can actively build a collaborative and mutual support network learning platform, give full play to the advantages of virtual simulation and network platforms, to create a better learning atmosphere. Specifically, the platform can set up an online student exchange area, so that students can discuss the problems in the training process, share learning experiences, provide assistance, and realize experience and resource sharing. It is also possible to develop some small programs to assist learning, such as operation demonstration system, knowledge checking system, homework questioning system, etc., to enrich the way of students' independent learning. At the same time, the platform can record the specific operation data of students in the virtual training environment, summary analysis, generation of visual learning reports, so that students can fully understand their own learning situation and find deficiencies. Teachers can also be based on the report for targeted guidance. In addition, the establishment of an online Q&A system allows students to ask questions when they encounter specific problems, and teachers can provide timely answers. Through the creation of integrated communication, monitoring, data statistics, assessment and feedback in one of the virtual simulation network collaboration platform, you can really realize the student-centred virtual training mode, launch the students' initiative to help each other to learn the enthusiasm, so that each student can be in a resource-rich, well-monitored, interactive learning environment to obtain the most effective training for their own. This also provides design ideas for schools to build personalized and collaborative virtual practical training learning platform.

Acknowledgement. The research is funded by Key Research Base of Humanities and Social Sciences in Universities of Guangdong Province: Research Base for Digital Transformation of Manufacturing Enterprises (2023WZJD012).

References

1. Circular of the general office of the ministry of education on the construction of exemplary virtual simulation experimental teaching program in 2017–2020. Lab. Sci. **20**(04), 190+196+193+30+216+3+59+106+206+220+80+231 (2017)
2. Wu, B.G.: Exploration of teaching reform of economic management specialties in colleges and universities. Old Brand Mark. **19**, 179–181 (2023)
3. Zi, C.F., Xie, X.L.: Teaching analysis of interdisciplinary virtual simulation comprehensive training course for economics and management. Sci. Technol. Entrep. Monthly **35**(01), 141–144 (2022)
4. Chen, M.Y., Lin, G.C.: Empirical analysis of the teaching effect of inter-disciplinary virtual simulation comprehensive experiment in economics and management. J. Jilin Coll. Agric. Sci. Technol. **31**(05), 79–82 (2022)
5. Li, J.Z.: Design of interdisciplinary virtual simulation comprehensive training course for economics and management under the background of new business studies. Innov. Entrepreneurship Theory Res. Pract. **3**(17), 187–188 (2020)
6. Jiang, Y.J., Li, Y.: Teaching effect analysis of teaching practice of economics and management on virtual simulation platform - based on VBSE interdisciplinary comprehensive practical training. Educ. Observ. **11**(01), 83–86 (2022). https://doi.org/10.16070/j.cnki.cn45-1388/g4s.2022.01.033
7. He, X.Q., Wu, Q.F.: Research on comprehensive evaluation of the quality of virtual simulation cross-disciplinary comprehensive training platform based on MEBS. Mark. World **20**, 189–190 (2020)
8. Zeng, Y.: Construction and exploration of interdisciplinary simulation comprehensive training platform for economics and management-taking heyuan vocational and technical college as an example. Educ. Observ. **7**(23), 104–106 (2018). https://doi.org/10.16070/j.cnki.cn45-1388/g4s.2018.23.035
9. Li, H.: Construction and practice of national virtual simulation experimental teaching center for economics and management. Lab. Res. Expl. **35**(06), 139–142 (2016)
10. Yang, H.J.: Analysis of the construction of national virtual simulation experimental teaching center for economics and management based on rooted theory. Popular Stand. **14**, 139–140 (2019)
11. Liu, C., Duan, Z.G.: Research on the origin and evolution of Delphi method based on reference publication year mapping. Chin. J. Soc. Med. **40**(03), 373–377 (2023)

12. Fan, G.G.: Research on risk identification and response of "Belt and Road" international engineering projects based on Delphi method and AHP method. Kunming University of Science and Technology (2022). https://doi.org/10.27200/d.cnki.gkmlu.2022.001525
13. Zhang, C.: An analysis of the application of hierarchical analysis (AHP) method in landslide hazard risk assessment. Energy Environ. (05), 132–134+149 (2023)
14. Xie, Q.: Study on the measurement of factors influencing the generation of social science theory talents in colleges and universities in the new era - based on hierarchical analysis. J. Jiangsu Econ. Trade Vocat. Tech. Coll. 05, 24–27 (2023). https://doi.org/10.16335/j.cnki.iss n1672-2604.2023.05.007

Author Index

A

Aguirre, Joel 38, 189, 285, 310
Almeida, Pedro 142
Alves, Mariana 142

B

Bai, Xiangtian 259
Ball, Roger 354
Becker, Valdecir 268

C

Cantoni, Lorenzo 107
Cavalcanti, Daniel de Queiroz 268
Chen, Jialing 217, 232
Chen, Xiaoshi 371
Chen, Yali 201
Chen, Yiqi 53
Cruz, Filipe 3

D

da Rocha Filho, Edvaldo Vasconcelos 268
de Almeida, Fábio 22
de Sá, Felipe Melo Feliciano 268
Du, Xiaoxi 217, 232

F

Falconi, Fiorella 38, 189, 285, 310
Fan, Hao 68, 175
Fang, Yuzhe 53

G

Guo, Xinhao 217, 232

H

Huang, Xintong 53
Huang, Zhangchenlong 68

J

Jiang, Ao 68, 121, 175

K

Kato, Yukina 88
Kumagai, Naoya 300

L

Lecaros, Adrian 38, 189, 285, 310
Li, Chenyu 53
Li, Fanhao 259
Li, Lingyu 354
Li, Manhai 248
Liu, Joanna 107
Liu, Mengke 53
Liu, Wei 53
Liu, Yixuan 248
Liu, Yiyang 53
Liu, Yonghong 259
Lou, Yukun 121

M

Macêdo, João Marcelo Alves 268
Moquillaza, Arturo 38, 189, 285, 310

N

Nakajima, Tatsuo 88
Neves, Marco 3

O

Ohtsuka, Shuma 300

P

Paz, Freddy 38, 189, 285, 310
Paz-Sifuentes, Freddy-Asrael 310
Pedro, Luís 142

Q

Qiu, Dan 53

R

Rafael, Sónia 22
Ramos, Carlos 38, 189, 285, 310

Rong, Qu 53
Russo, Alessia 324

S
Sugaya, Midori 300
Sun, Shihua 53

T
Tan, Qi 132
Tian, Yuanqing 354
Tu, Chanjuan 324
Tu, Xin 201

V
Velhinho, Ana 142

W
Wan, Yu 338
Wang, LiMin 160
Wang, Tianyu 53
Wang, Xiang 53
Wen, Jiazhi 53

Wu, Xiaofan 53
Wu, Zeyu 53

X
Xue, Chengqi 217, 232

Y
Yang, Yuwei 53
Yu, DanDan 160
Yu, Kun 68, 121, 175

Z
Zhang, Ying 160, 324
Zhang, Zhongbo 53
Zhao, Liangliang 175
Zhao, Yan 68, 175
Zhou, Haihai 121
Zhou, Xiaozhou 217, 232
Zhou, Xuan 53
Zhou, Yide 338
Zhu, Jixu 371

Printed in the United States
by Baker & Taylor Publisher Services